The Definitive Guide to Grails

Graeme Keith Rocher

The Definitive Guide to Grails

Copyright © 2006 by Graeme Keith Rocher

ISBN-13 (pbk): 978-1-59059-758-3

ISBN-10 (pbk): 1-59059-758-3

Printed and bound in the United States of America 9 8 7 6 5 4 3 2 1

Lead Editor: Steve Anglin
Technical Reviewers: Guillaume Laforge, Dierk König
Editorial Board: Steve Anglin, Ewan Buckingham, Gary Cornell, Jason Gilmore, Jonathan Gennick,
    Jonathan Hassell, James Huddleston, Chris Mills, Matthew Moodie, Dominic Shakeshaft, Jim Sumser,
    Keir Thomas, Matt Wade
Project Manager: Kylie Johnston
Copy Edit Manager: Nicole Flores
Copy Editors: Jennifer Whipple, Ami Knox
Assistant Production Director: Kari Brooks-Copony
Production Editor: Lori Bring
Compositor: Susan Glinert
Proofreader: Nancy Sixsmith
Indexer: Joy Dean Lee
Artist: Kinetic Publishing Services, LLC
Cover Designer: Kurt Krames
Cover Art: Arthur Smit
Manufacturing Director: Tom Debolski

Distributed to the book trade worldwide by Springer-Verlag New York, Inc., 233 Spring Street, 6th Floor, New York, NY 10013. Phone 1-800-SPRINGER, fax 201-348-4505, e-mail orders-ny@springer-sbm.com, or visit http://www.springeronline.com.

For information on translations, please contact Apress directly at 2560 Ninth Street, Suite 219, Berkeley, CA 94710. Phone 510-549-5930, fax 510-549-5939, e-mail info@apress.com, or visit http://www.apress.com.

The source code for this book is available to readers at http://www.apress.com in the Source Code/Download section.

*To my amazing wife, Birjinia, for your love and support,
and for managing to live with a bit of a geek. Maitia zatut.*

Contents at a Glance

Contents

Foreword

Once upon a time, in a galaxy far, far away lived a people who could create web applications in no time . . . .

Enterprise-ready and built on proven and scalable open source frameworks such as Spring, Hibernate, Quartz, and SiteMesh, Grails is an MVC web framework that actually helps you build applications faster than the good, old, pure Java "elephant."

Taking inspiration from recent and innovative frameworks such as Ruby on Rails, or the likes of Django or TurboGears, Grails makes simple things simpler and harder things possible, by following the paradigm of "convention over configuration." Not only that, it brings back the fun of creating web applications.

Grails is so versatile that you can build an early prototype of your application in a few hours to validate the underlying domain model, or discuss possibilities or potential problems with your customers, without leaving them in the fog for months before something concrete appears before their eyes.

Leveraging the Java platform and the wealth of open source components, Grails has the ability to run applications on commodity hardware with open source servlet containers or large-scale, clustered commercial application servers. You can safely protect the investment your company has made in software and hardware. But you also take advantage of the skills of your teams knowledgeable in Java, Spring, and Hibernate, without requiring long and expensive training plans to be proficient with the technology and the tools. Though Grails hides the complexity of the underlying frameworks, it still lets you take control when the need arises for a finer-grained usage of those components, such as when you need to integrate with "legacy."

Graeme Rocher and his team decided not only to use off-the-shelf, bulletproof components, but to base Grails on Groovy. Grails takes advantage of advanced dynamic features provided by Groovy, the dynamic language that best integrates with the Java platform. This choice is also very clever because Groovy offers Java developers an almost flat learning curve for a new language because of Groovy's Java-like nature. People can code in Groovy as in Java, with few modifications; and as they learn the language further, they can start using more powerful and dynamic features of the language, while still benefiting from the Java background and all the possibilities offered by the Grails framework.

Grails definitely has an ambitious name for being the Holy Grail all application developers have sought so far. But more than having mere ambition, Grails fulfills its promises by letting you be more productive than you could have ever thought. Graeme Rocher, project lead of Grails and the author of this book, has done a tremendous job at creating a lovely and powerful platform for creating web apps, and has also fostered a welcoming and helpful community around this project. And from whose mouth would you best learn how to ride such a great horse than from the horse's mouth itself?

The Definitive Guide to Grails is another great achievement of Graeme Rocher, who not only did the lion's share of work on the framework, but also provided its excellent online documentation. In this book, Graeme will guide you through the best of his knowledge in developing applications, and will give you all the cards of the game to turn you into an expert of the Grails framework and the Groovy dynamic programming language.

We both feel very fortunate for having had the opportunity to work with Graeme on Grails and on this book.

For anyone who seeks guidance in using Grails and wants to share the fun of programming that we have experienced with it, you have the right book in your hands.

May the source be with you!

Guillaume Laforge
Groovy Project Manager

Dierk König
Lead author of Groovy in Action

About the Author

GRAEME KEITH ROCHER is a software architect and chief technology officer at Skills Matter (`http://www.skillsmatter.com`), a skills transfer company specializing in open source technology and agile software development. In his current role as CTO, Graeme is in charge of Skills Matter's courseware development strategy and general technical direction. As part of this role he actively works with a wide range of experts from the open source community and speaks at industry conferences whenever possible on subjects related to Groovy, Grails, and dynamic languages in Java.

Graeme started his career in the e-learning sector as part of a team developing scalable enterprise learning management systems based on J2EE technology. He later branched into the digital TV arena, where he was faced with increasingly complex requirements that required an agile approach as the ever-changing and young digital TV platforms evolved. This is where Graeme was first exposed to Groovy and he began combining Groovy with Cocoon to deliver dynamic multichannel content management systems targeted at digital TV platforms.

Seeing an increasing trend for web delivery of services and the complexity it brought, Graeme embarked on another project to simplify it and founded Grails. Grails is a framework with the essence of Ruby on Rails, but targeted at tight Java integration. Graeme is the current project lead of Grails and is a member of the Groovy JSR-241 executive committee.

Before Skills Matter, Graeme worked at Knowledge Pool, where using Groovy he produced a rapid e-learning development toolkit called Originate. Originate incorporated Groovy as the glue language to bring together a diverse range of technologies, including Visual Basic, Microsoft Word, XSLT, the JavaScript language, and XSL-FO.

Graeme's major achievement, however, are his two beautiful children, Lexeia and Alex, and his wife, Birjinia, who he marvels at every day.

About the Technical Reviewers

GUILLAUME LAFORGE is the official Groovy project manager and spec lead of JSR-241, which is standardizing the Groovy scripting language. He spends his spare time bringing a versatile and agile environment to the masses, having initiated a year ago the discussions about Grails, which has its architecture based on Groovy and Spring.

He also contributed to Manning Publications' *Groovy in Action* with Dierk König, one of the passionate Groovy developers.

In his professional life, Guillaume is a software architect and an open source consultant, working for OCTO Technology, a French-based consultancy focusing on architecture of software and information systems.

DIERK KÖNIG works as a senior programmer, mentor, and coach. He is the lead author of *Groovy in Action* and is committed to both Groovy and Grails. He founded the popular open source Canoo WebTest project and has been managing it ever since. Dierk regularly speaks at international conferences and publishes in leading magazines. He works for Canoo Engineering AG in Basel, Switzerland, where he is founding partner and member of the executive board.

Acknowledgments

First and foremost, I'd like to thank my wife, Birjinia, for her beauty, wisdom, and continued love and support. You are the best. Also, to my kids, Alex and Lexeia, who wanted to extract me from my laptop on many occasions while I was writing this book, but had the patience to let me complete it. Thanks to my mum, my father (I miss you), my sister, and to all of Birjinia's amazing family who mean so much to me.

At Apress, thanks to Steve Anglin for having the initial vision and incite to approach me about doing a Grails book. Even though other publishers enquired later, it says volumes for Steve and Apress that they were able to foresee the potential of Grails months before others.

Also, thanks to all on the Apress production team that I have worked with, such as Jennifer Whipple and Ami Knox (my copy editors), Nancy Sixsmith (proofreader), Lori Bring (production editor), and, in particular, Kylie Johnston (project manager) for putting up with some of my badgering.

Needless to say, special thanks must go out to the technical reviewers of this book, Guillaume Laforge (Groovy project lead) and Dierk Konig (lead author of *Groovy in Action*) who provided a steady stream of useful insight and suggestions throughout the whole process.

Since all of this would not be possible without all those who have contributed to Grails over the past year or so, I would like to thank Steven Devijver of Interface21 and Guillaume again for joining me in getting Grails going when it was just a bunch of ideas in an e-mail.

To Marc Palmer for providing a voice of reason, intelligent debate, and continued valuable contribution to Grails. To Micha Kujszo for his contributions toward Quartz support. To Dierk again and Canoo (http://canoo.com) for providing the Grails continuous integration server and testing infrastructure. To the core members of the Groovy team, such as John "Tug" Wilson and Jochen "blackdrag" Theodorou, whose continued responsiveness makes Grails' existence possible.

Thanks to Arthur Smit at The Hermit Design (http://www.thehermitdesign.co.uk) for designing the original Grails logo and much of the Grails artwork, including the starburst on the cover of this book. If you ever need creative treatment of a brand or any graphics work, he is your man.

Also, without the support of the Grails community in general, we wouldn't have gotten very far. So thanks to all the Grails users and in particular Sven Haiges for producing the Grails podcast and screencasts, and to Jason Rudolph for writing so many fantastic articles about Grails on sites such as InfoQ.

Moving back in time, thanks to the original core members of the Futuremedia team, who taught me so much and continue to be valuable fountains of knowledge—guys like Jeremy Aston, Piers Geyman, Phil Horton, and Nathan Summers, with a special mention for Pete Bergin (RIP). We miss you, man.

Thanks too to Tugdual Grall at Oracle for doing so much to push Grails both within Oracle and at major events such as JavaOne and JavaPolis. Last, but most certainly not least, thanks to Wendy Devolder at Skills Matter for seeing the potential of Grails and granting me the privilege of working with her fantastic company.

Introduction

In the late '90s I was working on a project developing large-scale enterprise learning management systems using early J2EE technologies such as EJB 1.0 and the Servlet framework. The Java hype machine was in full swing and references to "EJB that, and Java this" were on the cover of every major IT publication out there.

Even though what we were doing—and learning as we did it—felt so horribly wrong, the industry kept telling us we were doing the right thing. EJB was going to solve all our problems, and servlets (even without a view technology at the time) were the right thing to use. My, how times have changed.

Nowadays, Java and J2EE are long forgotten buzzwords, and the hype machine is throwing other complex acronyms at us such as SOA and ESB. In my experience, developers are on a continued mission to write less code. The monolithic J2EE specifications, like those adopted by the development community in the early days, didn't help. If a framework or a specification is overcomplex and requires you to write reams of repetitive code, it should be an immediate big red flag. Why did we have to write so much repetitive boilerplate code? Surely there was a better way.

In the end, developers often influence the direction of technology more than they know. Why do so many developers favor REST over SOAP for web services? Or Hibernate over EJB for persistence? Or Spring over JNDI for Inversion of Control? In the end, simplicity often wins the day.

Certainly, working with Spring and Hibernate feels a lot better than traditional J2EE approaches; in fact, I strove to use them whenever possible, usually in combination with WebWork, and delivered a number of successful projects with this stack. Nevertheless, I still felt I had to deal with the surrounding infrastructural issues and configuration, rather than the problem at hand. After all, the more efficient I could be as a developer when doing "real" work, the more time I would have to do what should be driving every developer: spending time with your loved ones and learning new and exciting technologies.

In 2003, Groovy entered the picture. I had always been fond of looser rules governing dynamic languages in certain contexts, having worked extensively with Perl, Visual Basic, and JavaScript in the past, and after quickly hacking the WebWork source code, I was able to write MVC controllers (or *actions* in WebWork lingo) with Groovy in no time.

Groovy was perfect for controllers whose sole responsibility should be to delegate to business logic implemented by a service and then display an appropriate view. I was starting to have even more time for the good things in life. Then came the storm of dynamic language–based frameworks led by Ruby on Rails.

Unfortunately, it was all a little late. Java, the community, the tools, the frameworks, and the mindshare are well-embedded. The size that Java has grown to is quite staggering, and having been in the training business for many years, I see it asx showing no signs of slowing, contrary to popular belief. Still, Java has its problems, and I wanted to write less code. Grails was born with this goal in mind in the summer of 2005 after I, Steven Devijver, and Guillaume Laforge kicked off a discussion about its conception on the Groovy mailing list.

Fundamentally, there is nothing at all wrong with many of the specifications that form part of J2EE. They are, however, a rather low-level of abstraction. Frameworks such as Struts, WebWork, and more recently JSF have tried to resolve this issue; however, Java and its static typing don't help. Groovy, on the other hand, allows that higher level of abstraction. Having used it for controllers, it was now time to take it to every layer, from controllers to tag libraries, from persistence to the view technology.

The APIs you can create with Groovy's metaprogramming support are amazingly simple and concise. Grails uses every single dynamic trick, at both run time and compile time, from custom domain-specific languages to compile-time mixins, with two fundamental goals in mind: write less code and be Java friendly.

Are Groovy and Grails a replacement for Java, like other dynamic language frameworks? No, on the contrary they're designed to work with Java. To embrace it. To have Java at their very core. Grails is Java through and through, and it allows you to pick and choose which features to implement with dynamic typing, and which to better place in the safer hands of static typing.

Grails exists out of the acknowledgment that there is never only one tool for the job. Grails is about providing an entry point for the trivial tasks, while still allowing the power and flexibility to harness the full Java platform when needed. I hope you enjoy the book as much as I have enjoyed writing it and being part of the Grails community.

Who This Book Is For

Grails forms just one framework that is driving the movement toward dynamic language–based frameworks. In this sense, anyone who is interested in the dynamic language field, whether you are from a Perl, Ruby, or Python background, would gain something from reading this book, if just to acquire insight into what the alternatives are.

If platform is not a choice, and Java is the way your project is going, Grails can provide features like no other framework. In this circumstance, Grails may have the answers you are looking for. Primarily, however, this book will provide the most benefit to those who know and love the Java platform, those who see the Java language for all of its strong points but want something better as a web framework.

Grails is providing the answers to the long search for something better in the Java world by presenting a framework that solves the common problems in an unobtrusive, elegant manner. This is not to say the subject matter within this book is trivial.

I'll be challenging you with advanced usages of the Groovy language and real-world examples. Furthermore, you'll be pushing the boundaries of what is possible with a dynamic language like Groovy, extending it into every tier of a typical web application from the view layer with Ajax-enabled technology, to the persistence tier with rich domain models. For experienced Java developers, it should be an enlightening experience, as features not found in Java such as closures, builders, and metaprogramming are explored.

Through all this, however, although the subject matter and examples are advanced, the solutions are simple, and along the way you may learn a new way to approach web application development.

How This Book Is Structured

This book is divided into 11 chapters, starting with the overview and introductions and extending to advanced topics in the final chapter. You'll start the journey through Grails in Chapter 1 by understanding the motivations behind it and what makes it so special.

In Chapter 2, you'll take a tour of the Groovy language features, if you haven't been exposed to them before. Although I cover some of the advanced language features, most of what you will learn about Groovy when applied to real-world situations is scattered throughout the remainder of the book.

Chapter 3 covers what a Grails project looks like, and you'll create your first one, which is the example you'll follow throughout the entire book. In Chapter 4, you'll start to look at what makes up a domain model and how Grails builds on advanced ORM technologies such as Hibernate to provide a robust domain-driven programming model. In this chapter you'll start to construct the domain model for the example application and understand how this relates to the underlying persistence model.

It starts to get really exciting in Chapter 5, as you create a working application automatically from the code in the domain model. This chapter introduces a concept called *scaffolding* that will not only help you become more productive but will serve as an invaluable learning tool.

Before we get too far ahead of ourselves, in Chapter 6 we'll tackle the issue of unit and functional testing within Grails and see how to apply advanced techniques such as closure currying and mock objects to write effective tests.

The book will then dive straight into the nitty-gritty details of Grails in Chapter 7 by exploring what controllers mean to you as a developer in the grand scheme of things and how to work with Grails' advanced view technology, GSP, in Chapter 8.

I then tackle a very *now* issue in Grails' support for Ajax technology in Chapter 9, and you'll see how to apply Ajax techniques to improve the usability of the example application that you'll be developing throughout the book.

It starts to get a little more advanced in Chapter 10, when the book introduces how Grails makes integration of services and jobs trivial. Finally, in Chapter 11, I introduce what is really the essence of Grails: its ability to integrate seamlessly with Java.

Conventions

This book uses a diverse range of languages, including HTML, XML, JavaScript, Groovy, and Java. Nonetheless, each example is introduced appropriately and appears in a fixed-width Courier font. I also endeavor to be consistent in the use of naming conventions throughout the book to make the examples as clear as possible.

In many cases, the original source code has been reformatted to fit within the available page space, with additional line breaks and modified code indentation being common. To increase the clarity of the code, some examples omit code where it is seen as unnecessary. In cases where the code is omitted between two blocks of code, an ellipsis (…) is used to indicate where the missing code would have been.

Prerequisites

This book goes through the installation of Grails; in the examples I use the 0.3 release. However, Grails itself is dependant on the existence of an installed Java Virtual Machine. As a minimum, you will need to install JDK 1.4 or above for the examples in this book to work.

Installation of an application server, such as Tomcat, and a database server, such as MySQL, is entirely optional, as Grails comes bundled with an embedded server and database. Nevertheless, to use Grails in production, you may want to at least set up a database server.

Downloading the Code

The code for the examples in this book is available to readers in the Source Code/Download section of the Apress web site at http://www.apress.com. The examples are presented in three flavors that cover the use of different persistence techniques.

Contacting the Author

Graeme is an active member of the open source community and welcomes any comments and/or communication. You can reach him via e-mail at graeme.rocher@gmail.com or via his blog at http://graemerocher.blogspot.com. Alternatively, you can simply pop a message on the Grails mailing lists, the details for which can be found here: http://grails.org/Mailing+lists.

■■■

## CHAPTER 1

The Search for the Holy Grail(s)

Grails is one of the upcoming new wave of dynamic language-based web frameworks. In this chapter we'll explore the history behind Grails' inception and why you should be interested in it and its alternatives.

Grails specifically is a next-generation web application framework for Java that leverages the Groovy language to promote simplicity and convention. Grails leverages as many existing projects as possible to create a full stack framework that is in stark contrast to many existing frameworks for Java that present the user with an anemic[1] API.

Grails arrives at a time when web applications are getting ever more complex with the onset of Web 2.0 and Ajax, a topic I'll be discussing in greater detail later in the book. Before we get ahead of ourselves, let's explore the reasoning and user experiences of other frameworks that have led to the emergence of frameworks such as Grails.

Trouble in Paradise

Have you ever wanted a Java web application framework that required less configuration? Maybe one that magically reads your mind and guesses what you want to achieve based on the business logic rather than mountains of surrounding configuration. The amount of work it takes to develop web applications in current Java web application frameworks has seen a dramatic rise in code-generation utilities whose sole purpose is to generate surrounding configuration or jump-start application development. If you're reading this book as a developer interested in Grails I hazard a guess that you've experienced the often cumbersome multistep process it can be to work with web frameworks on the Java platform.

Trust me though, you're not alone. The search has been on for years to transform the landscape of the way we develop web applications with the Java platform and extends way beyond just the frameworks themselves, but into the entire stack. It started with the initial specification of the much heralded Java 2 Enterprise Edition (J2EE) stack, described lovingly by Bruce Tate[2] as an "elephant." The specification created a configuration-heavy, time-consuming environment, and acknowledgement of these mistakes were made particular in the area of Enterprise JavaBeans (EJB).

---

1. Anemic APIs are a common antipattern encapsulated by Martin Fowler in an article about domain models titled "Anemic Domain Model" (`http://www.martinfowler.com/bliki/AnemicDomainModel.html`).
2. Bruce Tate is a big critic of Java's current development process and has written a number of books on the topic, including *Bitter Java, Better, Faster, Lighter Java*, and *Beyond Java*. His article on the "elephant" can be found at `http://today.java.net/pub/a/today/2004/06/15/ejb3.html`.

Before the mistakes could be corrected, the open source community reacted with frameworks such as Spring, inspired by Rod Johnson's book *J2EE Development Without EJB*, allowing simplified development models, while ease of use in the object-relational mapping (ORM) arena was driven by simplified POJO (Plain Old Java Object) frameworks such as Hibernate.

It was not, however, the statically typed Java world that prompted the real innovation in web framework design. Dynamic languages were already gaining prominence in other arenas, but thanks to frameworks such as Ruby on Rails (henceforth simply referred to as Rails), Django, and TurboGears, particular focus has been placed on their usage as web application frameworks. After years of being ridiculed as toys, dynamic languages finally started to turn heads and kick-start a rethink into how web applications can be simplified.

Built with scripting languages such as Ruby and Python, this new generation of web frameworks introduced the concept of "convention over configuration" in an object-oriented environment. Instead of configuring everything via reams of XML, the convention within the files or code itself dictated how the application was configured. Suddenly there was no need to configure, and with that, the time spent on a typical development cycle was dramatically reduced. Given their dynamic nature, the frameworks in question provided the ability to save a particular class or resource and have the changes automatically propagated without any need to restart an application server. Applications could be developed with a save/reload paradigm, and state could be maintained; agile and iterative development had finally arrived.

Since much of the functionality of these frameworks can be configured and dispatched at runtime, the available APIs are significantly richer and often more domain-specific.

Scripting languages themselves have always been popular for the development of web applications because of their ability to realize changes immediately (no deployment step) and their often more simple and concise syntax. Unfortunately they've rarely been seen as appropriate for usage on large-scale systems, usually due to a lack of object-oriented features and issues with performance and scalability and/or legacy integration.

Given the advancements in the platforms in which these languages operate and the hardware on which they are executing, these issues have become less and less of a problem. Modern, dynamic virtual machines (VMs) suffer from fewer of these deficiencies and have become a real viable alternative, attracting many Java developers away from the Java platform.

The Arrival of Web 2.0 Applications

Over the past few years the web has seen significant change. The Internet bubble burst, search became the doorway to the web, and the rise of weblogs and open information saw the web become even more opinionated. On the technology front, one of the most significant changes to occur was the appearance of web applications that come close to rivaling the desktop environment. Web developers had long been dismissed as mere hackers compared to their counterparts in the desktop GUI programming world. But this was all about to change, and it all started with essentially one object: the `XMLHttpRequest`.

The `XMLHttpRequest` object has, in reality, been around for quite some time. Microsoft started the revolution by including it as a custom ActiveX object to support its Outlook web access service that integrated with Microsoft's Exchange Server.

Essentially it allowed the client (the browser) to query the server without the necessity to reload the whole page. It achieved this feat by sending an *asynchronous* request to the server via JavaScript. Although, strictly speaking, anything could be sent and received using the technology, XML was the initial technique used. Web applications could suddenly be event-driven, use drag-and-drop, perform autocompletion that integrates with server components, and do all sorts of fancy things previously only seen in frameworks such as Swing. Applications such as Gmail and Flickr even prompted users to stop using their desktop equivalents for mail and photo organization, respectively.

Since then, the word *Ajax* (Asynchronous JavaScript and XML) was coined and the web has been abuzz with it ever since; Web 2.0 was born. The significance of this technology cannot be underestimated. It has brought capabilities to web browsers thought only possible in desktop environments. However, it has also increased the complexity, development time, and expertise required to develop web applications.

Luckily, with this influx of software engineering expertise into the client-side programming world, JavaScript libraries have advanced at a staggering pace, adopting object-oriented techniques to create simple reusable components. However, it is not just the client side that has had to adapt; a much unwanted side effect of Ajax applications is the increased number of requests that they produce. Ajax applications are for the most part loathed by network administrators because of the load placed on the servers, but equally undesirable for developers because the frameworks and tools we know and love are designed around a sequential request/response model.

Furthermore, existing Java frameworks have followed the traditional *develop-compile-deploy* paradigm, a process that becomes slower as the number of requests increase and the size of the project grows. Since Ajax applications inevitably end up being larger, in terms of project size, than traditional web applications, this has huge implications on the compilation and packaging time required to deploy a web application.

To compound these already significant factors, testing rich application flows started to become problematic. With much of the state held on the client, having to reload your browser due to an application restart could set you several steps back in any given use case. The reality was that the frameworks needed to adapt. Adapting is not the easiest thing to achieve in the statically typed world of the Java Virtual Machine (JVM) where classes tend to be compiled once. This is in complete contrast to dynamic languages that follow either an interpreted model or automatically update resources for you at run time.

The timing of the arrival of Ajax was perfect for the aforementioned dynamic-language-based frameworks as they began offering solutions that wowed developers with support for developing Ajax applications and automatic reloading. Tight integration with JavaScript libraries such as Prototype and Script.aculo.us allowed developers to easily perform asynchronous requests, implement element observers, and perform interesting effects.

In addition, features such as the iterative nature of development, no configuration or deployment cycle, and the convention-based approach meant that it was an extremely appealing environment to develop with.

Are the changing times a sign of not only a shift in the way we build applications, but also the technologies we use to build them? Is this the end of Java as we know it? And is Java venturing down the road to become the next COBOL? Many believe so; but the reality is quite different.

The Power of Java

Unfortunately, however wonderful these dynamic frameworks are, they remain inaccessible to thousands upon thousands of organizations for one simple reason: they do not integrate seamlessly with Java. Java integration itself goes far beyond simply executing within the context of the JVM. It means API integration, architectural integration (security, profiling, debugging, etc.), object model integration, Java Enterprise Edition integration, and knowledge and mindshare integration (yes company X already has dozens of Java developers if not more).

Organizations across the world have a significant investment in Java technology as a platform for their business. They've invested in application servers, support contracts, training materials, employees, and hardware optimized for the JVM. All of this amounts to too much to just walk away from to embrace the latest hot framework.

The Java industry is a huge multibillion dollar behemoth that encompasses not only web applications but server applications, desktop applications, smart cards, handheld devices, mobile phones, set-top boxes—this list could go on forever. Conferences dedicated to Java are some of the largest technology events in the world, proving to be the envy of other technology industries.

The size of the industry is sometimes difficult to fathom and it's built on the strength of the *platform*—a platform that has ensured the Java language has more open source libraries than any other language on the planet.

Need a library to programmatically create PDF documents? You have FOP or iText. Want a choice of web frameworks that cover every potential use case? Java has dozens. Need a platform to build service-oriented architecture (SOA) applications? The Java platform has the solution for you.

For many, Java and its sibling in the enterprise world, Java Enterprise Edition, have been the platform of choice, having reached an unrivalled level of maturity and industry support. Java application servers have become robust, scalable managed environments with advanced deployment capabilities, security controls, and web services integration.

Unfortunately, with all this power, Java web applications can be a pain to develop when compared to their dynamic rivals from Ruby, Python, and PHP. Much of the time involved in creating one of these beasts is spent on configuration, the build process, and deployment. Java developers have strived to create build automation tools that make this process easier, including tools that generate source code. This has improved even further with the advent of Java 5 annotations support. But developing Java web applications for the most part remains quite a complex, configuration-heavy experience.

Nevertheless it would be simply unjust if the Java community were denied access to a framework with the same capability as those available on dynamic language platforms.

Since there are several dynamic languages that run happily on top of the JVM, such as Jython, JRuby, and Groovy, it seems imminently possible. Luckily the Java community tends to take the good ideas and make them better; enter Grails.

Grails: The Story So Far

The formation of Grails came on the back of the fabulous progress made in the Groovy language in the summer of 2005. A small group of Groovy enthusiasts who had been astounded by the power of dynamic languages, but unable to take advantage of them due to an existing investment in Java, formed the then-named Groovy on Rails in honor of Ruby on Rails. The Groovy language itself was finally reaching a level of maturity where it was usable as a dynamic language in enterprise environments, making the timing of this formation perfect.

The goal of Grails was to go beyond what other languages and their associated frameworks could offer in the web application space. Grails aimed to do the following:

- Integrate tightly with the Java platform

- Be simple on the surface but retain flexibility to access the powerful underlying Java frameworks and features

- Learn from the mistakes already made on the mature Java platform

By utilizing Groovy as the starting point for the framework, it gave Grails a huge head start. Groovy's goal was to create a language that is a seamless transition for Java developers into the dynamically typed scripting world, bringing advanced features impossible to implement with statically typed languages.

Groovy's goals as a general-purpose language for the Java platform are very much inline with those of Grails as a web framework: to make the transition into the dynamically typed world as painless a learning experience as possible.

The creators of Groovy recognized that for Java developers to be truly productive when using a dynamic language it should not require a huge mental shift to go from language to language. Thanks to this, Groovy uses a strikingly similar syntax and the same APIs available to you in the JDK.

Groovy compiles directly down to byte code, thus ensuring that it also shares the same object model as that used within the JVM. A Groovy object *is* a Java object and does not have any specialized interpreter or VM.

Java Integration

Groovy's ability to seamlessly integrate with Java, along with its Java-like syntax, is the No. 1 reason so much hype was generated around its conception. Here we had a language with similar capabilities to languages such as Ruby and Smalltalk running directly in the JVM. The potential is obvious, and the ability to intermingle Java code with dynamic Groovy code is huge.

In addition, Groovy allowed you to mix static types and dynamic types, providing the safety of static types with the power and flexibility to opt out of using static typing where deemed necessary.

This level of Java integration is what drives Groovy's continued popularity, and the world of web applications is no different. Across different programming platforms there are varying idioms to express essentially the same concept. In the Java world we have servlets, filters, tag libraries, and Java Server Pages (JSP). Moving to a new platform requires relearning all of these concepts and their equivalent APIs or idioms—easy for some, a challenge for others.

Not that learning new things is bad, but the problem is that there is a cost attached to knowledge gain in the real world, and this can be a major stumbling block in the adoption of any new technology that deviates from the standards or conventions defined within the Java platform and the enterprise.

In addition, there are standards within Java for deployment, management, security, naming, and more. The goal of Grails is to create a platform with the essence of frameworks like Ruby on Rails that embraces the mature environment that is the Java Enterprise Edition and associated APIs.

Simplicity and Power

Clearly embracing all of these wonderful features within the Java platform should not come at the cost of simplicity, and this is where the expressiveness of Groovy really shines through.

Groovy is one of the very few languages available on the Java platform that provides both tight Java integration and syntactic expressiveness. However, frequently, simplicity and convention will only get you so far. Grails aims to provide the flexibility to leverage the underlying "power features" of the Java platform.

To ensure this flexibility is available, careful choices were made regarding technologies that would power Grails. Reinvention of the wheel is not a phrase that sits well in the Java community, and hence the underlying infrastructure within Grails is powered by the most popular open source technologies in their respective categories:

Hibernate: The de facto standard for ORM in the Java world

Spring: The hugely popular open source Inversion of Control (IoC) container and wrapper framework for Java

Quartz: An enterprise-ready, job-scheduling framework allowing flexibility and durable execution of scheduled tasks

SiteMesh: A robust and stable layout-rendering framework

For some readers the concept of ORM and IoC may seem a little alien. As an explanation, ORM simply serves as a way to map objects from the object-oriented world onto tables in a relational database. ORM provides an additional abstraction above SQL, allowing developers to think about their domain model instead of getting wrapped up in reams of SQL.

IoC, also known as *dependency injection*, is a way of "wiring" together objects so that their dependencies are available at run time. As an example, an object that performs persistence may require access to a data source. IoC provides a way to take the responsibility of obtaining a reference to the data source off the developer. Nevertheless, don't get too wrapped up in these concepts for the moment, as their usage will become clear later in the book.

Moving on, Grails exposes each of the aforementioned frameworks capabilities via a simplified interface, but still allows the usage of them using their documented configuration and development capabilities. Figure 1-1 illustrates how Grails relates to these frameworks and the Java enterprise stack.

At Grails' core lies the JVM, which both the Java and Groovy languages compile to via byte code. The leveraged frameworks, such as Spring, Hibernate, and Quartz (to name a few), are built on the strength of the Java language and the JVM. Groovy can work with these APIs outside of Grails, but Grails harnesses Groovy's advanced features combined with the Java Enterprise Edition environment to provide a simplified environment for building web applications.

The APIs for many of the frameworks depicted in Figure 1-1 are often criticized for being overly complex even though they're often spoken of as representing a *lightweight* approach to Java web application development. One of the primary aims of Grails is to provide an additional abstraction layer over these frameworks that takes advantage of the dynamic nature of Groovy.

However, the full underlying power of these frameworks is still readily available to harness should you so choose. Having all this power is one thing, but it would be rather silly if Grails didn't learn from some of the mistakes in previous generations of web frameworks.

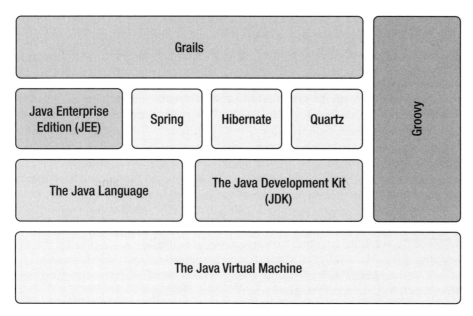

Figure 1-1. *How Grails stacks up*

Lessons Learned

Java web development practices and methodologies have been refined and optimized over a number of years. Mistakes have been made in both the frameworks and the specifications themselves. These have been slowly rectified over time in their various revisions based on the experiences and feedback from the Java community.

The dynamic language platforms are not entirely devoid of these mistakes themselves—things like cleanly separating logic so that the view does not contain scriptlet code, and providing a clean, clear model-view-controller (MVC) architecture where business logic is separated from view logic. The MVC architecture is designed to minimize this risk, but clearly it is still possible to fall into this trap within the constraints of an MVC application.

Grails aims to provide the necessary infrastructure to cleanly separate this logic and includes concepts more familiar in the Java space such as tag libraries, a service tier, and domain-driven development.

Why You Should Be Interested in Grails

So you've read a bit of the background, but the question is, why should you be interested in using it? Every solution is born out of a problem. The repetitive nature of web development and the common issues within it, such as application state, converting from text to object representation, and dealing with its multithreaded nature, are just some of the things faced by today's web application developers.

These are only growing more complex as the usage of technologies such as Ajax increase the complexity of the application state and push the number of requests into the stratosphere. A dynamic framework can help in reducing the strain of the development cycle at a more simplistic level.

However, there is a lot to be said for the benefits of static typing, advanced IDE support, and refactoring that is available on the Java platform and its associated development environments. As your application grows in complexity you begin to realize just how important these features are. Grails allows a blended approach by mixing both statically typed Java code and the dynamic nature of a language such as Groovy.

To this end, Grails allows you to scale up your application as it grows—scaling not in terms of performance, but in terms of *application complexity*. Have a particular piece of logic that is better suited to a Java implementation? No problem. Groovy and Grails work seamlessly with Java to enable this and thus allow you to continue using IDEs such as Eclipse and IntelliJ IDEA for code navigation, analysis, and refactoring.

Grails could be the solution that you've been looking for in the Java space. Even if you're already developing in one of the other aforementioned frameworks, Grails is worth a look because of the power and flexibility it offers, the ability to use a blended approach by mixing static and dynamic typing, and tight integration with the Java platform.

In addition, being able to integrate with Java and the JVM is only part of the story. Why dump all your knowledge of frameworks such as Spring and Hibernate? Grails is built on top of these, and their existing APIs are fully available for you to call just as in Java code. These frameworks are also written in Java themselves, so you get the benefit of that in terms of the performance they offer over their rivals.

Heard enough? Can't wait to get started? Let's start our journey into the Grails universe by installing it first.

Getting Started with Grails

As with any software, the first thing you need to do with Grails is install it. To do so follow these steps:

1. Download the latest Grails distribution from the web site `grails.org`.

2. Extract the relevant archive into a convenient location. If you're organized, this could be in a development sandbox or even simply on your desktop.

3. Set the `GRAILS_HOME` environment variable to the location where you extracted the Grails distribution. Setting environment variables is a rather platform-specific activity, but in Windows this can be via the Advanced tab in the properties of My Computer. Alternatively, if you're running Mac OS X you could add a `GRAILS_HOME` variable to your `.profile` file within your home directory (i.e., `cd ~`).

4. In addition, to get the Grails scripts to work from a terminal or command window you need to add the bin directory within Grails to your PATH that will make the Grails scripts visible to the window. To do this, take these steps:

   a. On Windows append %GRAILS_HOME%\bin to the Path variable.

   b. On Unix append $GRAILS_HOME/bin to the PATH variable.

To validate your installation, open a command window and type the command **grails**. If you have successfully installed Grails, the command will output the usage help executed in Listing 1-1.

■Note This listing introduces a convention that will be used throughout the book by using **bold** to highlight user input.

Listing 1-1. *Grails Command-Line Help*

```
>grails
```

```
help:
 Usage: grails [target]

Targets:
"create-app"            - Create a new grails app
"create-controller"     - Create a new controller
"create-service"        - Create a new service
"create-domain-class"   - Create a new domain class
"create-taglib"         - Create a new tag library class
"create-test-suite"     - Create a new test suite
"create-job"            - Create a quartz scheduled job
"generate-controller"   - Generates a controller from a domain class
"generate-views"        - Generates the views from a domain class
"generate-all"          - Generates all artifacts from a domain class
"test-app"              - Run current app's unit tests
"run-app"               - Run the application locally and wait
"create-webtest"        - Create the functional test layout
"run-webtest"           - Run the functional tests for a running app
"shell"                 - Opens the Grails interactive command line shell
"console"               - Opens the Grails interactive swing console
"war"                   - Create a deployable Web Application Archive (WAR)
```

It may be interesting to note at this point that Grails uses the Apache Ant (`http://ant.apache.org`) build system to power these targets, and throughout the book I will be referring to them as *targets* (as opposed to *commands* or *operations*).

Note Ant is supported by every modern IDE on the market and is the ubiquitous build system for the Java platform. The advantage being that there is an extremely high level of knowledge of Ant within the Java community, making the Grails build easily customizable if additional functionality is required by your development process.

Now that you've seen what targets are available, let's find out how to run them. Running the targets is a prerequisite to be able to effectively use Grails, so getting this step right will benefit you greatly in the long run. Luckily, it's pretty simple, as you'll see next.

Running the Targets

To execute the Grails targets you simply have to run the `grails` command followed by the name of the target. For example, to create a new Grails application, you could run the `grails create-app` command.

An additional feature of Ant is that you can combine targets. For example, if you need to test your application and then create a web application archive (WAR) file for deployment onto an application server you could type this:

```
grails test-app war
```

What this will do is execute the `test-app` target first and if successful will continue on to the `war` target. This becomes more useful as you get familiar with all the targets available and how they can be combined. It may be worth conducting some experiments of your own to get an idea of what's possible.

Looking back at the list of targets, the `create-*` targets are convenience targets for setting up a Grails application and creating Grails artifacts. However, unlike a few other frameworks, the targets themselves don't perform any special configuration of their own in the background. This is significant as it allows you to start off using the `create-*` targets as a learning tool to advance your knowledge of Grails.

Then once you are familiar enough with where everything goes you can create the various classes yourself using your favorite IDE if you so choose. Moving on, the `generate-*` targets are extremely powerful, allowing the generation of boilerplate code, which is great for both the learning process and getting started quickly. These will be discussed in detail in Chapter 5, which delves into a concept called *scaffolding*.

Of the remaining targets, the most useful are those for executing the Grails application (using the included Jetty application server) for running unit and functional web tests and creating web application archives.

The Obligatory "Hello World!"

So let's get started creating our first Grails application. As is traditional, no book would be complete without a "Hello World!" example, so here it is. To complete your journey through creating a "Hello World!" application you're going to step through the following tasks:

1. Execute the `grails create-app` command to create a basic Grails application.

2. Create something called a *controller* that will handle a web request.

3. Use the controller to display some text.

4. Run the Grails application and view what you achieved in a web browser.

So let's get going. First up is the creation of a project. Grails provides a target to do just this. Having a common project infrastructure across projects is hugely beneficial, as it ensures newcomers to a project who are already familiar with the way Grails projects are laid out can get up to speed quickly. This allows a developer to immediately focus his attention on the code instead of focusing on understanding how a project fits together.

Projects such as Maven (`http://maven.apache.org`) have introduced this concept in the Java world. Unfortunately the vast majority of projects still use a custom build system via Ant. It represents one of the graver mistakes made by the designers of the Java Enterprise Edition specification because every Java web project tends to have a different structure and resource layout. Needless to say, this is one mistake that can't be corrected easily, hence Grails ensures that projects are structured in a common way.

To create our "hello" application we need to run the `create-app` target. This will prompt you for the name of the application you wish to create. Enter the word **hello** and hit the return key as per the example in Listing 1-2.

Listing 1-2. *Running the create-app Target*

```
>grails create-app
init-props:

create-app:
    [input] Enter application name:
hello
```

Upon completion, the target will have created the "hello" Grails application and the necessary directory structure. The next step is to navigate to the newly created application in the command window using the shell command:

```
cd hello
```

At this point you have a clean slate—a newly created Grails application—with the default settings in place. A screenshot of the structure of a Grails application can be seen in Figure 1-2.

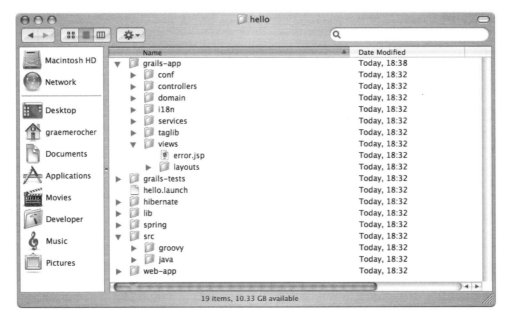

Figure 1-2. *The "hello" application structure*

We will delve more into the details of the structure of a Grails application and the roles of the various files and directories in Chapter 3. You will notice, however, how Grails contains directories for controllers, domain objects (models), and views.

Grails is an MVC framework and has models, views, and controllers to cleanly separate concerns. Nevertheless, to display a simple "Hello World!" we only need to be concerned with controllers for the moment.

Controllers are core to any MVC framework, Grails being no different; and in fact the only way to handle a request in Grails is to create a controller. Out of convenience, Grails provides a target to do just this. To create a controller, run the `create-controller` target and enter **hello** as the name of your controller followed by the Enter key. Listing 1-3 demonstrates this in action.

Listing 1-3. *Running the create-controller Target*

```
>grails create-controller
    [input] Enter controller name:
hello
```

This will create a new controller called `HelloController` within the `grails-app/controllers` directory of the Grails application as well as an associated unit test case called `grails-test/HelloTests.groovy`. As mentioned previously you could have created the controller with an IDE or text editor. Regardless, the resulting controller created for you will resemble something like this:

```
class HelloController {
    def index = { }
}
```

At the moment it contains only a single action called index. Yes, controllers have actions that they delegate to (another thing you'll learn about later in the book). Just to provide some clarity, the effect you want to achieve is depicted in the screenshot in Figure 1-3.

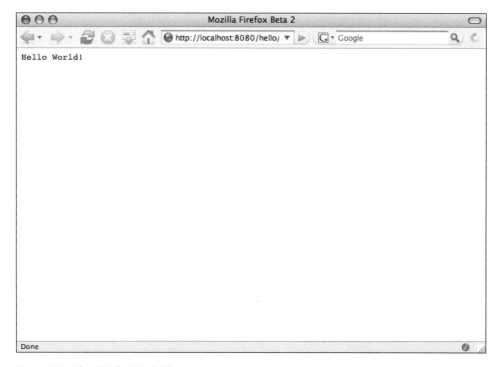

Figure 1-3. *The "Hello World!" response*

In order to create the response depicted in Figure 1-3, you're going to make some modifications to the HelloController and add a new action called world to it. Actions are both *closures* and *properties*. In the coming chapters you'll begin to understand more what this means at a practical level. Listing 1-4 demonstrates how to create the world action.

Listing 1-4. *The world Action*

```
class HelloController {
    // each action is a closure property
    def world = {
        render 'Hello World!' // render response
    }
}
```

The previous example defines a single action called world that renders the text "Hello World!" to the response. It does this using one of Grails' built-in methods called render, the details of which you'll learn about in Chapter 7. To try the "Hello World!" example, start the Grails application by running the following target:

```
grails run-app
```

Once the application has loaded, open a browser and navigate to the address shown in Figure 1-4 by typing the URL into the address bar (by default Grails starts up on port 8080).

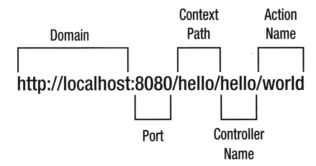

Figure 1-4. *The Grails URL format*

As the diagram illustrates, Grails uses a convention to automatically configure the path to a particular action. Following Figure 1-4, the *context path* is the root of the application and could be removed altogether if the final deployment environment is the root application. The *controller name* part of the URL is taken from the first part of the HelloController class's name. Essentially, the controller name is calculated as the controller class name minus the Controller suffix and the first letter in lowercase. Finally, the *action name* at the end of the URL shown in the figure maps to an *action* within the controller. In this case the URL will call the world action defined in Listing 1-4.

The result is that the text "Hello World!" will be displayed within the browser as depicted in Figure 1-5. Now, say instead of merely saying hello to the user you want to do something rather more useful such as displaying the current date and time.

To get the controller to display a message as well as the date and time, you need to open up the controller again and modify the world action as shown in Listing 1-5.

Listing 1-5. *Modified HelloController.groovy*

```groovy
class HelloController {
    def world = {
        render "Hello World it's " + new java.util.Date()
    }
}
```

Figure 1-5. *"Hello World!" plus the date*

The world action in Listing 1-5 concatenates the string "Hello World!" with an instance of the class java.util.Date, the standard class for handling dates in the JDK. Once the modification has been made don't stop the server, simply hit the Refresh button on the browser and note how your changes are immediately available with the action printing the "Hello World!" text followed by the current date and time. No recompilation step, no build to run, and no packaging required. Grails automatically reloads the controller at run time without you, the developer, needing to restart the server.

This simple example demonstrates some of the key features of Grails, including a glimpse into its MVC architecture, the tight integration with Java (I used java.util.Date), and the iterative development made possible by autoreloading.

This is just the taster, however, and in future chapters we'll explore Grails with more concrete examples.

The Unit Tests

Yes, it seems nowadays that no code can be written without an associated test, and rightly so. Fortunately, Grails has already created a test case for us called grails-test/HelloTests. groovy. The initial code for this unit test is the following:

```
class HelloTests extends GroovyTestCase {
    void testSomething() {
        // test code goes here!
    }
}
```

As you can see there is a testSomething method just waiting for us to populate it. Neverthe-less, there is an entire upcoming chapter dedicated to testing in Grails that tackles concepts such as basic unit testing, mock objects, and more. Hence, I'll defer going into any great detail about testing here until later. If you can't wait, the chapter in question is Chapter 6.

Summary

So far you learned how to create a Grails application, took a brief look at rendering responses with controllers, and had a glimpse at the Grails command-line targets. Clearly I only brushed the surface of Grails with the first example, and introducing the framework this way is little bit like plunging into the deep end of the Groovy and Grails world on Groovy.

In the next chapter I will go through an overview of the Groovy language and its key features, particularly those that are significant during Grails development. Feel free to skip Chapter 2 if you think you're already an expert on Groovy.

Chapter 2 is by no means a complete detail of the entire Groovy language, as that warrants a book by itself (and funny enough, there is one: Groovy in Action produced by Manning Publi-cations), however it will give you a feel of the language and why it is such a great fit for web application development.

CHAPTER 2

■■■

The Groovy Language

Groovy is an all-purpose programming language for the JVM. It was born in 2003 when James Strachan and Bob McWhirter founded the Groovy project with the goal of creating a glue language to easily combine existing frameworks and components. Groovy is a language that aims to bring the expressiveness of languages such as Ruby, Lisp, and Python to the Java platform while still remaining Java-friendly.

It attracted much excitement due to these ambitious goals, as the majority of other scripting languages on the Java platform either used an entirely alien syntax and APIs, or were simply Java without the need to specify types.

Despite its young age, thanks to the Java Specification Request (JSR-241), Groovy is a stable, feature-rich language that forms the perfect base for Grails. This can only be seen as a fantastic achievement, given the limited resources available to an open source project such as Groovy.

In terms of Grails, Groovy was an obvious choice as a platform for the framework, as it provides the necessary underlying infrastructure to create the diverse range of miniature domain-specific languages utilized throughout Grails.

Note Martin Fowler wrote an excellent article on the topic of domain-specific language: http://www.martinfowler.com/bliki/DomainSpecificLanguage.html.

What does this mean? Well the syntax you see used throughout this book is often magically enhanced and shortened by using a combination of Groovy's already-concise syntax and its support for metaprogramming. Groovy performs a lot of magic under the covers, removing the burden from the programmer who would otherwise be required to write reams of unnecessary, repetitive code.

Before you start your journey through the diverse syntax offered by Groovy, it is worth understanding how it compares to its Java brethren. In the next section you will see how seamlessly Groovy integrates with Java at the syntax level.

Groovy and Java: A Comparison

Groovy's resemblance to Java is often quite striking. Some Groovy code is almost indiscernible from Java. If your Groovy code looks too much like Java, you can improve its expressiveness by writing more idiomatic Groovy. Let's take a look at the key similarities and differences between Groovy and the Java language.

What's the Same?

There are actually many similarities between Java and Groovy. This is what makes Groovy so appealing from a Java developer's perspective. There is no huge mental shift necessary to start working with Groovy. The Groovy syntax can almost be seen as a superset of the Java language (although this is not the case), with the following taken directly from Java's syntax:

- Keywords and statements

- Try/catch/finally exception handling

- Class, interface, field, and method definitions

- Instantiation of objects using the new operator

- Packaging and imports

- Operators, expressions, and assignment

- Control structures

- Comments

More importantly though, Groovy shares the same object and runtime model as Java, meaning the infrastructure within which you are operating (the JVM) is the same. What does this mean? Well, although Groovy is a dynamic language similar in nature to Ruby or Python, it is *not* interpreted. All Groovy code, be it executed as a script or a fully qualified class, is compiled down to byte code and then executed.

The significance of this shouldn't be underestimated, as it means that a Groovy class *is* a Java class and they can interoperate with each other. A Java class can call methods on an interface implemented by Groovy without ever knowing any different.

So that's what is the same; again, I've given a brief overview, but really the similarities become obvious quite quickly once you start working with Groovy. Of equal significance, however, is what is *different* about Groovy.

What's Different?

What makes Groovy different is that there are a number of things that are optional in Groovy, including parentheses, return statements, and semicolons at the end of statements.

In addition, some `import` statements are optional, as Groovy automatically imports the following packages for you:

- `groovy.lang.*`
- `groovy.util.*`
- `java.lang.*`
- `java.util.*`
- `java.util.regex.*`
- `java.net.*`
- `java.io.*`
- `java.math.BigDecimal, java.math.BigInteger`

At the time of this writing Groovy did not support the classic `'for(init;test;inc)'` Java for loop. Support for this construct may be added in a future release of Groovy, however, due to Groovy's support for ranges it is not completely necessary, other than to placate the Java developers who feel more at home using this construct.

Over and above these differences, Groovy's main goal is to add features that make the common tasks faced by Java developers trivial. To facilitate this, Groovy supports the following:

- Closures (similar to anonymous code blocks, but with different scoping rules)
- Advanced string support with GStrings (described in the "Groovy Strings" section of this chapter), regular expressions, and template generation
- True object orientation with autoboxing/unboxing
- Operator overloading and syntactic structures to ease access to existing Java classes
- Improved syntax for existing data types augmented by news types
- An extended library of methods onto existing Java classes

At this point we've tackled many of the similarities and differences with Java but have yet to see any actual code. In the next section you start your journey into Groovy by getting the basics right first.

The Basics

The Groovy syntax is extremely closely aligned to that of Java; this does not mean that you can copy and paste Java code into Groovy and vice versa (although in some cases this does work), but it does mean that it all feels very familiar.

Fundamentally, Groovy can either be written in classes or as a script. Implementing the "Hello World!" example as a Groovy script would involve one line of code:

```
println 'Hello World!'
```

Assuming that you've saved this code into a file called `Hello.groovy`, executing this code is trivial too:

```
groovy Hello.groovy
```

Groovy automatically creates an executable *class* from the script. The reason this is highlighted is that it is important to note that even though no class has been declared, the previous code will inevitably still become a class that extends `groovy.lang.Script`, the superclass used by Groovy to provide support for running arbitrary snippets of code as scripts.

Like Java, everything in Groovy must be a class.

Declaring Classes

Class declaration is simple and familiar enough; in fact you've already seen an example of this in `HelloController`. Listing 2-1 serves as a reminder of the `HelloController` class definition.

Listing 2-1. *HelloController.groovy*

```
class HelloController {
    def world = {
        render "Hello World it's " + new java.util.Date()
    }
}
```

Here I have defined a class called `HelloController` that contains a single property called `world`. The property itself has been assigned a value, which is a closure. Java developers may be a little confused at the moment as to how this simple declaration can be a property given the verbosity of the property syntax in Java.

Essentially, another difference from Java is that Groovy has no concept of default visibility (also known as *package-level visibility*). Instead, properties declared at the default level, without any explicit modifiers such as `private`, `protected`, or `public`, are assumed to be JavaBean properties, and the appropriate getters and setters are generated for you.

The lack of default visibility also becomes clear when defining methods, as methods are assumed to be public if no modifier is specified. In the next few sections we'll be taking a look at some of these, as well as some of the other powerful features that Groovy offers, starting with built-in assertions.

Language-Level Assertions

Assertions are a concept introduced to the Java language in Java 5 that allow you to verify application state at a certain point. Like Java, Groovy has an `assert` keyword, however, unlike Java, it is not reliant on having a Java 5 virtual machine in place.

Assertions are primarily useful to avoid the scenario where code is executed under an invalid state and, to this end, is a useful debugging tool. In terms of this book, assertions are also useful for revealing what the current state of an executing Groovy program is. An example of an assertion in action can be seen in Listing 2-2.

Listing 2-2. *Groovy Assertions*

```
def num = 1
...
assert num == 1
```

Here we simply verify that the variable called num still has a value of 1 at the point of execution in the code. Assertions will be utilized throughout many of the following examples, including in our coverage of Groovy strings, which we'll look at next.

Groovy Strings

Groovy supports a concept found in many other languages such as Perl and Ruby called *string interpolation.* As this is rather a mouthful in Groovy-land they're simply (or comically, depending on which way you look at it) known as GStrings.

A GString is just like a normal string, but it allows embedding of variables within it, using the familiar ${..} syntax found in many popular Java frameworks including Spring, Apache Ant, and an array of different view technologies. The curly braces can actually be omitted if it is simply the variable name that is required. Listing 2-3 demonstrates another powerful feature of Groovy's string support: multiline strings. These are defined with the triple-quotation syntax.

Listing 2-3. *GStrings in Action*

```
def person = "John"

println """
${new Date()}

Dear $person,

This is a Groovy letter!

Yours Sincerely,
The XYZ Company
"""
```

On the first line of the listing, I define a variable called `person` that is then later referenced from the string itself. The multiline string can span several lines and includes all new line characters, tabs, and spaces in its output. The resulting output of the listing can be seen here:

```
Thu Sep 14 06:20:58 BST 2006

Dear John,

This is a Groovy letter!

Yours Sincerely,
The XYZ Company
```

Coming from Java, where every new line has to be closed with a quote and contain the + concatenation character, this example comes as rather a relief. This also brings us nicely to another difference from Java in the way that Groovy interprets strings vs. characters. In Java, a character is defined using the single-quotation syntax, while in Groovy it could either represent a regular string (i.e., one not of the GString variety) or a character. For example the declarations in Listing 2-4 are all valid in Groovy, while in Java the first and third would produce compilation errors.

Listing 2-4. *String and Characters in Groovy*

```
String hello = 'Hello' // a regular String
String greeting = "$hello World!" // a GString
def c = '\n' as char // A java.lang.Character new line character
char c = '\n' // the same as above
```

Believe it or not there is yet another alternative for declaring strings in Groovy. It is known as the *slashy* syntax and allows easy definition of regular expressions (regex) without the need to introduce escape characters as with Java.

■**Note** *Regular expressions* are a way of doing pattern matching against strings. Commonly referred to as *regex* they define a set of matching operators that can be used to match almost any pattern in a string. A full discussion on regex is beyond the scope of this book, but there are many references available online about the topic.

This allows you to omit the backslash (\) escape character that cripples Java's regex support. Consider the example in Listing 2-5.

Listing 2-5. *Groovy vs. Java Regex*

```
def file = /C:\this\will\need\escaping\afile.pdf/
// This is what you need in Java
assert file ==~ "\\w{1}:\\\\.+\\\\.+\\\\.+\\\\.+\\.pdf"
// And here is how you do it in Groovy
assert file ==~ /\w{1}:\\.+\\.+\\.+\\.+\.pdf/
```

Here we have an example of an attempt to match a file reference on a Windows system. Since Windows uses the backslash character in file references it means that you would need to escape every one of these in the Java regex expression on line 3 twice—once because Java requires you to, and again because regex does too.

But thanks to Groovy's slashy syntax, on line 5 you are able to avoid this particular nightmare by at least having to only escape the backslash character once.

In addition to the slashy syntax, Groovy's regex support goes even further, with support for specialized regex operators, some examples of which can be seen in Listing 2-6.

Listing 2-6. *Groovy Regular Expressions*

```
1  import java.util.regex.*
2
3  // usage of the matching operator which returns a Boolean
4  assert 'abababab' ==~ /(ab)+/
5
6
7    // Here the pattern operator is used
8    // to create a java.util.regex.Pattern instances
9    def pattern = ~/foo/
10   assert pattern instanceof Pattern
11
12  // The matcher operator allows you to create a
13  // java.util.regex.Matcher instance
14  def matcher = "cheesecheese" =~ /cheese/
15  assert matcher instanceof Matcher
```

The first example on line 4 uses the match ==~ operator that will attempt to match the entire string against the provided regex. Next, line 9 demonstrates how to create an instance of java.util.regex.Pattern using the pattern operator.

Essentially by starting a string with the ~ character, it creates the Pattern instance instead of a string. The pattern operator is commonly seen applied directly before slashy stings in the format ~/.../, but can in fact be applied to any string.

Note It is important to notice the space between the equals sign and the ~ character that differentiates the pattern operator from the find =~ operator on line 14.

Lastly, the find =~ operator on line 14 will find the first match in the supplied string and, if used in an assignment as seen in the example, will return a java.util.regex.Matcher instance. A full discussion on regular expressions is rather beyond the scope of this book; nevertheless, what you have seen so far serves to introduce the capabilities Groovy has to offer in terms of regex support.

The next section should be pretty interesting as we explore Groovy's closure support. The closure, as a construct, is beginning to get much attention among the software development community as the benefits (and also the limitations of languages that don't have them) have started to become abundantly clearer.

Closures

Closures can essentially be seen as reusable code blocks (often called *anonymous code blocks*). At a simplistic level they are a sequence of statements surrounded by curly braces. They can be quite difficult to understand in the beginning at a conceptual level, but once you begin using them it becomes hard to comprehend how you ever lived without them.[1] Let's take a look at a basic example shown in Listing 2-7.

Listing 2-7. *Simple Closure*

```
def square = { it * it }
assert [1,4,9] == [1,2,3].collect(square)
```

The previous example can be seen as a similar concept to creating a function pointer in C, although the behavior of closures differs significantly. First you define a closure and assign it to a variable called square that takes the default argument and multiplies it by itself. The default argument in Groovy is called it and is useful for simple definitions.

The square closure is then passed to another one of Groovy's built-in methods called collect that will collect each element from the list and apply the passed closure to its value. In this case the result is a list of numbers that represent the square root of each element in the original list.

Clearly it's useful to be able to pass blocks of code around in this fashion, however, another useful way to use closures is inline as an argument to a method. This can be seen as similar to using an anonymous inner class in Java, except the syntax is significantly more elegant, as Listing 2-8 demonstrates.

Listing 2-8. *Groovy step Method*

```
def lastRevision = 0.9

0.1.step(lastRevision, 0.1) { currentRevision ->
    println( currentRevision )
}
```

---

1. There are a number who feel now is the time for Java to introduce closure support and this may happen in the future. See http://mindprod.com/jgloss/closure.html for information on why Java doesn't at present support closures.

The previous code steps through all the revisions of an imaginary version control repository and outputs each revision number. The last argument of the method is a closure, which is executed on each iteration (or *step* if we're using the method's verb).

■**Note** The `step` method itself actually takes three arguments. The last of these arguments is a closure instance. Note how Groovy allows the closure to be specified at the end of the expression.

Clearly closures take some getting used to when coming from Java, but if you think of them as a type of anonymous inner class it will go a long way to aid your understanding. You'll see many more examples of their usage in the coming chapters as well as see them combined with another powerful Groovy concept: builders.

In the next section we'll look at how Groovy greatly simplifies the Java collections API by providing language-level constructs for common Java types, as well as one of its own.

Lists and Maps

Groovy contains first-class constructs for two of the most commonly used collections in Java: list and map. This new syntax combined with operator overloading and additional methods that use closures (provided by Groovy to extend the Java collection API) are a powerful combination best illustrated with some examples, shown in Listing 2-9.

Listing 2-9. *Collections in Action*

```
1    // prints 1 2 3 separated by new lines to standard out
2    [1,2,3].each { num -> println num }
3    // create an empty list
4    def list = []
5    // use overloaded left shift operator to append items
6    list << 'one' << 'two' << 'three'
7    // check that we have 3 items
8    assert list.size() == 3
9    // Use Groovy's findAll method to find all words containing the letter "o"
10   assert list.findAll { item -> item.contains('o') }.size() == 2
11   // Merges a list into a string using the supplied string
12   assert list.join(',') == 'one,two,three'
13
14   // map of contact numbers
15   def contacts = [ Fred : '903-0200-1565',
16                    Wilma: '903-0207-7401' ]
17   contacts.each { key, value ->
18       println "calling $key on $value"
19   }
20   // add new contact
21   contacts.Dino = '903-0207-0349'
22   assert contacts.size() == 3
```

Here you can see various usages of Groovy lists and maps. First, in line 2 there is an example of using Groovy's each method to iterate over a list of integer values:

```
2   [1,2,3].each { num -> println num }
```

The example calls each directly on the list definition and prints out each element of the list using println, resulting in this output:

```
1
2
3
```

Next, there is an interesting use of the left shift << operator to append elements to the list. In Groovy the left shift operator is generally available on all objects that have the concept of *appending* such as lists, buffers, and streams:

```
6   list << 'one' << 'two' << 'three'
```

Groovy then checks the size of the list using the size method. The size method is interesting in that even though it does exist for collections it can be used on pretty much any object that has the concept of size or length. Java is extremely inconsistent in its handling of size and length, and there are different ways to obtain this information, depending on whether you are working with strings, arrays, or collections. Groovy attempts to unify this into a single method:

```
8   assert list.size() == 3
```

There is another example of closures in action, which I will be introducing further in the next section. Here, on line 10 Groovy's findAll method is used on the list to locate all strings within the list that contain the letter *O*. The closure passed to findAll is evaluated as the criteria on each element of the list:

```
10  assert list.findAll { item -> item.contains('o') }.size() == 2
```

Another useful method in the toolbox is join, which allows you to merge any list or array into a string using the passed arguments as the separator. Here you create a comma-separated string of all elements in the collection:

```
12  assert list.join(',') == 'one,two,three'
```

The next example demonstrates Groovy's built-in syntax for defining maps:

```
15  def contacts = [ Fred : '903-0200-1565',
16                   Wilma: '903-0207-7401' ]
```

Here you create a java.util.Map that has two elements representing contact information for Fred and Wilma. Groovy allows you to omit the quotes around keys within the map syntax so the keys Fred and Wilma in the example translate into strings.

■**Note** The map concept in Java is equivalent to what is known as a *hash* in many other languages. In fact, the default implementation used is `java.util.HashMap`.

Sometimes you want to use something other than a string as the key and want to resolve an object from the surrounding scope as the key. If this is the case, you need to surround the key with parentheses (`...`).

Lines 17-19 in the example demonstrate how you can use the each method to iterate over a map in the same way you do other collection objects, with the key and value coming in as arguments to the method. More interestingly, however, is the use of the dereference operator on line 21:

```
21 contacts.Dino = '903-0207-0349'
```

This will actually create a new key called Dino, with the value being the telephone number. Why is this interesting? Well it allows you to treat maps almost like dynamic objects. Speaking of dynamic objects, there is a particular type of Groovy object called Expando.

Expando Objects

It is often useful to be able to create an object dynamically at run time, particularly if it is not a frequently used one that warrants a class definition. This is where Expando comes in handy. Consider the example in Listing 2-10.

Listing 2-10. *Expando in Action*

```
fred = new Expando()

fred.firstName = "Fred"
fred.lastName = "Flintstone"

fred.age = 45
fred.happyBirthday = {
    fred.age++
}

fred.happyBirthday()
assert fred.age == 46
```

As you can see Expando allows you to programmatically define an object, its properties, and its methods at run time. This example creates an Expando object called `fred`, then simply goes about assigning some properties with some initial values. A method is defined by setting a closure to a property that can be later called like a regular method.

So far you've seen quite a range of Groovy features, and with that particular pun out of the way we're going to move onto another type introduced by Groovy: ranges.

Ranges

Groovy supports the concept of inclusive and exclusive ranges at the language level. Ranges at a conceptual level are a left and right value with a strategy for how to move from left to right. Ranges can be used on numbers, strings, dates, and any other object that implements the Comparable interface and defines next and previous methods.

■Note The java.lang.Comparable interface is Java's way of comparing two objects. It defines a single method called compareTo(Object) that returns an integer. The method should return 1 if the passed object is greater than this object, -1 if it is less than this object, and 0 if they are equal.

Listing 2-11 shows some examples of using ranges in combination with Groovy's advanced switch statement.

Listing 2-11. *Ranges in Action*

```
def person = Expando()
person.name = "Fred"
person.age = 45

def child = 0..16 // inclusive range
def adult = 17.<66 // exclusive range
def senior = 66..120 //

switch(fred.age) {
    case child:
        println "You're too young ${fred.name}!"
    break
    case adult:
        println "Welcome ${fred.name}!"
    break
    case senior:
        println "Welcome ${fred.name}! Take a look at our senior citizen rates!"
    break
}
```

In this example there are three ranges plus Groovy's advanced switch capabilities to print different messages depending on the age of the user. Ranges are commonly used in Groovy as a replacement for the traditional Java for loop using Groovy's for..in syntax and in combination with the subscript operator.

Listing 2-12 shows how to use the for loop with a range applied to a string using the subscript operator.

Listing 2-12. *The Groovy for Loop and Ranges*

```
def text = 'print me'
for(i in 0..<text[0..4]) {
    println text[i]
}
assert 'print' == text[0..4]
```

Here you're looping through the first four characters of the supplied text (remember the previous example is an inclusive range) and printing out each character. The output of the for loop equates to the following:

```
p
r
i
n
```

And that sums up this whirlwind tour of Groovy basics. You've explored a lot, and although this section is by no means comprehensive, it should give you an idea of what Groovy is capable of as a general-purpose language.

In the next section you'll start to explore the features that make Grails a possibility. What you've seen so far is great, but there is so much more to Groovy that makes it one of the most dynamic languages available on the JVM today.

Groovy Power Features

The next sections are by no means a prerequisite for using Groovy but will aid you in understanding what makes Groovy so powerful when compared to some of its dynamic sister languages that exist on the JVM.

Three features that we're going to explore in particular detail are the following:

- True object orientation

- Metaprogramming

- Builders

Everything Is an Object

Unlike Java, which mixes primitive and reference types, in Groovy everything is an object. How is it possible that Groovy does this while maintaining integration with Java? Well, before Java 5.0 was even introduced with Generics and autoboxing, Groovy was doing this for you in Java 1.4.

When a primitive type gets passed into the Groovy world it is automatically "boxed" into its object equivalent and vice versa. This allows Groovy to support some interesting concepts, which I will cover in the following sections:

- Methods on Primitives

- Operator Overloading

- The Groovy Truth

In this respect Groovy is far more true to object-oriented languages such as Smalltalk than Java, since even operators such as ==, !=, +, and – are translated into method calls at run time.

■Note Groovy's == operator differs from Java's in that it does not evaluate object identity, but delegates to the object's `equals` method. For object identity, Groovy introduces a special `is` method: `left.is(right)`.

To get you on your way to understanding the implications and possibilities that true object orientation offers, the first thing we're going to look at is Groovy's ability to support methods on "primitives."

Methods on Primitives

Since Groovy performs autoboxing at run time, you then automatically have all the methods available in the concrete class equivalent (the Java primitive type `int` becomes `java.lang.Integer`, for example) as well as some additional ones provided by Groovy.

Combine this feature with Groovy's closure support and it provides some interesting use cases. Listing 2-13 provides various examples of calling methods on integers.

Listing 2-13. *Methods on Numbers*

```
3.times {
    println it
}
// iterates from 3 to 9
3.upto(9) {
    println it
}
// iterates from 3 to 9 in increments of 3
3.step(9,3) {
    println it
}
```

The previous examples provide a little taster of what allowing methods on primitive types means to Java developers. For others this may not seem so revolutionary; nevertheless it's another string on the Groovy bow.

Operator Overloading

Operator overloading, which has a love/hate relationship in the world of C++, has been incorporated into the Groovy language in an extremely elegant fashion. As mentioned previously, Groovy is a true object-oriented language, and this extends into the operators themselves. Operators in Groovy are actually simply method calls that follow a naming convention.

Table 2-1 lists the Groovy operators and their equivalent methods. To utilize operators simply add the necessary method to your object.

Table 2-1. *Groovy Operator Method Names*

Operator	Method
a + b	a.plus(b)
a - b	a.minus(b)
a * b	a.multiply(b)
a / b	a.divide(b)
a++ or ++a	a.next()
a-- or --a	a.previous()
a[b]	a.getAt(b)
a[b] = c	a.putAt(b, c)
a << b	a.leftShift(b)

It doesn't end here however. Groovy also uses operator overloading to overload the comparison operators. Table 2-2 shows these operators and the methods or expressions they evaluate to.

Table 2-2. *Groovy Comparison Operator Method Names*

Operator	Method
a == b	a.equals(b)
a != b	! a.equals(b)
a <=> b	a.compareTo(b)
a > b	a.compareTo(b) > 0
a >= b	a.compareTo(b) >= 0
a < b	a.compareTo(b) < 0
a <= b	a.compareTo(b) <= 0

In addition, Groovy provides a number of built-in operators on common Java types that let you work with them in intuitive ways. As an illustration, the left shift `<<` operator can be used to do the following:

- Append an item to a `java.util.List`

- Output data to a `java.io.Writer` or a `java.io.OutputStream`

- Append characters onto a `java.lang.StringBuffer`

There are many more such operators that Groovy provides across the JDK classes—too many to list here—hence it is worthwhile to explore available operators within the Groovy documentation and source code. As your knowledge of Groovy grows, you will find yourself using them more and more and even providing your own.

The Groovy Truth

What is true and what isn't is very different in Groovy in comparison to Java, but not in a bad way. The term "the Groovy Truth" was coined by Dierk Koenig, Groovy committer and author of *Groovy in Action* published by Manning Publications, to differentiate Groovy's concept of what is true and what is not. As an example, the following, by no means comprehensive, list can be passed to `if` statements in Groovy and will evaluate to `false`:

- A `null` reference

- An empty or `null` string

- The number zero

- A regex `Matcher` that doesn't match

This makes for infinitely cleaner code and decreases the burden on the programmer to make sure that `null` checks are valid, that they're checking that a string is not `null` and is not zero length (boy that's a mouthful), and a whole hoard of other possibilities that cause error-prone code.

In the context of web applications this is extremely useful given the amount of string evaluation necessary (remember request parameters come in as strings).

Using the Groovy Truth, the `if`, `while`, and `assert` statements become rather more intelligent than their equivalents in Java. However, it simply wouldn't be Groovy if it wasn't taken even further. In Java the `switch` statement is rarely used. Why? Well it's fairly limiting in that it only operates in conjunction with the `int` or `char` primitive types (as well as `Enum` since Java 5).

In Groovy, however, the `switch` statement is your best friend and one of the more frequently used constructs. Groovy's `switch` accepts *any* object that implements the method `isCase`. Default implementations of `isCase` are provided for many of the commonly used types; if none is provided, it simply delegates to the `equals` method. Listing 2-14 shows the `switch` statement in action and how it can be used in conjunction with a variety of types.

Listing 2-14. *Usage of Groovy switch*

```
switch (x) {
  case 'Graeme':
    println "yes it's me"
    break
  case 18..65:
    println "ok you're old enough"
    break
  case ~/Gw?+e/:
    println 'your name starts with G and ends in e!'
    break
  case Date:
    println 'got a Date instance'
    break
  case ['John', 'Ringo', 'Paul', 'George']:
    println "It's one of the beatles! "
    break
  default:
    println "That is something entirely different"
}
```

The previous example is just a taster of what is possible with the Groovy switch. Try doing some experiments of your own to get used to the behavior of switch and how isCase behaves for each type.

Given what you've seen so far with Groovy's ability to dynamically dispatch operators and methods and box primitive types in objects, you would think that I've covered the parts that make Groovy truly dynamic. Not quite. In the next section you'll look at Groovy's metaprogramming support, which makes Groovy extremely compelling and powerful and helps put it on an even keel with languages such as Ruby and Python.

Metaprogramming

Any concept that has a colorful name such as *metaprogramming* sounds scary, but fundamentally, metaprogramming in Groovy is the ability to add behavior to classes at run time. You've already seen this in action a countless number of times already with Groovy's seemingly magical ability to add new methods to existing Java classes.

Given that the Java's class loading mechanism dictates that classes, once loaded, cannot be changed, you may be wondering how this is possible at all.

What Groovy does is that for every class loaded by the Groovy runtime there is an associated MetaClass that is used when dispatching methods to the class itself. Think of it in terms of a proxy that delegates to the actual implementation. The remarkable thing with Groovy, however, is that it doesn't just cover method dispatching. Constructors, fields, operators (due to operator overloading), properties, static, and instance methods can all be added, intercepted, or modified at run time thanks to Groovy's Meta Object Protocol (MOP).

Outside of Groovy, the way this is done is through software such as AspectJ, an implementation of Aspect-Oriented Programming (AOP) for Java, which does byte code weaving. In Groovy, byte code manipulation is unnecessary, and through Groovy's metafacility, Grails is able to perform a lot of magic in one line of code that would otherwise be reams of complicated Java code.

A full discussion of the implementation details and possibilities of `MetaClass` within Groovy is beyond the scope of this book, but it is, however, important to understand what a powerful concept this is and how it is leveraged within Grails.

None of Grails' classes extend any special framework-specific classes, and the necessary behavior is instead injected into your classes at run time via the `MetaClass`. The `MetaClass` concept in combination with Groovy's advanced syntax is also what enables a concept called *builders*. In the next section we look at what builders are, what's the driving force behind their conception, and why they're so important to the overall picture.

Understanding Builders

A *builder* is an object that implements the builder pattern. The Gang of Four's book (*Design Patterns: Elements of Reusable Object-Oriented Software* by Erich Gamma, Richard Helm, Ralph Johnson, and John Vlissides) introduces one particular pattern known as the *builder* pattern. The idea behind it is to construct complex objects from another object or builder. For example, you may need to build a complex markup hierarchy with the root object being the document itself. A builder would encapsulate the logic to construct or *build* this object for you.

The builder pattern is actually extremely difficult (some would say impossible, and that current implementations are merely mimicking a true builder, although efforts have been made in projects such as Commons CLI and IntelliJ IDEA PSI) to implement in Java due to the limitations of the syntax. Groovy, however, has no such problem, thanks to its support for named arguments, closures, and optional parentheses.

■**Note** Groovy doesn't support true named arguments, but allows the method to specify a map as the only argument, hence mimicking this capability. This limitation is mainly down to Java byte code itself, which does not associate names (only types) with method parameters.

Groovy ships with a number of builders built-in, including but not limited to the following:

- The MarkupBuilder for constructing, typically XML, markup

- The DOMBuilder for constructing W3C DOM trees

- The AntBuilder to provide scripting for Apache Ant

- The SwingBuilder and an SWT builder (as a module) for constructing GUI interfaces

As an example we'll take a look at usage of the MarkupBuilder, shown in Listing 2-15, which allows construction of markup documents such as XML or HTML.

Listing 2-15. *MarkupBuilder in Action*

```
// construct builder that outputs to standard out
def mkp = new groovy.xml.MarkupBuilder()

// write mark-up
mkp.authors {
     author(name:'Stephen King') {
         book( title:'The Shining')
         book( title:'The Stand')
     }
     author(name: 'James Patterson') {
         book( title:'Along Came a Spider' )
     }
}
```

The previous example demonstrates the construction of a groovy.xml.MarkupBuilder instance using standard out and the usage of closures and named arguments to represent the markup. The result is shown in Listing 2-16.

Listing 2-16. *Result of MarkupBuilder*

```
<authors>
     <author name="Stephen King">
         <book title="The Shining" />
         <book title="The Stand" />
     </author>
     <author name="James Patterson">
         <book title="Along Came a Spider" />
     </author>
</authors>
```

It is interesting at this point to just step back a moment and take a closer look at Listing 2-15. In this example we passed an "anonymous" closure to the authors() method of the MarkupBuilder instance; but imagine for the moment the possibility of assigning this closure to a variable and then passing as an argument the same closure to different builders, one that renders XML and another that outputs the same data as a PDF document or renders it in a GUI.

Unlike the produced XML in Listing 2-16, the builder code in Listing 2-15 is pure Groovy code and can therefore leverage the full power of the language: conditionals, looping, referencing, inheritance, and so on.

Builders are an extremely powerful concept, and if you're willing to delve into some Groovy development by extending the BuilderSupport class to create your own builders, you can create some pretty amazing constructs that could end up as domain-specific languages within your application.

Grails utilizes builders all over the place, from constructing Hibernate criteria to rendering markup to the HTTP response. Builders are a key element to the conciseness and power that Grails brings to web application development.

Summary

That completes this whiz through the Groovy language. As previously mentioned, this is by no means comprehensive. Groovy has many more fantastic features; hence it is really worth investing the time in learning more aspects of Groovy. But this should give you an idea of why some of the features within Groovy are so important to Grails and how they make life easier developing today's web applications.

You saw that Groovy looks pretty much like Java at first glance, allowing a smooth transition into the new world of dynamic programming. Since Groovy is fully integrated into the Java platform and works directly on JDK objects, your investment in learning Java and your experience with the platform is fully protected.

What's new is that Groovy gives you more immediate control over types such as lists and maps, making programming feel more like having a horse on short reins. New concepts such as closures and ranges perfectly complete the picture. The combination of syntax enhancements, new types, improvements to JDK classes, and metaprogramming leads to an idiomatic Groovy style that is both simple and powerful. Next you're going to dive straight into Grails by going through a brief introduction and then looking at its project infrastructure.

CHAPTER 3

■■■

The Grails Project Infrastructure

Have you ever started a new Java web development project and asked yourself where to put the sources? What about the tests? Configuration anyone? Or maybe it was a project that was already up and running: did you understand the directory layout and purpose? It was brushed upon before, but it is worth re-emphasizing that a major downfall in Java projects is that there is no specification that dictates *how* a web application project should be structured. Hence, moving from project to project causes some difficulty, particularly between companies with different methodologies, build systems, and development processes.

Grails aims to circumvent this problem by providing this information and structure for you. Every Grails project is structured in the same manner; therefore, finding the code you need to change to maintain a Grails project becomes that much simpler once you are familiar with what goes where.

With that in mind let's look at the overall structure of a Grails project and what each bit does.

Overview of a Grails Project

You've already seen in the "Hello World!" example in Chapter 1 exactly how to go about creating a Grails application, but what I didn't cover is what each bit does and what it means to you as a budding Grails developer.

Just to recap what you learned previously, and to start off the sample application that you'll be following throughout the whole book (a social bookmarking application), I'm going to run through the process of creating a Grails application again.

■**Note** *Social bookmarking* is a popular concept pioneered by sites such as `http://del.icio.us/`, which allows users to share bookmarks with each other by making them public and attaching tags to them.

If you recall from the first chapter, Grails has a special target that manages this tedious process for you. The target in question is called `create-app` and we'll use it now to create the bookmarks application by running it using `grails create-app`, as shown in Listing 3-1.

Listing 3-1. *Creating the Bookmarks Application*

```
>grails create-app
init-props:

create-app:
    [input] Enter application name:
bookmarks
```

Once again the areas of user input are highlighted in bold. After the target has completed execution, a number of new directories will be created and files copied, all sitting snugly within a bookmarks directory. The screenshot in Figure 3-1, from a Windows system, illustrates this.

■**Tip** By default the grails create-app target creates a Servlet 2.4–compliant Grails application, but you can create a Grails application for Servlet 2.3 and 2.5 environments too. Simply pass the servlet. version argument to the run-app target: grails -Dservlet.version=2.5 run-app.

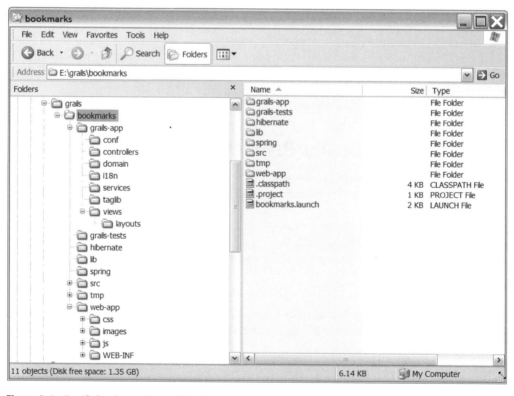

Figure 3-1. *Grails bookmarks application*

Essentially, the core of a Grails application resides within the `grails-app` directory, which contains all of the core artifacts such as controllers, domain models, and so on.

Web application resources such as static HTML, JavaScript, and CSS reside within the `web-app` directory as well as other resources such as the `web.xml` file required to conform to the Servlet specification.

Table 3-1 shows a breakdown of each directory and what it represents within a Grails application.

Table 3-1. *Grails Project Directories*

Directory Name	Description
grails-app	Directory containing core Grails artifacts
+ conf	Configuration elements, such as the `DevelopmentDataSource.groovy`
+ controllers	Controllers that handle requests (covered in Chapter 7)
+ domain	The location of the domain model (covered in Chapter 4)
+ i18n	Internationalization message bundles
+ services	Services that encapsulate business logic (covered in Chapter 10)
+ taglib	Dynamic tag libraries to aid in view rendering (covered in Chapter 8)
+ views	Groovy Server Pages (GSP) or JSP views
+ layouts	GSP or JSP layouts powered by SiteMesh (covered in Chapter 8)
grails-test	Application unit tests
hibernate	Optional Hibernate configuration (covered in Chapter 11)
lib	JAR archives
spring	Optional Spring configuration (covered in Chapter 11)
src	Directory for other Groovy and Java sources
+ java	Further Java sources for compilation
+ groovy	Further Groovy sources for compilation
web-app	Remaining web application resources (CSS, JavaScript, etc.)

Note that the configuration files found within the `spring`, `hibernate`, and `web-app/WEB-INF` directories require no configuration for pure Grails development. If you're not concerned with the intricacies of these, just leave them alone. Alternatively, feel free to harness the underlying power of configuration if you need it. This is the essence of Grails.

Nevertheless, we will be looking at some more of the advanced configuration options in greater detail when we get into the optional topic of integrating Grails with Java servlets, services, and domain models in Chapter 11.

Grails and the MVC Pattern

As you may have noted already, Grails organizes an application in the MVC pattern that separates the application's domain model, user interface (or view), and controller logic.

This allows for the separation of concerns and minimizes the risk of mixing logic between components. If you're already familiar with the pattern, feel free to skip the following sections, although it may be of use to observe how the pattern relates to Grails. A diagram of the MVC pattern is shown in Figure 3-2.

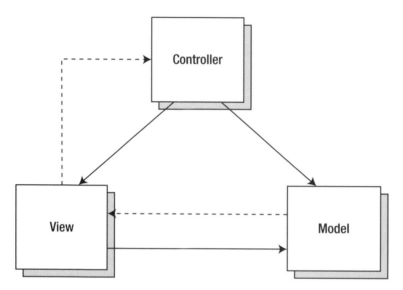

Figure 3-2. *MVC pattern diagram*

To facilitate the separation of concerns that MVC provides within the grails-app directory, controllers are placed within the controllers directory, views within the views directory, and the domain model within the domain directory.

The *M* in MVC

The *domain model* is the core of your application where your business entities are defined. As an example, if you were modeling a bookshop you may have entities such as Book and Author. These entities hold the state of your application and are more often than not persistent. They also implement behavior (the verbs within your application) and are related to each other in some way: one-to-many, many-to-one, one-to-one, or many-to-many. You will take a closer look at Grails' support for implementing domain models in Chapter 4.

Note Users of Rails may be interested to note that the `models` directory is called `domain` in Grails. Within the Java world, and indeed within Grails, the approach to developing applications is through *domain-driven* development, where the core of your application is defined and driven by a *domain model*. This is common through most ORM solutions and differs greatly from the Rails approach where the core of your application is the database itself.

The *V* in MVC

The *view* is responsible for rendering the interface, typically HTML, in a web application. The view often needs a model to render the user interface and this is passed to the view by the controller. Views are covered in Chapter 8.

The *C* in MVC

Controllers are the dictators of your application and handle user actions. They coordinate requests via actions and compile a model and delegate or create a view. Controllers sometimes interact with the domain model and often perform changes to the model. At other times they simply delegate or redirect to another view or action. Controllers are clearly important and so are covered in depth in Chapter 7.

Beyond MVC

The MVC pattern is just part of the story, as you can see by the directory structure. The reality is the complexity of modern web applications results in the need for further layers of abstraction. At a controller level this could be moving some controller logic into a shareable service class that could be used from multiple places featured in Chapter 10.

Views would have a big job on their hands without a little help, thus the need for *view helpers* that in Grails take the shape of dynamic tag libraries covered in Chapter 8. Web applications also have to deal in some way with internationalization (i18n) and maintenance, hence there are message bundles (Chapter 8) and job scheduling (Chapter 10).

If web applications were as simple as the MVC pattern, all this would be unnecessary. As it is, they're not, and Grails provides the features to ease commonly recurring problems. In the next section we'll take a look at how Grails deals with the concept of multiple environments.

Being Environmentally Friendly

Typically in any web application production team you have a development configuration for the application that may be configured to work with a locally installed database. This configuration sometimes even differs from developer to developer, depending on their specific desktop configuration.

In addition, QA staff that test the work produced by developers have a separate machine that is configured in a similar way to the production environment. So far, we know of two environments already, but then there is the third example of having a configuration for production when the system goes live.

This scenario is ubiquitous across pretty much every development project, with each development team spinning custom solutions via Ant or another custom build system, instead of being provided the solution by the framework itself.

By default Grails supports the concept of development, test, and production environments and will configure itself accordingly when executed. Some of this is done completely transparently to the developer. For example, when configured in development mode, auto-reloading is enabled, while in production mode this feature is disabled to increase performance and minimize any potential security risk (however small).

Executing Grails under different environments is remarkably simple. For instance the following command will run a Grails application with the production settings:

```
grails prod run-app
```

Here I use the prod target in combination with run-app; this in combination with the dev and test targets allows you to easily execute Grails within the desired environment. All these three targets do, however, is set a Java system property called grails.env to production, development, and test respectively. With this in mind it is equally possible to configure additional environments by explicitly passing this property as an argument:

```
grails -Dgrails.env=myenvironment test-app
```

Here you execute the Grails test cases using an environment called myenvironment. All this environment switching is handy, but what does it actually mean in practical terms? Well for one thing it allows you to configure different databases for different environments, which we'll look at in the next section.

Data Source Configuration

Armed with your newly acquired knowledge of environments and how to switch between them, the implications of this knowledge should become abundantly clear when you start configuring data sources. What initial configuration steps are required to get a Grails application up and running? Well, none actually. That's right; you don't have to configure a thing. Even configuration of the data source is optional; if you don't configure one, Grails will start up with an in-memory HSQLDB database.

This is actually highly advantageous to begin with, particularly in terms of testing, as an application can be started with a fresh set of data on each load. However, for our purposes, it would be helpful to delve into configuration of the data sources, as it is the one area where configuration is certain to take place and will aid in developing our knowledge of environments.

When creating a Grails application, Grails will automatically create three different data sources in the grails-app/conf directory. Each data source represents a configuration for a specific environment and uses the convention within the name of the data source to identify which particular data source it is for.

To aid you in your understanding of this, the screenshot in Figure 3-3 shows the three data sources for development, test, and production that are created by default.

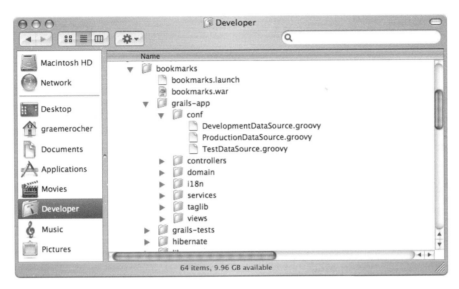

Figure 3-3. *Grails data sources*

As you can see, the *convention* in the file name, and hence class name, is used to configure the data source to be loaded dependant on the environment. Creating a new data source for an environment that is not predefined as those in the screenshot is a simple matter of creating a new class, `AppleDataSource.groovy` for example, and then specifying the environment in one of the targets:

```
grails -Dgrails.env=apple run-app
```

Defining a data source is one area where building on the strength of the Java platform becomes apparent. Java's database connectivity technology, JDBC, is extremely mature, with drivers available for pretty much every database on the market. In fact, if a database provider does not provide quality, stable JDBC drivers, its product is unlikely to be taken seriously in the marketplace.

A data source definition is translated into a `javax.sql.DataSource` instance that supplies JDBC `Connection` objects. If you've ever used JDBC before, the process will be strangely familiar, with the first step ensuring that the driver classes, normally packaged within a JAR archive, are available on the classpath. For the purposes of this example, let's assume you're going to use the latest MySQL driver for use in the test and production environments.

The development environment is by default configured to use an in-memory HSQLDB and to clear and re-create the database on each application load. Listing 3-2 demonstrates this configuration.

Listing 3-2. *Development In-Memory Database*

```
class DevelopmentDataSource {
    boolean pooling = true
    String dbCreate = "create-drop" // one of 'create', 'create-drop','update'
    String url = "jdbc:hsqldb:mem:devDB"
    String driverClassName = "org.hsqldb.jdbcDriver"
    String username = "sa"
    String password = ""
}
```

Using an in-memory database is useful as it allows you to execute Grails without the need to install any database product, thus allowing you to be immediately productive. In addition, in development it is often useful to start off with a clean slate of data, which this approach allows.

Moving on to the production and test data sources, what you need is the ability to communicate with MySQL. Since you're using JDBC, this requires a suitable driver. Drivers are available to download from the MySQL web site at http://www.mysql.com. In this book's examples I'm using version 3.1 of the MySQL connector for Java. To configure the driver, drop the driver's JAR file into the lib directory of the bookmarks application, as shown in Figure 3-4.

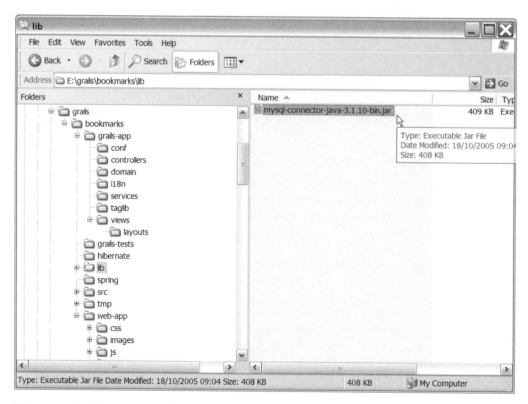

Figure 3-4. *MySQL driver installation*

With the driver in place, the next thing on the list is to configure the Grails data source to use the settings defined by the driver's documentation. This is common practice with JDBC (and equivalent technologies on other platforms) and essentially requires the following information:

- The driver class name

- The URL of the database

- The username to log in with

- The password for the username

The necessary properties to configure a data source are already prepopulated, and by default the ProductionDataSource.groovy file is configured to use an HSQLDB where the schema is updated if possible, as shown in Listing 3-3.

Listing 3-3. *The Grails ProductionDataSource*

```
class ProductionDataSource {
boolean pooling = true
    String dbCreate = "update" // one of 'create', 'create-drop','update'
    String url = "jdbc:hsqldb:file:prodDb"
    String driverClassName = "org.hsqldb.jdbcDriver"
    String username = "sa"
    String password = ""
}
```

This ensures that at least the database is persistent across application restarts and data isn't wiped on each load, but doesn't necessarily provide the optimal solution for production deployment. The majority of the properties to configure within the data source should be fairly obvious, but just to provide a little clarity let's apply the necessary settings, shown in Listing 3-4, to get up and running with MySQL.

Listing 3-4. *ProductionDataSource Configured for MySQL*

```
class ProductionDataSource {
    boolean pooling = true
    String dbCreate = "update"

    String url = "jdbc:mysql://localhost/bookmarks"
    String driverClassName = "com.mysql.jdbc.Driver"
    String username = "root"
    String password = ""
}
```

Note that the previous configuration assumes a blank password for the root user, which clearly will need to be changed in a real production environment. In addition, make sure you have created the bookmarks database (or *catalog* in MySQL terms).

You may have noted that the data source contains two properties that are not generally standard JDBC fair. The first is the `pooling` property, which allows you to configure whether to use a connection pool or not. Clearly, it is better to leave this set to `true` under the majority of circumstances.

The more interesting property of the two, however, is the `dbCreate` property. This uses a feature of the underlying Hibernate subsystem to autogenerate the database schema at run time. The available settings for this property are as follows:

- `create-drop`: Drops and re-creates the database schema on each application load

- `create`: Creates the database on application load

- `update`: Creates and attempts an update to existing tables on application load

- `<not defined>`: Does nothing

Using `create-drop` is again useful for testing purposes while `update` or `create` can be configured on production systems to create the database schema automatically. If this sounds a bit scary and you feel more comfortable doing these things manually, simply remove this property altogether.

That is it for data sources for the moment; note that in some circumstances, network administrators are not comfortable with passwords being embedded directly in plain text files such as the previous Groovy data source classes. In this circumstance, Grails can be configured to use a JNDI data source, which we will explore in Chapter 11.

Supported Databases

Since Grails leverages Hibernate, it supports every database that Hibernate supports, and given how Hibernate has become almost a de facto standard within the industry it has been tried and tested against many different databases and versions.

As it stands, the core Hibernate team performs regular integration tests against the following database products:

- DB2 7.1, 7.2, 8.1

- HSQLDB

- HypersonicSQL 1.61, 1.7.0, 1.7.2, 1.8

- Microsoft SQL Server 2000

- MySQL 3.23, 4.0, 4.1, 5.0

- Oracle 8*i*, 9*i*, 10*g*

- PostgreSQL 7.1.2, 7.2, 7.3, 7.4, 8.0, 8.1

- SAP DB 7.3

- Sybase 12.5 (JConnect 5.5)

- Timesten 5.1

In addition, although not included in the Hibernate QA team's testing processes, Hibernate is often provided with community-led support for the following database products:

- Apache Derby

- HP NonStop SQL/MX 2.0

- Firebird 1.5 with JayBird 1.01

- FrontBase

- Informix

- Ingres

- InterBase 6.0.1

- Mckoi SQL

- PointBase Embedded 4.3

- Progress 9

- Microsoft Access 95, 97, 2000, XP, 2002, and 2003

- Corel Paradox version from 3.0, 3.5, 4.x, 5.x, and 7.x to 11.x

- A number of generic file formats including flat text, CSV, TSV, and fixed-length and variable-length binary files

- XBase (any dBASE, Visual dBASE, SIx Driver, SoftC, CodeBase, Clipper, FoxBase, FoxPro, Visual Fox Pro 3.0, 5.0, 7.0, 8.0, 9.0, and 10.0, xHarbour, Halcyon, Apollo, GoldMine, or BDE-compatible database)

- Microsoft Excel 5.0, 95, 97, 98, 2000, 2001, 2002, 2003, and 2004

A few, mostly older, database products that don't support JDBC metadata, which allows a database to expose information about itself, need information about the Hibernate *dialect* to use to communicate with the database. In the next section you'll see how to register a custom dialect.

Configuring a Custom Dialect

Given that different database products often support variations of the ANSI SQL standard, in order for Hibernate to communicate successfully with a database it needs to know how to "talk the talk." Hibernate does this through a dialect, and in most cases this is auto-configured for you.

However, occasionally certain database products don't provide enough information about the database in order for the dialect to be detected. In this case you need to explicitly specify the dialect in the Grails data source class.

To define a custom dialect, create a `dialect` property that references one of the classes in the `org.hibernate.dialect` package. As an example, you may want to use the MySQL InnoDB engine to communicate with MySQL instead of the default. Hibernate allows you to use this engine simply by specifying a different dialect by adding the following property to a Grails data source class:

```
def dialect = org.hibernate.dialect.MySQLInnoDBDialect
```

There are a number of other dialect classes within the `org.hibernate.dialect` package for you to explore, and occasionally a database vendor might provide its own dialect, in which case it's worth checking the documentation for your database product. For the moment, however, let's find out how you can use Grails bootstrap classes to programmatically load data into your database.

Bootstrapping a Grails Application

Any given Grails application can have one or many *bootstrap classes*. What is a bootstrap class? Quite simply it is a class that can perform any configuration on application load. By default Grails creates a single bootsrap class in the `grails-app/conf` directory called `ApplicationBootStrap.groovy`.

Listing 3-5 shows what the bootstrap classes looks like when first created.

Listing 3-5. *The ApplicationBootstrap Class*

```
class ApplicationBootStrap {
  def init = { servletContext ->

  }
  def destroy = {
  }
}
```

As seen in the previous listing the `ApplicationBootStrap` class defines two closure properties called `init` and `destroy` that are called on application load and shut down respectively.

■**Note** Although the `destroy` method is there, it assumes a graceful shut down on the application server and therefore shouldn't be relied upon for anything critical.

What you actually do within the body of these closures is up to you. You could for example populate the database with some initial state. You could even make your database population code quite intelligent by having code that evaluates the initial state of the database and only creates the missing or needed data; hence it is far more valuable than a "dumb" script.

Nevertheless, it is one more feature that helps in easing the burden for the developer when faced with the problem of how to get an application into an appropriate state at load time. In the next section you'll see how to work with Grails' flexible underlying logging system.

Configuring Logging

Under the hood, Grails uses the popular logging framework Log4j to output information to the console. Grails is initially configured to write only basic information to the console. The amount of information written to the console is configured using a *log level*. In Log4j the log levels are debug, info, warn, error, and fatal. Each level, from debug to fatal, provides a decreasing amount of output to the console. You can increase the default log level if you so choose, which will result in much more activity appearing in the console when executing the run-app target.

Log4j uses a standard Java properties file to configure itself, and in Grails this can be found in the directory web-app\WEB-INF and is called log4j.properties. If you open up this file in a text editor the initial configuration will look something like Listing 3-6.

Listing 3-6. *Default Log4j Configuration*

```
log4j.appender.stdout=org.apache.log4j.ConsoleAppender
log4j.appender.stdout.layout=org.apache.log4j.PatternLayout
# Enable logging for everything. Rarely useful
log4j.rootLogger=error, stdout


# Enable this logger to log Hibernate output
# handy to see its database interaction activity
#log4j.logger.org.hibernate=debug,stdout
#log4j.additivity.org.hibernate=false

# Enable this logger to see what Spring does, occasionally useful
#log4j.logger.org.springframework=info,stdout
#log4j.additivity.org.springframework=false

# This logger covers all of Grails' internals
# Enable to see what's going on underneath.
log4j.logger.org.codehaus.groovy.grails=info,stdout
log4j.additivity.org.codehaus.groovy.grails=false

# This logger is useful if you just want to see what Grails
# configures with Spring at runtime. Setting to debug will show
# each bean that is configured
log4j.logger.org.codehaus.groovy.grails.commons.spring=info,stdout
log4j.additivity.org.codehaus.groovy.grails.commons.spring=false

# Interesting Logger to see what some of the Grails factory beans are doing
log4j.logger.org.codehaus.groovy.grails.beans.factory=info,stdout
log4j.additivity.org.codehaus.groovy.grails.beans.factory=false

# This logger is for Grails' public APIs within the grails. package
log4j.logger.grails=info,stdout
log4j.additivity.grails=false
```

So what does this all mean? Well, essentially the file has configured a number of different loggers: the root logger that covers all packages, various package-level loggers for different libraries, and specific Grails loggers for the org.codehaus.groovy.grails and grails packages. The root logger is configured to output at the error level, while the Grails loggers are set to output a little more information at the info level. You can, of course, lower the log level of the Grails loggers if the messages are too verbose for your liking.

Log4j is a very flexible logging system and has quite a breadth of features, including strategies that can output via a text file, or XML, or even e-mail. It is worth taking a look at the documentation at http://logging.apache.org/log4j/docs/ to get a better understanding of what it is capable of, but as an example, suppose you want to trace what exactly the Hibernate ORM system is doing (SQL queries, domain mapping, etc.). Log4j makes this simple enough; all you have to do is provide another logger for the org.hibernate package:

```
log4j.logger.org.hibernate=debug
```

This will allow you to view all of the interesting things that Hibernate is doing in the background if you are that way inclined. If on the other hand you merely want to log the SQL that Hibernate creates, there is another more accessible way to do so that we'll look at next.

Enabling SQL Logging

It is often handy to be able to see only the SQL activity going on in the background that Hibernate is responsible for. This is simple enough to enable; to do so, open up the relevant data source, say DevelopmentDataSource.groovy, and add the following property:

```
def logSql = true
```

That's it. You're done. All SQL communication will now appear in the console window.

Logging and Environments

More often than not it becomes useful to have differing log configurations depending on the environment. By default Grails supplies only a single log4j.properties file, but if you need specific logging for a particular environment you can simply create a file in the format log4j. environment_name.properties.

For example, a Log4j configuration for the production environment would be log4j. production.properties. The settings in this file would override any defined in the regular log4j.properties file.

That about wraps it up for logging. In the next section I'll start to dig deeper into what the various command-line targets offer.

The Grails Command-Line Utilities

I've already touched on some of the command-line utilities during our adventures creating a "Hello World!" example in Chapter 1. Now let's have a more comprehensive look at some of the other ones and point out where the rest will be addressed within this book.

Table 3-2 details all the targets and provides the chapter where they are covered. Remember that they are all powered by Ant and hence easily customizable.

That should whet your appetite for what is coming up ahead. For the moment though, let's take a look at some handy targets that you may need to know straight away, starting with how to get Grails to load on a different port, thus avoiding any nasty port conflicts.

Table 3-2. *Grails Targets*

Target Name	Relevant Chapter
create-app	This chapter
create-controller	Chapter 7
create-domain-class	Chapter 4
create-test-suite	Chapter 6
create-taglib	Chapter 8
generate-controller	Chapter 5
generate-views	Chapter 5
generate-all	Chapter 5
test-app	Chapter 6
run-app	This chapter
create-webtest	Chapter 6
run-webtest	Chapter 6
console	This chapter
shell	This chapter
war	This chapter

Running on a Different Port

The run-app command executes by default on port 8080, which may or may not be convenient depending on your environment. To change the default port, an argument can be passed to the command using Java's -Darg syntax:

```
> grails -Dserver.port=9090 run-app
```

The previous code will start Grails' embedded Jetty server on port 9090. This may be handy at times when you're running a test machine that may already have something like Tomcat on port 8080. As an alternative, instead of forcing the Jetty server to run on a different port you could just package your Grails application up and deploy it to Tomcat. In the next section we'll look at how to create a deployment-ready WAR archive.

Packaging a WAR Archive

When you execute a Grails application using the run-app command, Grails configures the application to be reloaded upon changes at run time, hence allowing quick iterative development. This does however have an effect on the performance of your application.

The run-app command is hence best suited for development only. For deployment onto a production system a packaged WAR should be used. This follows Java's mature deployment strategy and separation of roles in terms of developers and administrators.

To create a WAR archive, run the war target as follows:

```
> grails war
```

Grails will package your application ready for deployment within an archive located in the root of your project as demonstrated in the screenshot in Figure 3-5.

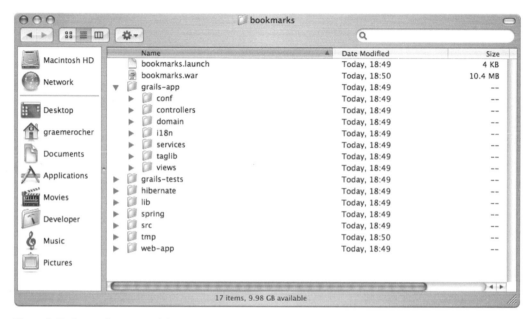

Figure 3-5. *Created WAR archive*

Here you see the deployment-ready WAR file created for you in the root of the project. This can subsequently be deployed using the mechanism defined by your application server. This may be a simple case of dropping it in a directory such as with Tomcat or even via a web-based server management interface as found in some commercial products.

Using the Grails Console and Shell

Grails comes with extended editions of the Groovy command-line shell and interactive swing console. These allow you to interact with the artifacts within a Grails application from the command line or via a Swing GUI interface. Throughout the book it will become handy to try out code samples via the console, so it is recommended that you become familiar with either the interactive shell or the console.

Using the Command-Line Shell

To operate the command-line shell, open a terminal or command window from the root of a Grails application such as the one you just created and type the following command:

```
> grails shell
```

It will take a moment, but once loaded you will see a command-line interface similar to the screenshot in Figure 3-6.

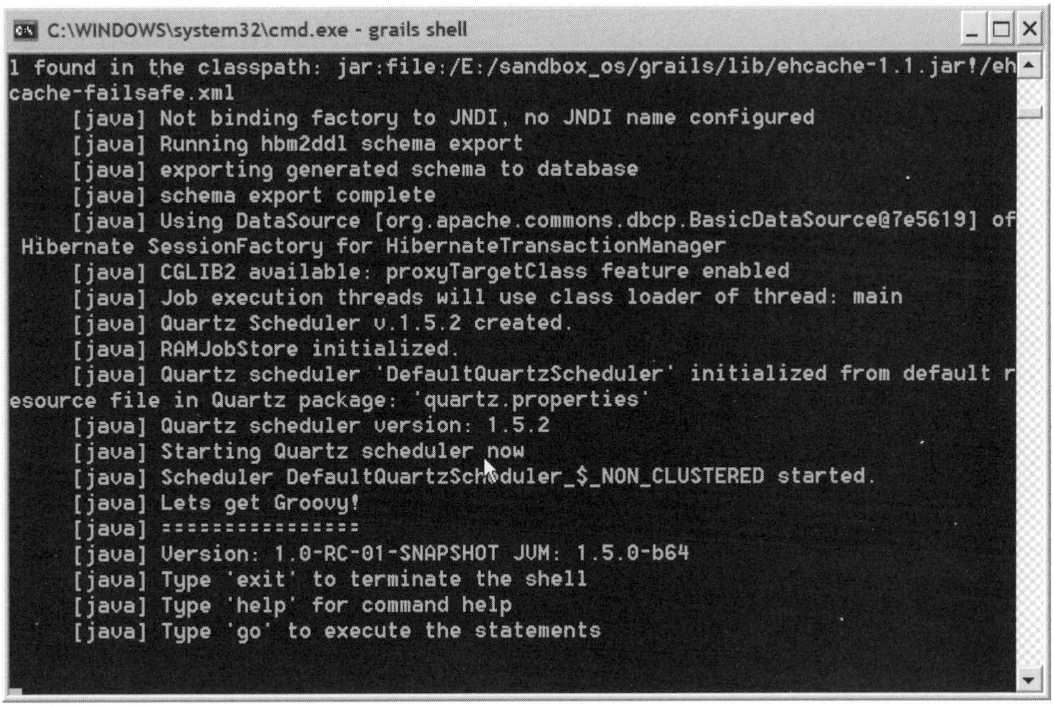

Figure 3-6. *Grails command-line shell*

Help is available via the command line by typing **help** and hitting the Enter key; however, the basic usage pattern is to essentially type the Groovy code you wish to execute into the shell, separating statements by carriage returns (i.e., hitting Enter/Return). Once you have assembled the commands to be executed, type **go** and hit the Enter key, and the commands will be executed with the output written to the terminal window.

The Grails Console

If you have a GUI available to you, it may be preferable to use the Grails Swing console. To load the console, type the following command followed by the Enter key:

```
> grails console
```

Once loaded, the console will appear in a small window, as shown in Figure 3-7, which, like the command-line shell, allows you to enter arbitrary Groovy statements to be executed.

To use the console, simply type your statements and then either click Actions ➤ Run on the menu to run the code, or simply use the available keyboard shortcuts which are CTRL+R or CTRL+Enter.

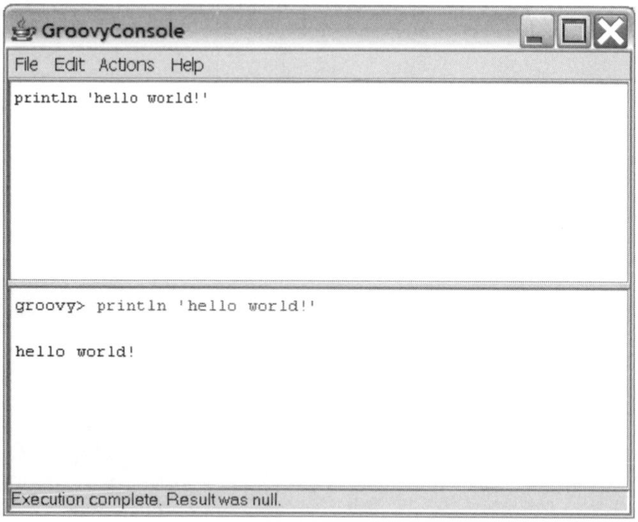

Figure 3-7. *The Grails console*

IDE Integration

Integrated development environments (IDEs) have come a long way in recent years. It all started with IntelliJ IDEA, which really set the bar for others to follow, and for the most part they have. Open source IDE offerings such as Eclipse and NetBeans have provided developers with rich toolsets to develop applications with no upfront cost.

The power that an IDE gives you in terms of the ability to refactor code, perform code completion, and automate common tasks is undoubtedly a huge selling point and a feature sadly lacking in the world of dynamically typed languages.

The problem remains that the lack of types in languages such as Ruby and Python mean that full support for features such as refactoring and advanced code navigation in modern Java IDEs are harder to achieve. In this sense Groovy does have an advantage in that it is able to mix both statically and dynamically typed code. With this capability, the potential is there to build an IDE that is capable of performing Groovy refactorings.

However, even without this capability, Grails allows you to mix Groovy and Java code so seamlessly that you can take a blended approach to web application development (you'll see more of this in Chapter 11).

Regardless, IDE support is clearly important, and big strides have been made in this area recently. In particular we will be taking a look at how Grails integrates with Eclipse through the Groovy-Eclipse plug-in.

In addition to the Eclipse plug-in, other plug-ins are available that bring varying levels of Groovy support to other popular IDEs, including the following:

- *GroovyJ*: An IntelliJ IDEA plug-in (http://groovy.codehaus.org/IntelliJ+IDEA+Plugin)

- *The Coyote Project*: A plug-in that adds scripting support to the NetBeans platform for a number of languages, including Groovy (http://coyote.dev.java.net/)

- *jEdit*: A Swing-based text editor that supports Groovy syntax highlighting and features a plug-in for executing Groovy scripts (http://jedit.org)

Installing the Groovy-Eclipse Plug-in

The Eclipse plug-in is available from the Groovy web site at `http://groovy.codehaus.org/Eclipse+Plugin` where there are instructions on how to install it.

It is still under active development, and progress is fast, so I would recommend going down the route of retrieving it from Groovy's Subversion repository, building it, and installing it per the instructions on the site. This will allow you to get the most benefit out of the currently implemented features. Alternatively, the Update Site at the aforementioned web site is kept reasonably up-to-date.

The installation process with Eclipse is merely to drop the plug-in ZIP file into the `plugins` directory located within your Eclipse installation. Once this is complete, simply restart the IDE, and the plug-in will be activated.

Importing a Grails Project

Once you have the plug-in installed, the next step is to import your Grails project. Luckily Grails automatically creates Eclipse project and classpath files for you when you create the project. So to import the project, right-click within the Package Explorer and select the Import option, at which point the dialog box shown in Figure 3-8 will appear.

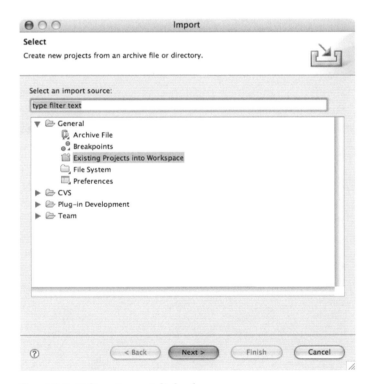

Figure 3-8. *Eclipse Import dialog box*

Select the Existing Projects into Workspace option and click the Next button. Now browse to the project you created earlier by clicking the Browse button, as shown in Figure 3-9, and click Choose/OK.

Figure 3-9. *Importing a Grails project*

Once you have chosen the directory where the project is located, Eclipse will automatically detect that there are Eclipse project files within the specified root directory and even in subdirectories within the root. The result is that Eclipse displays a list of projects that you can potentially import, shown in Figure 3-10.

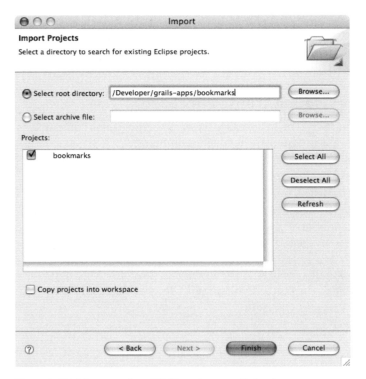

Figure 3-10. *The populated Eclipse Import dialog box*

Now click the Finish button to complete the import. Don't be surprised that the book-marks project appears in the Package Explorer as "not compiling" and the Problems view contains a number of entries. Once the import is complete there is one final step. Every Grails Eclipse project anticipates the existence of a GRAILS_HOME Eclipse variable; to create this (if it doesn't already exist) perform the following steps:

1. Right-click the project and select Properties.

2. Select Java Build Path on the left menu.

3. Click the Libraries tab.

4. Click the Add Variable button.

5. Click the Configure Variables button.

6. Within the dialog box that appears click New.

7. Enter **GRAILS_HOME** into the Name field.

8. Click the Folder button and browse to the location where Grails is installed.

9. Keep clicking OK until the changes are applied through all dialog boxes.

At this point your project will be configured with the correct source directories, classpath, and, most importantly, a run configuration. Yes, not only does Grails create the necessary project files, it sets up the appropriate configuration for you to run the Grails application embedded within the IDE.

Running the Grails Application from Eclipse

Running a Grails application requires you to first package it for the required environment. This can be done via the terminal window by typing the following command:

```
grails dev war
```

This is only required the *first* time you run a Grails application, as once loaded, all changes made in Eclipse will be automatically reloaded at run time in the same way as the `grails run-app` target. If you stop the application server within Eclipse it is recommended that you repeat the previous step before starting it up again. This requirement may be eliminated in a future version of Grails.

Nevertheless, to run the bookmarks application, open the Run drop-down menu by clicking the small down arrow next to the Run button, then click Run, as shown in Figure 3-11.

Figure 3-11. *How to access the Run dialog box*

This will open the Eclipse Run dialog box. The Run dialog box in Eclipse is responsible for managing various run configurations. Since Grails provides a run configuration right out of the box, the Run dialog box automatically detects this. The run configuration is then displayed within the Java Application menu on the left. The Java Application menu can be expanded and the run configuration Grails provides is the one matching the project name, in this case *bookmarks*, as shown in Figure 3-12.

By clicking the bookmarks Java application you will note that the import process has set up all the necessary classpath references. These can be configured further as necessary if you have additional JAR libraries in your `lib` directory or you need particular resources on the classpath at run time.

You could also configure what arguments are passed to the class, using the Arguments tab. Using this feature you can provide the `grails.env` argument that allows you to configure which environment to execute Grails under, although this is rarely needed, since by default Grails will execute using the development environment and associated configuration.

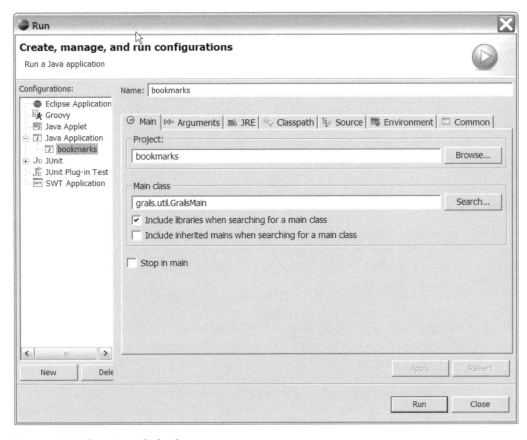

Figure 3-12. *Eclipse Run dialog box*

Needless to say there are several options for you to explore in the various tabs that allow a fair amount of flexibility. To execute the bookmarks application, simply click the Run button and the bookmarks application will start up, embedded in the IDE. The output from the server will be displayed in Eclipse's console view. All output that you send to either Log4j loggers or standard out will appear in this view so it comes in handy. The screenshot in Figure 3-13 illustrates a typical console view.

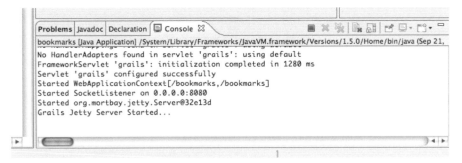

Figure 3-13. *Grails embedded in Eclipse*

Now that Grails has been started you can access the application via the browser in exactly the same manner described earlier, and all changes made within the IDE will be automatically reloaded. Although the need for an IDE is greatly reduced in dynamic languages such as Groovy, one advantage of Grails is the ability to use a *blended* approach to development by using Groovy *and* Java where necessary.

Dynamically typed and statically typed languages have very different strengths and weaknesses, and by approaching development with a blend you have greater choice in deciding the best tool for the job.

IDE support enables an easy transition between languages and reduces *task switching*, a common activity known to reduce productivity.

Summary

Grails follows the usual MVC pattern and allows easy definition of models, views, and controllers by simply putting the respective Groovy files in their directories. This simple work becomes even easier with scaffolding (discussed in Chapter 5), which generates the requested artifacts in the required place.

The Grails command-line utilities do all the automation work for scaffolding and other development activities such as `run-app`, `war`, and so on.

With the bookmarks application being created with the help of the command-line utilities, you have even more options for working with it: you can use the interactive Grails shell and console, or you can work with convenient IDE support. Setting up a Grails application in Eclipse is particularly easy since the Eclipse-specific files are already generated by Grails.

In this chapter I covered the basics of working with a Grails project and setting up the bookmarks application. I also discussed Grails' support for development environments such as Eclipse. This chapter went into quite a bit of detail about the more configuration-heavy aspects (and they're really not very heavy!) of Grails, but the amazing thing is that none of the configuration discussed in this chapter is really necessary to get started since all you have to do is type **grails run-app**. However, the material in this chapter will help you get to grips with using Grails in different environments and understanding the configuration options that do exist.

The next chapters should be interesting, as we begin to tackle the various Grails artifacts and understand how the power of convention can save you a bundle load of time. Next stop: the application domain.

CHAPTER 4

■■■

The Application Domain

Object-oriented applications of any kind, whether they are desktop, server, or mobile applications, are developed with a *domain model* central to the application. The domain model defines the core business entities within the application. These are drawn from the nouns in the requirements definition and model real-world or abstract objects. For example, you could have a Book object in a bookstore application or an Order object in a purchasing system. These business entities have relationships between each other. An Author may have authored many Books for example. In general, these artifacts tend be persistent; in other words, their state can be saved to a location and restored at a later date. In the server-side world of web applications, this tends to be handled by a relational database management system (RDBMS), which for the purposes of clarity I'll hence forth simply refer to as a *database*.

As wonderful as many of the database products are, the format in which the data is stored is very different from its runtime representation in an object-oriented application. In OO programming there are objects with properties, fields, and methods, while a database has tables with columns and primary keys. There have been a number of efforts to create systems that bridge this gap, including EJB entity beans with their rather verbose XML descriptors and container-managed persistence (CMP); pure OO databases that dump the concept of tables all together; and object-relational mapping (ORM) solutions that map the object model onto its relational representation.

Possibly the most successful and widely used of these is an open source ORM library called Hibernate. Hibernate promotes the use of POJOs—Java classes that don't extend any special class or implement any special interface—that follow the JavaBean convention of allowing mapping properties onto columns in a database. This simplified approach has helped Hibernate achieve mass adoption, a buzzing community, and a mature code base. Given Hibernate's level of popularity, some almost see it as the de facto industry standard until EJB3 achieves wider adoption. It is this solid foundation that Grails builds upon to support the creation of the application domain.

Simplified ORM with Grails Object-Relational Mapping (GORM)

Grails uses Hibernate's highly customizable configuration APIs to allow for even easier ORM mapping by utilizing the power of convention with a new mapping strategy called Grails Object-Relational Mapping (GORM). Instead of the mappings being defined in some external form, such as XML for example, GORM uses the convention in the classes themselves to perform the mapping. To demonstrate this let's build on our bookmarks application by creating the domain objects for it. Clearly, the most obvious one is Bookmark, which is an object that defines the URL location of the bookmark and associated information such as notes, tags, and the like.

Since this is a shared web application you want some way of associating a set of bookmarks with a user. To facilitate this we are going to have the ubiquitous User object.

So far you have users, bookmarks, and tags, and before this gets too complicated let's take a moment to visualize this in the form of a UML class diagram, which is depicted in Figure 4-1.

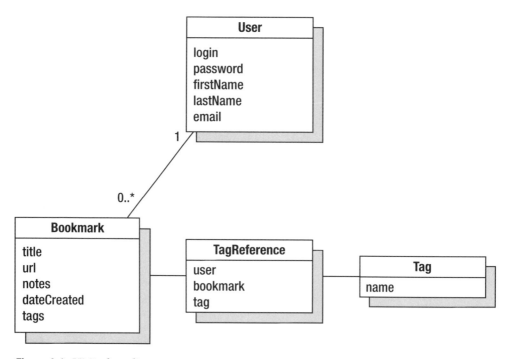

Figure 4-1. *UML class diagram*

This UML class diagram should give you an idea of the domain model you are trying to achieve. As mentioned, you have a User class that has many Bookmark instances. Bookmarks can have tags attached to them, but of course several bookmarks might share the same tag, so there is an intermediate class called TagReference that serves a number of purposes. Firstly, it relates a specific bookmark to a specific tag. It also, however, relates the tag to a user allowing you to find out all the tags a user has used as well as all the tags a bookmark might have.

GORM Basics

To create the Bookmark class, Grails provides a convenience target, however this step is not entirely necessary. If you prefer to create the domain class with your favorite text editor or IDE, feel free. It is however a very powerful way to learn Grails as it helps you to establish where everything goes and how the conventions work. Regardless of the method you use, to create the Bookmark class, run the create-domain-class target via the command line from the root of the bookmarks application as demonstrated in Listing 4-1.

Listing 4-1. *Creating a Domain Class*

```
>grails create-domain-class
create-domain-class:
    [input] Enter domain class name:
bookmark
```

When prompted, enter **bookmark** and hit the Enter key. Grails will create a domain class called `grails-app/domain/Bookmark.groovy` within the bookmarks application. Note that the first letter of the class name is automatically capitalized and what you will get is a class that looks roughly like the one in Listing 4-2.

Listing 4-2. *Bookmark Domain Class*

```
class Bookmark {
}
```

One point to note is that a Grails domain class doesn't extend or implement any Grails-specific framework parent class or interface. Grails injects all the necessary behavior at run time. An often-asked question is why doesn't Grails use inheritance? Well, needless to say, there are obvious benefits to not having a parent class, given Java's, and hence Groovy's, single-class inheritance model. A better description of the reasoning, however, can be gathered from an answer that was well received in a Grails mailing list entry covering this exact topic: The Grails model is actually closer to aspect-oriented programming (AOP) than anything. If you go back to the early lessons on OO, inheritance essentially defines an "is a" relationship. Now imagine for a moment that you create a class that inherits its attributes from a `Frog` parent class. For all intents and purposes your class *is* a frog. Clearly your subclass will jump like a frog, croak like a frog, and exhibit all the usual froglike mannerisms. But one day your class decides "Hey, I don't want to be a frog. I want to be a prince." Well your frog is out of luck, unfortunately; it can't very well go off and be a prince when it's already a frog.

The Grails and AOP approach is to take a regular, quite plain object or class (a POJO or POGO (Plain Old Groovy Object) maybe?) and *inject* the necessary behavior into the class at run time. This approach means that your class behaves as it should in the context or environment (i.e., the Grails runtime environment) it is operating in. Think of Grails as the princess that kisses your object to turn it into a prince without it even having to be a frog in the first place. Outside of the Grails environment your domain object can be whoever or whatever it wants without having to carry all the frog baggage into another world.

Now, returning to our `Bookmark` class—clearly, due to the notable sparseness of the class it doesn't do very much at this point. What you need to do is attach properties and behaviors to your domain model to make it a little more interesting. So what do bookmarks have? Well they definitely have a URL, but the URL is often more meaningful when associated with a title. Adding notes can also be good, just in case the title is not descriptive enough, and it may be worth recording further information that will remind you of the relevance of the bookmark. So all in all, you end up with something like the example in Listing 4-3.

Listing 4-3. *Bookmark Mark 2*

```
class Bookmark {
        URL url
        String title
        String notes
        Date dateCreated
}
```

Now it's getting interesting; but before we get too excited, let's stop for a moment to understand exactly how the previous domain class relates to a table in a relational database. The default convention used by Hibernate and extended by Grails is as follows:

1. The class name is the table name in lowercase with camel case[1] converted to underscores.

2. Each property is a column with the camel casing of the property name converted to underscores.

3. There is an implicit id property added that represents the native database identifier.

4. There is an additional version property that is used by Hibernate to ensure transactional integrity and support optimistic locking.

To illustrate the previous steps, the diagram in Figure 4-2 represents the Unified Modeling Language (UML) notation for the Bookmark class and how it relates to the database table representation.

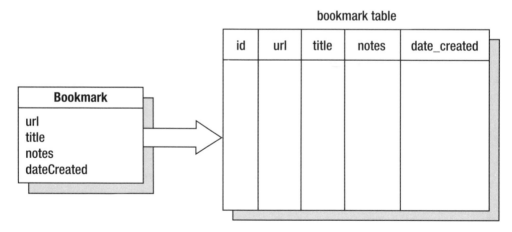

Figure 4-2. *Class-to-table mapping*

I imagine the interesting part of all this is the mention of implicit id and version properties and their appearance in the previous table. GORM, as per the Don't Repeat Yourself (DRY)

---

1. Camel case is the practice of writing words joined without spaces (e.g., PoweredByGrails). The name comes from the uppercase "bumps" in the middle of the word, suggestive of the humps of a camel.

principle, does its best to minimize the amount of boilerplate code written. Having a database identifier is, in general, good practice, so GORM adds this automatically, as it would become repetitive in nature if it had to be entered manually every time. Thanks to Hibernate, transactions become simpler, too, with the additional version column in the database.

GORM in combination with Hibernate takes the burden off the developer by managing the state of these properties for you. We will be looking in more detail at the id property in the section "Querying the Domain Model"; for the moment just be aware that it is there.

In the next section we'll explore ways to further configure GORM by allowing properties to be made optional.

Making Properties Optional

By default, in GORM all properties are required. In other words, they cannot have a null value when stored in the database. This is not always desirable or indeed necessary. Hence GORM provides the ability to specify those properties, which are optional. As an example, in the Bookmark class it is unlikely that a user will always make notes about their bookmarks, so making this property optional is probably a good thing. To do this, create a static property called optionals, as shown in Listing 4-4, that is assigned a list of the names of the properties you wish to make optional.

Listing 4-4. *Making Properties Optional*

```
class Bookmark {
     static optionals = ['notes']
     //...
}
```

The previous example uses Groovy's list syntax with string values for each property name to make the notes property optional. And with that ridiculously trivial example let's move on to how to work with relationships in GORM.

Relationships with GORM

To make your bookmarks application even more useful it would be handy to be able to attach tags or labels to a bookmark. Tags are a way of organizing information without actually placing objects into any formal hierarchy or tree structure, which are often limiting in that objects can only be placed within one node (think files in directories). As an example, if you find a great recipe explaining how to go about creating the ultimate risotto you could attach a more specific tag such as risotto or a more generic term such as recipe or Italian food.

From this you can gather that a bookmark could have many tags, and tags can have many bookmarks, as illustrated in the previous UML diagram. On that occasion we used a special class to manage the relationship, but for purposes of the following examples we shall skip the creation of the class and revisit it at a later date.

In other words, we're going to create a direct one-to-many relationship between the Bookmark and Tag classes. Before we do so and before we get ahead of ourselves we need to create the Tag class by following the same steps performed when creating the Bookmark class. A Tag then has a *name* and the Bookmark it relates to, making this relationship bidirectional.

If we omit the bookmark property shown in Listing 4-5, the relationship would be a simple unidirectional one-to-many.

Listing 4-5. *The Tag Class*

```
class Tag {
        static belongsTo = Bookmark

        Bookmark bookmark
        String name
}
```

There are two important aspects to note about the previous class. First, the belongsTo definition tells GORM that the Tag class is owned by the Bookmark class. This is important because imagine a circumstance when a Bookmark is deleted; you would want all of the tags associated with that Bookmark to be removed too. However, imagine the inverse situation when a Tag is deleted; clearly you don't want the Tag to delete its owner, the Bookmark. For GORM to take the appropriate action it needs to know *who* the owner is.

Second, because Groovy supports static as well as dynamic typing, the bookmark property is automatically recognized as being the one side of the one-to-many relationship without requiring any additional settings.

Now imagine for a moment that all the bookmarks for a particular tag name need to be located. This is simply a matter of querying by the tag name and using another Groovy feature called GPath to retrieve the results via the object graph, a concept we will look at in more detail in the section "Querying the Domain Model."

Of course, to make this relationship bidirectional, the other side of the relationship needs to be defined. To do this we need to revisit the Bookmark class and modify it as per Listing 4-6.

Listing 4-6. *Bookmark with Tag Relationship*

```
class Bookmark {
        static hasMany = [tags:Tag] // addition of hasMany here

        URL url
        String title
        String notes
        Date dateCreated = new Date()
}
```

What the hasMany property does is tell GORM that a Bookmark has many Tag instances and, in another instance of reducing repetitive work, GORM creates an implicit tags property that is of type java.util.Set to access all the tags for a particular bookmark. Not only that, GORM also automatically provides an implementation of an addTag method that makes it easy to work with the association. This is best illustrated by a few examples, shown in Listing 4-7, which you can try out yourself by opening up the Grails console as discussed previously in Chapter 3.

Listing 4-7. *Working with Relationships*

```
// create a new bookmark
def b = new Bookmark(url: new URL('http://grails.org'),
                                title:'Grails',
                                notes:'Groovy-based web framework')

// now add some tags
b.addTag( new Tag(name: 'grails') )
 .addTag( new Tag(name: 'web framework') )

// iterative of the bookmarks tags and print their names // to standard out
b.tags.each { println it.name }
```

So you've seen how to create a bidirectional one-to-many relationship; the other types of relationships are quite simply variations of the previous. Grails supports the creation of the following types of relationships:

- one-to-many

- many-to-one

- one-to-one

Of course, all these relationships can either be unidirectional or bidirectional, but remember to be sure to set the owning side of the relationship using the belongsTo property, as seen previously in Listing 4-5.

■**Note** As of this writing, many-to-many relationships are not directly supported by GORM. This can be worked around by using an intermediate mapping class as we have done in the UML class diagram of our eventual model.

Performing CRUD Operations

The fundamental interactions necessary in any database-driven application can essentially be broken down into four operations:

- Create

- Read

- Update

- Delete

As you may have already gathered, they form a commonly used acronym called CRUD. Interestingly, performing these operations in GORM doesn't involve any additional supporting API or SQL. Everything is handled through dynamic methods that are injected into our classes by Groovy's Meta Object Protocol that was introduced in Chapter 2.

Creating Bookmarks

Let's jump right in and see this in action by creating some bookmarks. First of all, load up the Grails console or interactive shell and try out the code in Listing 4-8.

Listing 4-8. *Using the Save Method*

```
// create a new bookmark
def b = new Bookmark(url: new URL('http://grails.org'),
                                 title:'Grails',
                                 notes:'Groovy-based web framework')
// save the bookmark
b.save()
```

This listing uses the dynamic save method to persist a Bookmark instance to the database at which point the instance gets automatically assigned a database identifier. That's it; no SQL operations; no interaction with an external API. It is that simple.

Reading a Bookmark

OK, now that we have a Bookmark persisted to the database, it might be handy at some point to get it back. Clearly, queries come in useful in this area, which will be addressed shortly; but a common way to read an instance back is via the database identifier mentioned previously. Listing 4-9 demonstrates the usage of the get method.

Listing 4-9. *Using the get Method*

```
// get the bookmark back
def b = Bookmark.get(1)

// output the URL
println b.url
```

The static get method allows retrieval of persistent instances using the database identifier. It will attempt to retrieve the instance for the specified identifier (in this case 1), otherwise it will simply return null.

Updating the Bookmark

Needless to say, it will inevitably become valuable to update one's bookmarks. Again, Grails has the answer, which bears a striking resemblance to what we have seen already. Listing 4-10 shows how you can use the save method to update a persistent instance retrieved using the get method.

Listing 4-10. *Updating the Bookmark*

```
// get the bookmark back
def b = Bookmark.get(1)

// update the URL to point directly at the home page
b.url = new URL('http://grails.org/Home')

// save the bookmark
b.save()
```

It is important to understand how the semantics of saving a new instance and updating an existing instance differ when used with Grails. It is actually possible to omit the call to the save method entirely from the previous listing, and Grails will still commit the change to the database. As soon as you modify a persistent instance it is seen as being *dirty*, in other words it has changes and is automatically saved.

When you start to look at validating your domain model with constraints as described in the section "Validating the Domain" later in the chapter, it will become clear how this isn't always desirable behavior and how you can handle updates in scenarios when your domain model is not valid.

Deleting Bookmarks

Last but certainly not least, bookmarks eventually go out of date, or maybe the bookmarked site becomes less fashionable. At this point, deletion of the Bookmark is the way to go. Listing 4-11 shows how to delete a Bookmark with the aptly named delete method.

Listing 4-11. *Deleting the Bookmark*

```
// get the bookmark back
def b = Bookmark.get(1)

// delete bookmark
b.delete()
```

Querying the Domain Model

Clearly, it is not always possible to know the database identifier of an object beforehand, as demonstrated in previous examples with the get method. In the following sections, we'll be looking at the various ways to perform queries on objects in the database in order to retrieve one or possibly several objects from the database.

Basic Retrieval with get and exists

We've already seen the get method in action in the previous section, however it's worth covering again alongside its close sibling exists.

The get method, as already mentioned, retrieves an instance for a specified identifier or returns null if the instance isn't found. The exists method on the other hand will return true if it exists and `false` if it doesn't. The `exists` method is generally utilized within `if` statements, however, the two methods are actually interchangeable due to Groovy's advanced `if` capability.

Essentially, `null` evaluates to `false` in Groovy, so you could just as well use `get` in place of `exists`. However, the `exists` method, shown in action in Listing 4-12, reads better and is arguably more performant.

Listing 4-12. *Usage of exists and get*

```
// get the bookmark back
if(Bookmark.exists(1)) {
   def b = Bookmark.get(1)
}
// the same as above but with duplication of get call
if(Bookmark.get(1)) {
   def b = Bookmark.get(1)
}
// as an alternative
def b = Bookmark.get(1)
if(b) {
   // do something with the bookmark
}
```

Listing, Sorting, and Counting

A common way to retrieve items from a database is to simply list them. Clearly it is not always desirable to list every instance, and the order in which they are returned is often important. GORM provides a `list` method, which takes a number of named arguments such as `max`, `offset`, `sort`, and `order` to customize the results, the definitions of which are listed here:

- *max*: The maximum number of instances to return

- *offset*: The offset relative to 0 of the first result to return

- *sort*: The property name to sort by

- *order*: The order of the results, either `asc` or `desc` for ascending and descending order respectively

In addition to `list`, and often used in combination with it, is the `count` method, which counts the total number of instances in the database. To demonstrate these let's look at some examples of their usage as shown in Listing 4-13.

Listing 4-13. *Using the list Method*

```
// get all the bookmarks, careful there might be many!
def allBookmarks = Bookmark.list()

// get the ten most recently created bookmarks
def topTen = Bookmark.list(max:10,sort:'dateCreated')
```

```
// get the last ten in descending order of creation
def lastTen = Bookmark.list(offset:Bookmark.count()-10,
                                    sort:'dateCreated',
          order:'desc')
```

As you can imagine it is fairly trivial to use the list method to perform pagination of results simply by customizing the offset argument, which we will explore more in Chapter 8.

In addition, there is a set of listOrderBy* methods that are variations on the list method. The listOrderBy* methods are the first introduction to dynamic methods that use the properties on the class itself in their signatures. They are unique to each domain class, but it is just a matter of understanding the convention for using them.

An example of one of these methods, shown in Listing 4-14, uses the dateCreated property of the Bookmark class as part of the method signature.

Listing 4-14. *Using listOrderBy**

```
// all bookmarks ordered by creation date
def allByDate = Bookmark.listOrderByDateCreated()
```

The previous code lists all bookmarks ordered by the date they were created. The property name is appended onto the end of the method signature starting with a capital letter that follows the standard naming convention for Java method signatures. You'll see more methods of this ilk in the next section on dynamic finders, including a variation of the count method.

Querying with Dynamic Finders

Dynamic finders are one of the most powerful concepts of GORM; as with the previously mentioned listOrderBy* method they use the property names of the class to perform queries. However, they are even more flexible than this, as they allow logical queries such as and, or, and not to form so-called method expressions. There can be literally hundreds of combinations for any given class, but again they're fairly simple to remember if you know the convention.

Let's look at an example findBy* method first, shown in Figure 4-3, which locates a unique instance for the specified method expression.

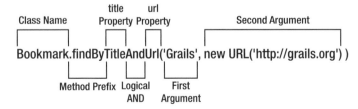

Figure 4-3. *Dynamic finder diagram*

The diagram uses the title and url properties to look up a Bookmark instance. There is a logical And expression in the middle to ensure both values need to be equal in the query. This could be replaced with a logical Or to look up a bookmark that either has the title Grails or the URL http://grails.org.

I have, however, only brushed on what is possible with dynamic finders and method expressions. Dynamic finders support a wide range of expressions that allow greater than/less than, like, and between queries, to name just a few, simply by appending an additional expression on the end of the property name. Listing 4-15 shows some of these in action.

Listing 4-15. *Dynamic Finders in Action*

```
// retrieve a bookmark where the title begins with Grails
def bookmark = Bookmark.findByTitleLike('Grails%')

// get a bookmark created in last 10 days
def today = new Date()
def last10Days = Bookmark
.findByDateCreatedBetween(today-10,today)

// a bookmark not about Grails?
def somethingElse =   Bookmark
.findByTitleNotEqual('Grails')
```

Table 4-1 illustrates all the possible expressions that can be appended, the number of arguments they expect, and an example of each in action.

Table 4-1. *Available Dynamic Finder Method Expressions*

Expression	Arguments	Example
Between	2	Bookmark.findByDateCreatedBetween(today-10,today)
Equals	1	Bookmark.findByTitleEquals('Grails')
GreaterThan	1	Bookmark.findByDateCreatedGreaterThan(lastMonth)
GreaterThanOrEqual	1	Bookmark.findByDateCreatedGreaterThanOrEqual(lastMonth)
IsNull	0	Bookmark.findByNotesIsNull()
IsNotNull	0	Bookmark.findByNotesIsNotNull()
LessThan	1	Bookmark.findByDateCreatedLessThan(lastMonth)
LessThanOrEqual	1	Bookmark.findByDateCreatedLessThanOrEqual(lastMonth)
Like	1	Bookmark.findByTitleLike('Grails%')
NotEqual	1	Bookmark.findByTitleNotEqual('Grails')

The findBy* method has two cousins that accept the same method expressions you've already seen. The first is findAllBy* which retrieves all the instances that match the method expression as a java.util.List. Finally, there is the countBy* method which returns the total number of instances found by the method expression as an integer.

It is worth opening up the Grails console once again and having a play with these methods to experiment with the different combinations and discover just how easy they are to use.

Querying with HQL

Another way to perform queries is via the Hibernate Query Language (HQL), which is a highly flexible object-oriented alternative to SQL. A full discussion on HQL is beyond the scope of this book, however the Hibernate documentation does cover it splendidly well at `http://www.hibernate.org/hib_docs/reference/en/html/queryhql.html`. We will look at some basic examples of how GORM supports HQL via more built-in methods.

Those who know SQL should not find it hard to adapt to HQL, as the syntactic differences are minimal. GORM provides three methods for working with HQL queries: `find`, `findAll`, and `executeQuery`. Each method, when passed a string, will assume it's an HQL query. The example in Listing 4-16 presents the most basic case combined with `findAll`.

Listing 4-16. *HQL via the findAll Method*

```
// query for all bookmarks
def allBookmarks = Bookmark.findAll('from Bookmark')
```

In addition, JDBC-style IN parameters (queries with question mark [?] placeholders) are supported by passing a list as the second argument. Thanks to Groovy's concise syntax for expressing lists, the result is very readable as presented in Listing 4-17.

Listing 4-17. *HQL with Parameters*

```
// query for the Grails bookmark
def grailsBookmark = Bookmark.find(
'from Bookmark as b where b.title = ?',
['Grails'])
```

The methods `find` and `findAll` assume the query is a query specific to the `Bookmark` class and will validate that this is so. It is possible, however, to execute other HQL queries via the `executeQuery` method, as shown in Listing 4-18.

Listing 4-18. *HQL via executeQuery*

```
// get all the tags
def tags = Bookmark.executeQuery('select elements(b.tags) from Bookmark as b')
```

Clearly, there is a lot to cover with HQL, since it is possible to perform more-advanced queries using joins, aggregate functions, and subqueries. Luckily the aforementioned documentation on the Hibernate web site is an excellent overview of what is possible and can help you on your way.

Querying by Example

An alternative to HQL queries is to pass an instance of the class you're looking for to the `find` or `findAll` methods. This is an interesting option when used in conjunction with Groovy's additional implicit constructor for JavaBeans, as shown in Listing 4-19.

Listing 4-19. *Query by Example*

```
def bookmark = Bookmark.find( new Bookmark(title:'Grails') )
```

Query by example is a little limiting, as you don't have access to some of the more-advanced expressions such as like, between, and greater-than when passing in the example. It is however another useful addition to your toolbox.

One form of querying that is most certainly not limiting is the usage of criteria. In the next section we explore how Grails makes criteria more accessible via concise builder syntax.

Querying with Criteria

Possibly one of the most powerful mechanisms for querying is with criteria. This is the first time we'll be exposed to a "mini" domain-specific language (DSL) for creating queries using Groovy's builder support.

A builder in Groovy is essentially a hierarchy of method calls and closures that make it perfect for "building" treelike structures such as XML or a graphical user interface (GUI). This also makes it a good candidate for constructing queries, particularly dynamic queries, which are often constructed with the horrifically error-prone StringBuffer.

The Hibernate Criteria API is meant to reduce the risk of errors by providing a programmatic way to construct "criteria" queries. However, Groovy's expressive syntax and powerful meta-programming support has taken this to a new level of conciseness.

Let's start off by looking at basic usage patterns of criteria, after which we can move on to some more-advanced examples. Firstly, before you can perform a criteria query, you need a criteria instance for the class you want to query. To facilitate this, GORM provides a createCriteria static method on each domain class. Once you have acquired the criteria instance, one of four methods can be invoked, each of which expects a closure argument:

- get: Locates a unique instance for the query

- list: Returns a list of instances for the query

- scroll: Returns a ScrollableResults instance for the query

- count: Returns the total results as an integer for the query

The most common use case is to use the list method on the criteria instance to perform the query, as shown in Listing 4-20.

Listing 4-20. *Simple Criteria Example*

```
def c = Bookmark.createCriteria()

def results = c.list {
      like('title', 'Grails%')
      between('dateCreated', new Date()-10, new Date())
}
```

The previous example lists all the bookmarks with the title starting with Grails for the last ten days. The nested method calls within the closure block translate into method calls on Hibernate's org.hibernate.criterion.Restrictions class, the API for which is too long to list here. Nevertheless, the `like` and `between` methods seen here are just two of many for performing all the typical queries found in query languages such as SQL and HQL.

It is worth taking a look at the API on the Hibernate web site (http://www.hibernate.org) to see what is available and to get a better understanding of the power that is at your fingertips. Of course, you can accomplish similar queries as those in Listing 4-20 with dynamic finder methods. What you haven't really explored is the power of closures, and building the query up dynamically.

Consider for the moment that a closure is just a block of code and can be assigned to a variable. Also, consider that a closure can reference variables within its enclosing scope. Put the two together and you have a pretty powerful mechanism for reusing dynamically constructed queries.

As an example, say you have a map whose keys define the property names to be queried, and the values define the value (note I haven't mentioned that Grails controllers pass in request parameters as a map since we haven't reached that topic yet, but you can imagine where this is going). A query could easily be built up from this map and assigned to a variable. Listing 4-21 provides an example of this concept in action.

Listing 4-21. *Dynamic Querying with Criteria*

```
1 def today = new Date()
2 def queryMap =   [ title: 'Grails%', dateCreated: [today-10,today]  ]

3 def query = {
4             // go through the query map
5             queryMap.each { key, value ->
6                     // if we have a list assume a between query
7                     if(value instanceof List) {
8                             // use the spread operator to invoke
9                             between(key, *value)
10                    }
11                    else {
12                            like(key,value)
13                    }
14            }
15 }
16
17 // create a criteria instance
18 def criteria = Bookmark.createCriteria()
19
20 // count the results
21 println( criteria.count(query) )
22
23 // re-use again to get a unique result
24 println( criteria.get(query) )
25
26 // re-use again to list all
27 criteria.list(query).each { println it }
28
```

```
29 // use scrollable results
30 def scrollable = criteria.scroll(query)
31 def next = scrollable.next()
32 while(next) {
33         println(scrollable.getString('title'))
34         next = scrollable.next()
35 }
```

That's a fairly long example, the longest we've had so far in fact, and includes some fairly advanced concepts. To simplify your understanding of it I've included line numbers and I'll go through it step-by-step.

The first two lines in the following code define a date instance from the current time, and a map using Groovy's map syntax that will dictate which properties you're going to query. The map's keys are the property names to query, and the values define the value to query by:

```
1 def today = new Date()
2 def queryMap =   [ title: 'Grails%', dateCreated: [today-10,today]   ]
```

Tip In the previous code example, to calculate the date range to be the last ten days, I took a java. util.Date instance and subtracted 10 from it. This is an example of one implementation of Groovy's operator overloading facility to simplify date operations.

On line 3 we assign a closure to the query variable, which will be used in conjunction with the criteria. The closure's closing bracket is on line 15, but there is some important stuff going on in the body of the closure:

```
3  def query = {
       ...
15 }
```

Firstly, we're using an inbuilt GDK method called each that uses a closure for iteration. Essentially the method iterates through each element in the map and passes the key and value to the closure as arguments.

```
5    queryMap.each { key, value ->
           ...
14   }
```

Next up we're using the familiar (to Java developers that is) instanceof operator to check whether the value passed is a List. If the value passed is a List you invoke the between method passing the key and the value. The value is split into two arguments using Groovy's * spread operator:

```
7              if(value instanceof List) {
8                      // use the spread operator to invoke
9                      between(key, *value)
10             }
```

```
11                     else {
12                             like(key,value)
13                     }
```

The * spread operator's job is to split apart a list or an array and pass the separated values to the target. In this case the between method, which actually takes three arguments not two, is correctly called, with the first element of the list being the second argument, and the second element being the third argument.

Now let's start to look at how the query, in the form of a closure, works with a criteria instance as a reusable code block. As usual, of course, you have to create the criteria instance, which is accomplished on line 18:

```
18 def criteria = Bookmark.createCriteria()
```

The various methods of the criteria instance are then utilized using the same closure:

```
21 println( criteria.count(query) )
24 println( criteria.get(query) )
27 criteria.list(query).each { println it }
```

The first, on line 21, counts all the results for the query; the next prints out a unique result (if there is one), and finally, the last lists all the results for the query and then iterates through them with the already encountered each method printing each one to standard out.

There is one more usage on line 30, which uses the scroll method on criteria. This returns an instance of the Hibernate class called org.hibernate.ScrollableResults, which has a similar interface to a JDBC java.sql.ResultSet and shares many of the same methods. One major difference, however, is that the columns of results are indexed from 0 and not 1 as in JDBC.

Querying Associations

Often it is useful to execute a query that uses the state of an association as its criteria. So far we have only performed queries against a single class and not its associations. So how do we go about querying an association?

Grails' criteria builder allows querying associations by using a nested criteria method call whose name matches the property name. The closure argument passed to the method contains nested criteria calls that relate to the *association* and not the criteria class.

For example, say we wanted to find all bookmarks that are tagged with the name Grails. The criteria shown in Listing 4-22 would perform exactly this.

Listing 4-22. *Querying Assocations with Criteria*

```
def criteria = Bookmark.createCriteria()
def results = criteria.list {
        tags {
                ilike('name', 'Grails')
        }
}
```

This is a fairly trivial example, but all the criteria you've already seen so far can be nested within the nested `tags` call seen in the code listing. Combine this with how criteria can be built up from logical code blocks and it results in a pretty powerful mechanism for querying associations.

■**Tip** You can also combine association criteria as seen in Listing 4-22 with regular criteria on the class itself.

Querying with Projections

Projections allow the results of criteria queries to be customized in some way. For example, you may want to only count the number of results as opposed to retrieving each one. In other words, they are equivalent to SQL functions such as `count`, `distinct`, and `sum`.

With criteria queries, specifying a `projections` method call that again takes a closure, provides support for these types of queries. Instead of criteria, however, the method calls within it map to another Hibernate class called `org.hibernate.criterion.Projections`.

Let's adapt the example in Listing 4-23 by adding a project that results in counting the distinct URLs that are tagged with `Grails`.

Listing 4-23. *Querying with Projections*

```
def criteria = Bookmark.createCriteria()
def results = criteria.list {
        projections {
            countDistinct('url')
        }
        tags {
            ilike('name', 'Grails')
        }
}
```

In all the examples we have seen so far, the queries executed have assumed that relationships will be loaded *lazily*. In the next section we find out how this behavior can be altered.

Lazy vs. Eager Loading

By default, in Grails, relationships assume *lazy loading*. What this means is that when retrieving a persistent instance, the associated classes in a one-to-many or one-to-one scenario are not loaded until requested. For many circumstances this is fine, but it can result in what is commonly referred to as the *N+1 select problem*. To describe this problem, imagine a scenario where you load an individual bookmark using one query. The `Bookmark` instance in question has, in a hypothetical scenario, thousands of `Tag` instances associated with it via the `tags` relationship.

What happens is you get a single select for retrieving the `Bookmark` instance, and then if you access the `tags` relationship you get an additional select for *each* `Tag` instance. To avoid this pitfall what you need to do is *eagerly* fetch the association as part of the query. In HQL you would do the following:

```
def bookmarks = Bookmark.findAll("from Bookmark b inner join fetch b.tags")
```

This example uses an *inner join* in combination with the fetch operator to retrieve the tags association eagerly. The resulting bookmarks will have their collections initialized and hence avoid the N+1 problem.

Another technique is to use a dynamic finder in combination with the fetch argument. This is useful when you want to use the convenience of dynamic finders but still use eager fetching:

```
def bookmarks = Bookmark.findAllByTitle("Grails",[fetch:[tags:"eager"]])
```

In the previous code example you simply specify that the tags relationship should be *eager*; the rest is handled for you. Lastly, if you're using a criteria query you can also specify eager fetching. Listing 4-24 shows how this is done.

Listing 4-24. *Specifying the fetch Mode in Criteria*

```
import org.hibernate.FetchMode as FM
...

def criteria = Bookmark.createCritera()
def bookmarks = criteria.list {
    eq("title","Grails")
    fetchMode("tags", FM.EAGER)
}
```

Here I explicitly use the org.hibernate.FetchMode class to set the fetch mode on the criteria instance for the tags relationship.

■**Tip** The example in Listing 4-24 demonstrates a neat feature of Groovy imports. You can specify an alias for an import using the as keyword, which is handy for referencing static constants and methods. It also reduces the code change to a single line: the import. This is handy if the referenced class ever moves package or gets renamed as a result of a refactor.

That wraps it up for eager fetching for the moment. Although Grails, as of this writing, doesn't support declarative eager fetching, there is enough flexibility in the querying APIs to offset the need for this feature. And if you *really* need declarative eager fetching you could always map your domain class with Hibernate XML or EJB3 annotations, which we'll explore in Chapter 11.

In the next section, however, we're going to move onto the topic of inheritance and how Grails, thanks to Hibernate, handles polymorphic queries and inheritance hierarchies.

Mapping Inheritance

Inheritance has been traditionally troublesome to map onto the relatively flat structure of database tables. Hibernate itself includes a number of different strategies to map inheritance, including table-per-hierarchy, table-per-concrete-class, and table-per-subclass. Each of these requires different notation in the XML configuration for Hibernate, which can end up being quite verbose. However, it is a powerful feature, particularly when used in conjunction with polymorphic queries.

GORM attempts to simplify inheritance as much as possible, by using table-per-hierarchy inheritance. What this means is that each class in the hierarchy shares the same table and the subclasses are differentiated with an additional `class` column. The downside of this is that subclass properties cannot be required (in other words they can be `null`) due to the fact the table is shared. This is not a huge problem, however, as Grails has its own strategy for performing validation, which we will look at in a moment.

Now let's say for example we want to differentiate bookmarks in some way for different types of sites. For example, it may be useful to search only bookmarked weblogs (or *blogs* as they're most often referred to) or possibly only bookmarked news feeds[2] that are in the Really Simple Syndication (RSS) or Atom formats. These new `Bookmark` types might have specific information that differs them from other bookmarks, such as whether they are an RSS or an Atom feed for example.

To better understand this I'll expand on the UML class diagram you saw earlier and add a couple of subclasses of the `Bookmark` class, as shown in Figure 4-4.

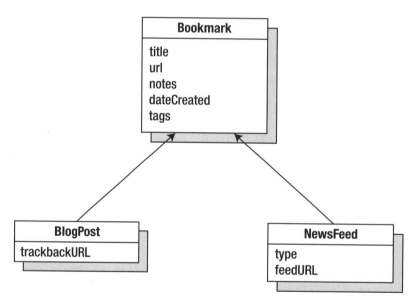

Figure 4-4. *Inheritance class diagram*

Here we have added two new subclasses, one for creating bookmarks for news feeds and the other for blog postings. The `NewsFeed` class has a new property called `type`, which stores the feedback type (either RSS or Atom). The `BlogPost` class contains an additional property for the TrackBack URL that is used by bloggers to reference each other's posts.

So how does this work from a code perspective? It is actually remarkably simple. Just create two new domain classes for our new types that extend the `Bookmark` class and add the additional properties to each, as shown in Listing 4-25.

---

2. A news feed is a document (often XML-based) that contains content items, often summaries of stories or weblog posts with web links to longer versions.

Listing 4-25. *Inheritance with GORM*

```
class NewsFeed extends Bookmark {
      String type
}
class BlogPost extends Bookmark {
      URL trackbackUrl
}
```

This is where it gets interesting because GORM, thanks to Hibernate, supports polymorphic querying. What does this mean? Well, if I use the dynamic finder method `findAll` as per the example in Listing 4-26, it will return not only `Bookmark` instances, but `NewsFeed` and `BlogPost` instances too.

Listing 4-26. *Inheritance in Action*

```
// return all bookmark types
def bookmarks = Bookmark.findAll()

// retrieve only blog posts
def blogPosts = BlogPost.findAll()

// retrieve atom feeds
def atomFeeds = NewsFeed.findAllByType('atom')

// it works with HQL queries and criteria too!
def grailsBookmarks =
      Bookmark.findAll( 'from Bookmark as b where b.title like ?',
                               '%Grails%'] )
```

Inheritance is extremely powerful and simple to use with GORM, which takes care of the entire underlying configuration for you at run time, thanks to the use of convention.

Next we're going to look at validating your domain model to ensure that the data you have stored is always the data you expect.

Validating the Domain

Validation is an important part of any application, and in the web space it is a complicated problem to address as it often spans multiple tiers within an MVC application. Validation can occur on the client side using JavaScript via the controller and against the domain model. One thing is certain however, the domain model is the center of an application and it should always validate.

To this end, Grails provides a flexible mechanism to specify *constraints* against your domain model. These constraints are then validated at run time. The `save` method performs validation automatically and will not persist the object if it doesn't validate against the specified constraints.

Applying Domain Constraints

In yet another instance of Groovy's builder syntax, constraints are defined within the domain class itself. To take a look at how this works let's create the User class for the bookmarks application, as shown in Listing 4-27.

Listing 4-27. *User Class*

```
class User {
        String login
        String password
        String firstName
        String lastName
        String email
}
```

There are clearly some properties contained within the User class that are required or need some form of validation. It would be error-prone and repetitive to have to perform manual validation of each property. Luckily, Grails will handle the logic for you using the constraints builder, as shown in Listing 4-28.

Listing 4-28. *Applying Domain Constraints*

```
1 class User {
2           String login
3           String password
4           String firstName
5           String lastName
6           String email
7
8         static constraints = {
9              login(unique:true,length:5..15)
10             password(matches:/[\w\d]+/, length:6..12)
11             email(email:true)
12             firstName(blank:false)
13             lastName(blank:false)
14         }
15 }
```

To fully explain how this works I'll go through it line by line.

First you define a static property called constraints that is a closure. The body of the closure has a number of builder nodes (method calls, in reality) that relate to each property name within the class. In other words, the login property has a node called login(..).

```
8     static constraints = {
              //...
14    }
```

The previous `constraints` ensures that the login is unique within the database and restricts the value of the `login` property to be between 5 and 15 characters in length using Groovy's range syntax:

```
9          login(unique,length:5..15)
```

Next up you have a constraint for the `password` property, which uses a regular expression to ensure that it is only made of alphanumeric characters and that its length is between 6 and 12 characters:

```
10         password(matches:/[\w\d]+/, length:6..12)
```

The `email` property uses an `email` constraint that ensures it is a valid e-mail address in the form `address@domain`:

```
11          email(email:true)
```

The `firstName` and `lastName` properties both use the `blank` constraint, which ensures that they cannot be blank strings or `null`:

```
12         firstName(blank:false)
13         lastName(blank:false)
```

The examples so far are just a small taste of what is possible. Table 4-2 lists the supported constraints with descriptions and examples.

Table 4-2. *Domain Constraints Table*

Name	Example	Description
blank	login(blank:false)	Set to false if a string value cannot be blank
email	email(email:true)	Set to true if the value must be an e-mail address
inList	login(inList:["Joe", "Fred"])	Value must be contained within the given list
length	login(length:5..15)	Uses a range to restrict the length of a string or array
min	age(min:new Date())	Sets the minimum value
minLength	login(minLength:5)	Sets the minimum length of a string or array property
minSize	children(minSize:5)	Sets the minimum size of a collection or number property
matches	login(matches:/[a-zA-Z]/)	Matches the supplied regular expression
max	age(max:new Date())	Sets the maximum value
maxLength	login(maxLength:5)	Sets the maximum length of a string or array property

Table 4-2. *Domain Constraints Table (Continued)*

Name	Example	Description
maxSize	`children(maxSize:25)`	Sets the maximum size of a collection or number property
notEqual	`login(notEqual:"Bob")`	Must not equal the specified value
nullable	`age(nullable:false)`	Set to `false` if the property value cannot be `null`
range	`age(range:minAge..maxAge)`	Must occur within the specified range
size	`children(size:5..15)`	Uses a range to restrict the size of a collection or number
unique	`login(unique:true)`	Set to `true` if the property must be unique
url	`url(url:true)`	Set to `true` if a string value is a URL address

Armed with this knowledge on how to apply constraints let's move straight onto exploring their practical usage by learning how to validate against specified constraints.

Validating Against Constraints

Defining the constraints is one thing, but you still need to validate against them. First of all, as mentioned previously, the save method will automatically validate against the specified constraints. When validation fails, the save method will return null; this allows you to write conditional code that takes into account validation, as shown in Listing 4-29.

Listing 4-29. *Validating onsave*

```
def user = new User(login:'Graeme',
                           password:'letmein',
                           email:'graeme@grails.org',
                           firstName:'Graeme',
                           lastName:'Rocher')

if(user.save()) {
        println "User $user created!"
}
else {
        user.errors.allErrors.each { println it.defaultMessage }
}
```

An interesting aspect to note about the previous code is the usage of the errors property on domain classes. This property is an instance of the Spring Framework's org.springframework. validation.Errors interface, thus allowing advanced querying of the validation errors that did occur. In the previous example, if validation fails, which in this case it won't, you're simply getting a list of all the errors that occurred and printing them to standard out. Listing 4-30 shows some of the more useful methods of the Spring Errors interface (note there are more methods, but the examples in this listing represent the most useful ones).

Listing 4-30. *The Spring Errors Interface*

```
package org.springframework.validation;
class Errors {
    List getAllErrors();
    int getErrorCount();
    FieldError getFieldError(String fieldName);
    int getFieldErrorCount();
    List getFieldErrors(String fieldName);
    Object getObjectName();
    boolean hasErrors();
    boolean hasFieldErrors(String fieldName);
    // ...x remaining methods
}
```

As you can see there are a number of useful methods for retrieving errors. Using getAllErrors(), you can retrieve all the validation errors or, alternatively, if you only want errors for a specific field you can use getFieldErrors(Sring fieldName). In the majority of cases, however, you won't need to work directly with this interface, with Grails handling all those intricacies for you.

Occasionally it is useful to perform changes to the domain model before committing to the save method. In this case Grails provides a validate method, which simply returns a Boolean value to indicate whether validation was successful. The semantics are exactly the same as in the previous example with the save method, except, of course, that the validate method doesn't perform any persistent calls.

Defining Custom Constraints

With the breadth of different built-in validators you would think it would be sufficient to cover all possible use cases. It is impossible, however, to predict every feasible domain model, as software spans such a wide range of industries and use cases.

Needless to say, Grails provides a way to specify custom validation constraints when the built-in ones don't suffice. To do so, provide a closure as the final argument to any constraint, as shown in Listing 4-31.

Listing 4-31. *A Custom Constraint*

```
class User {
    ...
    static constraints = {
        password(unique:true,length:5..15, validator: { val, obj ->
            if(val?.equalsIgnoreCase(obj.firstName)) {
                return false
            }
```

```
    })
        ...
    }
}
```

In the code listing you check, for security reasons of course, that the user isn't using a silly password such as his first name. As per the example, if validation fails, the closure should return `false`, otherwise it should return `true`. The first argument passed to the closure is the object to be validated in its current state. Using this mechanism, the error code, used to pick up the error message from the `grails-app/i18n/messages.properties` resource bundle, will be resolved as `className.propertyName.validator.invalid`. For example, in the previous case, the error code would be `user.password.validator.invalid`.

Alternatively, if your custom validation code is more complex and requires multiple different error messages, you can return a string, which is appended to the sequence `className.propertyName` to create the error code as shown in Listing 4-32.

Listing 4-32. *Specifying Message Codes*

```
class User {
    ...
    static constraints = {
        password(unique:true,length:5..15, validator:{ val, obj ->
            if(val?.equalsIgnoreCase(obj.firstName)) {
                return 'passwordEqualsFirstName'
            }
            else if(val?.equalsIgnoreCase(obj.lastName)) {
                return ['passwordEqualsLastName', lastName]
            }
        })
}
```

In this case if a string is returned, validation fails, otherwise the closure should return `true` as usual. The error code produced here is either `user.password.EqualsFirstName` or `user.password.EqualsLastName` depending on which validation check failed.

In the `second` return statement, however, a list is returned instead of a string:

```
    return ['passwordEqualsLastName', lastName]
```

This allows arguments to be passed to the message within the bundle using the standard `java.text.MessageFormat` format. For example, a message within the property bundle for the previous code and arguments could be something like the following:

```
user.password.EqualsLastName=Your password cannot be {3} as it is your last name!
```

The index to retrieve passed arguments starts from the number 3 because the first three arguments available to all messages are always the property name, class name, and property value.

Performing Updates Revisited

Earlier we looked at how GORM performs updates to persistent instances. Just to recap an important fact about the way GORM deals with updates, it is *not* necessary to call the save method for the updates to take effect. GORM, thanks to the underlying Hibernate runtime, will realize that the instance has changed and will perform these updates for you automatically when no exceptions occur.

Given that we've just been talking about data integrity and validation it is important to understand why this is not always desired behavior. If an instance does not validate clearly, you don't want the changes to be persisted. Luckily, calling the save method in GORM neatly handles this problem. Essentially, if you do call save and the object does not validate, any changes made to the object will not be saved.

In this sense it is important to understand how save differs from validate. The validate method *will not* discard changes if validation fails, thus allowing you to rectify those changes at run time and still have the object persisted. To understand this better Listing 4-33 shows a few examples that fail to validate.

Listing 4-33. *Validating on save*

```
// get four hypothetical users from the database
def u1 = User.get(1)
def u2 = User.get(2)
def u3 = User.get(3)
def u4 = User.get(4)

// make the invalid
u1.login = null // cannot have a null login
u2.email = 'an_invalid_email' // set an invalid email
u3.firstName = '' // first name cannot be blank
u4.password = 'with spaces' // Password can't have spaces

// fails to validate, will not be saved
u2.save()
// fails to validate, but will still attempt to save
u3.validate()
// explicitly discarding a change
if(!u4.validate()) {
        u4.discard()
}
```

The previous code will exhibit the following behavior when run in the Grails environment:

- Grails will attempt to save the instance u1 automatically (which will fail anyway as the login property is required by default at the database level).

- The save method on the instance u2 will perform validation first, which will fail and the changes will be discarded.

- The `validate` method is called on instance u3 which fails, but Grails will still attempt to autosave the instance.

- Finally, the instance u4 fails to validate, but the explicit `discard` method is used to discard the changes and hence it is not saved.

If you consider these semantics for the moment they do make sense and exist in this way for a very good reason. Clearly it is valuable from both a code clarity point of view and for validation that the `save` method is invoked explicitly during updates, but the autosave feature is still there for the more simple cases. Also, the `validate` method exists for code to be able to programmatically correct itself following a validation error and, if successful, to either call `save` or else `discard`.

The semantics are not difficult to understand but are important to grasp, as they can lead to surprises if not followed correctly.

In Chapters 7 and 8 we will look at how to display and tailor the error messages that are causes by validation errors.

Summary

This chapter covered quite a bit of ground by introducing the application domain and how it facilitates domain-driven development with Grails. GORM is tremendously simple when compared to other approaches to object-relational mapping, and thanks to Groovy's dynamic capabilities it is made even simpler by dynamic methods and GPath.

Remember, a great way to familiarize yourself with GORM is to load up the Grails console (as discussed in Chapter 3) and try out dynamic methods for yourself. This interactive approach is a good way to learn Grails and better understand your own domain model.

CHAPTER 5

■■■

Scaffolding

S_caffolding_ is the name coined by the Rails framework for the generation of the artifacts that make up a usable interface to perform CRUD operations. This term has been further extended and generalized to basically mean the generation of an interface to fulfill a use case based on the convention within a project. This is in part due to a number of extensions being added for creating authentication/authorization code, unit tests, and the like, simply by recognizing that there is a convention in place.

Scaffolding is something better demonstrated and explained visually so before I bore you with too much detail and technical definitions let's get started straight away and see the book-mark*s* application in action that we constructed in the previous chapter.

Dynamic Scaffolding

Scaffolding comes in two flavors: dynamic (or runtime), and static (or template-driven). First we'll look at *dynamic* scaffolding, where a CRUD application's controller logic and views are generated at run time. Dynamic scaffolding does not use boilerplate code or templates; it uses more advanced techniques such as reflection and Groovy's MetaClass to achieve its goals.

Before we can start using scaffolding, we need a controller. We had a brief introduction to controllers in Chapter 1. The controller code necessary to enable scaffolding is minimal. We're going to dynamically scaffold the Bookmark class, hence we need a controller for this class, which you can either create manually or via the command line as shown in Listing 5-1.

Listing 5-1. *Creating the Bookmark Controller*

```
>grails create-controller
    [input] Enter controller name:
bookmark
```

As demonstrated in the code listing, when prompted, enter **bookmark** into the terminal window and hit the Return key. Grails will create a file called grails-app/controllers/ BookmarkController.groovy which, when opened, will have contents such as the example in Listing 5-2.

Listing 5-2. *The Bookmark Controller*

```
class BookmarkController {
      def index = {}
}
```

To enable scaffolding, create a `scaffold` property with the name of the target class as its value, in this case the `Bookmark` class, as shown in Listing 5-3.

Listing 5-3. *The Bookmark Controller with Scaffolding Enabled*

```
class BookmarkController {
        def scaffold = Bookmark
}
```

Note Groovy automatically resolves class names, such as with `Bookmark` in Listing 5-3, to the `java.lang.Class` instance without requiring the `.class` suffix as with Java. In other words `Bookmark ==` `Bookmark.class`.

That's it, we're done. What we have told Grails is that a set of actions to perform CRUD operations on the `Bookmark` class are to be provided at run time, and that a set of views to interact with those actions should be generated. Now start Grails by running the `grails run-app` command from the root of the bookmarks project and open up a web browser. Navigate to the address `http://localhost:8080/bookmarks` via a browser, and the Grails welcome page will appear, displaying a comforting welcome message, as shown in Figure 5-1.

Figure 5-1. *The Grails welcome page*

More usefully, however, you will notice that the welcome page lists the controller you created in the previous step. Click the BookmarkController link and out of nowhere a page will appear listing your Bookmark objects (none, as the case may be) as depicted in Figure 5-2. It is fairly remarkable that you've made it this far given the BookmarkController encompasses a grand total of three lines of code.

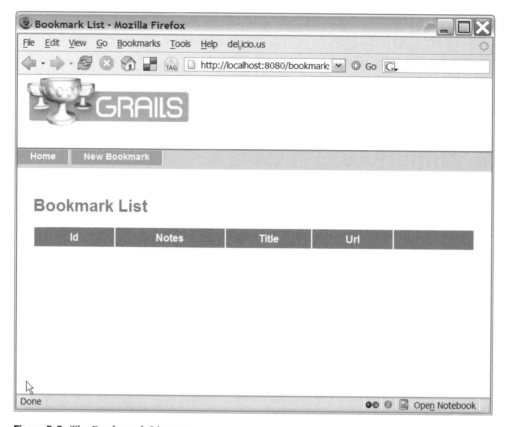

Figure 5-2. *The Bookmark List page*

Create Operation

The magic doesn't end here. By clicking the New Bookmark link at the top of the screen, new bookmarks can be *created*, thus representing the first word represented in the CRUD acronym. While generating the views, Grails does its best in trying to guess what type of field is required to edit a property's value. As an example, if it finds a string it will create a text field, while if the property value is a java.util.Date, it will render drop-down select boxes to specify the date and time instead. Constraints can also effect how the interface is rendered, including the order in which fields are displayed and the type of field that is rendered; but for now let's take a look at what the Create Bookmark screen, shown in Figure 5-3, looks like.

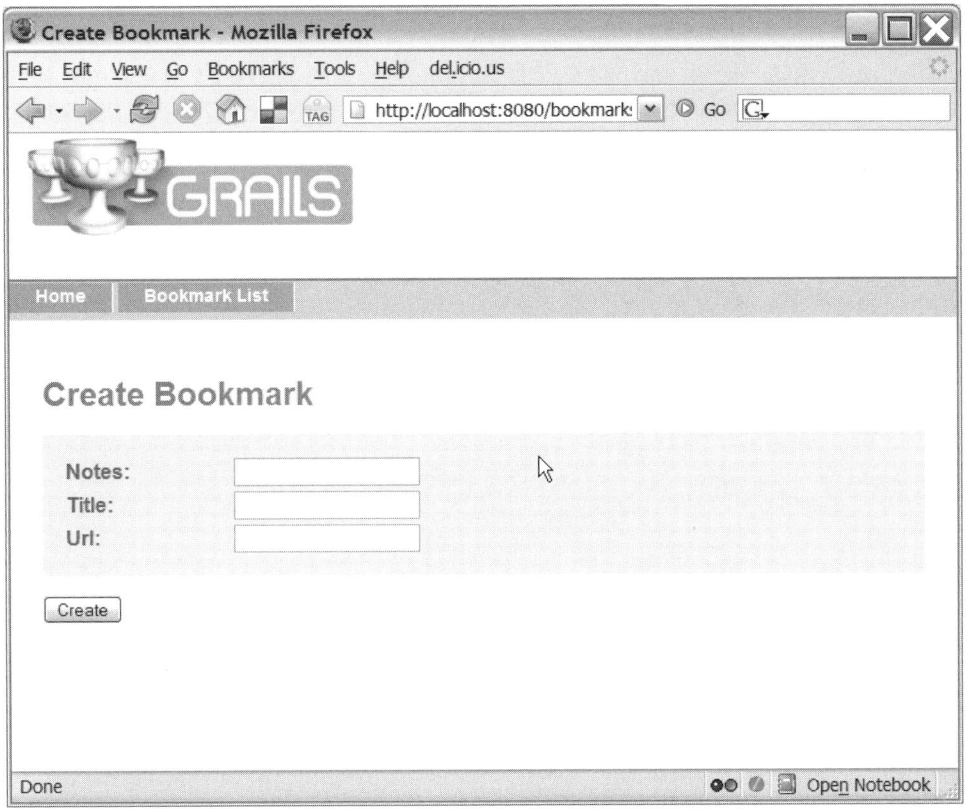

Figure 5-3. *The Create Bookmark page*

Notice how the fields don't exactly appear in the desired order. This is where constraints come in handy. The constraints builder syntax serves not only to define validation constraints, but also affects the rendering of scaffolding. To see this in action open up the Bookmark class and add the constraints in Listing 5-4.

Listing 5-4. *Bookmark Constraints*

```
class Bookmark {
    . . .
    static constraints = {
        url(url:true)
        title(blank:false)
    }
}
```

Save your changes and return to your browser window and hit the Refresh button or key combination (generally the F5 key performs a refresh on most browsers). Not only has the previous constraints definition ensured that the url property is a valid URL and that the title property cannot be blank, but the resulting screen has reordered the fields based on the order of the nodes in the constraints builder, as shown in Figure 5-4.

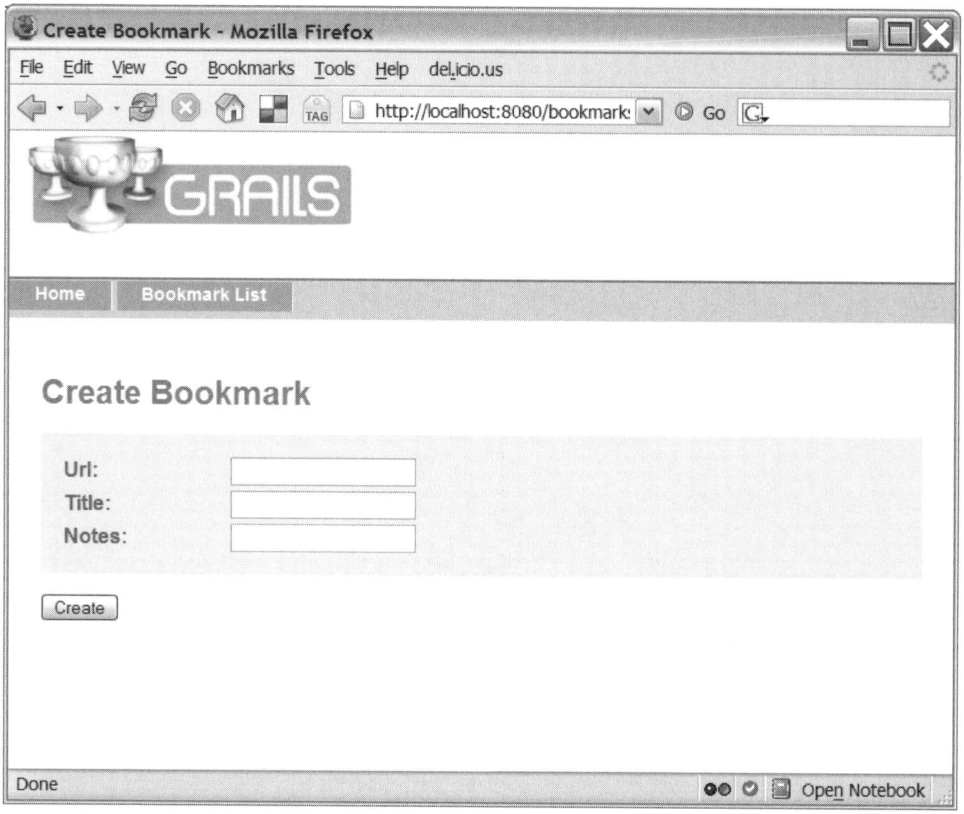

Figure 5-4. *Reordering with constraints*

Now that the order of the fields has been rectified, try clicking the Create button without having entered any information. The result will be an error message similar to that which is displayed in Figure 5-5.

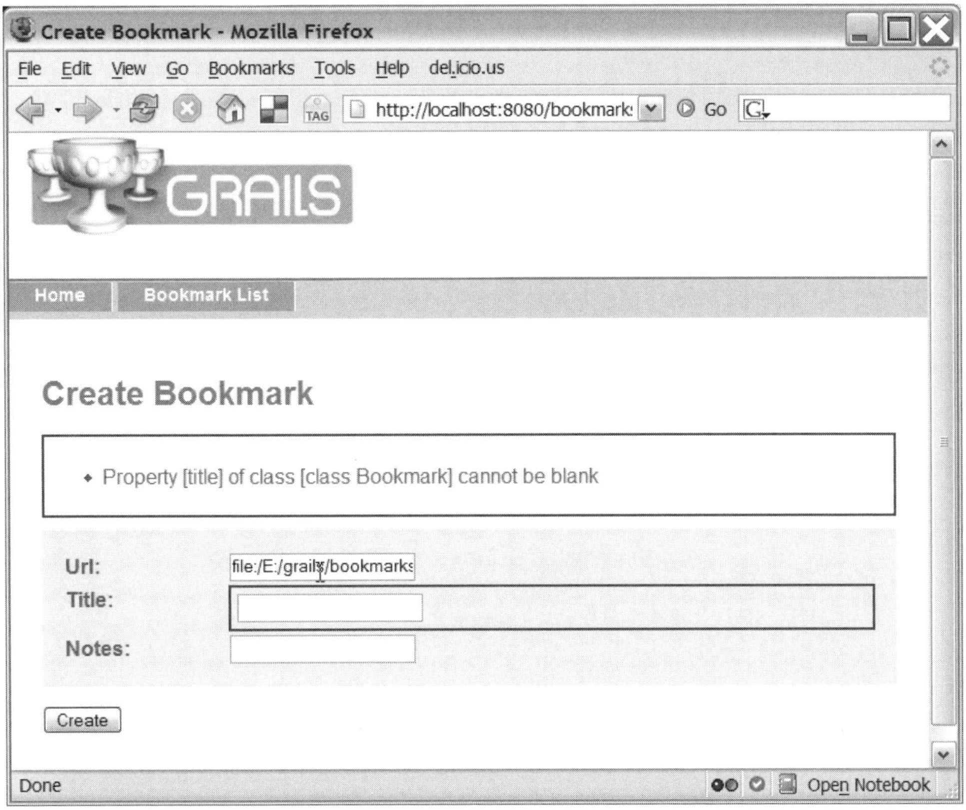

Figure 5-5. *A validation error message*

Notice how the field that caused the error is highlighted with a red border, indicating where the problem lies. The error message is loaded from the defaults found in the `grails-app/i18n/messages.properties` message bundle. You could obviously customize the message at this point, but for now the defaults will do. (This will be covered in greater detail in Chapter 8.)

Moving on, let's create a bookmark to the Grails web site using the following data:

- *URL*: `http://grails.org`

- *Title*: Grails

- *Notes*: An agile web framework for the Groovy language

Once done click the Create button again, which will create and then display the bookmark. This time no errors occur and you end up at a view that displays your newly created bookmark and the values you populated previously.

Read Operation

The Show Bookmark screen (yes, we're on to the second letter of CRUD, which stands for *read*), shown in Figure 5-6, displays the details of the Bookmark and an additional two buttons that allow you to edit and, if you so choose, delete this Bookmark.

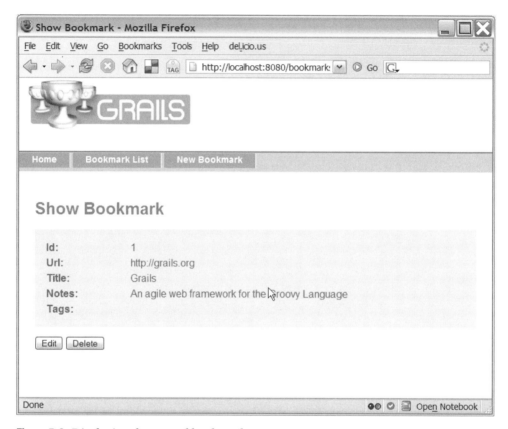

Figure 5-6. *Displaying the created bookmark*

Notably the Tags field is blank, as you have not yet applied any tags to the Bookmark. Remember that a tag is modeled using a Tag domain class, and a Bookmark can have many tags. So how do you go about establishing this relationship (a bidirectional one-to-many, as the case may be) between the Grails Bookmark and some tags?

Update Operation

Firstly, click the Edit button, which will display the Edit Bookmark screen and a button that represents the third letter in CRUD, *update*. Figure 5-7 demonstrates this; as you can see, the form appears prepopulated with the values from the bookmark you are editing. Opposite the Tags field's label, however, there is an Add Tag link. Grails is intelligent enough to know that this is a relationship and that the relationship is defined by another class called Tag and hence links across to another controller called TagController which manages this class.

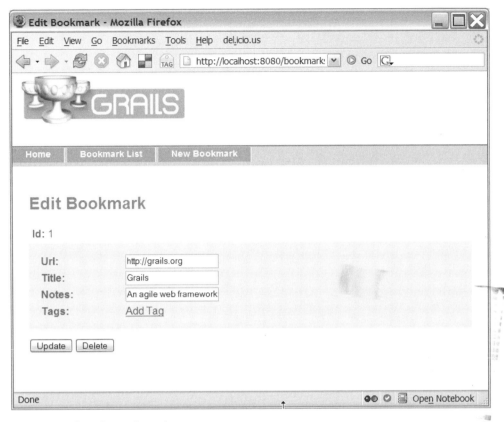

Figure 5-7. *The Edit Bookmark page*

Unfortunately, you only created a BookmarkController, so at the moment there is no TagController in existence, hence the result would be a "page not found (404) error" from the web server. No problem, we simply need to create one, which again involves the following steps already covered when we created the BookmarkController:

1. Run the grails create-controller target.

2. Type in the name **tag** when prompted, followed by the Return key.

3. Add a scaffold property and set its value to the Tag class.

The result of performing these steps can be seen here:

```
class TagController {
    def scaffold = Tag
}
```

Once the TagController is created, clicking the Add Tag link will no longer result in a nasty "404," but instead a rather pleasant Create Tag screen will appear with the value of the Bookmark drop-down already set to the correct controller, as shown in Figure 5-8.

Figure 5-8. *The Create Tag page*

Interestingly, the value of the drop-down reads Bookmark: 1. This is the default toString() method implementation provided by domain classes; to alter this, simply override toString() as shown in Listing 5-5.

Listing 5-5. *Updated toString() on Bookmark*

```
class Bookmark {
    . . .
    String toString() {
        return "$title - $url"
    }
}
```

The `toString()` method definition uses a Groovy GString (aka *string interpolation* for Ruby/Perl users) to format a string representation of a bookmark as the title followed by a hyphen character and then the URL. If you hit Refresh on your browser again, the field should say `Grails - http://grails.org`, as shown in Figure 5-9.

■**Note** If you are using the default in-memory database, modifying a domain class and refreshing the browser will cause all data to be cleared, as essentially a new in-memory database will be created. If this becomes too inconvenient it is probably more practical to switch to a more permanent store as explained in Chapter 3.

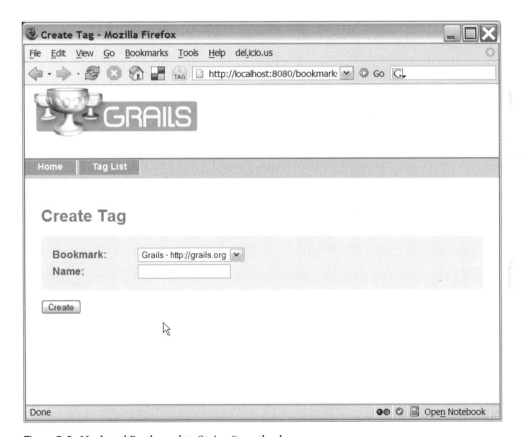

Figure 5-9. *Updated Bookmark toString() method*

Given that you now know which `Bookmark` is which, you can go ahead and start tagging them to your hearts content. Following the example, let's tag the Grails site with three tags named `groovy`, `web framework`, and `agile`, thus allowing you to group the `Bookmark` with others that are related to these topics. The result will appear something like Figure 5-10 when you return the Show Bookmark screen.

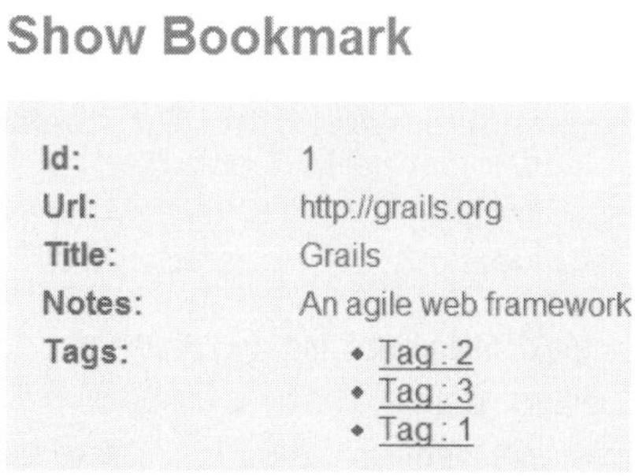

Show Bookmark

Id:	1
Url:	http://grails.org
Title:	Grails
Notes:	An agile web framework
Tags:	• Tag : 2
	• Tag : 3
	• Tag : 1

Figure 5-10. *Show Bookmark screen with tags*

But wait. It seems as if we have another toString() method to specify on the Tag class so that we can differentiate them by name rather than database identifier. Listing 5-8 shows the addition of the toString() method to the Tag class.

Listing 5-8. *Updated Tag toString() method*

```
class Tag {
    . . .
    String toString() { name }
}
```

In this case, because the string representation is so simple (just the name property) it fits nicely onto one line with the return statement omitted as another optional keyword in Groovy. The result is that we can now decipher which tag is which as reflected in Figure 5-11.

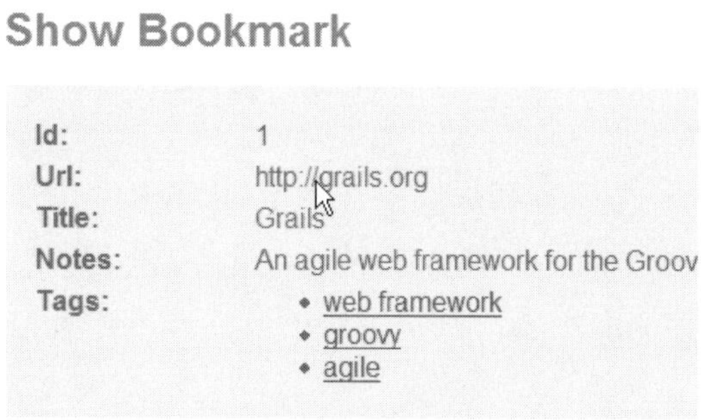

Show Bookmark

Id:	1
Url:	http://grails.org
Title:	Grails
Notes:	An agile web framework for the Groov
Tags:	• web framework
	• groovy
	• agile

Figure 5-11. *Show Bookmark screen with tags and updated toString() method*

Clearly, there is a lot of refinement that could go on, but fundamentally what we have is the basics of our bookmarks application. OK, it might not quite reach the same heights of usability as some of the Ajax-enabled commercial social bookmarking applications, but it is a start. In total you have written nine lines of code to achieve a basic application that manages bookmarks. That is a lot of payoff for the little bit of work you have done so far.

Delete Operation

There is still, however, one last letter of the CRUD acronym to address: D for *delete*. What if you want to delete a Bookmark or a tag? Well you already saw the Delete button when you started viewing and editing the Grails bookmark. Clicking Delete will delete the bookmark and take you back to the list of bookmarks and display a confirmation message, as shown in Figure 5-12.

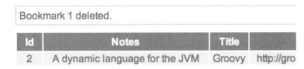

Figure 5-12. *Confirmation following delete*

Overriding CRUD Operations

As mentioned previously, Grails' scaffolding implementation is truly dynamic and utilizes no code generation strategies at the controller level. An interesting side effect of this is the ability to mix *real* controller actions with those dynamically created via scaffolding. One approach to this is to override the individual scaffolded actions themselves.

As an example, you may want to restrict what bookmarks can be saved based on the protocol used in the URL. Clearly the cleanest way to resolve this is to provide custom validation as described in Chapter 4. For the purposes of this example, however, you could override the save action in the controller to perform this validation for you, as shown in Listing 5-6.

Listing 5-6. *Overriding the save Action*

```
class BookmarkController {

    def scaffold = Bookmark

    def save = {
        def b = new Bookmark(params)
        if( ['http', 'https'].contains( b.url?.protocol ) ) {
            // save bookmark
            . . .
        }
        else {
            flash.message = 'Invalid bookmark'
            redirect(action:create)
        }
    }
}
```

The previous example checks whether the java.net.URL instance's protocol is contained within a list of supported protocols and if it does, redirects back to the create action, which is actually a scaffolded action and doesn't exist in the code at all.

■**Note** For clarity this book keeps the examples simple, but in a real-world situation, the list of supported protocols is actually better represented as a static constant or even loaded from an external properties file.

Note the usage of Groovy's safe dereference operator to safeguard against the infamous NullPointerException. The expression b.url?.protocol will essentially evaluate the whole expression as null when the url property is null instead of throwing a NullPointerException. It is quite remarkable what a huge difference this one operator makes, not only to the length of your code, but to the quality, simply by dramatically reducing the amount of null checking the programmer is required to perform.

Returning to action overriding: in order to override actions you need to know the names of them to begin with. Clearly you could establish the names by trying out the application and taking note of the actions used via the URL in the browser. However, if you're not into taking on such a research project, Table 5-1 shows a list of the actions Grails' scaffolding mechanism provides at run time and their associated descriptions.

Table 5-1. *Actions Provided by Scaffolding*

Action Name	Example URI	Description
list	/bookmark/list	Lists all instances of the scaffolded class
create	/bookmark/create	Displays the create view
save	/bookmark/save	Saves a new instance to the database and displays it
show	/bookmark/show/1	Shows an instance for the specified identifier
edit	/bookmark/edit/1	Displays the edit view for the specified identifier
update	/bookmark/update/1	Updates an instance to the database
delete	/bookmark/delete/1	Deletes an instance from the database

Customizing Fields with Constraints

You've already seen how the order in which constraints are defined affects the order of the fields when they are rendered in the view. The power constraints wield over how the view is generated extends even further, however, with the length, range and inList constraints rendering different editors in the following ways:

- The length constraint will display a text area if the maximum length is beyond 255 characters.

- The range constraint will display a select box with the allowed values in the range as values.

- The inList constraint will display a select box with the allowed values.

For example, say hypothetically one day new features are added to the bookmarks application that allow bookmarks to be placed in categories, based on type, and rated with values between 1 and 10. To do so, new properties are added to the Bookmark class to represent the type and rating, as shown in Listing 5-7.

Listing 5-7. *Updated Bookmark class*

```
class Bookmark {
    . . .
    Integer rating
    String type

    static constraints = {
        url(url:true)
        title(blank:false)
        rating(range:1..10)
        type(inList:['blog', 'article', 'general', 'news'])
        notes(maxLength:1000)
    }
}
```

In addition to the aforementioned features, we've increased the maximum length of the notes property's allowed value to 1,000 characters. Now when you refresh the browser, the new fields are added, but the Rating and Type fields are represented with selects and the Notes with a text area, as shown in Figure 5-13.

It's worth conducting your own little experiments with these constraints to see how you can customize the generated interface. The examples seen already should give you an idea of the control available to you via constraints that extend beyond the view and into the validation of your domain model.

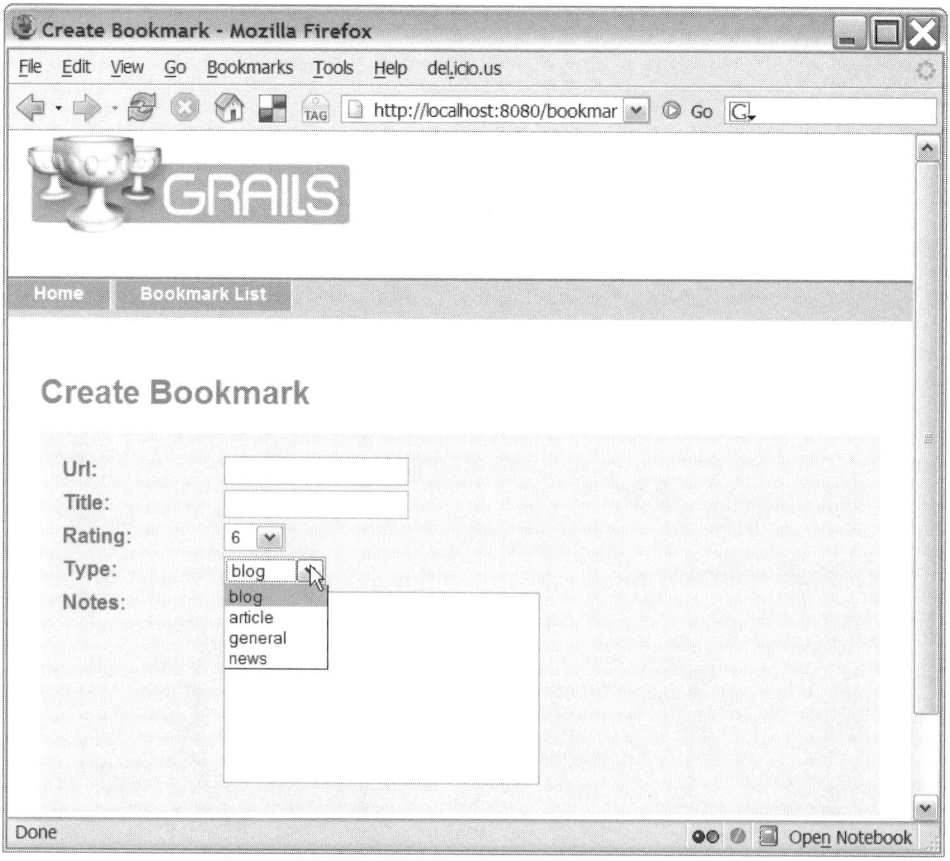

Figure 5-13. *Customizing generated fields*

Static Scaffolding

Dynamic scaffolding can serve a number of purposes from creating administration interfaces to providing the basis of a real application. However, it more often than not becomes useful to take customization to a new level, particularly in terms of views. Fortunately Grails provides the ability to take a domain class and generate a controller and associated views from the command line through the following targets:

- `grails generate-views`: Generates views for the specified domain class

- `grails generate-controller`: Generates a controller for the specified domain class

- `grails generate-all`: Generates both a controller and associated views

They are split out in this way, as it is frequently useful to only generate the views and continue to use dynamic scaffolding with the controller, or vice versa.

■**Note** Command-line scaffolding is a fantastic way to learn how to write Grails controllers, as it generates a ready-made controller example that relates to *your* domain model. This is a powerful concept, as it allows you to relate what the controller is doing to the business objects within your application. There is much debate in the community as to whether boilerplate code is a good thing or not, but there is no denying the power scaffolding offers as a learning tool.

Generating a Controller

Let's generate a controller for one of your domain classes. Doing this requires you to delete one of the existing controllers, as the generate-controller target will wisely not override any pre-existing controllers. You're going to generate a new TagController, and since there is already an existing TagController, you will need to delete it first to see the code generation take effect.

Once you've deleted the grails-app/controllers/TagController.groovy file, type **grails generate-controller** into a command window from the root of the bookmarks project, and when prompted enter **tag** as the name of the domain class. The result will resemble something like Figure 5-14, with Grails kindly informing you where it has placed the newly generated controller.

Figure 5-14. *Generating a controller*

At this point it is probably useful to go and examine the contents of this mysterious controller to see how many thousands of lines of code have been generated. If you're coming from a traditional Java web development background you may expect to at least have to implement a few different classes. For example you would likely need a controller that calls a business interface that in turn invokes a Data Access Object (DAO) that performs the CRUD operations.

Surely there will be mountains of ORM framework code in the DAO, and maybe a few lines of JDBC mixed in for good measure. Surprisingly (or unsurprisingly, depending on your perspective), the code is extremely concise and is well under 100 lines—still not quite short enough to list in full here, but we will step through each action in the generated controller to understand what each is doing.

The index action is the default action, which is executed if no action is specified in the controller URI. It simply redirects to the list action passing any parameters along with it:

```
def index = {
    redirect(action:list,params:params)
}
```

To get a list of all tags there is the list action. Note how it gets passed the params object, which the list method can then inspect for max, offset, and sort arguments, hence allowing pagination of results. The list method has already been covered in Chapter 4, and pagination of results, in terms of how it relates to the view, will be revisited in Chapter 8:

```
def list = {
    [ tagList: Tag.list( params ) ]
}
```

The show action takes the id parameter from the params object and passes it to the get method of the Tag class and places the returned instance in the model for display:

```
def show = {
    [ tag : Tag.get( params.id ) ]
}
```

The action that handles deletion of tags is the aptly named delete action, which will retrieve a tag for the specified id parameter and, if it exists, delete it and redirect it to the list action:

```
def delete = {
    def tag = Tag.get( params.id )
    if(tag) {
        tag.delete()
        flash.message = "Tag ${params.id} deleted."
    }
    else {
        flash.message = "Tag not found with id ${params.id}"
    }
    redirect(action:list)
}
```

While similar to the show action, which simply displays a tag's property values, the edit action delegates to an edit view, which will render fields to edit a tag's properties:

```
def edit = {
    def tag = Tag.get( params.id )

    if(!tag) {
            flash.message = "Tag not found with id ${params.id}"
            redirect(action:list)
    }
    else {
        return [ tag : tag ]
    }
}
```

For updating there is the update action, which again looks strikingly similar to what we've seen already due to the pattern developing around usage of the static get method. In this case, however, it updates the tag's properties and attempts a call to the save() method:

```
def update = {
    def tag = Tag.get( params.id )
    if(tag) {
        tag.properties = params
        if(tag.save()) {
            redirect(action:show,id:tag.id)
        }
        else {
            render(view:'edit',model:[tag:tag])
        }
    }
    else {
        flash.message = "Tag not found with id ${params.id}"
        redirect(action:edit,id:params.id)
    }
}
```

To facilitate the creation of new tags, the create action will delegate to the create view, which like the edit view will display appropriate editing fields. Note that it inserts a new Tag instance into the model to ensure that field values are populated from request parameters:

```
def create = {
    [ tag: new Tag(params) ]
}
```

And, finally, the save action will attempt to create a new Tag instance and save it to the database:

```
def save = {
    def tag = new Tag(params)
    if(tag.save()) {
        redirect(action:show,id:tag.id)
    }
    else {
        render(view:'create',model:[tag:tag])
    }
}
```

In both the save and update actions you alternate between using the redirect or render method. These will be covered in more depth in Chapter 7 on controllers, but just as a brief explanation, the redirect method redirects the entire request to a different action while the render method renders a selected view to the response of the current request.

Clearly, I've only provided a brief overview of the various CRUD operations and what they do, but have single-handedly failed to elaborate further on a lot of the magic that is going on here. There is, however, method in the madness. The nitty-gritty details of controllers and how they work is being saved for Chapter 7. For the moment, however, let's progress and try out our newly generated controller by running the bookmarks application once again via the grails run-app target.

Once the server has loaded, navigate your browser to the tag controller at the address http://localhost:8080/bookmarks/tag. What happens? Well, not a great deal, actually. The result is a "page not found (404)" error returned to the browser because the generated controller is not using dynamic scaffolding. Dynamic scaffolding renders the views at run time, but what you have here is actually just a plain old controller, nothing special about it, and there are no views.

■**Note** We can of course set the scaffold property to the Tag class, and the views will be generated with each action overridden.

Generating Views

It would be nice to have some views for our actions to delegate to. Fortunately, we can generate them via the grails generate-views target, which is executed following the same process described earlier in the section "Generating a Controller." The resulting output from the command window will resemble something like that which is represented in Figure 5-15.

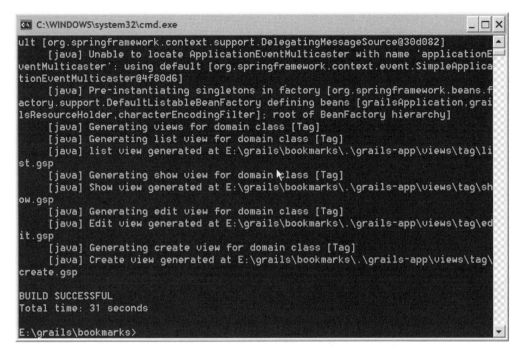

Figure 5-15. *Result of generate-views target*

Again, the target will inform you exactly where the views have been placed. All in all, there are four generated views:

- `list.gsp`: Used by the `list` action to display a list of `Tag` instances

- `show.gsp`: Used by the `show` action to display an individual `Tag` instance

- `edit.gsp`: Used by the `edit` action to edit a `Tag` instance's properties

- `create.gsp`: Used by the `create` action to create a new `Tag` instance

■**Note** All of the views use the main layout found at `grails-app/views/layouts/main.gsp`. This includes the placement of title, logo, and any included style sheets. The main layout is what you'll likely want to use to customize the look and feel of a web site.

As it stands you now have a controller and views to perform CRUD. So what have you achieved beyond what you saw in dynamic scaffolding? Well nothing yet. The power of command-line scaffolding is that it allows you a starting point to build your application. Having started off with nothing, you now have a controller to place your own custom business logic into.

You have views, which you can customize to your heart's content—all this while writing minimal amounts of code. In general, the developers I know are on a constant mission to write less code, and scaffolding is a useful item in the toolbox to win this very battle.

With the TagController and associated views in place, delete the existing BookmarkController and repeat the steps in Figures 5-14 and 5-15 to generate a controller and views for the Bookmark domain class. You're going to need the generated code in the coming chapters as we build on the basic CRUD functionality developed so far.

Summary

When planning this book, I originally had scaffolding as one of the later chapters, but it is an extremely powerful learning tool and therefore is best introduced early. It also has a great deal of visual impact and wow factor. In general, it is fairly common to start heavily customizing controllers and views generated by scaffolding. What it does do, however, is provide the necessary momentum and a starting point to get a project up and running quickly.

Scaffolding also provides you with an interactive way to learn Grails. You generate *real* working code that relates to *your* domain model. This is a tremendous aid in understanding how Grails fits together as a framework. Over and above this, scaffolding can help you quickly prototype an application to gather requirements and feedback without incurring a large amount of development cost. In addition, it is not unheard of to use controllers and views generated by scaffolding to provide administrative interfaces (or those that don't require that designer touch) for your application.

Needless to say, this chapter did generate a lot of code, and before you start digging deeper into understanding the workings of the code, you need to tackle the subject of *testing*. Automated testing is so crucial to modern web applications. It is a shame that many dynamic web frameworks ignore this important aspect of development.

In the next chapter I cover the topic of testing and how Grails applications can be tested at the unit and functional level.

CHAPTER 6

■■■

Testing, Testing, Testing

So far in this book we have already generated a lot of functionality, but we have yet to write a single test! This chapter aims to rectify this serious (some might even say horrific) problem and help get you in the mindset of writing good, solid, automated tests for your application.

The software industry has seen a lot of changes recently, one of these being a shift away from the traditional waterfall approach, in which design and analysis is done up front, to being agile and embracing change. You may have noticed that the Grails framework professes to be an *agile* web framework. What exactly does this mean?

Well, Grails in itself is not agile, as no tool on its own can be agile. However, it does fit very well within agile methodologies. *Agile methodologies* are techniques for developing software that promote a number of best practice principles.

Grails complements many of these practices including the following:

Be adaptive to change: Thanks to Grails' autoreloading mechanism and dynamic nature, it embraces change and iterative development.

Delivery of working software early: Grails' simplicity allows a Rapid Application Development (RAD) approach, increasing the chances of early delivery. In addition, Grails promotes unit testing by automating the creation of tests, heightening developer awareness of their importance.

Simplicity is essential: The Grails team aims to deliver absolute simplicity over anything else. Grails takes complex concepts like ORM and wraps them in a simple API.

Enthusiastic, self-organizing teams with the right environment: Since Grails allows developers to focus primarily on the business logic necessary to solve a particular issue, rather than the surrounding configurational issues, you're more likely to have happy, enthusiastic developers!

Many frameworks misuse the term "agile" to latch onto much of the hype. I don't believe that this is the case with Grails, given how well it blends into an agile approach. Nevertheless, it is important to note that the agile principles are just that, a set of principles and not necessarily the gospel.

In my experience, businesses that have benefited most from agile methodologies are those that have chosen the aspects of these methodologies that best suit their business and needs. Pair programming, a concept from the eXtreme Programming (XP) methodology, is not necessarily for everyone.

This is not a book about agile methodologies, however, and in this chapter we'll mainly focus on one important aspect of agile methodologies: the way we write automated tests. In agile methodologies, this is normally done using *test-driven development* (TDD) or *test-first development* (TFD).

Although Grails creates tests for you while you are creating artifacts like controllers and domain classes, this is really not the essence of TDD. Essentially, with TDD you write a test first, get it to fail, and only then write code.

In fact, in TDD writing tests is seen as a *design* activity and not necessarily a testing activity. By writing the tests first, you are essentially trying out the future API of your application and hence getting a feel for how it will end up working before you have actually implemented the code.

In this sense, what you are doing is making decisions about class names and method signatures that are actually more related to the design of an application.

Whether you practice TDD or not, it will still be of value to write tests for your application, and in fact many organizations, and even developers, would not think of writing code nowadays without associated unit tests.

Nevertheless, the practicalities of TDD are not really suited to a book of this nature, and hence in most cases I will be presenting the examples first following by how you would test said examples. In the next section, we explore how to create unit tests, which are one of the more common types of tests.

Writing Effective Unit Tests

As with other Grails artifacts, a target exists that will create a unit test case for you. The target in question, called `grails create-test-suite`, will prompt you for the name of the test and place it within the `grails-test` directory of a Grails application. Figure 6-1 shows the results of this target in action.

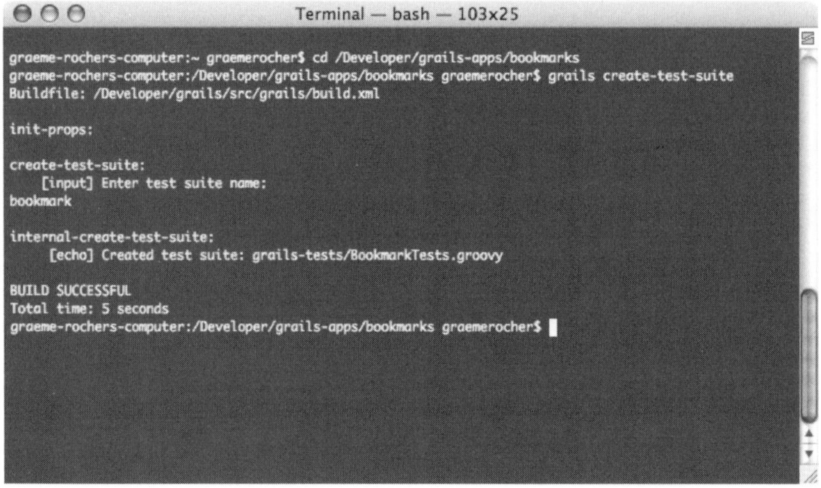

Figure 6-1. *Creating a test suite*

If we enter the name bookmark as shown in Figure 6-1, this creates a test suite called grails-tests/BookmarkTests.groovy. Initially, the result of this target will resemble something like the following:

```
class BookmarkTests extends GroovyTestCase {

    void testSomething() {

    }
}
```

Essentially, what we have here is a class (BookmarkTests) that extends a Groovy class called GroovyTestCase. A GroovyTestCase in turn extends the regular JUnit class known as TestCase, hence all the methods available within a regular JUnit test are available to you in a GroovyTestCase.

If you are unaware of what JUnit is, it is basically the de facto standard for unit testing within the Java world today. With regular JUnit, you extend a class called TestCase, and it provides a number of methods for performing various assertions. Interestingly, it uses a convention-based approach to figure out which methods are test methods. If a method starts with "test", it is considered to be a test method and will be executed as such.[1]

So far so good, but it just wouldn't be Groovy if there wasn't another twist to the tale! Recall from Chapter 2 that Groovy has a built-in assert keyword that performs assertions. Well, this can be used within Groovy test cases as a replacement for many of the JUnit methods.

Imagine for a second we had a method, or closure, that needed to retrieve all bookmark URLs sorted by a particular property. To implement this using Groovy, you could do something like the following:

```
def sortUrlsBy = {  property ->  Bookmark.findAll().sort { it."$property" }.url  }
```

To explain what the sortUrlsBy closure is doing, it essentially takes a property argument, finds a list of all Bookmark instances, and uses Groovy's sort method, which takes a closure. The closure passed to the sort method uses the property argument and a GString to reference the property name to sort by. Finally, once the list is sorted, it obtains all the url properties from each Bookmark in the list using GPath.

All in all, that's pretty concise and neat, but how do you know it actually works as expected? You could manually test the code by trying it out in the console, which you learned about in Chapter 3, as in Figure 6-2.

The unfortunate flaw with a manual strategy like the developer monitoring output from a console is that although the code may by chance work in isolation, how does it operate as part of a wider application? What about regression? How can you future-proof this code? The answer is to write automated tests that execute as part of a suite and preferably as part of a *continuous integration* platform like CruiseControl.

---

1. JUnit 4 has gone beyond this restriction, but Grails still uses JUnit 3.8.

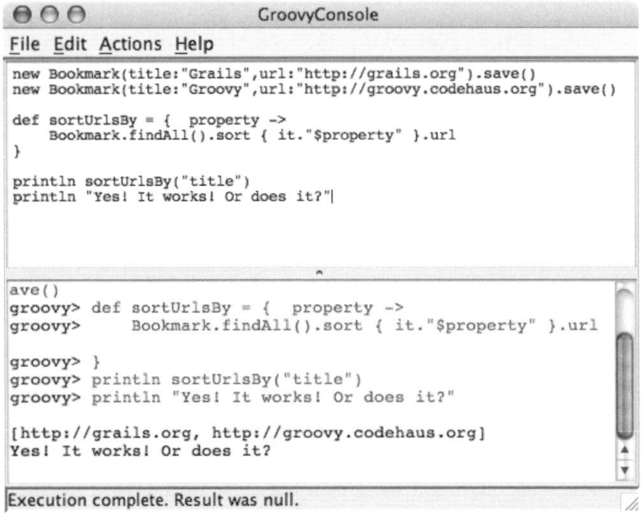

Figure 6-2. *Testing code out via the console*

■ **Note** CruiseControl is a continuous integration toolkit that allows you to set up a build server that monitors a version control repository for changes and initiates a new build every time there is a change. The build should also execute any unit tests and send notifications of failure to responsive developers. Grails' code base is monitored by a CruiseControl server hosted by Canoo (www.canoo.com). For more information, see http://grails.org/Continuous+Integration.

Having this kind of automated unit and integration testing is where unit tests truly come into play, and in the next section you find out about the Groovy solution to unit testing.

Using the assert Keyword

The assert keyword is not specifically targeted at unit testing and in fact can be used anywhere in a Groovy application to ensure application integrity. Nevertheless, it is commonplace to find assert spread all over Groovy unit tests.

You've already been introduced to what a GroovyTestCase looks like, but you need to know some important things about it. First, it is not required that you extend GroovyTestCase to write unit tests, but what it does give you is the ability to execute GroovyTestCase instances via the command line as Groovy scripts.

It also adds a number of new methods, which we'll explore shortly. First, however, take a look at Listing 6-1, which shows how assert can be used in a number of circumstances within a GroovyTestCase.

Listing 6-1. *Using the assert Keyword in Unit Testing*

```
1 class BookmarkTests extends GroovyTestCase {
2
3      void testSortBookmarks() {
4
5          Bookmark.list()*.delete()
6
7          new Bookmark(title:"Skills Matter",url:"http://skillsmatter.com").save()
8          new Bookmark(title:"Canoo",url:"http://canoo.com").save()
9          new Bookmark(title:"Grails",url:"http://grails.org").save()
10         new Bookmark(title:"Groovy",url:"http://groovy.codehaus.org").save()
11
12         def sortUrlsBy = {  property ->
13             Bookmark.findAll().sort { it."$property" }.url
14         }
15         def urls = sortUrlsBy("title")
16         assert urls
17         assert urls.size() == 4
18         assert urls[0].toString() == "http://www.canoo.com"
19         assert urls[1].toString() == "http://grails.org"
20     }
21 }
```

In Listing 6-1, we use the assert keyword several times on lines 16 to 19 to assert different conditions of the resulting list of URL objects. For simplicity's sake, we've defined the sortUrlsBy closure within the test itself, but in a real situation you would be testing a public API.

Note that although asserting comparisons between values as in lines 17 through 19 is a valid approach to using the assert keyword, it does have a major downside. Essentially, if the result of one of the assertions is a comparison failure, you won't be able to see the two values that cause the failure. In this circumstance, it is recommended that you use the standard JUnit assertEquals method instead, which takes two arguments for the left and right side of the comparison.

■**Tip** An interesting aspect of the code in Listing 6-1 is the usage of the * (spread) operator on line 5. Here the code Bookmark.list()*.delete() takes the list returned by the list method and, using the spread operator, invokes the delete method on each object within the list. Sure we could have used a query, but it seemed appropriate to introduce another one of Groovy's interesting features!

To execute the test, and indeed the other tests in your project, execute the grails test-app target. The test-app target will bootstrap the Grails environment and execute the tests within the project. A test report will be printed to the terminal windows upon completion of the tests. An example of an execution that successfully passed all tests can be seen in Figure 6-3.

```
test-app:
    [mkdir] Created dir: /Developer/grails-apps/bookmarks/tmp/war/WEB-INF/grails-app/tests
    [copy] Copying 3 files to /Developer/grails-apps/bookmarks/tmp/war/WEB-INF/grails-app/tests
    [echo] Running tests for environment: development
    [java] log4j:WARN No appenders could be found for logger (org.springframework.core.CollectionFactory).
    [java] log4j:WARN Please initialize the log4j system properly.
    [java] ....
    [java] Time: 0.403

    [java] OK (4 tests)

    [delete] Deleting directory /Developer/grails-apps/bookmarks/tmp/war/WEB-INF/grails-app/tests

BUILD SUCCESSFUL
Total time: 16 seconds
graeme-rochers-computer:/Developer/grails-apps/bookmarks graemerocher$ ▌
```

Figure 6-3. *A successful test execution*

On the other hand, when a test fails, Grails will print an error report to the console including such useful information like the following:

- The test where the failure occurred

- The line number of the failure

- The assertion that caused the failure

Figure 6-4 presents an example of a failure message containing this information.

```
    [java] Time: 0.405
    [java] There was 1 error:
    [java] 1) testSortBookmarks(BookmarkTests)java.lang.AssertionError: Expression: (urls[1].toString() ==
http://grails.org&)
    [java]     at org.codehaus.groovy.runtime.InvokerHelper.assertFailed(InvokerHelper.java:506)
    [java]     at org.codehaus.groovy.runtime.ScriptBytecodeAdapter.assertFailed(ScriptBytecodeAdapter.java
:553)
    [java]     at BookmarkTests.testSortBookmarks(BookmarkTests:22)
    [java]     at sun.reflect.NativeMethodAccessorImpl.invoke0(Native Method)
    [java]     at sun.reflect.NativeMethodAccessorImpl.invoke(NativeMethodAccessorImpl.java:39)
    [java]     at sun.reflect.DelegatingMethodAccessorImpl.invoke(DelegatingMethodAccessorImpl.java:25)
    [java]     at org.codehaus.groovy.grails.support.GrailsTestSuite.runTest(GrailsTestSuite.java:47)
    [java]     at grails.util.RunTests.main(RunTests.java:67)

    [java] FAILURES!!!
    [java] Tests run: 4,  Failures: 0,  Errors: 1
```

Figure 6-4. *A failing test case*

Now that you have an idea of how to execute tests and identify failures, in the next section we start to explore a better way to initialize test data.

Using Test Data

The previous example in Listing 6-1 demonstrated how to create test data using the Bookmark class's constructor combined with the save method. Still, even with this being quite concise, it will become a little tedious to have to re-create these instances for every test.

Never fear—like regular JUnit tests cases, Groovy test cases support the setUp and tearDown methods for doing initialization and post processing. Listing 6-1 could be amended with a setUp method as in the example in Listing 6-2.

Listing 6-2. *Using setUp to Initialize Data*

```
class BookmarkTests {

    void setUp() {
        new Bookmark(title:"SkillsMatter",url:"http://www.skillsmatter.com").save()
        new Bookmark(title:"Canoo",url:"http://www.canoo.com").save()
        new Bookmark(title:"Grails",url:"http://grails.org").save()
        new Bookmark(title:"Groovy",url:"http://groovy.codehaus.org").save()
    }
    ...
    void tearDown() {
            Bookmark.list()*.delete()
    }
}
```

Listing 6-2 shows how some test data is created inside the setUp method and then cleared in the tearDown method. Remember that, by default, Grails uses an in-memory database when executing tests, so every test starts with a clean slate.

With our data initialization in the right place, in the next section we'll be looking at what other features GroovyTestCase offers over a regular JUnit test.

Exploring GroovyTestCase

As well as providing the ability to execute a test as a script, GroovyTestCase also adds a number of new methods and features not found in the regular JUnit TestCase class. The additional methods complement Groovy's advanced syntax features and make testing more enjoyable. Table 6-1 lists the new methods available and what purpose they serve.

Table 6-1. *Additional Assertions in GroovyTestCase*

Method Name	Description
assertArrayEquals(Object[] expected, Object[] value)	Compares contents of each array
assertContains(char expected, char[] array)	Asserts that a given char array contains the specified char
assertContains(int expected, int[] array)	Asserts that a given int array contains the specified int
assertInspect(Object value, String expected)	Invokes inspect() on the object and compares with the expected value
assertLength(int length, char[] array)	Asserts length of a char array
assertLength(int length, int[] array)	Asserts length of int array
assertLength(int length, Object[] array)	Asserts length of an Object array
assertScript(String script)	Tries to run the proved script

Table 6-1. *Additional Assertions in GroovyTestCase (Continued)*

Method Name	Description
`assertToString(Object value, String expected)`	Calls `toString()` on the object and compares it with the expected value
`shouldFail( Closure code )`	Invokes the passed closure and asserts that it fails
`shouldFail( Class exception, Closure code )`	Invokes the passed closure and asserts that it throws the specified exception

The `assertScript` and `shouldFail` methods in particular play to Groovy's strengths by providing the ability to execute in-line scripts and wrap an entire block of code, a closure, in a failure assertion, respectively. A rather contrived example of `shouldFail` is presented in Listing 6-3.

Listing 6-3. *Using shouldFail*

```
void testBadUrl() {
    def badUrl = "aninvalidurl"
    def b = new Bookmark()
    shouldFail(MalformedURLException) {
        b.url = new URL(badUrl)
    }
}
```

In the example in Listing 6-3, we expect a `MailformedURLException` to be thrown given an attempt to assign an invalid URL to a `Bookmark` instance. If it is not thrown, the test should fail.

With this knowledge of `GroovyTestCase` fresh in your mind, let's tackle an example by writing some tests to test the logic in the controller that was generated in Chapter 5 on scaffolding.

Testing in Practice

In the previous chapter, we generated a `BookmarkController` that contained some basic CRUD operations. The actions themselves have names such as `save`, `delete`, `update`, `list`, and so on to represent the different CRUD operations.

The first thing we're going to do is test the `list` action to ensure that it correctly returns a list of `Bookmark` instances and that pagination works as expected. Just to recap what the `list` action looks like, Listing 6-4 shows what it does.

Listing 6-4. *The list Action*

```
def list = {
    [ bookmarkList: Bookmark.list( params ) ]
}
```

As you can see, the `list` action is one of the simpler actions. Nevertheless, that doesn't mean it shouldn't be tested! So what should be tested then? Everything that has either your own logic or is based on your assumptions should have some form of test. Here the code has no real application logic, and we don't really want to test foreign logic, but we do want to put our assumptions about the behavior of GORM to the test.

So to start off, let's write a simple test in the BookmarkTests class that simply tests the results returned from the list action.

We already have some data to work with as part of the setUp method covered in the section "Using Test Data." The only modification we need to make is to BookmarkController itself, as we need a way to customize the params object in the BookmarkController.

To do this, we need to create a params property within the BookmarkController that can be used by the test case. Later we'll also want to test the flash object so we can add a property for that, too. Listing 6-5 shows this small modification in place.

Listing 6-5. *Additions to the BookmarkController*

```
class BookmarkController {
    def params = [:]
    def flash = [:]
    ...
}
```

The need to manually add these properties may well have been resolved by the time of this writing. Nevertheless, it has no impact on the controller itself and merely helps us test the class. Listing 6-6 shows a simple test that asserts the results are of the correct quantity and contain the right data.

Listing 6-6. *Testing the list Action*

```
1 void testListAction() {
2     def bc = new BookmarkController()
3     def bookmarks = bc.list()?.bookmarkList
4     assert bookmarks != null
5     assertLength(4, bookmarks as Object[])
6     assert bookmarks[0].url?.toString() == "http://www.skillsmatter.com"
7     assert bookmarks[1].url?.toString() == "http://www.canoo.com"
8 }
```

The testListAction test case in Listing 6-6 creates a new BookmarkController instance and then calls the list action. The Bookmark list is retrieved from the model and an assertion executed ensuring it is not null:

```
3     def bookmarks = bc.list()?.bookmarkList
4     assert bookmarks != null
```

Given that we created and saved four instances in Listing 6-2, the next thing the test checks is that the list action retrieves the same number of bookmarks:

```
5     assertLength(4, bookmarks as Object[])
```

Note that in the preceding example you could have used assertEquals to check the size() of the bookmarks list. However, I used this example to illustrate Groovy's as keyword (in bold in the preceding line of code). This is necessary because the assertLength method accepts an Object[], not a java.util.List. Since Groovy uses dynamic method dispatching, using the as keyword is a way of casting to the correct type and hence ensures the correct method is called, particularly in cases where you need to call overloaded methods.

Finally, each Bookmark is checked on lines 6 and 10 to ensure that the URLs contain the same data as that which was created in the setUp method in Listing 6-2. To execute the tests, you can again run the grails test-app target, and the result will resemble something like the following:

```
Running tests for environment: development
  .....
  Time: 0.468

  OK (5 tests)
```

Success! Now let's add another test case that tests pagination of results using the max and offset parameters, which you'll learn more about in Chapter 8. Listing 6-7 demonstrates modifying the params object that the BookmarkController uses, thus customizing the results that are returned.

Listing 6-7. *Testing Pagination Controls*

```
void testListActionPaginate() {
        def bc = new BookmarkController()
        bc.params.offset = 2
        bc.params.max = 2

        def bookmarks = bc.list()?.bookmarkList
        assert bookmarks != null
        assertLength(2, bookmarks as Object[])
        assert bookmarks[0].url?.toString() == "http://grails.org"
        assert bookmarks[1].url?.toString() == "http://groovy.codehaus.org"
}
```

By manipulating the offset and max parameters, we are able to change the number and starting position (offset) of the results. In the example in Listing 6-7, we set the offset to 2, and thus the first element returned is the third object that was saved when creating the test data. The assertions that follow reflect our expectations of what the results should be.

OK, so far, so good. We have in place some handy tests that could potentially be included in a continuous integration build. We shouldn't stop here, however, and what would be really great is if we could test some of the more complex flows within the BookmarkController.

For example, the update action is one of the more complicated actions, and because much of the expected result within the body of the action is captured by the flow, it is not good enough to simply test what the resulting model is.

So how can we test logical flow? Well this is where *mocks* and *stubs* come in, and more specifically the Groovy Mock library. In the next section, we explore how to use mocks and stubs and how they differ in usage.

Using Mocks and Stubs

A *stub* is an object that mimics the behavior of a real object. Stubs are often used in unit tests as drop-in replacements when a framework object such as a database connection or `HttpServletRequest` instance is needed by the code. The stub will emulate the behavior of the framework object in order to add predictability to a unit test that would otherwise be dependent on the surrounding environment.

Stubs have what are known as *loose* expectations. In other words, stubs merely serve as a replacement for a collaborating object and don't really care whether they're called or not. A *mock*, on the other hand, has *strong* expectations and will fail a test if a *demanded* method is not called.

In this sense, mocks are useful for testing application flow and ensuring certain methods are called in certain scenarios. Some would argue that you should only be testing the result of a method. However, in certain situations, the result of a method or closure is encapsulated in the flow of its body.

For example, a controller action may decide at some point that it needs to redirect processing to another controller or action. Although the action has not really "returned" anything, it has produced a result by performing the redirect.

Easy-to-use frameworks such as jMock and EasyMock have popularized mocks and stubs, and in fact both are usable from Groovy test cases if you so choose. However, Groovy Mock presents a groovier alternative. It is based on the same concepts and ideas as EasyMock, but it takes advantages of Groovy's strengths like closures and method interception through `MetaClass`.

Mocks in Action

As mentioned in the previous section, the `update` action of the `BookmarkController` represents one of the more complex to test as it contains flow logic. Just to recap, Listing 6-8 shows the `update` action in its current form.

Listing 6-8. *The update Action*

```
def update = {
        def bookmark = Bookmark.get( params.id )
        if(bookmark) {
            bookmark.properties = params
            if(bookmark.save()) {
                redirect(action:show,id:bookmark.id)
            }
            else {
                render(view:'edit',model:[bookmark:bookmark])
            }
        }
        else {
            flash.message = "Bookmark not found with id ${params.id}"
            redirect(action:edit,id:params.id)
        }
    }
```

As Listing 6-8 demonstrates, there are a few logical flows that need to be tested in some way. To surmise, the following conditions could be reached during the flow of the update action:

- No Bookmark is found for the identifier and control is redirected to the edit action.

- A Bookmark is found and successfully updated, and flow is redirected to the show action.

- A Bookmark is found, but validation fails, and the create view is displayed again using the render method.

To test that these conditions all exhibit the correct behavior and redirect control appropriately, we're going to use a mock. However, to make it a little more exciting, we're going to explore a Groovy feature called *closure currying* along the way!

The first case to be tested is the simplest. What we want to do is make sure that flow is redirected to the edit action when a Bookmark instance is not found. Before we can start, we need to add an import statement to the top of the BookmarkTests class so that we can use the Groovy Mock library:

```
import groovy.mock.interceptor.*
```

This will allow us to use Groovy Mock's MockFor class to create dynamic mock objects. Unlike Java libraries such as EasyMock, no Java proxies are created. The magic happens through Groovy's dynamic runtime method dispatch and MetaClass facilities.

Listing 6-9 shows how to use Groovy Mock to test the first condition just discussed.

Listing 6-9. *Groovy Mock in Action*

```
1 void testUpdateNotFound() {
2       def bc
3       def mock = new MockFor(BookmarkController)
4       mock.demand.redirect { Map params ->
5           assert params.action == bc.edit
6       }
7       mock.use {
8               bc  = new BookmarkController()
9               bc.params.id = 5
10               bc.update.call()
11       }
12 }
```

So let's explore exactly what is happening here. On line 3, we create a new mock object that *mocks* the BookmarkController class:

```
3       def mock = new MockFor(BookmarkController)
```

We're using a mock here because to test application flow we need to use *strong* expectations. If you have a particular requirement for loose expectations, the StubFor class can be used as an alternative with the same API.

As discussed at the start of this section, mocks have *demands*, and on lines 4 through 6 we define a demand that *expects* the redirect method to be called. Since we have the power of closures at our fingertips, we can also assert that the action passed to the method is the edit action:

```
4        mock.demand.redirect { Map params ->
5            assert params.action == bc.edit
6        }
```

We then *use* the mock by utilizing a database identifier that we know doesn't exist (since we only created four test Bookmark objects) and calling the update closure.

```
7        mock.use {
8              bc  = new BookmarkController()
9              bc.params.id = 5
10              bc.update.call()
11       }
```

An interesting aspect about the preceding code, which is worth a little elaboration, is how we invoke the update closure using the call method on line 10. Remember that the mock created on line 3 mocks the behavior of the BookmarkController class and that the first *expected* method call is to the redirect method.

So if we called update directly as a method, it would fail the test, since calling update doesn't match the aforementioned expectation. To explain this in mock terminology, there is always a *caller* and a *collaborator*. The caller is the object calling the API being mocked, while the collaborator is the object doing the mocking.

Since the caller and the collaborator cannot be the same object, and in Listing 6-9 the collaborator is the BookmarkController, we cannot simply invoke the BookmarkController directly. By obtaining a reference to the update action on line 10 and then invoking call, the update closure becomes the *caller*.

What will then happen is within the body of the update action in Listing 6-8: the Bookmark instance will not be found, and the mocked redirect method in Listing 6-9 will be called. The mocked redirect method will validate that the action being redirected to is the edit action as expected; if not, the test will fail.

So that covers the simple test, but we also need to test the case where an update is successful and when validation fails. Since the code within the use closure on lines 7 to 10 is going to be very similar for all three cases, it makes sense to be able to reuse this somehow. In the next section, we explore how to use closure currying to reuse snippets of test code.

Defining Test Data with Closure Currying

The name may seem odd, but *currying* refers to applying arguments to a closure or method that then returns a new closure that takes the remaining arguments and returns the result. The name comes from the mathematician Haskell Curry, who developed the concept of partial functions.

Nevertheless, we're going to see curried closures applied within our test code to maximize code reuse and increase the robustness of our tests (as they will always be testing the same sequence of calls).

The first thing to do then is to assign the closure, previously on lines 7 through 10 of Listing 6-9, to a variable that can be reused within each test case. Since we may also need to check the state of the BookmarkController instance at any point, the BookmarkController instance needs to be a local field referenced by the closure. Listing 6-10 shows the test code in place.

Listing 6-10. *Using Closures for Test Code*

```
BookmarkController bc
final Closure UPDATE_TEST_CODE = {  id ->
    bc  = new BookmarkController()
    bc.params.id = id
    bc.update.call()
}
```

With the code refactored into a local variable called UPDATE_TEST_CODE, we can now update the testUpdateNotFound test case from Listing 6-9. The example in Listing 6-11 is our first exposure to closure currying.

Listing 6-11. *Reusing Test Code with Currying*

```
void testUpdateNotFound() {
    def mock = new MockFor(BookmarkController)
    mock.demand.redirect { Map params ->
        assert params.action == bc.edit
    }
    mock.use(UPDATE_TEST_CODE.curry(5))
}
```

The crucial bit of magic happens in the code highlighted in bold. The code uses a method called curry that accepts one or many arguments and returns a new closure. The effect of the expression in this case is a new closure that accepts no arguments. In addition to this change, in every place where the id argument was previously referenced in Listing 6-10, the new closure resolves the number 5 (the argument to the curry method).

Now let's see how we can harness this code reuse feature in a few additional tests, the first one being testUpdateSuccess in Listing 6-12.

Listing 6-12. *The testUpdateSuccess Test Case*

```
1 void testUpdateSuccess() {
2     def ctrlMock = new MockFor(BookmarkController)
3     def bookmarkStub = new StubFor(Bookmark)
4     def grailsBookmark= Bookmark.findByTitle('Grails')
5
6      bookmarkStub.demand.get {  grailsBookmark  }
7      ctrlMock.demand.redirect { Map params ->
8          assert params.action == bc.show
9          assert params.id == grailsBookmark?.id
10     }
11     ctrlMock.use {
12         bookmarkStub.use(UPDATE_TEST_CODE.curry(grailsBookmark?.id))
13     }
14 }
```

In this example we use a mock and a stub to mock the BookmarkController and Bookmark classes, respectively:

```
2       def ctrlMock = new MockFor(BookmarkController)
3       def bookmarkStub = new StubFor(Bookmark)
```

When the `Bookmark` class's static `get` method is called, the mocked version returns the `grailsBookmark` object, that was previously looked up on line 4, inside a closure on line 6:

```
6       bookmarkStub.demand.get { grailsBookmark  }
```

When the `redirect` method is called, instead of redirecting we simply assert that the arguments passed are redirecting to the right place. Remember that after an update occurs, the controller should redirect to the `show` action. The following assertions make sure this happens as expected:

```
7       ctrlMock.demand.redirect { Map params ->
8           assert params.action == bc.show
9          assert params.id == grailsBookmark?.id
10      }
```

In addition to asserting that the `show` action is executed next, the preceding code also checks that the `id` parameter is the same as the identifier of the `Bookmark` instance that was updated. Finally, since we're using two mocks here, we nest them within each other so they are both "used":

```
12      ctrlMock.use {
13          bookmarkStub.use(UPDATE_TEST_CODE.curry(grailsBookmark?.id))
14      }
```

The second mock gets passed the curried closure again, this time using the identifier of the previously looked-up `Bookmark` instance. To test the failure case is roughly similar, except instead of expecting the `redirect` method, we expect the `render` method. Listing 6-13 shows what the `testUpdateFailure` test case looks like in practice.

Listing 6-13. *The testUpdateFailure Test Case*

```
1 void testUpdateFailure() {
2       def ctrlMock = new MockFor(BookmarkController)
3       def bookmarkStub = new MockFor(Bookmark)
4         def grailsBookmark = Bookmark.findByTitle('Grails')
5         bookmarkStub.demand.get {
6             grailsBookmark.title = null
7             return grailsBookmark
8         }
9         mock1.demand.render { Map params ->
10            assert params.view == 'edit'
11            assert params.model?.bookmark == grailsBookmark
12        }
13        ctrlMock.use {
14            bookmarkStub.use(UPDATE_TEST_CODE.curry(grailsBookmark.id))
15        }
16 }
```

The differences between this test case and the testUpdateSuccess case in Listing 6-12 are shown in bold. Inside the mocked get method on line 6, we set the Bookmark instance's title property to null, thus causing validation failure. Then on lines 9 through 12, we set an expectation that the render method will be called with the correct parameters.

All and all we've achieved a lot in the last few sections, and you've learned how to use stubs and mocks to verify application flow and behavior in situations where merely testing the result of a method is not sufficient. The full listing of our endeavors can be seen here:

```groovy
import groovy.mock.interceptor.*
class BookmarkTests extends GroovyTestCase {

  BookmarkController bc
  final Closure UPDATE_TEST_CODE = {  id ->
    bc  = new BookmarkController()
    bc.params.id = id
    bc.update.call()
  }

  void setUp() {
    new Bookmark(title:"SkillsMatter",
                            url:"http://www.skillsmatter.com").save()
    new Bookmark(title:"Canoo",
                            url:"http://www.canoo.com").save()
    new Bookmark(title:"Grails",
                            url:"http://grails.org").save()
    new Bookmark(title:"Groovy",
                            url:"http://groovy.codehaus.org").save()
  }

  void testBadUrl() {
      def badUrl = "aninvalidurl"
      def b = new Bookmark()
      shouldFail(MalformedURLException) {
         b.url = new URL(badUrl)
      }
  }

  void testListAction() {
    def bc = new BookmarkController()
    def bookmarks = bc.list()?.bookmarkList
    assert bookmarks != null
    assertLength(4, bookmarks as Object[])
    assert bookmarks[0].url?.toString() == "http://www.skillsmatter.com"
    assert bookmarks[1].url?.toString() == "http://www.canoo.com"
  }
```

```
void testListActionPaginate() {
  def bc = new BookmarkController()
  bc.params.offset = 2
  bc.params.max = 2
  def bookmarks = bc.list()?.bookmarkList

  assert bookmarks != null
  assertLength(2, bookmarks as Object[])
  assert bookmarks[0].url?.toString() == "http://grails.org"
  assert bookmarks[1].url?.toString() == "http://groovy.codehaus.org"
}

 void testUpdateNotFound() {
   def mock = new MockFor(BookmarkController)
   mock.demand.redirect { Map params ->
        assert params.action == bc.edit
   }
   mock.use(UPDATE_TEST_CODE.curry(5))
 }

 void testUpdateSuccess() {
    def ctrlMock = new MockFor(BookmarkController)
    def bookmarkStub = new StubFor(Bookmark)
    def grailsBookmark= Bookmark.findByTitle('Grails')

    bookmarkStub.demand.get {   grailsBookmark  }
    ctrlMock.demand.redirect { Map params ->
        assert params.action == bc.show
        assert params.id == grailsBookmark?.id
    }
    ctrlMock.use {
         bookmarkStub.use(UPDATE_TEST_CODE.curry(grailsBookmark?.id))
    }
  }

  void testUpdateFailure() {
     def ctrlMock = new MockFor(BookmarkController)
     def bookmarkStub = new MockFor(Bookmark)
       def grailsBookmark = Bookmark.findByTitle('Grails')
       bookmarkStub.demand.get {
           grailsBookmark.title = null
           return grailsBookmark
       }
       mock1.demand.render { Map params ->
            assert params.view == 'edit'
            assert params.model?.bookmark == grailsBookmark
       }
```

```
            ctrlMock.use {
                bookmarkStub.use(UPDATE_TEST_CODE.curry(grailsBookmark.id))
            }
        }
    }

    void tearDown() {
        Bookmark.list()*.delete()
    }
}
```

Unit testing is, however, only a part of the testing story. Using mocks in this way is no substitute for testing the code in its native environment with all the unpredictability that it offers. With this mind, *functional testing* can help automate some of the integration tests that need to be carried out on software.

In the next section, we will look at what Grails has to offer in terms of functional testing and try to apply the concepts presented to the bookmarks application.

Functional Testing with WebTest

Unit tests are designed, and named as such, to test small units of functionality. They don't, however, replace manual testing of an application when running in its deployed environment. In fact, *nothing* replaces manual testing of some form, but automated functional tests can help reduce the scope that manual tests have to cover.

The amount of repetitive manual testing done allows quality assurance (QA) engineers to focus on corner cases and more obscure problems that are often the more serious issues.

Grails' functional testing capability is provided courtesy of Canoo WebTest (http:// webtest.canoo.com). WebTest allows you to programmatically call web pages and verify the results. It goes even further than that by allowing interaction with web pages like clicking links and submitting forms, all in an automated manner.

These functional tests can then be included as part of the build, with detailed reports of what went wrong and when produced by the WebTest reporting engine. To try this functionality out, we're going to automate the testing of the CRUD interface that was generated in Chapter 5.

Installing WebTest

First off, you need to create the WebTest project layout in the bookmarks project by executing the grails create-webtest target. This target will first go off and download the latest packaged version of WebTest from the Canoo web site. This can take a while as the release ZIP file is quite large, but you'll see a progress indicator that lets you know how much longer the download should take.

In addition, the target will create a new directory called webtest that contains the WebTest configuration, reports, and test cases. Figure 6-5 shows what the directory structure should look like.

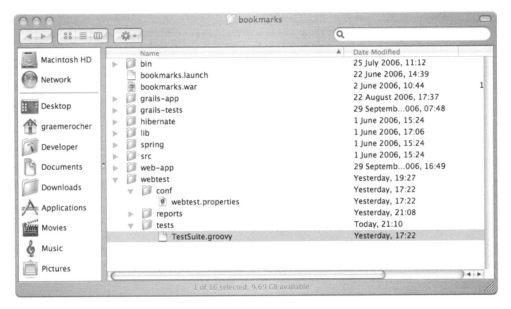

Figure 6-5. *The WebTest directory structure*

Figure 6-5 should make things a little clearer. The conf directory contains the webtest.
properties file used to configure various aspects of WebTest's behavior. Table 6-2 lists the
properties with their initial values and descriptions.

Table 6-2. *WebTest's webtest.properties File*

Name	Initial Value	Description
webtest_host	localhost	The name of the host server to start up on
webtest_port	8080	The port number to start the test server on
webtest_protocol	http	The protocol to use when communicating with server
webtest_summary	true	Whether to print a summary report
webtest_response	true	Whether to save responses for viewing from the report
webtest_resultpath	webtest/reports	The location to save reports to
webtest_resultfile	WebTestResult.xml	The name of the report results file
webtest_haltonerror	false	Whether to stop execution if an error occurs
webtest_errorproperty	webTestError	The name of the Ant property to set if an error occurred
webtest_haltonfailure	false	Whether to stop execution if a failure occurs

Table 6-2. *WebTest's webtest.properties File (Continued)*

Name	Initial Value	Description
webtest_failureproperty	webTestFailure	The name of the Ant property to set if a failure occurs
webtest_showhtmlparseroutput	true	Whether to show parsing warnings and errors in the terminal window

The various configuration options can in most cases be left as is, unless you have to customize the port settings for your environment. Nevertheless, they are there to play with should you so choose.

The other artifact generated was the TestSuite.groovy file, which merely loads all classes that end with WebTest. The code for this class looks something like the following:

```
import grails.util.WebTest

class TestSuite extends WebTest {

    static void main(args) {
        new TestSuite().runTests()
    }

    /**
        Scan through all test files and call their suite method.
    */
    void suite() {
        def scanner = ant.fileScanner {
            fileset(dir:'webtest/tests', includes:'**/*WebTest.groovy')
        }
    }
}
```

The suite method uses an Ant file scanner to load all of the tests into the suite for execution. You can also load web tests into the suite manually by constructing them and calling each one's suite method. Listing 6-14 shows this in action.

Listing 6-14. *Loading Web Tests Manually*

```
new DeleteBookmarkTest(ant:ant, configMap:configMap).suite()
new UpdateBookmarkTest(ant:ant, configMap:configMap).suite()
```

This technique allows you to define the order of execution of web tests as, unlike unit tests, functional web tests are executed sequentially and are dependent on order. Again, the TestSuite class is not something you necessarily need to play with, but it does grant you extra flexibility where required.

In the next section, we'll move on to actually writing a functional web test. However, as with many things, Grails is there to give us a helping hand by generating much of the code for you.

Generating a Web Test

That's right, Grails provides a target to generate much of the boilerplate code necessary to perform basic testing of a CRUD application. To execute the target, type `grails generate-webtest` into the terminal window and hit the Return key.

Grails will create a new class within the `webtest/tests` directory called `BookmarkWebTest` as presented in Figure 6-6.

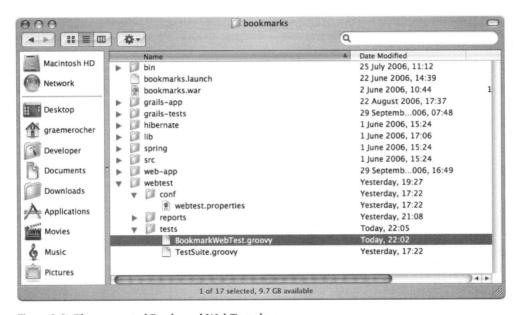

Figure 6-6. *The generated BookmarkWebTest class*

The generated web test itself contains the necessary steps in code to verify all the CRUD operations are working as expected. Listing 6-15 shows what the `BookmarkWebTest` currently does.

Listing 6-15. *The Generated BookmarkWebTest*

```
1 class BookmarkWebTest extends grails.util.WebTest {
2   void suite() {
3       testBookmarkListNewDelete()
4       // add tests for more operations here
5   }
6
7   def testBookmarkListNewDelete() {
8       webtest('Bookmark basic operations') {
9
10              invoke(url:'bookmark')
```

```
11                    verifyText(text:'Home')
12
13                    verifyListPage(0)
14
15                    clickLink(label:'New Bookmark')
16                    verifyText(text:'Create Bookmark')
17                    clickButton(label:'Create')
18                    verifyText(text:'Show Bookmark', description:'Detail page')
19                    clickLink(label:'List', description:'Back to list view')
20
21                    verifyListPage(1)
22
23                    group(description:'edit the one element') {
24                        clickLink(label:'Show', description:'go to detail view')
25                        clickButton(label:'Edit')
26                        verifyText(text:'Edit Bookmark')
27                        clickButton(label:'Update')
28                        verifyText(text:'Show Bookmark')
29                        clickLink(label:'List', description:'Back to list view')
30                    }
31
32                    verifyListPage(1)
33
34                    group(description:'delete the only element') {
35                        clickLink(label:'Show', description:'go to detail view')
36                        clickButton(label:'Delete')
37                        verifyXPath(xpath:"//div[@class='message']",
38                                        text:/Bookmark.*deleted./, regex:true)
39                    }
40
41                    verifyListPage(0)
42
43        }
44    }
45
46    String ROW_COUNT_XPATH = "count(//td[@class='actionButtons']/..)"
47
48    def verifyListPage(int count) {
49        ant.group(description:"verify Bookmark list view with $count row(s)"){
50            verifyText(text:'Bookmark List')
51            verifyXPath(xpath:ROW_COUNT_XPATH,
52                            text:count,
53                            description:"$count row(s) of data expected")
54        }
55    }
56 }
```

That's a pretty long listing! The code is doing a lot of testing though, and in order for you to understand exactly what is going on, we'll be going through the code by breaking it down into the steps that it tests:

1. The first step is to load the BookmarkController's default page and verify that the bookmark list contains no elements using the verifyListPage method.

    ```
    10              invoke(url:'bookmark')
    11              verifyText(text:'Home')
    12
    13              verifyListPage(0)
    ```

2. Next navigate to the Create Bookmark page and verify that you get there by testing for the text "Create Bookmark".

    ```
    15              clickLink(label:'New Bookmark')
    16              verifyText(text:'Create Bookmark')
    ```

3. Now click the Create button and verify that the Bookmark was successfully created. To do this, we verify that the text "Show Bookmark" appears on the page as expected. Once complete, the code navigates back to the Bookmark List page and uses the verifyListPage method to assert that the list contains one Bookmark.

    ```
    17              clickButton(label:'Create')
    18              verifyText(text:'Show Bookmark', description:'Detail page')
    19              clickLink(label:'List', description:'Back to list view')
    20
    21              verifyListPage(1)
    ```

4. Once back at the Bookmark List page, the code then groups together a set of related tests that test whether editing a bookmark works as expected. The group clicks on the Show link for a bookmark, clicks the Edit button followed by the Update button, and then verifies that the Show Bookmark page is displayed again.

    ```
    23              group(description:'edit the one element') {
    24                  clickLink(label:'Show', description:'go to detail view')
    25                  clickButton(label:'Edit')
    26                  verifyText(text:'Edit Bookmark')
    27                  clickButton(label:'Update')
    28                  verifyText(text:'Show Bookmark')
    29                  clickLink(label:'List', description:'Back to list view')
    30              }
    ```

5. Finally, another related group of tests is executed that verifies that a bookmark can be deleted by navigating to the Show Bookmark page and clicking the Delete button. The veryListPage method is then called again with an argument of 0 to check that the bookmark list is now empty.

```
34                group(description:'delete the only element') {
35                    clickLink(label:'Show', description:'go to detail view')
36                    clickButton(label:'Delete')
37                    verifyXPath(xpath:"//div[@class='message']",
38                                    text:/Bookmark.*deleted./, regex:true)
39                }
40
41            verifyListPage(0)
```

So that's how the test works, but how do we go about executing it? In the next section, we look at how to run web tests.

Executing Web Tests

As with most everything else in Grails, to execute a web test is a simple matter of running the appropriate target. In this case, the target in question is `grails run-webtest`, which will load up a Grails server instance and then execute the web tests against it.

WebTest will log its activity to the terminal window during test execution and at the end output a report for viewing. Figure 6-7 shows the typical console output following a WebTest execution.

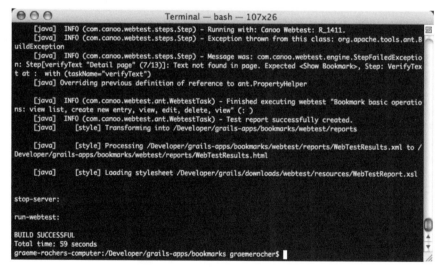

Figure 6-7. *WebTest terminal output*

Far more interesting than all of this console output is the report that WebTest spat out at the end of its execution. The report by default is located in the `webtest/reports` directory, which will also include all the captured responses. A typical `reports` directory following a WebTest execution cycle will look something like Figure 6-8.

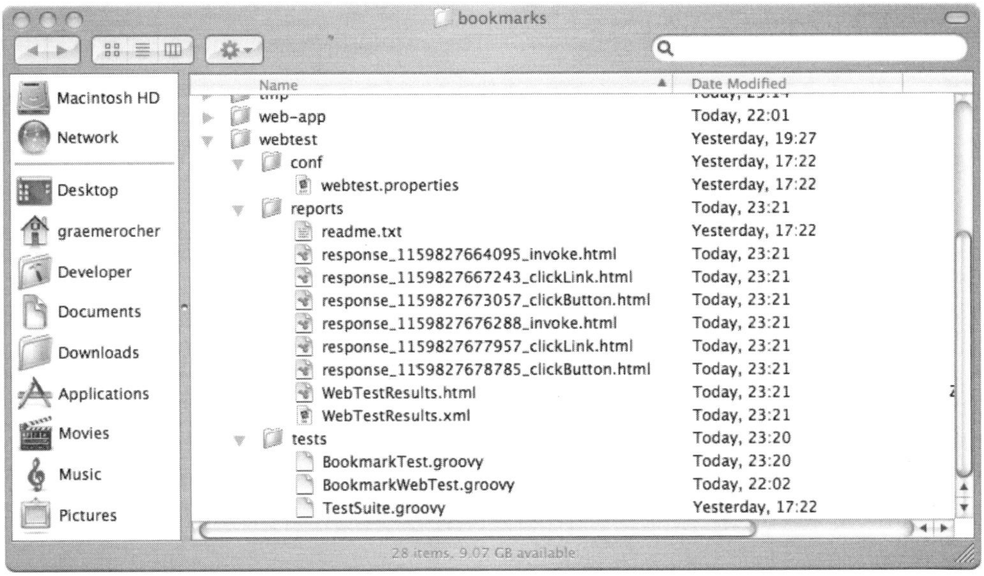
bookmarks
Macintosh HD
Network
Desktop
graemerocher
Developer
Documents
Downloads
Applications
Movies
Music
Pictures
Name
Date Modified
web-app Today, 22:01
webtest Yesterday, 19:27
conf Yesterday, 17:22
webtest.properties Yesterday, 17:22
reports Today, 23:21
readme.txt Yesterday, 17:22
response_1159827664095_invoke.html Today, 23:21
response_1159827667243_clickLink.html Today, 23:21
response_1159827673057_clickButton.html Today, 23:21
response_1159827676288_invoke.html Today, 23:21
response_1159827677957_clickLink.html Today, 23:21
response_1159827678785_clickButton.html Today, 23:21
WebTestResults.html Today, 23:21
WebTestResults.xml Today, 23:21
tests Today, 23:20
BookmarkTest.groovy Today, 23:20
BookmarkWebTest.groovy Today, 22:02
TestSuite.groovy Yesterday, 17:22
28 items, 9.07 GB available

Figure 6-8. *Generated WebTest reports*

The main report is the `WebTestResults.html` file, while each HTML page starting with "response_" represents a captured response. Interestingly enough, if you open up the `WebTestResult.html` file, you'll see there are currently test failures! Figure 6-9 shows a typical WebTest report containing failures.

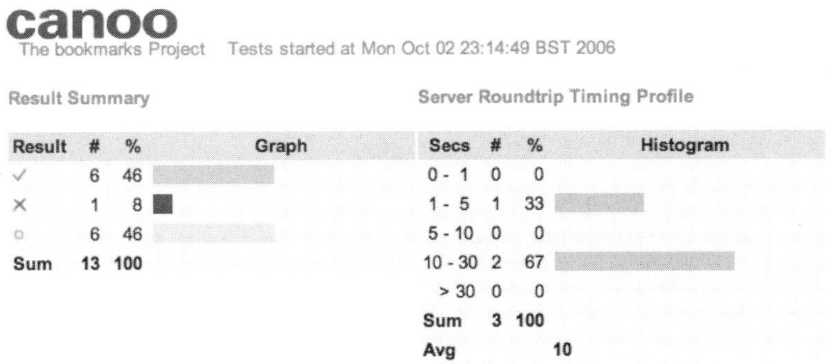
canoo
The bookmarks Project
Tests started at Mon Oct 02 23:14:49 BST 2006
Result Summary
Result # % Graph
✓ 6 46
× 1 8
○ 6 46
Sum 13 100
Server Roundtrip Timing Profile
Secs # % Histogram
0 - 1 0 0
1 - 5 1 33
5 - 10 0 0
10 - 30 2 67
> 30 0 0
Sum 3 100
Avg 10

Figure 6-9. *The WebTest results summary graphs*

As you probably already guessed, the topmost bar represents successfully completed web tests, while the second bar indicates those that failed miserably. The WebTest report gets even more detailed if you scroll down a bit, as it reveals the exact point of failure. Figure 6-10 shows a snippet of the report revealing the issue.

5	✓	**verifyText**	**text** Create Bookmark
6	✓	**clickButton** **label** Create	
		Resulting page	
7	✗ Error	**verifyText** Detail page	**text** Show Bookmark
8	▫	**clickLink** Back to list view	**label** List

Figure 6-10. *The WebTest failure report*

As you can probably gauge from this report, the test failed directly after the Create button was clicked. Clicking the Resulting page link often reveals some clues as to why the error occurred. Luckily, the failure in this case is pretty easy to resolve and requires you to obtain some knowledge about how to interact with forms, which you'll do in the next section.

Interacting with Forms

The failure in the previous section is down to WebTest submitting the form without actually populating it with any data! As we already know from the model we created in Chapter 4, Bookmark instances must have their title and url properties set to non-null values.

To resolve this issue, let's augment the existing test by adding the necessary form population code. Listing 6-16 shows how to set the value of input fields using WebTest before the Create button is clicked.

Listing 6-16. *Setting Input Fields*

```
...
17            setInputField(name:'url', 'http://grails.org')
18            setInputField(name:'title', 'Grails')
19            clickButton(label:'Create')
20            verifyText(text:'Show Bookmark', description:'Detail page')
...
```

Once these changes have been done, executing the grails run-webtest target will produce a report reflecting that the problem has been corrected as shown in Figure 6-11. This time we get only the topmost bar, exactly the desired result.

Note that this has only been a brief overview of the features that WebTest has on offer. There are many, many more that are beyond the scope of this book. As such, it's advisable to head over to the WebTest manual at http://webtest.canoo.com/webtest/manual/manualOverview.html. The manual has a more complete reference of all the possibilities as well as examples of usage in both XML and Groovy formats.

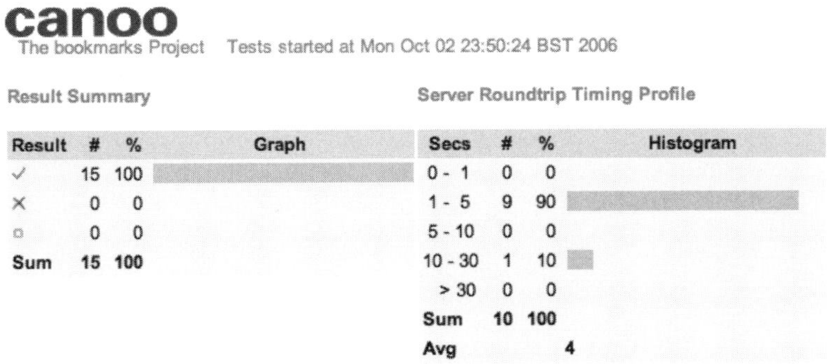

canoo
The bookmarks Project   Tests started at Mon Oct 02 23:50:24 BST 2006

Result Summary					Server Roundtrip Timing Profile			
Result	#	%	Graph		Secs	#	%	Histogram
✓	15	100			0 - 1	0	0	
✕	0	0			1 - 5	9	90	
▢	0	0			5 - 10	0	0	
Sum	15	100			10 - 30	1	10	
					> 30	0	0	
					Sum	10	100	
					Avg		4	

Figure 6-11. *WebTest successful report summary*

Summary

In this chapter, you experienced the usual lecture about how important testing is. More importantly, however, you learned how to apply unit testing on Grails artifacts like controllers. In addition, together we explored more-advanced testing techniques with mocks and even got to play around with an as yet unexplored Groovy feature in currying.

Finally, you learned about functional testing in contrast to unit testing and how to apply functional testing using Canoo WebTest and Grails. All in all, we covered a lot of ground in this section, but it does not mark the end of our testing endeavors. Throughout the following chapters, we'll be using testing to assert behavior and verify that the bookmark application that we've only really started to build is working as expected.

The next stop is Chapter 7, which will extend your currently limited insight into controllers by providing more detail on their usage patterns.

CHAPTER 7

■■■

Grails Controllers

Having already been exposed to controllers in Chapter 5 on scaffolding as well as in the "Hello World!" example in Chapter 1, it will come as no surprise that they are pretty core to Grails. Needless to say, this is even less surprising given that Grails follows the MVC pattern. Nevertheless I have only dealt with the *M* in MVC, the domain model, in any great depth in Chapter 4. This chapter aims to build on what you have seen so far by providing more detail surrounding controllers and the capabilities they offer.

Introduction to Controllers

A *controller* in Grails is a class that is responsible for dealing with requests issued by the client. Controllers are *prototype*, which means that a new controller instance is created for each request; therefore there is no need to worry about thread safety with local fields. The request itself can be dealt with in a number of ways, including the following:

- By simply delegating to an appropriate view

- By interacting with the domain, formulating a model, and passing it to a view for display

- By writing directly to the response's writer

- By redirecting to another action or controller

This is by no means an exhaustive list of possible activities, but gives you an idea of the kinds of jobs controllers are responsible for. The diagram in Figure 7-1 illustrates the previous points.

So what makes up a controller? A controller is quite simply a class found snugly within the `grails-app/controllers` directory whose class name ends with the convention `Controller`.

As with domain classes there is no parent class to inherit from; behavior is injected into these classes by Grails at run time. Again this can be seen as an abstraction from the framework itself, as controllers are not simply reserved for web applications. The MVC pattern is used in many other application types including desktop applications, although it is rather theoretical as to whether controllers can be reused for both desktop and web applications due to the very different architecture employed by each.

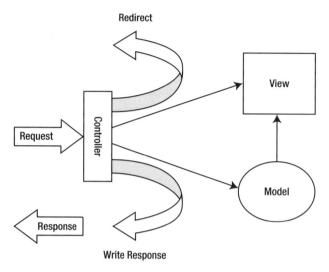

Figure 7-1. *Controller flow control*

Listing 7-1 is the class definition of the BookmarkController generated during scaffolding. The first part of the name (before the Controller suffix) maps to the first part of the URI after the context path (with its first letter in lowercase). For example, the BookmarkController within our bookmarks application would map to the URI /bookmarks/bookmark.

Listing 7-1. *The Bookmark Controller*

```
class BookmarkController {
        //...
}
```

Actions are defined using closure properties with each property name mapping to the third part of the URI. For example, an action called list would be mapped to /bookmarks/bookmark/list, as shown in Listing 7-2.

Listing 7-2. *An Action Example*

```
class BookmarkController {
        def list = { }
}
```

A frequently asked question is, why are closures chosen to define actions instead of simple method calls? There are a number of reasons:

- Closures in Groovy are much more dynamic than regular methods. Closures have three layers of delegation to resolve variables, including the closure itself, the enclosing scope, and a special *delegate*. The delegate is usually the enclosing class but can be changed at run time, making the possibilities with closures far greater.

- JavaBean properties are mutable, which allows for some interesting possibilities in terms of wrapping an existing action with another closure and then setting the closure as the new action on the controller, thus allowing action interception or use of the decorator pattern.

- Because actions are closures, references to the actions can be passed around and invoked from other places.

- Closure definitions, as seen in Listing 7-2, are JavaBean properties; they can be introspected by tools, IDEs, and configuration code.

Some of these points only really relate to the underlying Grails implementation and not to you as a user of Grails, but they have a great impact on the possibilities and features that can be offered by the framework itself.

Now let's start with basic controller usage, beginning with how to go about setting the default action that is executed when only the controller name is used in the URI.

Setting the Default Action

One of the first and most important things to understand is how Grails chooses the default action to execute if no action is specified in the URI path. The default action URI is the path to the controller, relative to the application context path, without any action suffix. For example, for the BookmarkController the default action's URI would be /bookmarks/bookmark. The rules that enable you to set the default action are as follows:

- If the controller defines only one action, it becomes the default action.

- If the controller defines an action called index, it becomes the default action.

- If a String property called defaultAction is defined, its value will be used as the default action name to execute.

The code in Listing 7-3 provides examples of the three techniques in action with three versions of the BookmarkController class:

Listing 7-3. *The Default Action*

```
// Here the 'list' action is the default as there is only one action defined
class BookmarkController {
        def list = {}
}
// In this example 'index' is the default by convention
class BookmarkController {
        def list = {}
        def index = {}
}
// Here list is explicitly set as the default
class BookmarkController {
        def defaultAction = 'list'
        def list = {}
        def index = {}
}
```

The mechanism you choose to set the default action is really up to you, but Grails provides enough flexibility in this area to grant you a few choices. In most cases you could simply implement an index action that performs a redirect. For example, the code in Listing 7-4 will execute the default action and then redirect to the list action.

Listing 7-4. *A Default Action with a Redirect*

```
class BookmarkController {
    def index = {
        redirect(action:list)
    }
    def list = {}
}
```

We'll be looking at redirects in greater detail in the section "Controlling Flow with Redirects." First, however, let's take a look at how to go about accessing request attributes such as parameters.

Accessing Request Attributes

Grails is built on top of the highly extensible Spring MVC framework, which in turn is built on top of the standard servlet framework. Why am I emphasizing this? Well, what it means to you as a developer is that you don't have to learn any new APIs; you'll be happy to know, Grails uses the standard objects from the servlet API, including HttpServletRequest, HttpServletResponse, HttpSession, and ServletContext.

These are automatically injected into controllers at run time. There is, however, a twist. Grails provides a number of enhancements to these objects as well as some new ones that might not sound so familiar (unless you're a Rails user) such as the flash and params objects.

You'll have a look at usage and naming of the standard objects shortly, but first, Table 7-1 shows the attributes each action within a controller has access to.

Table 7-1. *Standard Request Attributes*

Attribute	Description
actionName	The name of the executing action
actionUri	The URI of the executing action
controllerName	The name of the executing controller
controllerUri	The URI of the executing controller
flash	The flash object for working with flash scope
log	An org.apache.commons.logging.Log instance
params	A map of request parameters
request	The HttpServletRequest instance
response	The HttpServletResponse instance
session	The HttpSession instance
servletContext	The ServletContext instance

Many of the previously listed attributes are standard servlet API objects, the documentation for which can be found on Sun's Java technology web site at http://java.sun.com/. It is, however, interesting to observe the difference in working with these objects from a Grails controller. A common way to interact with the request, for example, is to retrieve or set a request attribute. The session and servlet context also have attributes that can be set or retrieved. Grails unifies these by overriding the dot dereference and subscript operators. Table 7-2 shows the difference between accessing request, session, and servlet context attributes in regular Java servlets compared to Grails controllers.

Table 7-2. *Differences Between Request Attributes in Java Servlets and Grails Controllers*

Java Servlet	Grails Controller
request.getAttribute("myAttribute") ;	request.myAttribute
request.setAttribute("myAttribute", "myValue") ;	request.myAttribute = "myValue"
session.getAttribute("myAttribute") ;	session.myAttribute
session.setAttribute("myAttribute", "myValue") ;	session.myAttribute = "myValue"
servletContext.getAttribute("myAttribute") ;	servletContext.myAttribute
servletContext.setAttribute("myAttribute", "myValue") ;	servletContext.myAttribute = "myValue"

Of course, if you are used to writing code like that in the left column of the table, you can continue to do so; Grails just makes it a little bit easier. The log variable in Table 7-1 deserves special mention; therefore we will take a look at it next.

Using Logging

Logging is an important aspect of any web application and allows potential problems to be traced and critical errors to be logged. Unfortunately, with Java only including logging as part of the platform since JDK 1.4, it is too often the case that logging encompasses writing to standard out. Using standard out is an option, of course, but you will be much better served by using a flexible logging system.

Luckily every Grails controller includes a logging mechanism already; so now there is no excuse to not log information appropriately. The log property is an instance of org.apache. commons.logging.Log, the interface for which can be seen in Listing 7-5.

Listing 7-5. *The org.apache.commons.logging.Log Interface*

```
public interface Log {
        public void debug(Object msg);
        public void debug(Object msg, Throwable t);
        public void error(Object msg);
        public void error (Object msg, Throwable t);
        public void fatal(Object msg);
        public void fatal(Object msg, Throwable t);
```

```
        public void info(Object msg);
        public void info(Object msg, Throwable t);
        public void trace(Object msg);
        public void trace(Object msg, Throwable t);
        public void warn(Object msg);
        public void warn(Object msg, Throwable t);
        public boolean isDebugEnabled();
        public boolean isErrorEnabled();
        public boolean isFatalEnabled();
        public boolean isInfoEnabled();
        public boolean isTraceEnabled();
        public boolean isWarnEnabled();
}
```

As you can probably gather, the methods allow you to log messages at different log levels. Since Apache Commons Logging abstracts the actual logging implementation, you can configure logging with either Log4j or the built-in Java logging APIs. Grails comes packaged with Log4j; the Log4j configuration file can be found within the web-app/WEB-INF directory of any Grails application.

Grails creates a logger for each controller, so to configure the log output for the BookmarkController, for example, you would need to add the following lines to the log4j.properties file:

```
log4j.logger.BookmarkController=debug, stdout
```

This will configure the logger for the BookmarkController to log at the debug level to standard out, meaning that messages output with code such as the following will appear printed to the console:

```
log.debug('I am important debug information')
```

It is also interesting to note that Groovy only provides support for runtime exceptions with checked exceptions translated into runtime exceptions. The implication of this is that you can write code without any try/catch blocks whatsoever.

This is probably not the wisest decision in every circumstance, however; and when an exception does occur in your application it is good to log the exception so that it can be captured by one of your loggers.

In Listing 7-6 I have committed the ultimate sin of simply catching java.lang.Exception instead of a more specific exception, but what is important is to understand the concept of logging exceptions.

Listing 7-6. *Logging an Exception*

```
try {
   // do something that could throw an exception
   ...
}
```

```
catch(Exception e) {
    log.debug('I am important debug information', e)
    throw e
}
```

Also, note that although in the examples I configured Log4j to log to standard out, this does not necessarily have to be the case. Log4j provides a number of different types of *appenders* that allow you to log information to different places.

For example, you could log information at the info level to the console, while errors could be logged to a file somewhere. You could even log fatal errors to an e-mail appender that sends an e-mail to you or your system administrators when a problem occurs, or, if you are really fancy, you could use an e-mail-to-SMS gateway to send a text message to your mobile phone.

■**Note** For more information about log levels such as info, error, debug, and fatal, refer to the material in Chapter 3 on configuring logging.

One of the useful things to log is request parameters that have been sent from the client. In the next section we will look at how to access and work with request parameters.

Working with Request Parameters

Request parameters, or *CGI parameters*, depending on your lingo, are key/value pairs that get passed to a request from a URL or a form submission. In Java, the servlet API's HttpServletRequest object provides access to these, which you can, of course, use in Grails just as in standard servlet programming as demonstrated in Listing 7-7.

Listing 7-7. *Request Parameters via Standard Servlet API*

```
def id = request.getParameter('id')
println(id)
```

Grails does, however, offer an alternative: the params object. The params object is quite simply a map of the request parameters. Unlike normal request parameters the params object is mutable, meaning you can add or modify request parameters at will.

The params object also comes into play with *data binding*, which you will see in action in the section "Data Binding and Type Conversion." For the moment, however, let's take a look at usage of the params object.

Listing 7-8 demonstrates two techniques for accessing the id parameter. The first, on line 1, is using the dot dereference operator, while on the last line, I use the subscript operator with a string to access the id. While the former is a cleaner syntax the latter, is useful when the name of the parameter is not a valid Java identifier, such as those containing dots or other invalid characters, or when the name of the parameter is not known until run time.

Listing 7-8. *Using the params Object*

```
def id = params.id
println(id)
params.id = 2
println( params['id'] )
```

Another interesting thing to note is that the example is accessing a parameter called id. The id parameter is rather special in how it relates to URIs. Essentially the id property is the token after the action name of a Grails URI. Figure 7-2 illustrates this.

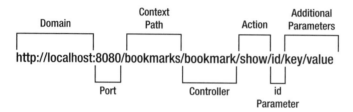

Figure 7-2. *The id parameter in URIs*

Here you see how Grails URIs also allow key/value pairs to be passed as part of the URI itself rather than using traditional ? query parameters. These, as well as the id parameter, appear in the params object at run time. The id parameter, as well as other parameters, can of course be passed as regular form data or query parameters, but the previous URI technique allows for some interesting, and possibly cleaner, combinations.

Now that you understand the params object, let's take a look at another object that is similar in usage but differs greatly in behavior: the flash object.

Understanding Flash Scope

Another object introduced by Grails, which Rails users will be familiar with, is the flash object. The flash object is also a map accessible in the same way as the params object, the fundamental difference being that key/value pairs stored in the flash object are stored in flash scope. What is flash scope? It's best explained with the problem it solves.

A common usage pattern in web applications is to do some processing and then *redirect* the request to another controller or servlet, or whatever. This is not an issue in itself, except, what happens when the request is redirected? It essentially creates a brand-new request, wiping out all previous data that may have resided in the request attributes. The target of the redirect often needs this data, but, unfortunately, the target action is out of luck.

Some have worked around this by instead storing this information in the session. This is all fine and well, however, the problem with the session is that people (yes, that means developers) forget to clear out this temporarily stored data and the burden is placed on the developer to explicitly manage this state.

Figure 7-3 illustrates this problem in action. The first request that comes in sets an attribute on the request called message. It then redirects the request by sending a redirect response back to the client. This creates a brand-new request instance, which is sent to the controller. Sadly, the message attribute is lost and evaluates to null.

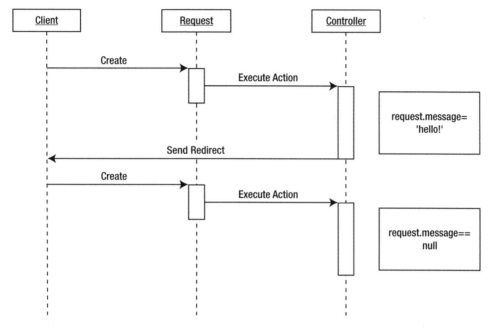

Figure 7-3. *Flash scope problem*

To get around this little annoyance, the `flash` object stores its values for the *next* request and the *next* request only, after which they automatically vanish. This manages the burden of this kind of use case for you and is another small but significant feature that allows you to focus on the problem at hand instead of the surrounding issues.

One of the more common use cases for flash scope is to store a message that will display when some form of validation fails. You'll see examples of this when you get to the section "Controlling Flow with Redirects," but for the moment, Listing 7-9 demonstrates how to store a hypothetical message in the `flash` object so it's available for the next request.

Listing 7-9. *Storing a Message in Flash Scope*

```
flash.message = 'I am available next time you request me!'
```

Remember that the `flash` object implements `java.util.Map` so all the regular methods of this class are also available, as well as the subscript operator syntax seen in Listing 7-8 when working with the `params` object. Figure 7-4 shows how flash scope solves the aforementioned problem.

Here, on the first request, you store a `message` variable to the `flash` object and then redirect the request. When the new request comes in, you are able to access this message, no problem. The `message` variable will then automatically be removed for the next request that comes in.

Note The `flash` object does still use the `HttpSession` instance internally to store itself, so if you require any kind of session affinity or clustering, remember that it applies to the `flash` object, too.

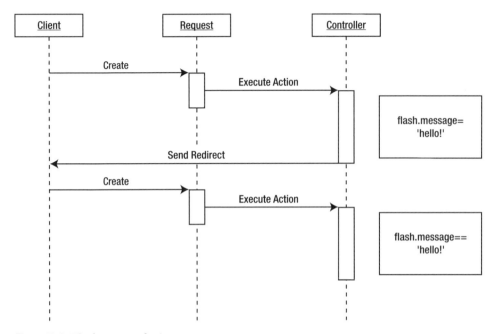

Figure 7-4. *Flash scope solution*

Storing variables in the flash object is a useful additional feature, but occasionally you just want to store variables in the request to be displayed by a view. In Grails this is called a *model*. In the next section you'll see how to create a model that can be rendered by a view.

Creating a Model

Of the many activities a controller is responsible for, one of the more fundamental ones is to formulate a model to be rendered by a view. A model is essentially a map of key/value pairs that can be referenced in the view. Listing 7-10 shows the show action of the BookmarkController that was generated in Chapter 5.

Listing 7-10. *The show Action*

```
class BookmarkController {
    ...
    def show = {
        [ bookmark : Bookmark.get( params.id ) ]
    }
    ...
}
```

So what does the previous code do? It is actually remarkably simple on closer inspection. First of all, the get method of the Bookmark class is invoked passing the id parameter from the params object. The result of this method is then assigned to a key with the string value of bookmark within a Groovy map. The result of the show action is a map with one element that has a key called Bookmark. There are a few interesting things to note about this code:

- Groovy allows you to omit the quotes in the keys of maps. If you want the key to be resolved from a variable in the enclosing scope, you need to surround the key with parentheses such as (Bookmark).

- Automatic type conversion occurs when passing the id from the params object. Remember, parameters arrive as strings, but the id of the Bookmark class is a Long.

- As Groovy allows you to omit return statements, the result is that the map is automatically returned, due to it being the last statement within the closure.

So a model is quite simply a map of key/value pairs; but a Grails action doesn't have to return a model, so what happens if no model is returned? The simple answer is that it depends on what the action does. If the action writes directly to response output, there is no model; conversely, if it simply delegates to the view with no model returned, the controller's properties automatically become the model. This allows you to write code like that in Listing 7-11 as an alternative to the show action you've already seen.

Listing 7-11. *The Controller as the Model*

```
class BookmarkController {
        Bookmark bookmark
        ...
        def show = {
                this.bookmark = Bookmark.get(params.id)
        }
        ...
}
```

The technique you choose to use is as much up to personal preference as anything else. Personally, I feel there is greater clarity in returning an explicitly defined map, but some may disagree. We'll be looking at how to reference elements within the model from views in the following chapter on Groovy Server Pages (GSP), but to continue your journey through the land of controllers, the next thing we'll be looking at is how to perform type conversion.

Data Binding and Type Conversion

A common problem in any web application environment is that request parameters, whether they are passed in via a query in the URI or via a form submission, arrive as strings. This becomes even more problematic in an OO environment where objects can define multiple properties, potentially with relationships and nested object graphs. This results in a good deal of a web application developer's time being spent handling this conversion and data-binding work instead of focusing on the core of the application and its business logic.

Luckily, Grails is built on the Spring MVC framework that takes data binding and type conversion seriously and, in addition, Grails provides a simplified interface onto the data-binding capability that Spring MVC offers.

Data Binding with Domain Models

A common activity is to set properties of domain objects from request parameters. Unfortunately, not all properties of domain objects are strings. So what do we do? Well, very little actually. Grails extends the default implicit constructor already added by Groovy, adding type-conversion capability powered by the Spring MVC infrastructure.

Even though you don't actually define any constructors in your domain model, Grails provides an implicit constructor that takes a java.util.Map, and if you recall, the params object is an instance of, you guessed it, java.util.Map.

I think you can probably imagine where this is going, but just in case: say, for example, you want to create a new Bookmark instance and set the url property from a request parameter. Of course, this property is an instance of java.net.URL, but you also want to set the dateCreated property from a string based on the current locale. The parameters are passed using the request's query parameters such as the following:

```
/bookmarks/bookmark/create?url=http://grails.org&dateCreated=01/06/2006
```

You could, of course, write the necessary logic to create a java.net.URL instance from the url parameter, catching any parsing exceptions. You would then need to write some more logic that uses java.text.SimpleDateFormat and an appropriate locale to perform the necessary date parsing from the dateCreated parameter.

Sounds like a lot of hassle, doesn't it? Alternatively, you can just use the domain classes' constructor in conjunction with the params object, as shown in Listing 7-12.

Listing 7-12. *Data Binding Using an Implicit Constructor*

```
import java.text.SimpleDateFormat

class BookmarkController {
  ...
  def create = {

    // create bookmark and bind from params
    def bookmark = new Bookmark( params )
    def df = new SimpleDateFormat('dd/MM/yyyy',request.locale)
    // perform a few assertions
    assert bookmark.url == new URL('http://grails.org')
    assert bookmark.dateCreated == df.parse('01/06/2006')
  }
}
```

In the line of code with the Bookmark constructor, there is some pretty complex logic. It has taken the parameters as strings, performed type conversion for the URL and set the url property, and used the request's locale to parse the passed date and set the dateCreated property. How does that compare to your previous experiences facing similar issues?

■**Caution** The features detailed so far can leave your web application open to URL attacks due to the automatic setting of properties from request parameters. This is a common issue among frameworks that perform such conversion (including Rails, Spring MVC, WebWork, and so on). If you are developing a web application with heightened security in mind, it is recommended that you use fine-grained control over data binding and stricter validation.

Occasionally it is useful to set properties on domain classes when they've already been constructed. Maybe they are persistent instances that have been retrieved using the faithful get method. In this case a domain class's `properties` property can be used in conjunction with the `params` object. The `properties` property is a `java.util.Map` instance that returns the properties of the domain object as key/value pairs, as shown in Listing 7-13.

Listing 7-13. *Data Binding with the properties Property*

```
class BookmarkController {
    ...
    def update = {
        // retrieve bookmark for id
        def bookmark = new Bookmark.get(params.id)
        // set properties using params object
        bookmark.properties = params
    }
}
```

Fortunately, as seen in the previous example, this is another one-liner. A persistent instance is retrieved and the properties are set, performing all the usual automagic type conversion, using the `properties` property. Note that the examples you have seen so far have again been taken directly from the generated controller from Chapter 5.

So what would happen if invalid data is passed and binding fails? Essentially the property would remain `null` and no binding would occur. However, remember that Chapter 4 discussed applying constraints and performing validation. Clearly it is then good practice to immediately validate after performing this kind of data binding. This can again be seen in action in the generated controller in Listing 7-14.

Listing 7-14. *Data Binding and Validation*

```
class BookmarkController {
    ...
    def update = {
        def bookmark = new Bookmark.get(params.id)
        bookmark.properties = params
```

```
            // validation called by save method
            if( bookmark.save() ) {
                    // validation sucessful. Show the bookmark
                    ...
            }
            else {
                    // handle validation errors
                    ...
            }
        }
    }
}
```

Remember that the save method automatically performs validation, and if it fails it returns null. If the previous Bookmark instance fails to validate, the else block will handle the errors that occur during data binding.

Data Binding with the bindData Method

Occasionally, it is useful to perform data binding like we have seen so far with objects other than domain classes. For instance you may want to perform data binding on the local properties of the controller itself. To help tackle this issue, Grails provides a bindData method that takes the object to bind the data to and a java.util.Map. The map should contain keys that match the property names of the target properties within the passed object. As an example, let's revisit what you have seen so far by having the dateCreated and url parameters bound to controller properties instead of a domain object.

The code in Listing 7-15 passes the *owner* of the closure, which is the BookmarkController instance, and the params object to the bindData method. The parameters are then set, using the same automatic type conversion facility, to the dateCreated and url properties of the BookmarkController.

Listing 7-15. *Using the bindData Method*

```
class BookmarkController {
        Date dateCreated
        URL url
        def bindAction = {
                bindData(owner, params)
                assert url == new java.net.URL('http://grails.org')
        }
}
```

In Listing 7-14 we revisited how to perform validation by demonstrating the use of an if/else block. What we didn't do is provide implementation details of what you do when validation is either successful or not, as the case may be.

One common way to handle a validation failure is to *redirect* control to another action or controller. In the next section we explore how to control application flow and perform redirects where necessary.

Controlling Flow with Redirects

As the dictator of your application, a controller often has to redirect requests between its actions or to another controller's actions. A redirect may be the result of a request that has been invalidated or simply natural application flow. A redirect will actually send a response to the client and create a brand-new request, so it should not be confused with request forwarding.

■**Note** You have already seen how redirecting differs from forwarding in the section "Understanding Flash Scope," which describes the `flash` object and the redirect problem.

Those familiar with the servlet API will of course be aware of the `sendRedirect` method available on the `response` object. However, Grails makes it a bit easier by providing a built-in `redirect` method on controllers that provides integration with Grails' concepts of controllers and actions. By referring back to our scaffolded bookmarks application, you can see some redirects in action, firstly in the `index` action, shown in Listing 7-16.

Listing 7-16. *Simple Redirect*

```
def index = {
        redirect(action:list, params:params)
}
```

The previous example `redirect` method takes two arguments. The first is the action to be redirected to, using the `action` argument, which in this case is actually passed a reference to the `list` closure itself. Essentially, the `action` argument either accepts a string, which is the name of the action, or a reference to the closure to redirect to. The second argument is the `params` argument, which passes request parameters from one action to the next using a map. In this case it is simply using the `params` object itself to pass all parameters.

Clearly the previous example is of the more simple variety. Luckily, the `redirect` method is flexible enough to cater to many other examples. Table 7-3 lists the arguments accepted by the `redirect` method.

Table 7-3. *Redirect Arguments*

Argument Name	Description
action	The name of or a reference to the action to redirect to
controller	The name of the controller to redirect to
id	The id parameter to pass in the redirect
params	A map of parameters to pass
uri	A relative URI to redirect to
url	An absolute URL to redirect to

Most of the arguments should be fairly self-explanatory; remember, however, that the uri and url arguments can only be used in conjunction with the params argument. Let's take a look at some additional examples of the redirect method, in Listing 7-17, using the aforementioned arguments.

Listing 7-17. *Redirects in Action*

```
// redirects to /bookmark/show/1
redirect(controller:'bookmark', action:'show', id:1)

// same as above with URI instead
redirect(uri:'/bookmark/show/1')

// redirect to grails site
redirect(url:'http://grails.org')

// usage of params
redirect(action:'list', params:[ max: 20, sort: 'url'])
```

There are some interesting things to note about the redirect method. Firstly, the controller name is specified without the Controller suffix and with the first letter in lowercase, following the convention. Also, if no controller is specified, it is assumed the action is within the currently executing controller.

Note that the params argument expects a map. Thanks to Groovy's special map syntax this not only allows you to easily pass parameters to a redirect, but also makes it remarkably trivial to pass existing parameters from one action to the next:

```
redirect(action:'show',params:params)
```

If you recall, I mentioned that the params object is a map; hence, to pass the same set of parameters from one action to the next, you simply provide the params object as the value of the params argument.

The redirect method is not the only way to pass control from one action to the next. The chain method is similar to the redirect method, but with a twist. In the next session we explore what the chain method offers as an alternative to a simple redirect.

Constructing a Model with Chaining

A closely related sibling of the redirect method is the chain method. The signature for the chain method is the same as that for redirect; it differs only in the addition of a model argument that takes a map, allowing you to build up your model across multiple actions. Remember, previously I discussed the problem of redirects and using flash scope to circumvent the issues surrounding losing request attributes when a new request is created. The chain method aids you even further by allowing the model to be passed from one action to the next, even though a redirect has occurred.

It does this, of course, by using flash scope internally. But the management of the flash scope is handled implicitly without the need for your intervention, and objects passed with the model argument will end up in the finally created model as if by magic. To help you understand this better, let's look at Listing 7-18, a reworked example of the scaffolded `save` and `create` actions that use chaining instead, followed by a diagram in Figure 7-5.

Listing 7-18. *Example of the chain Method in Action*

```
1 class BookmarkController {
2     ...
3     def save = {
4         def b = new Bookmark(params)
5         if(b.save()) {
6             redirect( action:show, id: b.id )
7         }
8         else {
9             chain(action:create,model: [ bookmark:b ] )
10        }
11    }
12    def create = {}
13    ...
14 }
```

Essentially, the previous example uses the `chain` method on line 9 when validation fails, chaining the model back to the `create` action. The invalid `Bookmark` instance will then be returned as part of the `create` action's model, even though the `create` action does not return any model at all. Of course, if the `create` action returns a model with a `Bookmark` instance in it already, the object passed via the `chain` method would be overridden.

In addition, if the `create` action returns another model, the model passed via the `chain` method would be *combined* with the model returned by the `create` action. This allows you to combine several calls to chain across multiple actions to build up the ultimately returned model. When chaining is used, a special `chainModel` request attribute is available that allows the currently executing action to access the model created by the previous call to `chain`. For example, accessing the bookmark from the `create` action would involve code such as the following:

```
println( chainModel.bookmark.url )
```

So without further ado, Figure 7-5 illustrates the `chain` method and how it affects application flow.

So how does it all work? Well, the `chain` method exists thanks to flash scope. The `flash` object is used internally by the `chain` method to pass the model from one action to the next. Otherwise it behaves exactly like a normal redirect.

Whether you use `chain` or `redirect` in the process of creating your model, ultimately a response will be written to the client. As you have already seen, Grails will automatically delegate to an appropriate view based on the conventions in the controller and actions name.

However, occasionally it is useful to have more explicit control over which view renders, or to render only a partial snippet of markup. In the next section you'll see how to do this via the extremely flexible `render` method.

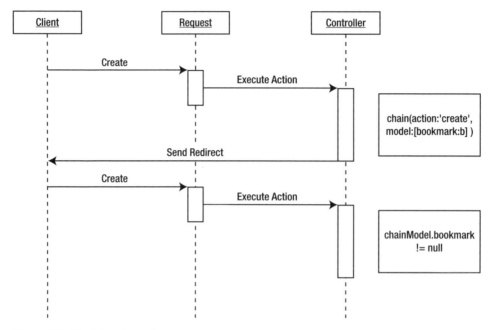

Figure 7-5. *Chaining in action*

Rendering a Response

On occasion (an occasion that is becoming more and more frequent as Ajax applications gain prominence, but we'll cover that in Chapter 9) it is useful for a controller action to write directly to the response, as opposed to delegating to a view. This of course can be achieved using standard servlet API calls such as the example in Listing 7-19, which uses the HttpServletResponse object to output binary data to the response in the form of a ZIP file.

Listing 7-19. *Writing Binary Data to the Response*

```
def createZip = {
  byte[] zip = ... // create the zip from some source
  response.contentType = "application/octet-stream"
  response.outputStream << zip
}
```

The previous code uses the response object's outputStream property in conjunction with Groovy's overloaded left shift << operator, which is present in a number of objects that output or append to something such as java.io.Writer and java.lang.StringBuffer to name just a couple.

Beyond these more explicit servlet API usages, Grails provides a more flexible and powerful means with which to write responses in the form of the render method.

The render method is an extremely flexible method that has multiple uses, which are best explained in the form of a series of examples covering a few use cases. However, I will not delve into all use cases here and will revisit the render method in subsequent chapters so you can see its usage in a number of contexts. First up, let's take a look at how to output simple text to the response.

Rendering Text

In its most basic form the `render` method can be used to output text to the response. You saw this in action as early as Chapter 1 when developing the "Hello World!" application, where the `render` method was used to output the current date:

```
render "Hello World it's ${new Date()}!"
```

For simple cases such as the previous, as with `println`, the parentheses can be omitted. This allows for greater clarity of code. By default the `render` method assumes a content type of `text/plain`. Using the `text` argument in conjunction with a `contentType` argument you can change the content type returned to whatever you choose:

```
render(text:"<hello>world</hello>", contentType:"text/xml")
```

Rendering a Specific View

Sometimes the logic of a controller action may dictate that a different view than the one delegated to by default is needed. To facilitate this, the `render` method provides a `view` argument:

```
render(view:"myView")
```

This will use a view called `myView.gsp` within the executing controller's views directory. Of course, sometimes a view requires a model in order to display correctly, thus the `render` method has a `model` argument, which takes a map that represents the model:

```
render(view:"myView",model: [ today:new Date() ] )
```

The `render` method is also useful for displaying *shared views*. Shared views are views that are used by multiple controllers. They can be located anywhere relative to the `grails-app/views` directory but are normally placed in the root of this directory. To access one of these views the `view` argument must start with a forward slash / character:

```
render(view: "/mySharedView")
```

The previous code will resolve a view called `mySharedView.gsp` within the `grails-app/views` directory. If you're organized, you can, of course, create shared views within a subdirectory; for example the following code looks for the `mySharedView.gsp` within a `shared` directory inside the `grails-app/views` directory:

```
render(view: "/shared/mySharedView")
```

Rendering Markup

Groovy's builder syntax is wonderful for creating structured representations of data including markup such as HTML or XML. To this end the `render` method provides support for creating markup by taking a closure argument, as shown in Listing 7-20.

Listing 7-20. *Rendering Markup*

```
render {
    html {
        head {
            title("Example Mark-up")
        }
        body {
            p("This is a single paragraph of mark-up!" )
        }
    }
}
```

The previous example takes a closure with each nested method call being translated into markup. The source of the resulting response of the previous call to render is the following:

```
<html>
    <head>
        <title>Example Mark-up</title>
    </head>
    <body>
        <p>This is a single paragraph of mark-up!</p>
    </body>
</html>
```

As seen earlier in this section with the text argument, the contentType argument can be used to change the content type. For example, to create XML markup you would use the following:

```
render(contentType: "text/xml" ) { ... }
```

We'll look in greater depth at rendering markup in Chapter 9 on Ajax, as it is a common usage pattern to render snippets of XML, JSON, or HTML when developing Ajax applications.

Using Action Interception

Frequently it is useful to catch the flow of method execution by *intercepting* calls to certain methods. This concept is the foundation of Aspect-Oriented Programming (AOP), which allows the definition of *point cuts* (execution points) to be intercepted. The intercepted execution can then be modified through the use of before, after, and around advice. *Advice* in AOP is code that can be executed either before or after an intercepted method call or can replace the method call entirely, which is called *around* advice.

AOP's great strength is providing support for implementing cross-cutting concerns. The example frequently used for this is the logging of method calls. Although Grails' interception mechanism by no means provides the same power and flexibility in terms of what point cuts can be intercepted, it does fulfill the basic need of intercepting calls to actions on controllers.

Controllers in Grails provide an interception mechanism that allows the implementation of cross-cutting concerns across controller actions. You can either intercept all actions or provide more fine-grained control by specifying which actions should be intercepted. To start off with, I will follow the lead of AOP in using logging or tracing as an example, after which I will show you a more thorough example by building on our bookmarks application.

Before Advice

Luckily, as with the rest of Grails, there is no hefty XML configuration or annotation trickery required, thanks to coding by convention. All it takes to define a before interceptor is to create a closure property named beforeInterceptor within the target controller, as shown in Listing 7-21.

Listing 7-21. *A beforeInterceptor*

```
def beforeInterceptor = {
        log.trace("Executing action $actionName with params $params")
}
```

The previous example uses the log object to output tracing information before any action within the BookmarkController is executed.

After Advice

After advice is defined using the unsurprisingly named afterInterceptor property that again takes a closure. The first argument passed to the closure is the resulting model from the action, as shown in Listing 7-22.

Listing 7-22. *An afterInterceptor Example*

```
def afterInterceptor = { model ->
        log.trace("Executed action $actionName which resulted in model: $model")
}
```

Again, in this rather trivial example, we have the result of any action executing being traced via the logging mechanism. Clearly logging is a rather basic example of the power that interceptors offer, but never fear, next we'll be looking at how to apply interceptors to one of the most common requirements in web applications: authentication.

Using Interceptors for Authentication

Returning to our ongoing example, clearly web applications are meant to support multiple users. As it stands, the bookmarks application allows you to create and list Bookmark instances; but in a typical multiuser scenario, clearly this would mean everyone is sharing the same bookmarks. So you need to make each Bookmark instance specific to a particular user and ensure when a user logs in to the system that the user sees only his or her bookmarks. To facilitate this, a user property is required on the Bookmark class, as shown in Listing 7-23.

Listing 7-23. *Updated Bookmark Class*

```
class Bookmark {
        def belongsTo = User
        User user

        ...
}
```

In addition, if a user is not logged in, you are going to have to redirect the user to a login screen to log in. Before this, however, you need to consider what happens if the user goes directly to a URL that is *secure*. This is where interception and interceptor conditions come in handy.

Firstly, let's create a new abstract base controller by running the grails create-controller command and using the name secure. By making the controller abstract it will not be exposed to the outside world as a regular controller, thus allowing you to safely subclass the controller. Next you need to modify the controller so that it defines the authenticating interceptor, as shown in Listing 7-24.

Listing 7-24. *Authenticating Controller*

```
1 abstract class SecureController {
2         def beforeInterceptor = [  action:   this.&auth,
3                                    except: [ 'handleLogin', 'login',
4                                              'handleRegistration', 'register' ]
5                                    ]
6
7       private auth() {
8               if(!session.user) {
9                       redirect(controller:'user',action: 'login')
10                      return false
11              }
12       }
13 }
```

Interestingly, the interceptor defined on lines 2 through 5 uses Groovy's map syntax to refer to a private auth method using Groovy's method closure syntax. The method closure syntax allows you to reference any normal method as if it were a closure.

The map also defines a second argument called except which makes sure the interceptor is executed for all actions *except* the login, register, handleRegistration, and handleLogin actions. As an alternative, you can use the only argument, which will apply the interceptor *only* to the specified actions. The following snippet illustrates an example of this by only executing the interceptor for an action called secureAction:

```
def beforeInterceptor = [  action: this.&auth, only: [ 'secureAction' ] ]
```

The auth method on line 7 essentially checks whether there is a User instance in the session and if no User instance is found redirects the request to the login action and returns false, which indicates to Grails that execution of the intercepted action should not continue. At this point the SecureController has successfully encapsulated the necessary authentication logic, but you still need to modify the BookmarkController to subclass the SecureController and modify the save and list actions slightly so that the User object stored in the session is used when interacting with bookmarks, as shown in Listing 7-25.

Listing 7-25. *Updated BookmarkController*

```
class BookmarkController extends SecureController {
    ...
    def save = {
        def b = new Bookmark(params)
        b.user = session.user
        ...
    }
            ...
            def list = {
                [ bookmarkList : Bookmark.findAllByUser( session.user, params ) ]
            }
}
```

Notice that the redirect we defined in Listing 7-24 redirected to a controller called user, which doesn't at this point exist. Remember that within a redirect you use the short name for the controller that has the first letter in lowercase and excludes the "Controller" suffix. In this case the controller redirected to is called UserController, which will handle various aspects having to do with users in the bookmarks application, including the crucial aspect of being logged in. What you need to do first is create this controller via the grails create-controller target. By now the usage of the Grails targets should be fairly familiar, with the resulting class looking something like Listing 7-26.

Listing 7-26. *The UserController*

```
class UserController {
        def index = {}
}
```

Of course, in order for users to log in, they're going to need an interface to enter their login details in the form of a login view. This will be your first exposure to developing a GSP, which we'll be looking into in greater depth in Chapter 8.

For the purposes of this example you need to create a new GSP view called login.gsp in the grails-app/views/user directory that was conveniently created for you by Grails when the create-controller target was executed earlier. Once created, populate the contents of the file as per the code in Listing 7-27.

Listing 7-27. *The login.gsp File*

```
<html>
    <head>
        <title>Login Page</title>
        <meta name="layout" content="main" />
        <style type="text/css" media="screen">
            form { width: 300px; }
            input {
                position: absolute;
                left: 130px;
            }
            p {  margin-left: 30px; }
            .button { margin-top: 30px; }
        </style>
    </head>
    <body>
        <div class="message">${flash.message}</div>
        <p>
            Welcome to Your Bookmarks. Login below or
            <g:link action="register">register here</g:link>.
        </p>
        <form action="handleLogin">
            <p>
                <label for="login">Login:</label>
                <input type="text" name="login" />
            </p>
            <p>
                <label for="password">Password:</label>
                <input type="password" name="password" />
            </p>
            <input type="submit" value="Login" />
        </form>
    </body>
</html>
```

Notice that there is a meta tag within the head tag that makes sure the main layout, located at grails-app/views/layouts/main.gsp, is used. This ensures that the login screen pulls in the Grails logo and look and feel, thus ensuring that the login screen doesn't look conspicuously like a dog's breakfast. I'll be covering layouts in greater detail in the next chapter on Groovy Server Pages, but feel free to work on the look and feel as much as you feel necessary. The screenshot in Figure 7-6 is what the login screen will end up looking like based on the code in Listing 7-27.

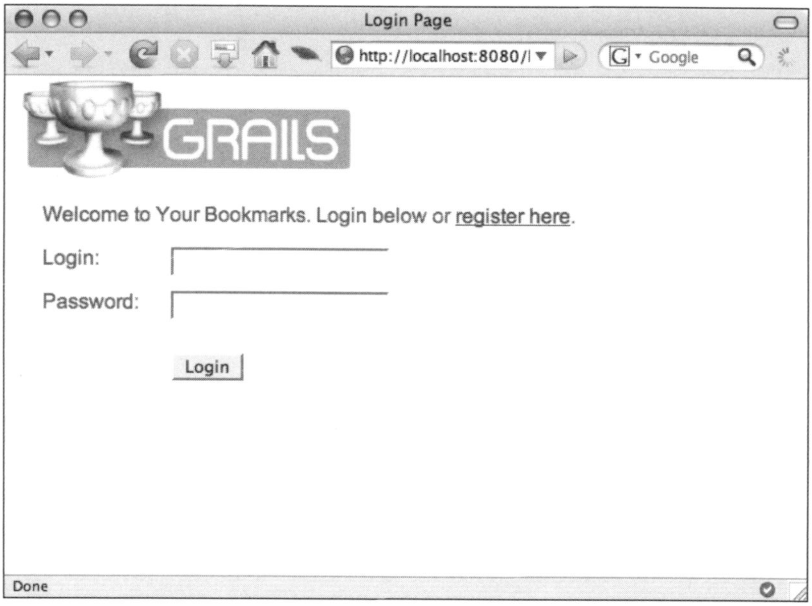

Figure 7-6. *The login view*

Next up you need to add actions that will deal with login processing. Firstly, you'll be creating a login action, which displays the login screen, and a handleLogin action, which processes a user login and subsequently redirects the user to his or her list of bookmarks if the login is successful, as shown in Listing 7-28.

Listing 7-28. *Handling Logins*

```
1 class UserController {
2
3   def login = {
4     if(session.user)  {
5         redirect(controller:'bookmark', action:'list')
6     }
7   }
8
9   def handleLogin = {
10    def user = User.findByLogin( params.login )
11    if(user)  {
12      if(user.password == params.password) {
13          session.user = user
14          redirect(controller:'bookmark', action:'list')
15        }
```

```
16        else {
17           flash.message = "Incorrect password for ${params.login}"
18           redirect(action:login)
19        }
20     }
21     else {
22        flash.message = "User not found for login ${params.login}"
23        redirect(action:login)
24     }
25  }
26 }
```

While the `login` action simply redirects users who are already logged in, the `handleLogin` action likely requires further elaboration, which I will go through now.

On line 10 of the previous listing, a user is looked up using a dynamic finder method passing a request parameter contained within the `params` object called `login`. The subsequent `if` statement on line 11 will redirect the request back to the login screen using the `flash` object to store a helpful message to be displayed if the user is not found.

The `if` statement in line 12 checks the user's stored password against the one passed by the request in the `params` object. If the password is correct, the `User` instance is stored in the `session` and the request is redirected to the bookmark controller's `list` action.

■**Note** This is an example of Groovy's operator overloading capability. The equals `==` operator does not imply object identity as in Java, but instead delegates to the object's `equals` method.

The `else` block will of course redirect the user back to the login screen with an appropriate message if the password is not entered correctly. So what you have so far is the capability to allow users to log in to the bookmarks application; but, of course, every secured login system needs some way of getting users registered so they can log in in the first place. As shown in Listing 7-29, you'll need to create another view that handles registration within the same directory as the login GSP created earlier.

Listing 7-29. *The register.gsp file*

```
<html>
    <head>
        <title>Registration Page</title>
        <meta name="layout" content="main" />
        <style type="text/css" media="screen">
            form { width: 300px; }
            input {
                position: absolute;
                left: 130px;
            }
```

```
                p {  margin-left: 30px; }
                .button { margin-top: 30px; }
            </style>
        </head>
        <body>
            <div class="errors">
                <g:renderErrors bean="${flash.user}" />
            </div>
            <p>Enter your details below to register for Your Bookmarks.</p>
            <form action="handleRegistration">
                <p>
                    <label for="login">Login:</label>
                    <input type="text" name="login" />
                </p>
                <p>
                    <label for="password">Password:</label>
                    <input type="password" name="password" />
                </p>
                <p>
                    <label for="confirm">Confirm Password:</label>
                    <input type="confirm" name="confirm" />
                </p>
                <p>
                    <label for="firstName">First Name:</label>
                    <input type="text" name="firstName" />
                </p>
                <p>
                    <label for="lastName">Last Name:</label>
                    <input type="text" name="lastName" />
                </p>
                <p>
                    <label for="email">Email:</label>
                    <input type="text" name="email" />
                </p>
                <input type="submit" value="Register" />
            </form>
        </body>
    </html>
```

Like the login page, the register page is just a simple form that submits to an action named handleRegistration and contains fields for the user to complete (see Figure 7-7).

An interesting aspect of the registration view is the usage of the g:renderErrors tag which takes a Grails domain instance and renders all the validation errors that have occurred following a call to the save or validate methods.

The instance is supplied via the bean attribute, which looks for a User instance that is stored in flash scope. The errors are then rendered as an HTML list with the messages looked up from the Grails message.properties resource bundle located in the grails-app\i18n directory. Again, you'll be taking a closer look at tags in the next chapter on GSP.

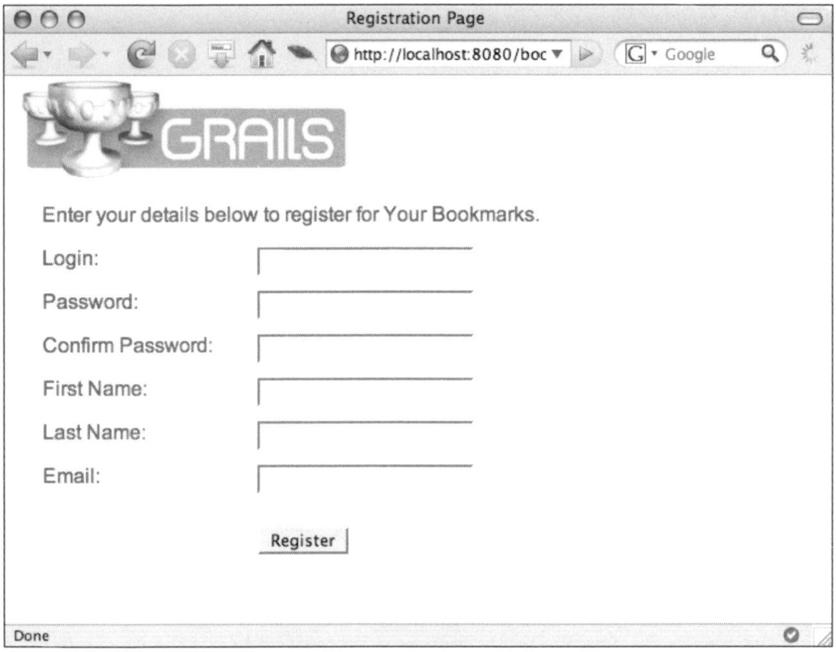

Figure 7-7. *The registration view*

Last but not least, the actions to handle user registrations need to be added to the
UserController. We're going to need a register action, which will render the register view and
an action to process user registrations called handleRegistration, as shown in Listing 7-30.

Listing 7-30. *The handleRegistration Action*

```
1 class UserController {
2  ...
3  def register = {}
4
5  def handleRegistration = {
6     def user = new User( params )
7     if(params.password != params.confirm) {
8       flash.message = "The two passwords you entered don't match!"
9       redirect(action:register)
10    }
11    else {
12      if( user.save() ) {
13        redirect(controller:'bookmark', action:'list')
14      }
15      else {
16        flash.user  = user
17        redirect(action:register)
18      }
```

```
19    }
20  }
21 }
```

The register action is remarkably simple and serves only to create the URI mapping and delegate to the register view, while the handleRegistration action is reminiscent of the save action generated by scaffolding. It first checks if the passwords that were entered matched the attempts to save a new User instance.

If validation fails (remember we applied constraints against the User class in Chapter 4) due to incorrectly entered data, the instance is placed in flash scope and the request is redirected back to the register action. The register view then has access to the instance stored within flash scope and can render the appropriate error list.

That's it! You've successfully created a login and registration process using Grails action interceptors for the bookmarks application. Clearly, authentication is not all that interceptors can be used for, and it's worth taking a look at your requirements to decipher where interceptors can be used to simplify cross-cutting concerns, because they can have a dramatic effect on the simplicity and robustness of an application.

That is, however, the end of this example. In the next section I'll take a different direction by showing you how to go about uploading files with Grails controllers.

Handling File Uploads

One of the more common use cases when developing web applications is to allow the user to upload a local file to the server using a multipart request. This is where Grails' solid foundation of Spring MVC starts to shine through. Spring has fantastic support for handling file uploads via an extension to the servlet API's HttpServletRequest interface called org.springframework. web.multipart.MultipartHttpServletRequest, the definition of which is in Listing 7-31.

Listing 7-31. *The org.springframework.web.multipart.MultipartHttpServletRequest Interface*

```
interface MultipartHttpServletRequest extends HttpServletRequest {
        public MultipartFile getFile(String name);
        public Map getFileMap();
        public Iterator getFileNames();
}
```

As is evident by the previous listing, the MultipartHttpServletRequest interface simply extends the default HttpServletRequest interface to provide useful methods to work with and manipulate files in the request.

Working with Multipart Requests

Essentially, whenever a multipart request is detected, a request object that implements the MultipartHttpSerlvetRequest interface is present in the controller instance. This provides access to the methods seen in Listing 7-31 to access files uploaded in a multipart request. Before we get ahead of ourselves let's take a look at what an upload form could look like in Listing 7-32.

Listing 7-32. *An Example Upload Form*

```
<form action="upload" enctype="multipart/form-data">
      <input type="file" name="myFile" />
      <input type="submit" value="Upload! " />
</form>
```

The important bits are in bold, but an upload form essentially requires two things:

- The enctype attribute set to the value multipart/form-data

- An input whose type attribute is set to the value file

In the previous case the name of the file input is myFile; this is crucial because this is the named reference that you work with when using the getFile method of the MultipartHttpSerlvetRequest interface. As an example, in Listing 7-33, the code within an upload action will retrieve the uploaded file from the request.

Listing 7-33. *Retrieving the Uploaded File*

```
def upload = {
        def file = request.getFile('myFile')
        // do something with the file
}
```

Note that the getFile method does not return a java.io.File, but returns an instance of org.springframework.web.multipart.MultipartFile, the interface that is detailed in Listing 7-34. If the file is not found in the request, the getFile method will return null.

Listing 7-34. *The org.springframework.web.multipart.MultipartFile interface*

```
interface MultipartFile {
    public byte[] getBytes();
    public String getContentType();
    public java.io.InputStream getInputStream();
    public String getName();
    public String getOriginalFilename();
    public long getSize();
    public boolean isEmpty();
    public void transferTo(java.io.File dest);
}
```

There are many useful methods defined in the MultipartFile interface; some of the use cases could be the following:

- Use the getSize() method to only allow uploads of certain file sizes

- Reject empty files using the isEmpty() method

- Read the file as a java.io.InputStream using the getInputStream() method

- Only allow certain file types to be uploaded using the `getContentType()` method

- Transfer the file onto the server using the `transferTo(dest)` method

As an example, the code in Listing 7-35 will upload a file to the server if it is not empty and less than 1024 bytes in size.

Listing 7-35. *File Uploads in Action*

```
def upload = {
    def file = request.getFile('myFile')
    if(file && !file.empty && file.size < 1024)  {
        file.transferTo( new java.io.File( "/local/server/path/${file.name}" ) )
    }
}
```

Working directly with a `MultipartHttpServletRequest` instance is one way to manage file uploads, but frequently you need to read the contents of a file. In the next section we'll look at how Grails makes this easier through data binding.

Uploads and Data Binding

In the section on Data Binding you saw how Grails performs automagic type conversion from strings to other common Java types. What wasn't discussed is how this capability extends to file uploads. Essentially, Grails, through Spring MVC, will automatically bind files uploaded to properties of domain class instances based on the following rules:

- If the target property is a `byte[]` the file's bytes will be bound

- If the target property is a `String` the file's contents as a string will be bound

As an example, say you want to allow users of the bookmarks application to store a photo of themselves within their profile upon registering. By adding a new property to the `User` domain class called `picture` of type `byte[]` you automatically have the capability to save the image data to the database, as shown in Listing 7-36.

Listing 7-36. *Adding the Picture Property*

```
class User {
    byte[] picture
    ...
}
```

To bind an uploaded file, you simply need to add a file upload field that matches the `picture` property name to the registration form and set the `enctype` attribute of the form to `multipart/form-data` as seen previously:

```
<input type="file" name="picture" />
```

The handleRegistration action, developed in the example on using interceptors for authentication in Listing 7-30, requires no updates whatsoever; the binding of the file to the byte[] is automatically handled by the following line:

```
6                 def user = new User( params )
```

Grails will automatically recognize the request as being multipart, retrieve the file, and bind the bytes that make up the file to the picture byte array property of the User class. This capability also extends to usage in conjunction with the properties property and bindData method discussed previously.

Summary

We covered a lot of ground in this chapter and hopefully you got a feel for how important controllers are to a Grails application. So far you should have a good understanding of how to go about creating controller actions to control requests, access request attributes, and redirect requests.

This chapter also explained how to use controllers to perform redirects, render different responses, forward to specific views, and create a model. In addition, you saw how controller interceptors can be used to build an authentication mechanism for your bookmarks sample application.

Believe it or not, this is not the end for controllers in terms of this book. You'll be seeing them again frequently in subsequent chapters covering Groovy Server Pages, Ajax applications, and Java integration.

You managed to get a taste of GSP in this chapter while creating the login and registration screens. In the next chapter you'll start to dig deeper into this view technology and see what it has to offer over traditional JSP pages.

■ ■ ■

## CHAPTER 8

Groovy Server Pages

View technologies for web applications in the open source world appear to be a rather popular topic, with a seemingly endless number available for Java. There always appears to be a newer, better one to learn if you grow tired of the incumbent JSP. The most popular view technology, JSP, has become the industry standard. It was produced by Sun to compete with Microsoft's Active Server Pages (ASP) and hence there is a high level of developer knowledge surrounding it.

JSP allows developers to mix traditional markup languages, such as HTML, with Java code (called *scriptlets*) to produce dynamic output. On the downside, this facility is extremely open to abuse; therefore there are custom tag libraries that add the ability to abstract logic from a JSP page via tags. Recently JSP has been augmented with two missing ingredients in the JSP Standard Tag Library (JSTL) and an expression language to bring it up to speed with some of its open source competitors.

So given JSP's maturity, robustness, and familiarity within the industry, why on earth would you need yet another view technology for Grails with Groovy Server Pages (GSP)? The answer lies with the Groovy runtime environment and essentially is answered by the following points:

- To fully take advantage of Grails, the view technology requires knowledge of Groovy's runtime environment and associated dynamic method dispatching.

- Groovy provides a far more powerful expression language, including GPath expressions, Groovy bean notation, and overridable operators.

- Other Groovy features such as regular expression support, GStrings, and an expressive syntax for maps and lists make it perfect for a view technology.

Of course, for any new view technology it is important not to fall into the same traps that JSP fell into in its early iterations. Mixing scriptlets and markup code is most definitely recognized as a bad thing, and to this end GSP provides a mechanism for creating custom tags just as JSP does, but without sacrificing any agility.

The Basics

You've already been exposed to GSP at various points throughout the book and I'm sure you are verging on the expert level already. Regardless, it will no doubt prove invaluable to start discussing the basics of GSP to help you fully grasp all the concepts within it. First of all, it is important to note that GSP is actually remarkably similar to JSP, and you may know from experience that with JSP, by default, there are a number of objects that are simply *available*. These include the request, response, and session objects and in fact are the same ones you saw in Chapter 7. If you recall, that particular discussion mentioned that there are a few additional objects available to controllers including the flash object. Well, you'll be pleased to know these can also be accessed from GSP views as well as an additional out attribute, which is a java.io.Writer instance representing the response output as shown in Table 8-1.

Table 8-1. *GSP Attributes*

Attribute	Description
application	The ServletContext instance
flash	The flash object for working with flash scope as discussed in Chapter 7
out	The response Writer instance
params	A map of request parameters
request	The HttpServletRequest instance
response	The HttpServletResponse instance
session	The HttpSession instance

You know how to get to these from controllers, but what about in views? Well, unsurprisingly, GSP supports the same constructs available in JSP as well as a few additional ones. This may start to look a little like a JSP 101 tutorial in the next few examples, but don't be confused—you're most definitely dealing with Groovy and not Java.

Understanding the Model

One of the fundamental activities in any MVC pattern, such as that which Grails employs, is to pass information (the model) to the view for rendering. In Chapter 7 on controllers you saw this in action, but just to recap, Listing 8-1 shows an example of how this is achieved in Grails.

Listing 8-1. *Creating the Model*

```
class BookmarkController {
    ...
    def list = {
        [ bookmarks : Bookmark.list( params ) ]
    }
}
```

In this listing (see the list action of the BookmarkController) the result is a map with one element, the key for which is a string with the value bookmarks. This key (and its value) is then placed in a GSP model (or *binding* for those more familiar with Groovy lingo), which means it is accessible as a variable in the same way as the page attributes you saw earlier in Table 8-1.

Throughout the following sections you will see examples of a bookmarks variable being referenced. The thing to remember is that this variable didn't appear by magic. It is passed to the view via the controller in code like in Listing 8-1.

Page Directives

GSP supports a limited subset of the page directives available in JSP. A page directive is an instruction that appears at the top of a GSP that performs an action that the page is reliant on. As an example, it could set the content type, perform an import, or set a page property, which could even be container-specific.

One of the more useful of these is the `contentType` directive, which allows you to set the content type of the response. This is useful in that it allows you to use GSP to output formats other than HTML markup such as XML or plain text. Usage of the directive is identical to JSP with the directive appearing at the top of the page and starting with `<%@`.

Listing 8-2 sets the content type to `text/xml` which allows you to output XML, which can be useful when working with technologies such as Ajax.

Listing 8-2. *The contentType Page Directive*

```
<%@ page contentType="text/xml" %>
```

Another page directive available is the `import` directive, which is analogous to the `import` statement in a Java or Groovy class. However, because Groovy imports many classes by default, and Grails encourages an MVC architecture where much of the logic should be placed in a controller and not the view, the usage of import is not too common. Nevertheless, Listing 8-3 shows an example of importing the `Time` class from the `java.sql.*` package.

Listing 8-3. *The import Page Directive*

```
<%@ page import="java.sql.Time" %>
```

Groovy Scriptlets

GSP tries to stay as true to JSP as possible, therefore it supports traditional JSP scriptlet blocks using the `<%...%>` syntax. Essentially, as soon as you type the opening `<%` declaration you have entered the world of Groovy and can type whatever Groovy code you so choose up until the closing `%>` declaration.

What this means is that you can use scriptlets to perform loops and logical `if` statements merely by combining scriptlet declarations, as shown in Listing 8-4.

Listing 8-4. *Scriptlets in Action*

```
<html>
    <body>
    <% 3.times { %>
        <p>I'm printed three times!</p>
    <%}%>
    </body>
</html>
```

This type of syntax will be familiar to users of Rails, as it bears a striking resemblance to Rails' view technology, RHTML (and indeed many other view technologies). However, it should be noted that scriptlets are available more to align the syntax with JSP and, in practice, are discouraged in favor of GSP tags, which you will see in the section "Built-in Grails Tags."

While the previous syntax allows arbitrary code to be inserted between the opening and closing declarations, it doesn't actually explicitly output anything when inside the scriptlet block. In other words, as with the previous example, you have to use a closing %> bracket to close the scriptlet expression in order to define what you want repeated three times. You can, however, use the out attribute mentioned earlier to output to the response:

```
<% out << "print me!" %>
```

The previous code will print the text print me! to the response using the out attribute. As you can imagine, having all of these out << statements all over the place can get a little tedious, so GSP supports another syntax inherited from JSP through the <%=...%> statement (note the equals sign directly after the opening declaration). Essentially, the following example is equivalent to what you saw in the previous code:

```
<%="print me!" %>
```

Here the = sign after the opening scriptlet bracket ensures that the result of whatever follows is printed to response. The response in general is a mix of markup and code that results in some text being sent to the browser or client. Now that you've seen GSP's similarities with JSP let's look at a feature you won't find in JSP: embedded GStrings.

GSP as GStrings

In recent times, since the introduction of JSTL, the usage of scriptlets and declarations such as those in the previous section has been rather looked down on. Instead, there is an expression language in JSP, which you can use in combination with the <c:out> standard tag to output values, as shown in Listing 8-5.

Listing 8-5. *JSP c:out Tag*

```
<%-- Output the bookmark title --%>
<p><c:out value="${bookmark.title}" /></p>
```

■**Tip** The previous JSP example uses the syntax <%--...--%> for comments that should not be present in the rendered response. These comments are also supported in GSP using exactly the same syntax.

In addition to the previous rather verbose tag, you would also need to import the tag library, which contains the <c:out> tag using a page directive at the top of the JSP. All this amounts to a lot of effort just to use a tag that lets you render values to the response. Luckily, with GSP it is a little bit simpler due to support for embedded GString values:

```
<p>${bookmark.title}</p>
```

A GSP, if you think about it, is essentially one big GString, thus allowing the same ${...} expressions nested within them as found in JSP. The expressions allowed within the GStrings are not, thankfully, limited to simply referencing properties. The full capability Groovy offers in terms of navigating object graphs is at your fingertips, which often becomes useful when iterating, as you will see in the next section.

Built-in Grails Tags

GSP has a number of built-in tags for performing basic operations such as looping, switching, and logical if statements. In general, tags are preferable to embedding scriptlets since they promote a cleaner separation of concerns and allow the creation of well-formed markup.

Each GSP tag requires the prefix g: before the tag name so that it is recognized as being a GSP tag. Unlike JSP, which requires directives to import tag libraries, no additional page directive is needed.

■**Note** At the time of this writing, GSP did not support JSP custom tag libraries. However, this is on the roadmap to make Grails integrate even more seamlessly to existing Java web components.

In the next few sections you'll see the tags that come built-in to Grails. These tags are there by default and require no extra work by the developer.

Setting Variables with Tags

Occasionally it is useful to set the value of a variable or define a new variable within the scope (commonly referred to as the *page context*) of a GSP page. Both use cases can be achieved via the <g:set> tag, which will set or define a variable in the page context regardless of whether it already exists. The <g:set> tag takes two attributes: the var attribute, which defines the name of the variable to set; and a value attribute, which is generally an expression:

```
<g:set var="bookmarkTitle" value="${bookmark.title}" />
```

Note that the <g:set> tag does not support any kind of scope attribute, and variables set with it are by default assumed to be within the page scope (or *binding*). Having said that, you can set a variable in the session scope simply by prefixing session followed by the dot dereference operator in front of the variable name:

```
<g:set var="session.user" value="${user}" />
```

Another fairly basic requirement, along with setting variables, is the ability to condition-ally display information. In the next section, you'll see how this can be achieved.

Logical Tags

As previously mentioned, it is often useful to display information based on a condition. At the most basic level it is useful to have basic programming constructs in the view such as if and else to facilitate this. GSP has the aptly named <g:if>, <g:elseif>, and <g:else> tags that, as with any regular programming construct, are used in conjunction with one another to condi-tionally display output.

The <g:if> and <g:elseif> tags take an attribute called test whose value can be an expression (i.e., statements surrounded by ${..}), as shown in Listing 8-6.

Listing 8-6. *Usage of Logical Blocks*

```
<g:if test="${bookmark?.url ==~ 'https://.+'}">
      Secure Site: <a href="${boomark.url}" target="_blank">${bookmark.title}</a>
</g:if>
<g:elseif test="${bookmark?.url ==~ 'ftp://.+'}">
      FTP Link: <a href="${boomark.url}">${bookmark.title}</a>
</g:elseif>
<g:else>
      Web Link: <a href="${boomark?.url}" target="_blank">${bookmark?.title}</a>
</g:else>
```

An interesting aspect of the previous code is the usage of Groovy's safe dereference operator, `?..` The operator really comes into its own when used in views, as it is often useful to navigate an object graph and only display information if all elements navigated through don't evaluate to `null`. If you look at the views generated during scaffolding, you will observe a lot of this in action. Yet another useful feature of the method is that it allows the optional execution of methods. For example, you may for some reason want the title of the bookmark in uppercase, in which case you would use an expression like the following:

```
${bookmark.title.toUpperCase()}
```

Unfortunately, if either the `bookmark` or the `title` of the `bookmark` in the previous code is `null` a horrid `NullPointerException` will be thrown. To circumvent this, the safe dereference operator comes to the rescue:

```
${bookmark?.title?.toUpperCase()}
```

Here the `toUpperCase` method is *only* executed if it can be reached, otherwise the entire expression evaluates to `null`. This is useful because `null` in GSP results in an empty string being printed to the response.

Following that little diversion, let's get back to the topic of the `<g:if>` tag. It is important to note that if you omit the enclosing `${...}` syntax when writing your expression, the value of the `test` attribute will be a string containing whatever is typed as the value. This can get confusing when testing for Boolean values in your model, because a nonempty string in Groovy evaluates to `true`, meaning that the first `if` block will always evaluate to `true` while the second example will not, as shown in Listing 8-7.

Listing 8-7. *Example of the if Pitfall*

```
<%-- Results in a String whose value is "bookmark.url ==~ 'http://.+'" --%>
<g:if test="bookmark.url ==~ 'http://.+'">
    I will always be displayed
</g:if>

<g:if test="${bookmark.url ==~ 'http://.+'}">
    I'm only displayed if the bookmark starts with http://
</g:if>
```

That's it for now on logical tags, although you will see their usage popping up throughout the book.

Iterative Tags

Iterating over collections of objects is one of the more common tasks when working with any view technology, GSP being no exception. Again, you could use scriptlets to achieve iteration, but why would you when you have GSP tags, which allow for a much cleaner transition between code and markup?

The first tag to be covered is the `<g:each>` tag, which is essentially the tag-equivalent of the Groovy each method and, in fact, simply delegates to this method internally as shown in Listing 8-8.

Listing 8-8. *Iterating with <g:each>*

```
<g:each in="${bookmark.tags?}">
    <span class="tag">${it.name}</span>
</g:each>
```

■Tip The safe dereference operator can also be used at the end of expressions, as in the previous example, which will not iterate if the `tags` property is `null`.

Like its closely related JSTL cousin, the `<g:each>` tag allows you to optionally specify the name of the object within the current iteration. The name, as with closures, defaults to an argument called it as seen in Listing 8-8. When using nested tags, however, it is good practice to name the variable being iterated over, which you can do with the var attribute, as shown in Listing 8-9.

Listing 8-9. *Iterating with <g:each> and a Named Variable*

```
<g:each var="tag" in="${bookmark.tags?}">
    <span class="tag">${tag.name}</span>
</g:each>
```

GSP tags are at their roots just closures; and in Groovy the variable it refers to the default argument of the *innermost* closure. If you use the `<g:each>` tag without declaring a var attribute and try to reference the default it variable within a nested GSP tag, it will result in evaluating it to the *current* innermost tag and not the surrounding `<g:each>` tag. By naming the variable used by `<g:each>` using the var attribute, you circumvent any conflicts such as this. If you remember that GSP tags are closures, you will have no issue at all adapting to the mindset.

Moving on, the next iterative tag GSP provides is the `<g:while>` tag that behaves like the traditional while loop by waiting for the expression specified within the test attribute to evaluate to false. As with any while loop, the condition should always end up evaluating to false at some point, otherwise you will end up in a never-ending loop, as shown in Listing 8-10.

Listing 8-10. *The <g:while> Tag*

```
<g:set var="i" expr="${bookmark.tags?.size()}" />
<g:while test="${i > 0}">
    <g:set var="i" expr="${i-1}" />
</g:while>
```

Here you get the total number of tags from the bookmark and store them in the variable i. You then start a <g:while> loop that will decrement the i variable on each iteration. The loop will continue until i reaches zero. The loop is equivalent to the following Groovy code:

```
while(i > 0) i-1
```

Using <g:each> and <g:while> are not the only way to loop over a collection. In the next section you'll see constructs that provide the powerful combination of filtering and iteration.

Filtering and Iteration

With some of the new methods that accept closures such as collect, findAll, and grep in Groovy that provide the powerful ability to filter and search collections, it would seem a shame if that power was not extended into GSP tags. Fear not; there are tag equivalents of these three that allow some pretty powerful filtering capabilities.

The collect Tag

The <g:collect> tag allows you to iterate over and collect properties of objects within a collection. Say for example you want the titles of all bookmarks; this can be achieved simply with <g:collect>, as shown in Listing 8-11.

Listing 8-11. *Using <g:collect> to Collect Values*

```
<ol>
    <g:collect in="${bookmarks}" expr="${it.title}">
            <li>${it}</li>
    </g:collect>
</ol>
```

In the previous example an HTML list of bookmark titles is created by passing a collection of bookmarks to the in attribute via the ${...} syntax. The second attribute, the expr attribute, contains an expression that is used to specify what should be collected (in this case the title property). Again you use the default it argument within the expression the same way you would in a closure. In fact, the previous code is equivalent to the scriptlet code in Listing 8-12.

Listing 8-12. *Equivalent Scriptlet Using a Closure*

```
<ol>
    <% bookmarks.collect{ it.title }.each { %>
            <li>${it}</li>
    <%}%>
</ol>
```

As you can see, the expression equates to what is found within the curly brackets of the `collect` closure. Whatever you can place in there can also be placed inside the `expr` attribute.

This, of course, could also be achieved with a GPath expression. If you recall what you learned about GPath so far, if you reference the `title` property and use the dereference operator on a *list* of bookmarks, it will produce a list of titles, as shown in Listing 8-13.

Listing 8-13. *Using GPath to Iterate Over Bookmark Titles*

```
<ol>
    <g:each in="${bookmarks.title}" >
            <li>${it}</li>
    </g:each>
</ol>
```

The `<g:collect>` tag does, however, give you another option and allows the logic within the `expr` attribute to be in your control.

The findAll Tag

Collecting properties from a collection via the object graph is handy, but sometimes you want to only iterate over values that meet a certain criteria. This is often achieved by iterating over all elements and having nested `if` statements; however, using `<g:findAll>`, as shown in Listing 8-14, is far more elegant.

Listing 8-14. *Using <g:findAll> to Locate Specific Elements*

```
<g:findAll in="${bookmarks}" expr="${it.tags?.name.contains('grails')}">
        <p>
            <a href="${it.url}">${it.title}</a>
        </p>
</g:findAll>
```

This is an interesting example, as it is another demonstration of the power of GPath, Groovy's expression language. The expression in bold references the default argument `it`, which is the current `Bookmark` instance being iterated over, and then uses GPath to retrieve a collection of all of the names of the tags.

The `tags` property itself is in fact a collection, too (a `java.util.Set` to be specific), and does not have a `name` property; but GPath magically recognizes that the reference to the `name` property is an attempt to retrieve a collection of `name` properties from the contained elements within the `tags` property.

Since the result is a collection, you can invoke the regular JDK `contains` method to look up all bookmarks that are tagged with the name `grails`. The result is far more readable than a bunch of nested `if` statements and is another case where you can see how a Groovy view technology such as GSP just makes a remarkable amount of sense.

Remember the power of the Groovy `switch` statement from Chapter 2? In the next section you'll see how to take advantage of its filtering capabilities with the `<g:grep>` tag.

The grep Tag

Yes, the fun most certainly hasn't ended with `<g:findAll>`, as there are yet more options available to you via the `<g:grep>` tag. The `<g:grep>` tag, again, is the cousin of the Groovy grep method, and like the two you've seen so far, it takes an `in` attribute combined with a `filter` attribute.

So what does `<g:grep>` do? If you remember in Chapter 2 on Groovy, I discussed how Groovy's `switch` statement is exponentially more useful than Java's, due to the way it allows switching between any object that implements the `isCase()` method. Well, grep also uses this feature and will take a collection and apply a given expression by invoking each object's `isCase()` method and thus filter the results.

Remember that Groovy provides mainly default implementations of `isCase()` for most common types, including things such as regular expressions shown in Listing 8-15.

Listing 8-15. *Powerful Filtering with <g:grep>*

```
<!-- Finds all tag names that match groovy, grails or agile -->
<g:grep in="${bookmarks.tags.name}" filter="${~/groovy|grails|agile/}">
    <p>${it}</p>
</g:grep>

<!-- Finds all bookmark instances that are of type Blog -->
Blogs:
<g:grep in="${bookmarks}" filter="${Blog}">
    <p>
        <a href="${it.url}">${it.title}</a>
    </p>
</g:grep>
```

As you can imagine, there are many possible usages of `<g:grep>`, and it can be an incredibly powerful way to filter and iterate over collections of objects. You could even extend the capability of `<g:grep>` further by implementing `isCase()` for your objects. In fact, let's do that right now by implementing `isCase()` so that you can filter bookmarks by tag name, as shown in Listing 8-16.

Listing 8-16. *Implementing isCase() to Provide Filtering*

```
class Bookmark {
    ...
    boolean isCase(value) {
        return tags?.name.contains(value) ? true : false
    }
}
```

What I have done here is add logic that checks whether the value passed by `isCase()` is one of the tag names assigned to the `Bookmark` instance and whether it is returned `true`. Now you can filter `Bookmark` instances by tag name with `<g:grep>`, as shown in Listing 8-17.

Listing 8-17. *Filtering by Tag Name with <g:grep>*

```
<!-- Get all the bookmarks tagged with a tag called "grails" -->
<g:grep in="${bookmarks}" filter="grails">
        <p>
            <a href="${it.url}">${it.title}</a>
        </p>
</g:grep>
```

You've seen quite a few options to perform different kinds of logical statements and itera-tion. Controlling the logical flow of a view is not, however, the only task you have when writing the view. One common activity is linking between controllers and actions, which you will look at next; but before that there is something important to note. This marks the end of the built-in tags. The tags seen so far are internally handled and optimized by GSP. The next section shifts focus to Grails dynamic tags and how they differ from the built-in tags.

Grails Dynamic Tags

Dynamic tags in Grails are those provided through classes called *tag libraries*, which can be found within the `grails-app/taglib` directory of any Grails project. Grails provides a number of tag libraries out of the box that you will see in the next few sections; then you will explore how to create your own tag libraries.

First, you need to understand what makes dynamic tags different from other tags besides the fact that they are provided by these libraries. Fundamentally, they can be used the same way as any other tag. For example, the `<g:link>` tag, which you'll see more of next, can be used like the built-in tags you saw previously, without requiring any import directive.

More interestingly, dynamic tags can also be invoked as methods from scriptlets and GString expressions. Why is this useful? To maintain a clean syntax it is best to avoid nesting tags within tag attributes. In JSP you often see code like that shown in Listing 8-18 that becomes difficult to read and is not well-formed markup.

Listing 8-18. *Unattractive JSP Example*

```
<a href="<c:out value="${application.contextPath}" />/show.jsp">A dynamic link</a>
```

Clearly, due to GSP's rather JSP-like nature, this problem could have been inherited if it was not for the dynamic nature of Groovy. So how would you invoke a GSP tag as a method call? Observe the example in Listing 8-19.

Listing 8-19. *An Example of a GSP Tag as a Method Call*

```
<!-- With a regular tag -->
<a href="<g:createLink action="list" />">A dynamic link</a>

<!-- As a method call -->
<a href="${createLink(action:'list')}">A dynamic link</a>
```

The two previous examples produce the same result. They call a tag called `createLink`, which creates a link to the `list` action. The second example is notably cleaner and produces well-formed markup. In addition, the body of the tag can be provided as the last argument to the method call.

An example of this is shown in action in the `create` and `edit` views generated in Chapter 5 on scaffolding. As part of form validation, these views highlight the problematic field by surrounding the offender with a red box. This is achieved through the `hasErrors` tags that will evaluate if a particular bean field has any validation errors and set a CSS class, the name of which is the last argument on the surrounding `div` element, if the field does contain errors, as shown in Listing 8-20.

Listing 8-20. *Field Validation Example*

```
<div class="${hasErrors(bean:bookmark,field:'title','errors')}">
    ...
</div>
```

These are just a few examples; and as you'll see in a moment, you can create your own tags that can be invoked in exactly the same manner. First, however, let's take a tour through the tags that are already available to you, starting with linking.

Linking Tags

With all these controllers and actions that end up being created it may become a little bit of a challenge to remember the URL patterns to link to them. Also, the context path of your application could change, depending which environment you deploy to. So how can you make sure you are always linking to the write place in a consistent manner? Well, luckily Grails provides a number of tags to handle linking in an elegant way, the first of which is the aptly named `<g:link>` tag.

The link Tag

The `<g:link>` tag will essentially create a simple HTML anchor tag based on the supplied attributes, which include the following:

- `controller`: The controller name to link to

- `action`: The action name to link to

- `id`: The identifier to append to the end of the URI

- `params`: Any parameters to pass as a map

One of either the `controller` attribute or the `action` attribute is required. If the `controller` attribute but no `action` attribute is specified, the tag will link to the default action of the controller. If, on the other hand, an `action` attribute but no `controller` attribute is specified, the *currently executing* controller will be linked to.

Beyond the previous attributes, the `<g:link>` tag also supports all attributes that the regular HTML anchor tag supports. These anchor tags can be added as required.

■**Tip** Since you've entered the world of GSP dynamic tags, you may want to take a look at the code that handles the `<g:link>` tag by checking out the source inside the `grails-app/taglib/ApplicationTagLib.groovy` class.

So on to some examples. The usage of `<g:link>` is actually pretty trivial and intuitive, and, of course, the values of the attributes could just as well be expressions of the ${...} kind if dynamic linking is required, as shown in Listing 8-21.

Listing 8-21. *Basic Linking with <g:link>*

```
<g:link controller="bookmark" action="list">List Bookmarks</g:link>
<g:link action="show" id="1">Show bookmark with id 1</g:link>
```

Of interest may be the `params` attribute, which takes a map of request parameters to pass via the link. In fact, the current request parameters can even be passed from one action to the other by using this attribute in combination with the `params` object, which if you recall is an instance of `java.util.Map`, as shown in Listing 8-22.

Listing 8-22. *Using Parameters with <g:link>*

```
<g:link controller="bookmark"
        action="list"
        params="[max:10,order:'title']">Show first ten ordered by Title</g:link>

<g:link action="create"
        params="${params}">Pass parameters from this action to next</g:link>
```

The first example uses the `params` attribute in conjunction with a map of parameters and provides your first exposure to another feature of GSP tags: attributes can be specified as maps with the `[key:value]` syntax. This allows for composite attribute values and minimizes the need for messy nested tags.

Finally, the second example demonstrates what was mentioned previously. Instead of specifying a map explicitly, you provide a reference to the `params` object via the ${...} expression syntax, which then allows passing parameters from the current page to the linked page. Next you'll see how to create links to other resources.

The createLink and createLinkTo Tags

The `<g:createLink>` tag has already been seen in action and probably needs less of an introduction. Simply put, if it's not clear from the examples, `<g:createLink>` takes the same arguments as the `<g:link>` tag, except it produces just the textual link and not an HTML anchor tag. In fact, the `<g:link>` tag actually delegates to `<g:createLink>` when creating its `href` attribute.

So what is this useful for? You could use it within a regular anchor tag, or possibly as a value for a JavaScript variable, as shown in Listing 8-23.

Listing 8-23. *Examples of createLink*

```
<a href="${createLink(action:'list')}">List Bookmarks</a>
<script type="text/javascript">
    var listBookmarksLink = "${createLink(action:'list')}";
</script>
```

Another tag, similar in both name and usage to `<g:createLink>`, is the `<g:createLinkTo>` tag, which allows convenient linking to resources within the web application's context path. This tag is most commonly used for linking to images and style sheets and again can be seen in action in the views generated by scaffolding:

```
<link rel="stylesheet" href="${createLinkTo(dir:'css',file:'main.css')}"></link>
```

As is apparent from the previous examples and Listing 8-23, both tags tend to be used via method calls as opposed to markup, as the values produced by them are usually nested within attributes of other tags. Now that linking has been covered, another common activity is to create forms so that users can enter data to be captured by server-side code. In the following section you'll see how Grails makes this easier.

Creating Forms and Fields

A form is most commonly a collection of fields that a user populates with data, although occasionally you find forms that consist entirely of hidden fields and no user interaction whatsoever. Nevertheless, how this is achieved depends on the type of field; in other words the user interacts differently depending on whether it is a text field, a drop-down select, or a radio button.

Clearly certain fields map nicely onto existing Java (and hence Groovy) types. Check boxes are great for Boolean values, text fields for strings, and selects are good when you have strings that can only be contained within a certain list of values (such as enums in Java 5).

To this end, most Java web frameworks provide some mechanism to make form elements (or fields) interoperate smoothly with Java types, Grails being no different. The benefit Grails and GSP have, however, is the advanced syntactic features available in Groovy in combination with dynamic tags.

Before you get too deeply involved in looking at the different kinds of fields, let's take care of the basics by looking at how Grails helps in defining forms.

The form Tag

Building on what you have seen in linking, the first tag you are going to look at is the `<g:form>` tag which is equivalent to the standard HTML `<form>` tag except it allows the same arguments as those seen with the `<g:link>` tag to allow easy submission to a specific controller and/or action as shown in Listing 8-24.

Listing 8-24. *An Example form Tag*

```
<g:form controller="bookmark" action="save">
    ...
</g:form>
```

By default the `<g:form>` tag uses the POST method for form submissions, meaning the previous example is roughly equivalent to the HTML definition (minus the closing tag):

```
<form action="/bookmarks/bookmark/save" method="POST">
    ...
</form>
```

As an alternative to Listing 8-24, the `<g:form>` tag can also be defined using a single url attribute that uses the map syntax to define the controller and action combination, as shown in Listing 8-25.

Listing 8-25. *A <g:form> Tag with url Attribute*

```
<g:form url="[controller:'bookmark', action:'save']">
    ...
</g:form>
```

Of course a form is of little use without some fields, the first of which to be discussed is the text field. In HTML most fields are handled by the `<input>` tag, which has a type attribute to change its behavior and appearance. The downside of this approach is that it is not clear from simply looking at the tag as to what its purpose is.

Grails provides a number of wrapper tags that encapsulate the different types of HTML inputs into more meaningful tags.

The textField Tag

First up is the `<g:textField>` tag that, unsurprisingly, handles entry of textual values. The `<g:textField>` tag takes a name attribute, representing the name of the parameter to send as part of the form submission, along with the associated value attribute, as shown in Listing 8-26.

Listing 8-26. *Example <g:textField> Usage*

```
<g:form controller="bookmark" action="save">
    <g:textField name="title" value="${bookmark?.title}" />
    ...
</g:form>
```

The previous `<g:textField>` definition will result in an HTML input such as the following:

```
<input type="text" name="title" value="A Bookmark's Title" />
```

Check Boxes and Radio Buttons

Check boxes are often used as a representation of Boolean values from a domain model. Unfortunately, many frameworks place a lot of burden onto the developer to both render check boxes in their correct state and to handle the server side processing as to whether the check boxes are checked or not.

Grails, on the other hand, provides a `<g:checkBox>` tag that accepts a Boolean `value` attribute and will render the tag in its correct state. In addition, Grails transparently handles check box processing through its automatic type conversion and data binding facility (discussed in Chapter 7 on controllers), as shown in Listing 8-27.

Listing 8-27. *Example <g:checkBox> Tag*

```
<g:checkBox name="aBooleanValue" value="${true}" />
```

Closely related to check boxes are *radio buttons*, which are used in groups, as they represent a one-from-many interaction. For example, two radio buttons must each be given the same name to be placed in the same group, and only one button can be selected at any one time.

Grails provides a `<g:radio>` tag that provides a convenient way to define radio buttons and also to calculate which one has been checked.

In Listing 8-28, two radio buttons are defined in the same group. The one that has been checked is calculated using the hypothetical `someValue` variable.

Listing 8-28. *Example <g:radio> Tags*

```
<p>
    <g:radio name="myGroup" value="1" checked="${someValue == 1}" /> Radio 1
</p>
<p>
    <g:radio name="myGroup value="2" checked="${someValue == 2}" /> Radio 2
</p>
```

Handling Lists of Values

When dealing with enumerated values (those that can only be of a specific set of values) it is often useful to constrain what the user can enter by presenting an HTML select box as opposed to a free text entry field.

To make the creation of selects much simpler, Grails provides a `<g:select>` tag, which accepts a list or range of values via a `from` attribute. The currently selected value can be set with the `value` attribute.

The example in Listing 8-29 creates two selects to modify the `rating` and `category` properties added to the `Bookmark` object in Chapter 5 on scaffolding.

Listing 8-29. *Example <g:select> Usages*

```
<g:select name="rating" from="${1..10}" value="${bookmark.rating}" />
<g:select name="category" from="${['blog', 'article', 'general', 'news']}"
          value="${bookmark.category}" />
```

The following is the resulting HTML select, given a bookmark with a rating of 2 and a category of blog:

```
<select name="rating">
    <option value="1">1</option>
    <option value="2" selected="selected">2</option>
    <option value="3">3</option>
    <option value="4">4</option>
    <option value="5">5</option>
   <option value="6">6</option>
   <option value="7">7</option>
   <option value="8">8</option>
   <option value="9">9</option>
   <option value="10">10</option>
</select>
<select name="category">
   <option value="blog" selected="selected">blog</option>
   <option value="article">article</option>
   <option value="general">general</option>
   <option value="news">news</option>
</select>
```

Clearly, just going by the two examples, using the `<g:select>` tag can save you writing a few lines of code. Its usefulness extends beyond this, thanks to two additional attributes that allow `<g:select>` to be used in combination with object graphs and relationships.

The first is the `optionKey` attribute, which allows customization of the value attribute within each option tag of an HTML select. This may seem a little odd that an `optionKey` attribute customizes an attribute called `value`, but if you think of each `<option>` element as a key/value pair, it begins to make sense. The `optionValue` attribute, on the other hand, allows customization of the value that appears within the body of each option tag.

Using these two in combination can, for example, allow you to create a select from a list of domain object instances as shown in Listing 8-30.

Listing 8-30. *Using <g:select> on a List of Domain Objects*

```
<g:select name="bookmark.id" from="${Bookmark.list()}"
                optionKey="id" optionValue="title"/>
```

The previous example takes a list of bookmarks and creates an HTML select where the `value` attribute within the option tag is the `id` of the `Bookmark`, and the value within the body of each option is the `title` property of each `Bookmark`. The result will resemble something like the following:

```
<select name="bookmark.id">
    <option value="1">Grails</option>
    ...
</select>
```

In addition to the general purpose `<g:select>` tag, Grails provides a few others that may come in handy. The `<g:currencySelect>`, `<g:localeSelect>`, and `<g:timeZoneSelect>` provide convenience tags for working with `java.util.Currency`, `java.util.Locale`, and `java.util.TimeZone` instances respectively.

Unlike the `<g:select>` tag, each of these takes only two attributes: a name attribute for the name of the select, and a value attribute, which takes an instance of one of the aforementioned classes, as shown in Listing 8-31.

Listing 8-31. *Currency, Locale, and Time Zone Selects*

```
<%-- Sets the currency to the currency of the Locale within the request --%>
<g:currencySelect
              name="myCurrency"
              value="${ Currency.getInstance(request.getLocale()) }" />

<%-- Sets the locale to the locale of the request --%>
<g:localeSelect name="myLocale" value="${ request.getLocale() }" />

<%-- Sets value to default time zone --%>
<g:timeZoneSelect name="myTimeZone" value="${ TimeZone.getDefault() }" />
```

As we're on the topic of the `java.util` package, there is also a specialized tag to handle one of the more commonly used objects within it: `java.util.Date`.

Working with Dates

Dates can be represented in a number of ways, from drop-down selects to advanced JavaScript calendars. One of the more common ways, due to its nonreliance on JavaScript, is to use a combination of HTML select boxes to specify the date or time, with each select representing a unit of time: year, month, day, minute, hour, and second.

Grails provides support for creating such fields (and automatically performing type conversion onto date instances) using the `<g:datePicker>` tag, as shown in Listing 8-32.

Listing 8-32. *A Basic Date Picker*

```
<g:datePicker name="myDate" value="${new Date()}" />
```

At its most basic level the `<g:datePicker>` tag takes a name attribute and a value attribute as a `java.util.Date` instance. In the previous example it creates a `<g:datePicker>` for the current time, which consists of selects for the year, month, day, minute, hour, *and* second.

Clearly it is not always useful to have that level of precision, so the `<g:datePicker>` tag provides the aptly named precision attribute for changing how many selects it renders. For example, to render only the year, month, and day selects, the following will suffice:

```
<g:datePicker name="myDate" value="${new Date()}" precision="day" />
```

All in all, Grails provides quite a few tools in your toolbox for simplifying the creation of forms. Given that forms allow users to enter data, often in a free-form fashion, implementing form handling is often one of the most challenging and error-prone activities in web application development.

To ensure data integrity, form validation is necessary and can be achieved on the client side using JavaScript. However, client-side validation should only ever be seen as a usability enhancement and not a replacement for server-side validation. Luckily, Grails provides solid support for performing validation with specialized validation and error-handling tags.

Validation and Error Handling

Having learned how to apply constraints to the domain model in Chapter 4, clearly it becomes useful at some point to display validation errors in the view when they occur. Of course, you could use scriptlets and iterate over the errors of a domain object and output them explicitly, but that's an awful lot of work that Grails can do for you. Just to recap on how validation works, take a look at the state diagram shown in Figure 8-1.

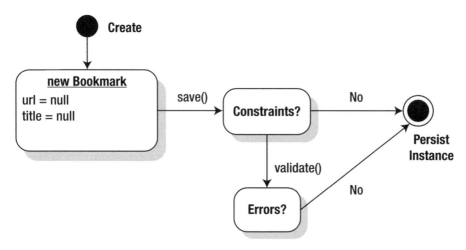

Figure 8-1. *Validation state diagram*

When an instance is persisted to the database using the save() method, validation is automatically called first, and if any validation errors occur, the object is not persisted. The save action of the BookmarkController generated by scaffolding demonstrates this flow, as shown in Listing 8-33.

Listing 8-33. *Example of Validation in Action*

```
if(bookmark.save()) {
    redirect(action:show,id:bookmark.id)
}
else {
    render(view:'create',model:[bookmark:bookmark])
}
```

The call to the render method within the else block, which is invoked if validation fails, is what you need to pay attention to, as this passes the Bookmark instance in the model of the create view. Since validation has failed, the instance has a number of errors attached to it. However, you need some way of displaying these errors, which is where Grails tags once again come to the rescue.

The hasErrors Tag

It is often useful to conditionally display information depending on whether there is an error. To this end, Grails provides a `<g:hasErrors>` tag which supports the following attributes:

- `bean`: A bean instance to inspect for errors

- `field`: The name of the field to check for errors

- `model`: An alternative to specifying a bean (an entire model [map] can be checked)

If you recall, you have already seen the `<g:hasErrors>` tag used as a method, but it is also equally applicable as a tag. Interestingly, if no attributes are specified whatsoever, the tag will scan the entire request scope for beans and check each object found for errors. Since the `<g:hasErrors>` tag is often used in conjunction with `<g:eachError>`, we'll look at that next, followed by an example.

The eachError Tag

If a bean instance does have errors, it is useful to iterate over them and display each in turn. This can be done simply with the `<g:eachError>` tag, which takes identical attributes to those expected by the `<g:hasErrors>` tag.

Building on the example controller code you saw in Listing 8-33, a `Bookmark` instance (a bean) would have been passed as the model. Clearly, if you've gotten this far, the bean in question must have some errors; but just to be sure you'll use `<g:hasErrors>` followed by `<g:eachError>` to display the relevant message, as shown in Listing 8-34.

Listing 8-34. *Displaying Errors*

```
<g:hasErrors bean="${bookmark}">
    <ul class="errors">
        <g:eachError bean="${bookmark}">
            <li>${it.defaultMessage}</li>
        </g:eachError>
    </ul>
</g:hasErrors>
```

In this instance, `<g:hasErrors>` checks if there are any errors in the first place, and if there are creates an HTML list. These errors are then iterated over via the `<g:eachError>` tag, which creates the list bullets using the *default message*. The default messages for validation errors can be found in the `grails-app/i18n/message.properties` message bundle.

If a list is all that is required, Grails makes it even easier to display errors via the `<g:renderErrors>` tag, which encapsulates everything you've just seen. Essentially, it takes the same arguments as the `<g:eachError>` tag, as well as an optional as attribute, which allows you to specify what to render the errors as. As of this writing, rendering as a list was all that was implemented; however, given the extensibility of Grails tags (which you will see when developing your own), there are sure to be more options in the future.

Nevertheless, to do what you saw in Listing 8-34 requires a single line of markup:

```
<g:renderErrors bean="${bookmark}" as="list" />
```

As noted previously, the examples seen so far use the *default message*. Clearly, the default message is not always what is desired, and it is often useful to provide specific messages for each property within a domain class. This is where the `<g:message>` tag comes into play with Grails' support for internationalization (i18n).

Internationalization Support

This whole section is dedicated to a single tag: `<g:message>`. Support for internationalization is often an afterthought in many frameworks, but thanks to Grails' solid foundation on Spring MVC, this is not the case. Grails uses Spring's underlying infrastructure to automatically detect the locale of the incoming request headers. This in turn allows Grails to pick up an appropriate message bundle based on this locale.

■Note A *locale* is an instance of `java.util.Locale`, and it represents a geographical, political, or cultural region. Locales are constructed from a language, a country, and a possible variant. For example, in England the locale is en_GB, where en is for *English* and GB is for *Great Britain*.

Message bundles are essentially just Java properties files containing key/value pairs. The default message bundle is found in the `grails-app/i18n/messages.properties` file. To create locale-specific message bundles that are loaded instead of the default when a specific locale is found in the request, you need to create a new message bundle with an underscore followed by the locale appended on the end.

For example, a message bundle for Spanish would need to be named `grails-app/i18n/messages_es.properties`, or a specific message bundle containing U.S. English spellings should be called `grails-app/i18n/messages_en_US.properties`. Once you have the various bundles required in place, messages can be read from them using the `<g:message>` tag.

The message Tag

Building on what you have already seen, Listing 8-35 shows how you add a welcome message to the default message bundle.

Listing 8-35. *grails-app/i18n/messages.properties*

```
welcome.message=Welcome to your Bookmarks!
```

You then add another welcome message to the Spanish bundle (called `grails-app/i18n/messages_es.properties`) with exactly the same code but with a different message, as shown in Listing 8-36.

Listing 8-36. *grails-app/i18n/messages_es.properties*

```
welcome.message=Bienvenido a sus Bookmarks!
```

The `<g:message>` tag itself is painfully simple. It takes one attribute—the `code` attribute—which is the name of the message code (or *key*) in a message bundle:

```
<g:message code="welcome.message" />
```

All the intricacies of reading the locale, loading the appropriate bundle, and retrieving the message are handled for you. All you have to remember is to populate the message bundle and use the `<g:message>` tag.

■**Tip** Remember, if no tag is found for a particular locale-specific bundle (such as the Spanish one), it will automatically look in the default message bundle.

We've covered quite a bit of the core Grails tag library and you are probably ready to plunge headfirst into creating your own views. Before you do, one important aspect when creating views is to be able to reuse them, which is exactly what you will be looking at next.

Using Layouts and Templates

There have been several techniques devised to maximize view reuse. The Gang of Four (Erich Gamma, Richard Helm, Ralph Johnson, and John Vlissides), however, first described one of the best ones—the decorator pattern—in *Design Patterns: Elements of Reusable Object-Oriented Software.*

You may be wondering why the reference to an object-oriented software design pattern when you're working with markup such as GSP. Well, if you think about creating views for a moment, it is often the case that the problem space, be it a form, a table, or whatever, is relatively small and simple, while the markup that renders the layout of the page can be large and unwieldy.

So what you want is something that takes your simple form or simple table and transforms it into something more complicated (a site with layout, navigation controls, etc.), thus allowing you to focus purely on the problem space. In other words, what you want is a decorator.

The diagram in Figure 8-2 serves as an example of this. The large section in the middle, a list of bookmarks, is the problem space being addressed by the page, while the shaded areas tackle a typical layout scenario with a header, a footer, and left navigation.

Clearly you don't want to have to repeat the shaded areas on each page, so you could separate them out into includes, for example. However, includes have their own issues, in that the developer still has to remember to place them in the view that is being developed and it is often a challenge to truly abstract the layout from the view.

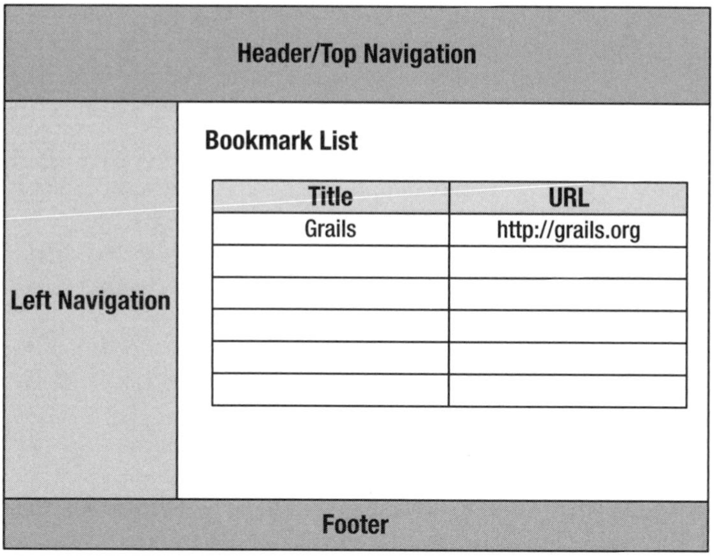

Figure 8-2. *Typical layout example*

This is where the strength of the decorator patterns becomes apparent, and Grails takes advantage of this by leveraging SiteMesh (http://www.opensymphony.com/sitemesh), one of the most popular and robust implementations of the decorator pattern.

In general, there are only a few areas of the page being developed that are interesting: the head tag with all the meta information, the script tags, and the attributes and content of the body tag.

SiteMesh makes all of this information available to the decorator (the page performing the layout), and Grails provides flexible ways to map decorators onto pages with the page needing little or no information about the decorator itself.

An Example Layout

Now that you've had a look at the concept of decorators, let's take a look at an example layout that will perform decoration on a page. Listing 8-37 demonstrates the layout that is being used currently by the bookmarks application.

Listing 8-37. *An Example Layout*

```
1 <html>
2    <head>
3        <title><g:layoutTitle default="Grails" /></title>
4        <link rel="stylesheet" href="${createLinkTo(dir:'css',file:'main.css')}" />
5        <g:layoutHead />
6    </head>
7    <body onload="${pageProperty(name:'body.onload')}">
8        <div class="logo">
10           <img src="${createLinkTo(dir:'images',file:'grails_logo.jpg')}"
```

```
11                        alt="Grails" />
12          </div>
13          <g:layoutBody />
14      </body>
15 </html>
```

The important parts are shown in bold, with this example demonstrating usages of all of the key tags used when creating a layout.

On line three there is the `<g:layoutTitle>` tag, which will place the title of the decorated page into the title tag; otherwise, if there isn't one, it will default to Grails. Figure 8-2 shows that the value placed in the HTML title tag would be Bookmark List.

Line 5 shows the extremely simple `<g:layoutHead>` tag that merely outputs the remaining contents of the `<head>` tag of the decorated page. This ensures that any `<script>` tags, `<style>` tags, or whatever else is included in the finally rendered page is added here.

Next, the `<g:pageProperty>` tag shown in Line 7 is able to read certain properties from the decorated page. In this case, it is used in the method call style. This tag has multiple applications. In the example, it's being used to read the `onload` attribute on the body tag, but you could use it to conditionally display information on the page based on the `meta` attributes on the target page. The following page attributes are available via this tag:

- `html`: All attributes of the `<html>` tag are converted to properties.

- `title`: The contents of the `<title>` tag are added as a property.

- `meta`: Each `<meta>` tag is available via a `meta` namespace. Each attribute is prefixed with `meta` followed by a dot and then the `name` attribute of the `<meta>` tag. The `content` attribute will be returned as the value when referencing a `meta` attribute. An example of this in action is shown in Listing 8-38.

- `body`: The attributes of the `<body>` tag are added as properties prefixed with `body`.

You could augment the previous layout with additional information read from meta tags as shown in Listing 8-38.

Listing 8-38. *Example of Meta Tag Usage*

```
...
<div class="description"><g:pageProperty name="meta.description" /></div>
<g:layoutBody />
<div class="copyright">Copyright 2006 <g:pageProperty name="meta.author" /></div>
...
```

Listing 8-38 reads description and copyright information via the meta tags contained within the decorated page. Returning to the original example in Listing 8-37, there is one last tag that has not been covered. In Line 13, the `<g:layoutBody>` is a very simple tag whose sole purpose is to output the body of the decorated page. With that, you are now ready to start creating some layouts. But hold on. One question does still remain: How do you apply this layout to your views?

Layout-by-Convention

The first point to note, regardless of the mechanism, is that all layouts reside either directly within the `grails-app/views/layouts` directory or within a subdirectory of that directory. This is convenient, as you'll always know where to find them.

Back to applying layouts though—the first and arguably most flexible way to use layouts is using layout-by-convention. The rules for layout-by-convention are as follows:

- If the target page has a meta tag (see the next section "Layout with Meta Tags"), the layout specified by the meta tag will be applied before all others.

- If you create a layout GSP with the same name as a controller, all views delegated to that controller will have this layout-by-convention and will have precedence over the main layout. For example, the `BookmarkController` could have a layout called `grails-app/layouts/bookmark.gsp`.

- If you create a layout within a directory with the same name as a controller that has the same name as one of the actions within a controller, this layout will be used by convention and will take precedence over the previously described controller-scoped layout. For example, the `list` action within the `BookmarkController` would have a layout called `grails-app/layouts/bookmark/list.gsp`.

In most cases, simply using the layout defined within a meta tag will be sufficient, but the mechanism discussed in this chapter does allow you to have more fine-grained control over which layouts are applied to which views or controllers.

Layout with Meta Tags

As an alternative to layout-by-convention, when you require even more fine-grained control you can use an HTML meta tag to specify which layout to be applied. This approach can potentially be more dynamic than the convention approach, as you could specify the value of the meta tag at run time via the controller's model.

As an example, by placing the meta tag within the `<head>` tag of your view, as per the following example, it will apply a layout called `grails-app/views/layouts/myLayout.gsp` to the view:

```
<meta name="layout" content="myLayout" />
```

Whichever approach you take is up to you, but using meta tags adds another string to your bow.

Layouts in Action

Now that you have a grasp of all this layout business, the time is right to start expanding on your bookmarks application by improving the interface and introducing new features. The features to be added are as follows:

- A descriptive title

- A new search bar for searching bookmarks

- A user profile pane

All of these features are to appear on every screen of the bookmarks application. So they are good candidates for being managed by a layout. A screenshot of roughly what you want to achieve is shown in Figure 8-3.

Figure 8-3. *Updated bookmarks application layout*

Since you have already implemented the necessary login and authentication mechanism, the information required to display the previous page is already conveniently located in the session. Revisiting the earlier diagram, however, it may be of use to again understand what is handled by the layout and what the page is responsible for.

The screenshot in Figure 8-4 shows that the nonshaded area is where the actual page functionality resides, and the remaining shaded areas are what the layout is going to be doing.

So what do you need to do to the layout to work these wonders? Opening up the grails-app/views/layouts/main.gsp file, the first thing you add is the text that displays whose bookmarks you're dealing with, as shown in Listing 8-39.

Listing 8-39. *Adding the Title Information*

```
<div class="logo">
    <g:if test="${session.user}">
        <h1>Bookmarks by ${session.user.firstName} ${session.user.lastName}</h1>
    </g:if>
      ...
</div>
```

Figure 8-4. *Screenshot with layout overlay*

Note that you add a check if the user is logged in because this layout is also used by the login and registration screens. Next you add the search bar that will handle searching for bookmarks, as shown in Listing 8-40.

Listing 8-40. *Adding the Search Bar*

```
<g:if test="${session.user}">
    <div class="searchbar">
    <div class="total">
       You have (${Bookmark.countByUser(session.user)}) bookmarks
    </div>
    <div class="search">
      <g:form action="search">
          <g:textField name="q" /> <g:submit value="search" />
      </g:form>
    </div>
     </div>
</g:if>
```

Again, you check for the user in the session; to display the number of bookmarks the user has you use the countBy* dynamic method. The search box is a simple field; the only thing you need to do is implement the search action, as shown in Listing 8-41.

Listing 8-41. *Implementing the Search Action*

```
1 class BookmarkController {
2        ...
3        def search = {
4              def criteria = Bookmark.createCriteria()
5                    def bookmarks
6                    if(params.q && !params.q?.indexOf('%')) {
7                          bookmarks = criteria.list {
8                                or {
9                                      ilike('title',"%${params.q}%")
10                                     ilike('notes',"%${params.q}%")
11                                       tags {
12                          I           like("name", params.q)
13                                       }
14                                }
15                          }
16                    }
17                    render(view:'list', model:[bookmarkList:bookmarks] )
18        }
19 }
```

The search action here uses a criteria instance that queries whether the title of a Bookmark instance, the notes in a Bookmark instance, or any of the Bookmark instance's tags match the search query.

The query utilizes an interesting feature of criteria querying when used with associations. If you recall, the Bookmark class has a tags property, and if you look at the criteria builder syntax on line 11 of Listing 8-41, there is a call to tags with nested criteria within it. What this does is allows you to apply criteria against the tags *association*. Essentially, it is saying that if any Bookmark instances have *associated* tags whose name properties are like the query, they should be included in the results.

Once the results have been retrieved, the render method is used to render the list view again, using the results from the search query. Next, you need to add the Your Profile panel that appears on the right and wrap the body in its own <div> tag, as shown in Listing 8-42.

Listing 8-42. *Adding the Your Profile Panel*

```
<div class="pageContent">
        <g:layoutBody />
</div>
<g:if test="${session.user}">
    <div class="userDetails">
        <h3>Your Profile</h3>
        <p><strong>Login</strong>: ${session.user.login}</p>
        <p><strong>First Name</strong>: ${session.user.firstName}</p>
        <p><strong>Last Name</strong>: ${session.user.lastName}</p>
        <p><strong>Email</strong>: ${session.user.email}</p>
    </div>
</g:if>
```

Finally, if you don't want the new look to appear like a horrific mess, a bit of CSS won't hurt, as shown in Listing 8-43.

Listing 8-43. *Adding Some Style*

```
<style type="text/css">
.searchbar {
     margin-top:10px;
     background-color: lightgrey;
     border:1px solid darkgrey;
     width:97%;
     height:30px;
     padding:5px;
}
.total {
     padding-top:5px;
     float:left;
     color:white;
}
.search {
     float:right;
     color:white;
}
.userDetails {
     position:absolute;
     right:10px;
     top: 180px;
     border:1px solid darkgrey;
     background-color:lightgrey;
     padding:10px;
     width:150px;
}
.pageContent {
     width:80%;
}
.logo h1 {
    float:right;
    margin:30px;
}
</style>
```

It is important to bear in mind that creating layouts does not exclude the use of using includes and breaking the page up into manageable chunks—quite the contrary, in fact. Includes are a perfect complement to layouts, and Grails provides a mechanism to use includes in the form of templates.

■Note Rails users will find the following sections strangely familiar. The major difference is that Rails users generally refer to templates as *partials* (as in a partial page).

Understanding Templates

Templates provide a mechanism to create reusable snippets of markup. In this way they are similar to JSP includes; but as you will see in a moment there is a twist. To help you understand how to create and use templates you're going to make further improvements to the bookmarks application.

Firstly, you're going to greatly simplify the bookmark list, because in reality all your users are going to want to do is click their bookmarks to get to the relevant link. As you are going about tweaking the way bookmarks are listed, you may as well separate how they are rendered into a template. Ideally, you want to achieve something that resembles Figure 8-5.

Figure 8-5. *A simplified bookmark list*

So to bring this more attractive looking list of bookmarks to life, the first thing to do is to create a template. Templates reside in the same directory as the view they are included in. In contrast to regular views, the name of each template starts with an underscore character. This allows you to easily differentiate which files are views and which are templates.

You're going to create the template for displaying bookmarks as discussed previously. To achieve this you create a new GSP called `grails-app/views/bookmarks/_bookmark.gsp`. The contents of this file can be seen in Listing 8-44.

Listing 8-44. *The Bookmark Template*

```
<div id="bookmark">
    <div id="link">
        <a href="${bookmark.url}">${bookmark.title}</a> -
        <g:link action="edit" id="${bookmark.id}">edit</g:link> |
        <g:link action="delete" id="${bookmark.id}"
                    onclick="return confirm('Delete this bookmark?')">delete</g:link>
    </div>
    <div id="notes">
        ${bookmark.notes}
    </div>
</div>
```

So how do you get this snippet to be rendered for each bookmark in the list? Well this is where the <g:render> tag comes in handy. Notice how in the template you reference a variable called bookmark several times? The <g:render> tag allows you to render a template for each item in a collection using a named variable. An example of this in action is shown in Listing 8-45 as you modify the grails-app/views/bookmark/list.gsp file to use your new template instead of creating a table.

Listing 8-45. *Rendering the Template with a Collection*

```
<g:render template="bookmark"
                var="bookmark"
                collection="${bookmarkList}" />
```

Note that when referencing the template via the template attribute, the underscore is omitted. The value of the var attribute, seen in bold, is used by the template as the bookmark reference seen earlier. Essentially, the <g:render> tag will iterate over each element of the collection and use the name bookmark as the name of the current variable being iterated over. It will then pass this variable to the template and output its contents to the view.

Furthermore, being the flexible beast that it is, the <g:render> tag is not just usable with collections. It has another two attributes that may come in handy, the first being the bean attribute, which allows the template to be rendered for a single bean instance:

```
<g:render template="bookmark" var="bookmark" bean="${bookmarkBean}" />
```

Here the same arguments are used, but the template is rendered for the single bean. This could be used, for example, to allow greater control over which bookmarks are displayed or not, as the case may be.

A second alternative is the model attribute, which takes a map instead, but, again, is only used to render a single occurrence of the template. The following example is equivalent to the previous usage of the bean attribute:

```
<g:render template="bookmark" model="[bookmark:bookmarkBean]" />
```

The major difference of course with the model attribute is that you could specify multiple model objects to pass into the template. As a rule of thumb, the collection attribute is useful when used in combination with collections or arrays of objects, while the bean attribute is helpful for rendering a single bean or object reference. The `model` attribute, on the other hand, provides extra flexibility with its ability to deal with multiple named beans.

In this section you explored some basic template usage and you saw how Grails uses a convention-based approach for the name and location of templates. One restriction of this approach, however, is that only views within the same directory can use a template, and sometimes it is handy to be able to share templates across controllers or views. You'll see how Grails makes this possible through shared templates as you explore the next section.

Shared Templates

Occasionally it becomes useful to share templates across controllers and views. Conceptually, what I'm talking about here is the ability to create global templates accessible to all. Grails provides a simple mechanism to do this that involves appending a forward slash character to the start of the template name.

For example, if you were to make the `bookmark` template global, you would need to change references to it as shown in Listing 8-46.

Listing 8-46. *Rendering the Template with a Collection*

```
<g:render template="/bookmark"
                var="bookmark"
                collection="${bookmarkList}" />
```

Note the forward slash in front of the name of the template within the `template` attribute. Once this has been done the `bookmark` template would need to be moved into the root of the views directory. In other words, its new home would be `grails-app/views/_bookmark.gsp`. This doesn't, however, mean that all shared templates need to be stored within the root views directory, as the forward slash can be followed by a relative path. For example, Listing 8-46 could be adjusted as shown in Listing 8-47.

Listing 8-47. *Rendering the Template with a Collection*

```
<g:render template="/shared/bookmark"
                var="bookmark"
                collection="${bookmarkList}" />
```

Here a `/shared/` path is added in front of the template name, which in turn translates to a template located in `grails-app/views/shared/_bookmark.gsp`. This mechanism is useful if you want to get a little more organized about where templates are located.

Note that in all of the examples so far, you have utilized templates via the view. In other words, you have been using the `<g:render>` tag from a GSP to display a template. This, however, is not the only way templates can be used. In the next section you will explore further possibilities that templates offer.

The Render Method Revisited

In Chapter 7 on controllers I went into quite a bit of depth about the `render` method. One bit of functionality that was not discussed, however, relates to templates and their usage from controllers. Now that you understand templates better, it is useful to know that they can be used directly from controller actions.

Why is this useful? Chapter 9 introduces and delves into Ajax technology that involves asynchronously updating page content. Ajax often involves rendering snippets of markup, which is exactly what the render method is useful for (among other things). For example, to render the bookmark template to the response using the render method you could do what is shown in Listing 8-48.

Listing 8-48. *Rendering Templates from Controllers*

```
class BookmarkController {
    ...
    def snippets = {
        render(template:"bookmark",
                var: "bookmark",
                collection:Bookmark.findAllbyUser( session.user ) )
    }
}
```

The snippets action will render the bookmark template for each Bookmark instance to the response. The render method, like the <g:render> tag, also supports the alternative bean and model arguments when working with single bean instances. You'll be exploring the render method and its capabilities further in Chapter 9 on Ajax, for now the previous example serves as a brief introduction to using it in combination with templates.

Since you're looking at the list of bookmarks at the moment, it may be worth brushing on another frequently encountered problem with web applications that deal with large amounts of data. Applications such as these clearly don't want to display every record to the user on a single page, as this could amount to millions of lines and a very long page, besides the obvious performance implications. In the next section, you'll see how to deal with this through pagination.

Paginating Data

Imagine for a moment that you have been using the bookmarks application for a while, happily storing thousands of your favorite sites in it. Clearly, it is going to become tedious for both the poor server and you to have to scroll through all these records if they're all rendered on a single page. The solution is to provide a mechanism that allows the user to move through the bookmarks from page to page using some navigational aid. This process is called *pagination*.

Pagination is a fairly common pattern in web applications and can be seen utilized in all sorts of applications from web mail to search engines. To help you on your way to dealing with this problem, Grails provides a special tag called <g:paginate> that is clever enough to create Previous and Next links plus a breadcrumb trail for you.

■**Tip** If the <g:paginate> tag doesn't render exactly what you want, you could always tweak it to your needs. It can be found in a tag library called `grails-app/taglib/RenderTagLib.groovy`.

At its most basic level the `<g:paginate>` only requires an attribute called `total` that defines the total number of records that it needs to paginate through:

```
<g:paginate total="1200" />
```

What this does is create a set of controls of paginating through 1,200 records for the *current* URI. To translate this into a more concrete example, let's take a look at how you would go about providing pagination of bookmarks.

First off, if you recall from Chapter 7 on controllers, the `list` action in the `BookmarkController` deals with preparing the model (a list of bookmarks) to be displayed in the view. To refresh your memory, the definition of the `list` action is shown in Listing 8-49.

Listing 8-49. *The list Action*

```
def list = {
    [bookmarkList: Bookmark.findAllByUser(session.user, params ) ]
}
```

What is interesting here is how the `params` object is passed as the last argument to the dynamic finder `findAllByUser`. This is significant because the `list` method and all `findAll*` methods can be passed a map that allows you to manipulate the offset and maximum number records to return.

The `offset` is the position of the first element to retrieve relative zero, while the `max` argument is the maximum number of records to retrieve. When used in combination, they allow you to paginate through sets of results. For example, an `offset` of 10 with a `max` of 20 will return bookmarks 10 to 20.

Unlike the `offset` argument, which has a default value of 0, the `max` argument has no default; hence, if you want, say, a maximum of ten results to be returned at any one time, you need to specify this. Since the current `list` action doesn't do this, you need to tweak it slightly to do so, as shown in Listing 8-50.

Listing 8-50. *The Updated list Action*

```
def list = {
    if(!params.max) params.max = 10
    [bookmarkList: Bookmark.findAllByUser(session.user, params ) ]
}
```

Here you check if there is already a specified maximum and add a `max` argument of 10 if there isn't. You are now able to control the bookmarks that get displayed via the URL. To test this out, try creating, say, 25 bookmarks and then typing the following URL into your browser's address bar:

```
http://localhost:8080/bookmarks/bookmark/list?offset=7&max=12
```

What you have done is added the ability to manually paginate data via the address bar. This is useful in itself, but clearly users needs to be able to control this themselves, and this is where the `<g:paginate>` tag comes in. To create a `<g:paginate>` tag that operates in conjunction with the list action, all you need to do is tell it the total number of bookmarks to paginate over:

```
<g:paginate total="${Bookmark.countByUser(session.user)}" />
```

Here you give it a total using the countByUser method, which will count the total number of bookmarks for the user. Note that this information could have equally been provided via the model passed by the controller or via a session attribute. The resulting control containing Previous/Next links and a breadcrumb will resemble something like Figure 8-6, depending on how many bookmarks you have.

Previous 1 2 3 4 5 6 Next

Figure 8-6. *Paginate tag controls*

The links in Figure 8-6 can be adapted using the following attributes:

- prev: Allows control over the text displayed by the Previous link

- next: Allows control over the Next link (the opposite of prev)

- breadcrumb: Control whether the breadcrumb is displayed when set to either true or false

These attributes control the display of the <g:paginate> tag and you can, of course, control how the links look via CSS if you so choose. Beyond this, as mentioned previously, using the <g:paginate> tag in its simple form will paginate the *current* action, but sometimes it is useful to reference another action or controller.

In this sense the <g:paginate> tag supports the same properties as the <g:link> tag. For example, if you want to be a bit more explicit in your definition of the <g:paginate> tag that uses the list action you could define it as follows:

```
<g:paginate controller="controller"
            action="list"
            total="${Bookmark.countByUser(session.user)}" />
```

If you require further customization of the <g:paginate> tag, you could always delve into the tag library and modify it to your needs. In fact, before you do so, take a look at the next section that digs further into Grails custom tags and how they work.

Creating Custom Tags

Custom tags in JSP are a wonderfully powerful feature. They provide the ability to cleanly separate concerns between the view and controller logic. In MVC terms they can be seen as view helpers. Unfortunately, for all their wonderful attributes they are tremendously complicated to develop. The reasons for this are understandable, as JSP tags attempt to account for every possible tag creation scenario including the following:

- Simple tags that only have attributes and no body

- Body tags that have both attributes and a body

- Tags that have parent/child relationships between one another

- Nested tags and a complete API for finding tag ancestors

The implication, however, is that the API for creating JSP custom tags is robust, to say the least. To compound matters, additional information is required about the tag in a tag library descriptor (TLD) file that is loaded on application startup. This makes tags difficult to reload without a server restart, as the application server utilizes this file to configure the tag library. As you can imagine, all this is not very agile and is rather a complete contradiction to the code-by-convention approach.

From a user's perspective, developers rarely go to the effort of creating tags themselves, and, typically, the ones used tend to be those provided by the frameworks and specifications, such as JSTL. This is rather a shame, as the concept is sound though the realization is not.

So what can Grails and, more specifically, GSP provide to make the creation of tags simpler? Clearly, supporting every tag type under the sun would result in a complicated API, much like that in JSP. In reality, the most commonly used tags can be broken down into three categories:

- *Simple tags*: Tags that have attributes but no body

- *Logical tags*: Tags that have a body, which executes conditionally

- *Iterative tags*: Tags that loop and execute the body of the tag one or more times

You will find that the majority of tags that you come across fall into one of the previous categories. Since Grails is all about making the common cases simple, creating a simplified API for these tag types seems only logical. The question is, Why create a new API at all? This is where Groovy and the power of closures start to shine.

Creating a Tag Library

Having already seen quite a few Grails tags throughout this discussion, it may well be that you've already browsed the source and have become familiar with what a Grails tag is all about. Regardless, it is important to understand how to create a tag library from scratch.

It is generally good practice to place tags inside a library that encapsulates their general function, kind of like a package does in Java. As an example, all the tags that provide helpers for HTML form elements can be found in the `grails-app/taglib/FormTagLib.groovy` tag library.

A *tag library* is quite simply a class that ends with the convention `TagLib` in the class name and resides snuggly in the `grails-app/taglib` directory. Like the other Grails artifacts you've seen, a convenience target exists for creating tag libraries. To create a new tag library for the bookmarks application, you can run the `grails create-taglib` target and type **bookmark**, as shown in Listing 8-51.

Listing 8-51. *Creating the Bookmark Tag Library*

```
$ grails create-taglib

init-props:

create-taglib:
    [input] Enter tag library name:
bookmark
    [copy] Copying 1 file to /Developer/grails-apps/bookmarks/grails-app/taglib
    [echo] Created taglib: grails-app/taglib/BookmarkTagLib.groovy
```

```
BUILD SUCCESSFUL
Total time: 8 seconds
```

The result will resemble something like the following:

```
class BookmarkTagLib {


}
```

To see how to go about making a tag library, you're going to look at a basic tag and then build some snazzy functionality into the bookmarks application that allows you to use *inline* editing to modify your bookmarks.

Custom Tag Basics

First off, let's look at the basics. A tag is essentially a closure property that takes two arguments: the tag attributes as a `java.util.Map`, and the body of the tag as a closure, as shown in Listing 8-52.

Listing 8-52. *An Example Tag*

```
class BookmarkTagLib {

    def repeat = { attrs, body ->
            attrs.times?.toInteger().times { n ->
                body(n)
            }
    }
}
```

In the example, I've defined a tag called `repeat` that looks for an attribute called `times`, which it attempts to convert to an integer and then use Groovy's built-in `times` method to execute the body multiple times.

As mentioned previously, the body is a closure and therefore can be invoked like a method. In addition, you pass the number of the current iteration, as the variable n, to the body as the first argument to the closure call. Why is this useful? It means that the number is available as the default it argument in the tag's body. As an example, let's try out the new tag in a GSP view as in Listing 8-53. Note that the name of the tag in the markup matches the property name defined in the library shown in Listing 8-52.

Listing 8-53. *Using the repeat Tag*

```
<g:repeat times="3">
        Hello number ${it}
</g:repeat>
```

As you can see, the tag uses the default it argument to reference the value passed when the tag calls the body closure. The resulting output will be the following:

```
Hello number 1
Hello number 2
Hello number 3
```

Not only are Grails tags amazingly concise when compared to their JSP brethren, but it is important to note that all changes to tags can be reloaded at run time just like with controllers: no need to configure tag library descriptors or restart servers, making Grails tags a far more interesting proposition.

Custom Tags in Action

Now let's explore a more advanced example. *Inline editing* is one of the offspring of the Web 2.0 technology revolution, using JavaScript to dynamically change a field and update the server without the need to refresh the page. To perform this amazing feat you're going to leverage the Scriptaculous JavaScript library (http://script.aculo.us), which comes bundled with Grails. Scriptaculous has done the hard work for you by implementing a JavaScript inline editor component, making your job a simple matter of encapsulating it as a tag.

You're going to expand on your increasingly impressive bookmarks application by adding inline editing of bookmark notes. The effect you want to achieve is the ability to click the notes text and for it to magically turn into an edit field, which you can then save without having to refresh the page, as shown in Figure 8-7.

Figure 8-7. *Inline editing of a bookmark*

The JavaScript, thanks to Scriptaculous, is already pretty concise, as the example in Listing 8-54 (taken from the Scriptaculous wiki) demonstrates.

Listing 8-54. *Inline Editing JavaScript*

```
<p id="editme">Click me, click me!</p>
<script type="text/javascript">
 new Ajax.InPlaceEditor('editme', '/demoajaxreturn.html');
</script>
```

In Listing 8-54, a paragraph of text is being set up for inline editing, which will allow the user to edit the text contained within the paragraph when it is clicked. Using Scriptaculous, this example constructs an instance of Ajax.InPlaceEditor and passes the ID of the element that should be enhanced with in-place editing functionality, and the URL (in this case a dummy) of the server-side code that will handle changes to the value. The mix of markup, content, and JavaScript can prove a little hard to remember, however, and tags tend to provide a cleaner more reusable approach. So let's abstract this little snippet into a dynamic tag called <g:editInPlace>, as shown in Listing 8-55.

Listing 8-55. *Edit-in-Place as a Tag*

```
1 class BookmarkTagLib {
2     ...
3     def editInPlace = { attrs, body ->
4         def rows = attrs.rows ? attrs.rows : 0
5         def cols = attrs.cols ? attrs.cols : 0
6         def id = attrs.remove('id')
7
8         out << "<span id='${id}'>"
9         body()
10         out << "</span>"
11         out << "<script type='text/javascript'>"
12         out << "new Ajax.InPlaceEditor('${id}', '"
13         createLink(attrs)
14         out << "',{"
15
16         if(rows)
17             out << "rows:${rows},"
18         if(cols)
19             out << "cols:${cols},"
20         if(attrs.paramName) {
21             out << "callback: " +
22             "function(form, value) { " +
23                 return '${attrs.paramName}=' + escape(value) " +
24             }"
25         }
```

```
26              out << "});"
27              out << "</script>"
28          }
29 }
```

The important bits can be seen in bold, the first being the call to the body of the tag. Essentially, the body of the tag is the editable content, so you wrap this in an inline span tag. The JavaScript is then programmatically created including a call to createLink to create the link to the action, thus reusing existing tags.

Tip One important thing you may have picked up on is that, again, tag libraries don't extend any super-class and yet you can call a tag, createLink, located in another library. This is a special feature of tag libraries; tags defined in one library can call tags in another library even with no reference to that library. This is another example of Groovy's MetaClass magic.

On lines 21 through 24 you utilize the Ajax.InPlaceEditor object's callback mechanism to allow the customization of the parameter name to be sent to the server. The remainder of the tags code adds additional features to allow customization of the edit-in-place field and the parameter name to send in the asynchronous request. So how do you put this marvel into action? You want to use it to edit the notes of bookmarks, so you need to edit the bookmark template (located at grails-app/views/bookmark/_bookmark.gsp) as shown in Listing 8-56.

Listing 8-56. *Edit-in-Place bookmark Template*

```
...
<div id="notes">
    <g:editInPlace id="notes${bookmark.id}"
                            url="[action:'updateNotes',id:id:bookmark.id]"
                            rows="5"
                            cols= "10"
                            paramName="notes">${bookmark.notes}</g:editInPlace>
</div>
```

Here you create a <g:editInPlace> tag that submits to an action called updateNotes with the identifier of the Bookmark. In addition, you alter the number of rows and columns the field has and change the parameter name to notes, using the paramName attribute, which is then sent in the request to the updateNotes action. The last thing to do is create the updateNotes action in the BookmarkController, which once again proves trivial, as shown in Listing 8-57.

Listing 8-57. *The updateNotes Action*

```
def updateNotes = {
    update.call()
    render( Bookmark.get(params.id)?.notes )
}
```

The first thing the updateNotes action does is call the update action. Since you already have an id within the params object coming in via the edit-in-place URL plus the updated notes parameter, the update action can be reused.

Tip Remember that actions are defined as closures that are instances of groovy.lang.Closure and define methods for invoking them, such as call() used in Listing 8-57. This allows you to reuse actions within controllers simply by invoking the necessary closures.

Finally, once update has been called, the render method is used to render the text within the notes back to the response, which will in turn be displayed by the edit-in-place field. Remember, that the notes property of the Bookmark class is a string, and the render method, when passed a string, simply outputs its value to the response. The edit-in-place field then takes the updated value from the response and updates the value of the field. And that, ladies and gentlemen, is it. Really, if you think how little code you have written to achieve something actually rather useful, it is quite remarkable and is a clear example of how a syntactically expressive language such as Groovy shines.

But remember, just because it's simple doesn't mean that it shouldn't be tested. In the next section you'll see how to go about testing the <g:editInPlace> tag.

Testing a Custom Tag

Tags, as you have seen in the previous sections, output their contents to a java.io.Writer instance called out. When used in a GSP, the out attribute equates to the Servlet framework's response writer. In test code, however, you need some way of simulating or *mocking* what is written to the out attribute, since you don't have access to the response writer. The response writer allows you to write character data back to the client's browser. Mock objects and their application in Groovy were first introduced in Chapter 6.

In the next few examples, you'll see how they can be put to use to test tag libraries. Before you get going, however, you need to create the test case in the grails-test directory. But hold on. The test is already there created for you as the appropriately named BookmarkTests.groovy. In fact, you've used it before to test the BookmarkController.

Nevertheless, let's add a new test case to the BookmarkTests class for testing the <g:editInPlace> tag, as shown in Listing 8-58.

Listing 8-58. *The editInPlace Test Case*

```
class BookmarkController {
    ...
    void testEditInPlace() throws Exception {
        ...
    }
}
```

Next you need to define the stub to be used to perform the mocking. To do this you use the groovy.mock.interceptor.StubFor class to create a stub for the BookmarkTagLib:

```
def tagLibStub = new groovy.mock.interceptor.StubFor(BookmarkTagLib)
```

Now you need to create some test data. To capture the result of the tag you're going to use a StringWriter that will mock the behavior of the response writer and you'll need a map representing the tags attributes:

```
def sw = new StringWriter()
def link = "http://grails.org"
def paramName = "testParam"
def testBody = "testBody"
def editorId = "testEditor"
def rowCount = 10
def colCount = 5
def attrs = [rows:rowCount, cols:colCount, paramName:paramName, id:editorId]
```

Now you're going to use the stub to mock the creation of the link. If you recall from Listing 8-55, the <g:editInPlace> tag uses another tag called by calling it as a method. The tag in question is createLink and it is used to actually formulate the link. You can mock this behavior by adding a demand to the stub:

```
tagLibStub.demand.createLink {  sw << link }
```

The idea here is that when the BookmarkTagLib class demands the createLink method call it will be substituted with a call to the closure that, in this case, outputs a dummy link to the StringWriter. Now it's time to use the stub by calling the appropriately named use method that takes a closure. Essentially, everything contained within the body of the use method will utilize the mocking facility provided by the stub:

```
tagLibStub.use {
     ...
}
```

Moving onto the body of the closure passed to the use method, you first need to create an instance of the BookmarkTagLib class and set its out property to use the StringWriter you created earlier. However, before you can do this, you need to add a *concrete* out property (as opposed to one dynamically injected) to the BookmarkTagLib class. Groovy Mock, as of this writing, did not support mocking of properties. Nevertheless, since Grails sets the out property at run time anyway, there is no harm in adding it yourself, as shown in Listing 8-59.

Listing 8-59. *Adding the out Property to BookmarkTagLib*

```
class BookmarkTagLib {
    Writer out
     ...
}
```

With the out property in place, you can now set it to use the StringWriter you defined earlier by wrapping the StringWriter in a PrintWriter instance. You can then call the editInPlace closure, passing it the test attributes and a mock body that is simply a closure that outputs some test data to the StringWriter:

```
def tl = new BookmarkTagLib()
tl.out = new PrintWriter(sw)
tl.editInPlace.call(attrs, { sw << testBody})
```

The resulting markup contained within the StringWriter will look something like the following (formatted for clarity):

```
<span id='testEditor'>test</span>
   <script type='text/javascript'>
       new Ajax.InPlaceEditor('testEditor',
                                   'http://grails.org',
                                   {rows:10,cols:5,
                                    callback: function(form, value) {
                                        return 'testParam=' + escape(value)
                                    }});
</script>
```

It is the previous markup that you need to test to ensure it is outputting what is expected. To do this, simply convert the StringWriter to a string and then add two assertions that verify the output against the test data:

```
def mkp = sw.toString()
assert mkp.startsWith("<span id='${editorId}'>${testBody}</span>")
assert mkp.
endsWith("<script type='text/javascript'>"+
         "new Ajax.InPlaceEditor('${editorId}',"+
         " '${link}'," +
         "{rows:${rowCount},cols:${colCount},"+
         "callback: function(form, value) {"+
             "return '${paramName}=' + escape(value) }"+
         "});</script>")
```

Notice how you use GStrings with embedded values that reference the original test data, thus ensuring that the output from the tag matches the test data passed into it. In the previous example, the string used in the second assertion has been split up over several lines for greater clarity, since the tag itself doesn't output any newline characters whatsoever.

The complete test case for the tag can be seen in the following results and is in fact longer than the code that handles the <g:editInPlace> tag in the first place:

```
void testEditInPlace() {
    def tagLibStub = new groovy.mock.interceptor.StubFor(BookmarkTagLib)

    def sw = new StringWriter()
    def link = "http://grails.org"
    def paramName = "testParam"
    def testBody = "testBody"
    def editorId = "testEditor"
    def rowCount = 10
    def colCount = 5
    def attrs = [rows:rowCount,cols:colCount,paramName:paramName,id:editorId]

    tagLibStub.demand.createLink { sw << link }

    tagLibStub.use {
        def tl = new BookmarkTagLib()
        tl.out = new PrintWriter(sw)
        tl.editInPlace.call(attrs, { sw << testBody})

        def mkp = sw.toString()
        assert mkp.startsWith("<span id='${editorId}'>${testBody}</span>")
        assert mkp.
        endsWith("<script type='text/javascript'>"+
                    "new Ajax.InPlaceEditor('${editorId}',"+
                    " '${link}'," +
                    "{rows:${rowCount},cols:${colCount},"+
                    "callback: function(form, value) {"+
                        "return '${paramName}=' + escape(value) }"+
                    "});</script>")
    }
}
```

And with that, you have successfully completed your first tag. This example demonstrates wrapping a more complex object (a JavaScript one at that) into a much simpler one and is analogous to a *façade* in pattern speak. This is just one potential use of tags and it's worth performing your own experiments to explore other possibilities offered by tags.

Summary

You have learned quite a bit in this chapter. You learned about Grails advanced alternative view technology, GSP, and the array of powerful tags that come packaged with it. You also learned how to build your own tags and further extended your knowledge of Groovy mocking in the process. You had a lot of ground to cover and you should now have a clear idea of how powerful GSP is. Thanks to GPath, as an expression language, and dynamic tag libraries, GSP has a lot to offer to increase your productivity and enjoyment levels.

You also had a little taster of Ajax technology while developing your first custom tag. The timing of this glimpse into the future is rather apt, since the next chapter covers, you guessed it, Ajax.

■ ■ ■

## CHAPTER 9

Ajax

Ajax is a technology that has rather taken the web by storm and prompted the Web 2.0 revolution. The technology was originally developed by Microsoft to power a web-based version of its Outlook e-mail software. Microsoft implemented Ajax as an ActiveX control that could be used by its browser, Internet Explorer, and be called from JavaScript to perform asynchronous browser requests.

The advantage of the approach is that the browser doesn't have to refresh the entire page to interact with the server, thus allowing the development of applications that bear a closer resemblance to their desktop counterparts. Since then, browsers other than Internet Explorer have standardized on a native JavaScript object called XMLHTTPRequest that has the same API as Microsoft's ActiveX control.

The Basics of Ajax

The implications of having different browsers is that you have to write specialized code that detects which browser you are operating in and loads the XMLHttpRequest, either as an ActiveX control or as a native object.

Note Microsoft plans to introduce a native JavaScript XMLHttpRequest object for the next iteration of the browser, called IE 7, which will be made available for all versions of Windows beyond XP.

A typical example of obtaining a reference to the XMLHttpRequest object in a cross-browser manner can be seen in Listing 9-1.

Listing 9-1. *Example of XmlHttpRequest in JavaScript*

```
var req = null;
if (window.XMLHttpRequest) {
      req = new XMLHttpRequest();
} else if (window.ActiveXObject) {
      req = new ActiveXObject("Microsoft.XMLHTTP");
}
if(req!=null) {
   // register an event handler
   req.onreadystatechange = processRequest ;
   // open connection
   req.open("GET",
           "http://localhost:8080/a/remote/location",
           true);
   req.send(); // send request
}
function processRequest(obj) {
      alert(obj.responseXML) // Get the result from the response object
}
```

The previous code will send an asynchronous request to the http://localhost:8080/a/remote/location address and then, using the onreadystatechange callback event, invoke the processRequest method. This method simply displays an alert box with the content of the response. To illustrate the previous code and help you better understand the flow of an Ajax request, take a look at the UML sequence diagram in Listing 9-1. Remember that Ajax calls are asynchronous.

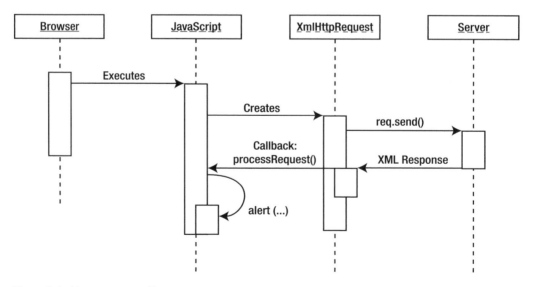

Figure 9-1. *Ajax sequence diagram*

As Figure 9-1 illustrates, the browser calls some JavaScript, which in turn creates the XMLHttpRequest object that is able to make the remote call. When the remote call has been made, the XMLHttpRequest object then invokes the callback (in this case the processRequest function), which in turn displays the alert.

Writing JavaScript code like that seen in Listing 9-1 can become rather repetitive and tedious. Fortunately there are Ajax frameworks that encapsulate much of this logic from the simple (such as JQuery) to the comprehensive (such as Dojo).

There are efforts underway to standardize on a JavaScript library, but as is always the case with any collaborative effort, this could be a long and painful process that will likely never satisfy everyone. The developers of Grails, however, feel that choice is a good thing and have chosen to provide support for a number of JavaScript libraries including the following:

Prototype/Scriptaculous: The pairing of Prototype and Scriptaculous has proven popular, thanks in part to the simplicity of its API, but also because it is the library used by Ruby on Rails.

Yahoo UI: The Yahoo library is a solid package with an open source license. Given that Yahoo is using it to power many of its sites, the stability and robustness of the library cannot be put to question.

Dojo Toolkit: Dojo is one of the more comprehensive Ajax toolkits, with its advanced packaging system and rich API of not only Ajax utilities but also UI components. Dojo has received the backing of many Java projects including Tapestry and WebWork (now Struts Action 2).

So how can Grails support all these libraries while still remaining clean and simple to use? The answer lies within the Grails tag libraries once again, with support for *adaptive* JavaScript tags that dynamically change, depending on the JavaScript library included in the page.

Before we delve into this world of Ajax tags, we need to revisit our bookmarks application, as we are going to be adding advanced Ajax features to once again improve on the user experience. The features we are going to implement to provide a bit of Ajax spice are as follows:

- The ability to asynchronously edit bookmark information

- A rollover preview link that asynchronously loads the target link into a small preview pane

- A feature that suggests tags to use for a particular URL as it is typed

To facilitate the addition of these advanced features, you're going to firstly progress your domain model from what you saw previously by creating the TagReference class seen originally in the UML class diagram in Chapter 4.

This will allow you to associate bookmarks with tags in a many-to-many relationship and allow tags to be shared among multiple users of your application. Just as a reminder, the UML diagram from Chapter 4 is shown again in Figure 9-2.

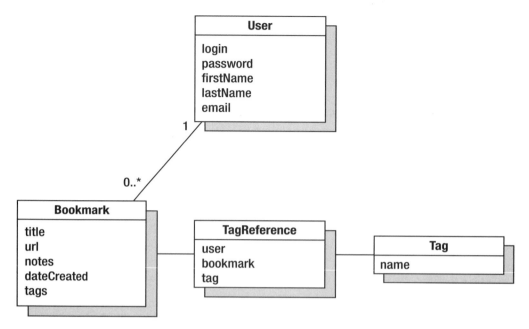

Figure 9-2. *UML class diagram*

Thanks to the simplicity of GORM, modifying your domain model proves rather trivial. The first thing you do is create the `TagReference` class using the `grails create-domain-class` target as per the code in Listing 9-2.

Listing 9-2. *Creating the TagReference Class*

```
>grails create-domain-class
create-domain-class:
     [input] Enter domain class name:
TagReference
```

Once the target in Listing 9-2 finishes executing, you can populate the `TagReference` class with the `user`, `bookmark`, and `tag` references shown in Figure 9-2. The final code for the `TagReference` class is shown in Listing 9-3.

Listing 9-3. *Updated BookmarkTag Class*

```
class TagReference {
     Bookmark bookmark
     Tag tag
     User user
}
```

Finally, the last thing to do is to update the relationship between the `Bookmark` class and the `Tag` class to reflect the changes you've made so far. By making the `Bookmark` class have many `TagReference` instances you can relate a bookmark to shared instances of the `Tag` class, thus allowing several bookmarks to share the same tag. Listing 9-4 illustrates the changes to the `tags` relationship.

Listing 9-4. *Updating the Bookmark Relationship*

```
class Bookmark {
    def hasMany = [tags:TagReference]
    ...
}
```

That's it! You're done. We can now move on to simplifying, creating, editing, and tagging bookmarks, Ajax style.

Ajax in Action

To begin with, what you're going to do is improve the creation of bookmarks and make them easier to tag. To do so you're going to create a new template called `grails-app/views/bookmark/_editor.gsp`, which will be responsible for rendering the fields necessary to create a bookmark.

Significantly, however, you are going to use a GSP tag called `<g:remoteField>` for the URL of the bookmark. The `<g:remoteField>` GSP tag uses Ajax to asynchronously send the value of a text field to the server as you type. You're going to use the value sent by the `<g:remoteField>` GSP tag to detect the URL typed in by the user, and provide suggestions as to which tags would be appropriate for the URL, based on the tags specified for this URL already by other users.

This will be the first introduction to the way in which Grails supports Ajax through its tag libraries. All the intricacies of performing the JavaScript calls are handled transparently through the tags, and, crucially, the tags are *adaptive*. What does this mean? Before you can use the `<g:remoteField>` tag you need to tell the GSP which library to use to perform the Ajax calls. Place the following line in the head tag of your GSP to tell it to use the Prototype JavaScript library:

```
<g:javascript library="prototype" />
```

Now imagine for a moment you want to switch to using Dojo instead. To do so you could simply change the previous definition to the following:

```
<g:javascript library="dojo" />
```

Like magic, all of the Ajax tags will change over to using Dojo instead. This also works with the Yahoo UI library by using a value of `yahoo`.

■**Note** The `<g:javascript>` tag can also be used with a tag body as a convenient alternative to the HTML `script` tag, which requires you to remember to set the `type` attribute to `text/javascript` on some browsers, as shown in this example: `<g:javascript>alert('hello!');</g:javascript>`.

The reasoning behind providing support for different libraries is simple. Each of the libraries has its respective strengths. Prototype is remarkable in its simplicity and ease of use, while Dojo has a rich API and set of UI components. On the other hand, Yahoo UI has a growing community and a rich set of widgets too. When you combine this with how remarkably simple it is to develop tags with Grails, it seems only fair to offer users a choice.

Returning to the bookmarks application, the first item we're going to implement is the suggestion feature. Essentially, the Create Bookmark screen, seen in Figure 9-3, should suggest recommended tags that would be appropriate to describe a particular link while the URL is being typed.

The suggestion feature will end up looking something like the screenshot depicted in Figure 9-3. The URL field will use the Ajax-enabled `<g:remoteField>` tag discussed at the beginning of this section to send the value that the user is typing to the server.

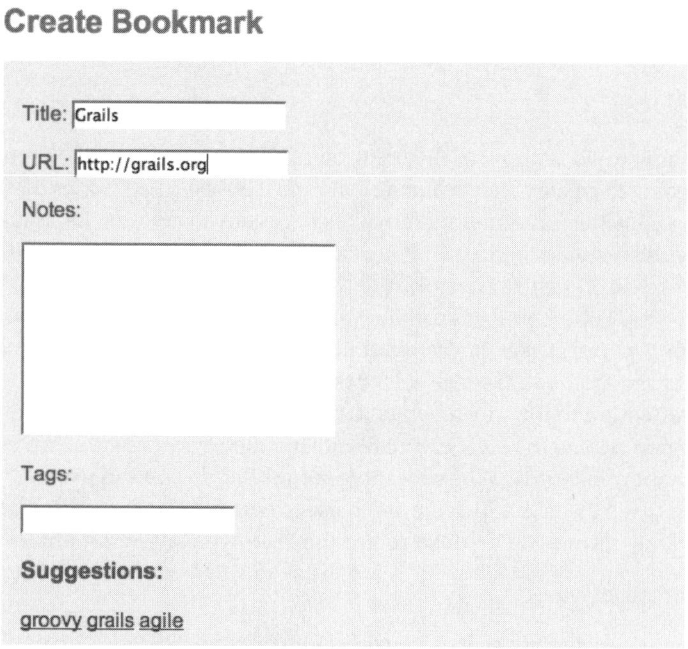

Create Bookmark

Title: Grails

URL: http://grails.org

Notes:

Tags:

Suggestions:

groovy grails agile

Figure 9-3. *The tag suggestion feature*

As Figure 9-3 demonstrates, when the user types in a URL, in this case http://grails.org, the suggestion feature creates a number of "suggestions" that will appear if other people using the application have also bookmarked (and tagged) the Grails web site URL. The user can then click each tag and it populates the Tags field with the clicked-on tags.

Eventually, when the bookmarks application starts to obtain more features, we will be able to start implementing some nice social networking features such as seeing the other links people have tagged as "grails" or "groovy." Very exciting stuff!

Before we get ahead of ourselves though, you need to actually implement the suggestion feature. So to start off with, let's take a look at the new editor template called grails-app/views/bookmark/_editor.gsp in Listing 9-5.

Listing 9-5. *The New editor Template*

```
1 <div id="editor">
2      <p>Title:
3        <g:textField name="title"
4                     value="${bookmark?.title}"/></p>
5      <p>URL:
6        <g:remoteField action="suggestTag"
7                       update="suggestions${bookmark?.id}"
8                       name="url"
9                       value="${bookmark?.url}"/>
10     </p>
11     <p>Notes:</p>
12     <p><textarea
13           name="notes"
14           col="1" row="1">
15              ${bookmark?.notes}
16        </textarea>
17     </p>
18     <p>Tags:</p>1
19     <p><g:textField
20           name="tagTokens"
21           id="tags${bookmark?.id}" />
22     </p>
23     <div id="suggestions${bookmark?.id}">
24       <g:each in="${suggestions?}">
25         <span class="suggestion">
26           <a href="javascript:void(0);"
27             onclick="$('tags${bookmark.id}').value+=
28               this.innerHTML+' ';this.style.display='none';">
29             ${it}</a>
30         </span>
31       </g:each>
32     </div>
33 </div>
```

The important parts are shown in bold, including the definition of the `<g:remoteField>` tag on lines 5 through 10. Here you create a field that will send its value to an action called `suggestTag` and update the `div` that has an `id` attribute of `suggestions`.

■Tip I am using a clever trick in Listing 9-5 with the safe-dereference operator, `?.`. Essentially the `update` attribute of the `<g:remoteField>` tag on line 7 is defined as `update="suggestions${bookmark?.id}"`; but of course, when you are creating a bookmark there is no `bookmark` variable so the GString expression evaluates to `null`. In GSP, `null` translates into an empty string resulting in a value of `suggestions`. However, when there is a bookmark field, the identifier of the bookmark will be appended on the end, thus allowing you to use the same template for both editing and creating (with and without an identifier).

On line 24 you iterate over each suggestion. Note the use of the safe-dereference operator, ?:

```
24                      <g:each in="${suggestions?}">
```

By appending the question mark at the end of the variable name inside the expression, you safeguard against any null pointer exceptions being thrown.

You then iterate over each suggested tag and output its value simply by referencing the default it argument with the syntax ${it} on line 29. Each tag is wrapped in an anchor tag on lines 26 through 29:

```
26    <a href="javascript:void(0);"
27       onclick="$('tags${bookmark.id}').value+=
28          this.innerHTML+' ';this.style.display='none';">
29       ${it}</a>
```

The HTML anchor tag has a JavaScript onclick event for each tag suggestion that appends the tag name to the list of tags when clicked upon and then hides the suggestion using display:none. This makes using the suggested tags a simple matter of clicking each one. Of course, to provide these suggestions when using the create view they would need to be placed in the model; hence, you need to update the create action to do so, as Listing 9-6 demonstrates.

Listing 9-6. *Updated create Action*

```
1 def create = {
2    def b = new Bookmark(params)
3    def suggestions = getSuggestions(b)
4    return [bookmark:b, suggestions:suggestions]
5 }
6 private getSuggestions(Bookmark bookmark) {
7   def tagRefs = TagReference
8                  .findAll('''from TagReference
9                     where bookmark.url = ? ''',
10                    [bookmark.url])
11   return tagRefs
12          .findAll { !bookmark.tags?.contains(it.tag) }
13          .tag
14          .unique()
15 }
```

The previous action demonstrates a number of key concepts. Firstly, note how the create action uses a private method called getSuggestions(bookmark), which is used to retrieve a list of suggestions for a URL. Methods are not visible to the outside world in the form of actions in the same way that closure properties are, hence they are useful for delegation.

In addition, on lines 7 to 10 of Listing 9-6, the code uses an HQL query to find all TagReference objects whose Bookmark properties match the query URL. The query is wrapped in the Groovy triple-quotes syntax for multiline strings to allow the query to span multiple lines. And, finally, on lines 11 through 14 you can see an example of the power of closures combined with GPath:

```
11   return tagRefs
12           .findAll { !bookmark.tags?.contains(it.tag) }
13           .tag
14           .unique()
```

In the previous example you use Groovy's findAll method to find all TagReference instances that *are not* already referenced by the bookmark. The logic to this is encapsulated by the closure directly after the call to findAll. The result of the expression is a java.util.List; however, by asking the List for its tag property, GPath automatically goes through all the TagReference instances in the List and collects each one's tag property.

The combination of querying with dynamic finders (or HQL) and GPath makes Groovy and Grails a powerful duo for sorting, filtering, and manipulating collections. Once you've learned all the different ways to deal with collections of objects in Groovy, you'll find yourself yearning for the same features when you return to Java.

Nevertheless, now that the necessary controller code is in place it is time to use the template defined in Listing 9-5. In order to do so, you need to update the create view located at grails-app/views/bookmark/create.gsp and replace the existing form fields with your editor template using the <g:render> tag. Listing 9-7 provides an example of the necessary changes.

Listing 9-7. *The Updated create View*

```
...
<g:form action="save" method="post" >
    <div class="dialog">
            <g:render template="editor" model="[bookmark:bookmark]" />
    </div>
...
```

Because you're now using a single field to specify tags, the save action needs to be changed to parse the sequence of tags from the tagTokens field and create TagReference instances. You also need to change the save action to take you directly back to the bookmark list after creating a bookmark; for our purposes, the show view is superfluous. Listing 9-8 shows the changes made to the save action.

Listing 9-8. *Updated save Action*

```
1 def save = {
2     def b = new Bookmark()
3     b.properties = params
4     b.user = session.user
5
6     if(b.save()) {
7       if(params.tagTokens) {
8           def tags = params.tagTokens.trim()
9           if(tags.indexOf(' ')) {
10              tags = tags.split(' ').toList().unique()
```

```
11         }
12         else {
13             tags = [tags]
14         }
15         tags.each {
16             Tag t = Tag.findByName(it)
17             if(!t)t = new Tag(name:it).save()
18             b.addTagReference(
19               new TagReference(bookmark:b,
20                                     tag:t,
21                                     user:b.user))
22         }
23           b.save()
24       }
25       redirect(action:list,id:b.id)
26     }
27   else {
28       render(view:'create',model:[bookmark:b])
29     }
30 }
```

The code added to the save action can be found between lines 7 and 22 in Listing 9-8, where you check for the tagTokens in the params object; then if there are spaces in the tagTokens, split the tag names up and create TagReference instances to each. Alternatively, if there are no spaces, just create a single TagReference to the specified tag.

A neat side effect of providing both automatic suggestion if the bookmark URL already exists and Ajax as-you-type suggestion is that you can make a convenient hyperlink to create new bookmarks. Try typing the following address into your browser address bar:

```
http://localhost:8080/bookmarks/bookmark/create?url=http://grails.org
```

The Create Bookmark page will appear with the URL already filled with http://grails.org and suggestions in place if other users have already bookmarked and tagged the Grails site. This convenient URL can be extended even further into a JavaScript hyperlink, commonly referred to as a *bookmarklet*. Try adding a bookmark to your browser with the following JavaScript hyperlink and call it Post to Bookmarks

```
javascript:location.href='http://localhost:8080/bookmarks/bookmark/create?url='+
encodeURIComponent(location.href)+'&title='+encodeURIComponent(document.title)
```

For example, in Firefox you could right-click the Bookmarks toolbar and select New Bookmark, which will load the New Bookmark dialog in Firefox shown in Figure 9-4.

Once the Post to Bookmarks button is created in the toolbar, navigate to your favorite site and click the Post to Bookmarks link. The result is that you get the Title and URL fields filled out for you plus any tag suggestions. The screenshot in Figure 9-5 illustrates what happens when visiting the Grails site and then clicking Post to Bookmarks. Bookmarking has never been easier!

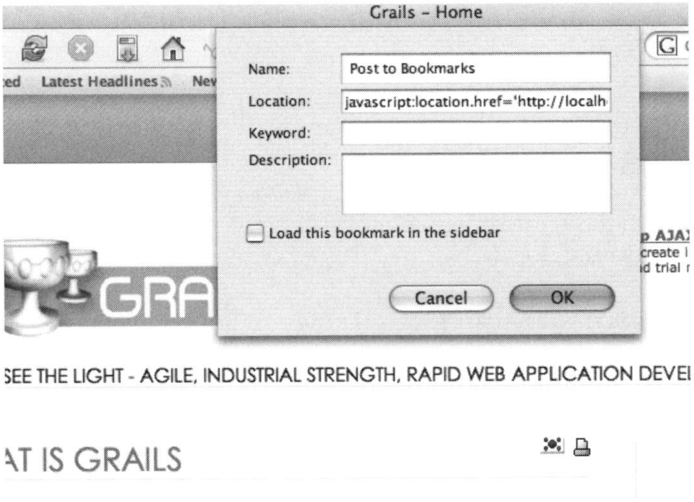

Figure 9-4. *Adding a JavaScript link to the bookmarks application*

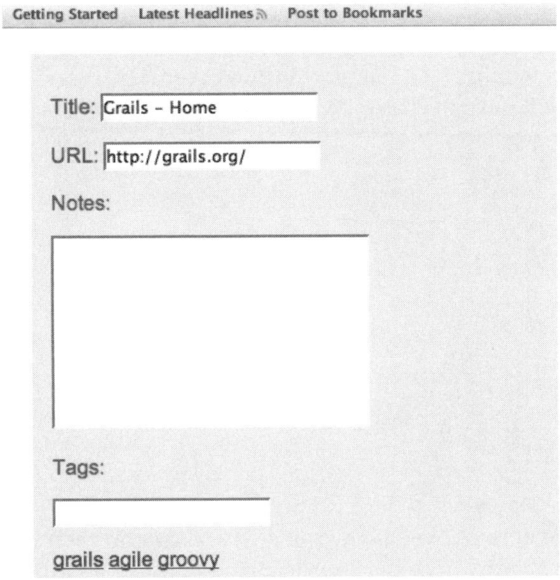

Figure 9-5. *Using the Post to Bookmarks link*

In order to get the Ajax tag suggestion feature working, you need to implement the suggestTag action in the BookmarkController. This will suggest appropriate tags to the user *as they type*. In other words, when they type in http://grails.org, the application should look for any appropriate tags and present them to the user. Listing 9-9 shows how the suggestTag action accomplishes the aforementioned use case.

Listing 9-9. *The suggestTag Action*

```
1 def suggestTag = {
2   if(params.value?.trim()) {
3     if(!params.value?.startsWith("http://"))
4         params.value = "http://${params.value}"
5     def bookmark = params.id ? Bookmark.get(params.id) : new Bookmark()
6     if(!bookmark.url) bookmark.url = params.value?.toUrl()
7     def tags = getSuggestions(bookmark)
8     render(template:'suggest',
9             model:[tags:tags,bookmark:bookmark])
10 }
```

The use of the ternary operator on line 5 of Listing 9-9 (also available in Java, of course) combined with Groovy's advanced concept of the truth is used either to look up an existing Bookmark instance or to create a new one entirely.

You then reuse the getSuggestions(bookmark) method defined in Listing 9-6 to retrieve a list of suggestions. Finally, the response is rendered using a suggest template:

```
7         render(template:'suggest',model:[tags:tags,bookmark:bookmark])
```

Templates are Ajax's best friend, as they allow you to render snippets of markup to the response. In this case, the render method is looking for a template located at grails-app/views/bookmark/_suggest.gsp, which you still need to create. As we're on a roll, let's go ahead and do just that, as you can see in Listing 9-10.

Listing 9-10. *The suggest Template*

```
<g:if test="${tags}"><h3>Suggestions:</h3></g:if>
<g:each var="t" in="${tags?}">
    <span id="${t.id}" class="suggestion">
        <a href="javascript:void(0);"
            onclick="$('tagTokens${bookmark?.id ? bookmark.id : ''}').value+=' '+
            this.innerHTML;this.style.display='none'">${t}</a>
    </span>
</g:each>
```

The template is simple enough and just iterates over the tags (if any) and creates each suggestion. As with the editor template seen earlier in this section, each suggestion is wrapped in an HTML anchor tag with an onclick event that populates the tagTokens field for you.

With that you've implemented an Ajax tag suggestion feature while writing very little JavaScript. To recap, in this section you learned about a useful Ajax tag called <g:remoteField> that lets you send the value of a field asynchronously to the server and update content on the page with the response.

■**Tip** By default, the parameter sent to the server is called `value`. You can alter this by using the `paramName` attribute: `<g:remoteField name="myField" paramName="myField" url= "[action:'myAction']" />`.

The `<g:remoteField>` tag is one of a collection of Ajax tags that accepts a similar set of attributes. I'll be covering the attributes that are applicable to the `<g:remoteField>` tag in the next few sections, but keep in mind that they are also equally relevant when working with the other tags, which I'll be covering in our next bookmarks application development cycle in the section "More on Updating Content."

Executing Code Before and After a Call

The `<g:remoteField>` tag supports two attributes called `before` and `after`, which allow the insertion of arbitrary JavaScript code to be executed before and after a remote call.

■**Note** The code within the `after` attribute will be executed regardless of whether the remote call is actually successful or not. In this sense it should not be compared to an `onComplete` event handler.

For example, you could use a `before` call to programmatically alter the value of the field in some way before it is sent to the server, as shown in Listing 9-11.

Listing 9-11. *Example before Attribute Usage*

```
<g:javascript>
    function transformUrl(field) {
        if(!field.value.match(/(http|https):\/\/.*/)) {
          field.value = "http://" + field.value
          }
    }
</g:javascript>
<p>URL: <g:remoteField action="suggestTag"
                        before="transformUrl(this);"
                        update="suggestions${bookmark?.id}"
                        name="url" value="${bookmark?.url}"/></p>
```

Here we add the `http://` prefix to the URL if it doesn't already exist, before the value of the URL field is sent to the server. It is important to understand that `before` and `after` are not event hooks. This becomes more apparent when using `after`, which will execute directly after an Ajax call and will not wait until it returns. In other words, it has no awareness as to whether the Ajax call is successful or not. Events are a different concept that I'll cover in detail in the next section.

Handling Events

An important aspect of Ajax development, and indeed any asynchronous development style, is the ability to receive and act on events. To this end, Grails' Ajax tags allow the registration of a number of different event handlers that you, the developer, are capable of consuming.

For example, a common use case in Ajax development is to provide some form of feedback to the user while an Ajax call is happening, be it an activity monitor, a progress bar, or a simple animated icon (such as a spinner or an hour glass).

To accomplish this for a single Ajax call, you could use the onLoading and onComplete events, as shown in Listing 9-12.

Listing 9-12. *Displaying a Progress Indicator*

```
<p>URL: <g:remoteField action="suggestTag"
                    onLoading="showProgress();"
                    onComplete="hideProgress();"
                    update="suggestions${bookmark?.id}"
                    name="url"
                    value="${bookmark?.url}"/></p>
```

Here I use two hypothetical JavaScript methods called showProgress() and hideProgress() to display feedback to the user. These could be as simple as displaying an animated graphic, or something more advanced, such as polling the server for the current state of a large operation and displaying a progress bar.

Table 9-1 shows the different events.

Table 9-1. *Table of Ajax Events*

Event Name	Description
onSuccess	Called when the remote call is successful
onFailure	Called when the remote call is not successful
onLoading	Called when the remote call begins to load the response
onLoaded	Called when the remote call has loaded the response, but prior to any page updates
onComplete	Called when the response has been received and any updates are completed
onERROR_CODE	Called for specific error codes such as "on404"

The last event in the table deserves special mention, as it allows you to handle specific error codes. This is often useful to display alert boxes or specific feedback to the user, such as certain codes when the server is down or being maintained. In the next section we'll be looking at more advanced ways to perform updates on content.

More on Updating Content

You've already seen how the `<g:remoteField>` can be used to update content; but what happens if the remote call fails? Maybe the server throws an error or, god forbid, goes down. You don't want the ugly error response to be placed into the content, and if a more graceful error is returned, you don't necessarily want this to appear in the same place either.

Luckily the `update` attribute is a bit more flexible than this and accepts a map as an alternative, as shown in Listing 9-13.

Listing 9-13. *Advanced Updating*

```
<p>URL:
    <g:remoteField action="suggestTag"
                   update="[success:'suggestions'+bookmark.id,
                            failure:'error']"
                   name="url"
                   value="${bookmark?.url}"/></p>
```

Here you pass a map to the `update` attribute with two keys. A success key tells the remote call what element to update if the call is successful. Alternatively, if the call is not successful, the element specified by the failure key, in this case an element with an `id` attribute of `error`, is updated with the value of the response.

So far you've seen the `<g:remoteField>` tag utilizing many of the features explored in the last few sections. In the next section on remote linking you'll see how another Ajax tag, `<g:remoteLink>`, uses the same attributes to create Ajax hyperlinks.

Remote Linking

The example we explored at the beginning of this chapter while building the Ajax tag suggestion feature uses a `<g:remoteField>` that sends its value to the server when you type. Having this capability is handy, but what if you just want to link to some remote content? In this case there are two techniques you can use; the first involves the `<g:remoteLink>` tag.

To demonstrate the use of `<g:remoteLink>` we are going to provide inline editing of bookmarks, rather than having to go off to a specific edit screen.

Firstly, we're going to change the `bookmark` template (located at grails-app/views/bookmark/_bookmark.gsp) to use a `<g:remoteLink>` tag instead of a normal link to the `edit` action as Listing 9-14 demonstrates.

Listing 9-14. *Updated bookmark Template*

```
<div id="bookmark${bookmark.id}">
    <div id="link${bookmark.id}">
        <a href="${bookmark.url}">${bookmark.title}</a> -
        <g:remoteLink
            action="edit"
            id="${bookmark.id}"
            update="bookmark${bookmark.id}">
          edit</g:remoteLink> |
...
```

The changes in Listing 9-14 are in bold, where the code gets the `<g:remoteLink>` to update the surrounding bookmark div with the contents of the response. Now if you change the edit view (located at `grails-app/views/bookmark/edit.gsp`) to simply display a partial snippet of HTML instead of the whole page, you can get your inline editing fields to appear when the Edit link is clicked. Listing 9-15 illustrates the changes made to the edit view.

Listing 9-15. *Updated edit View*

```
1 <div id="bookmark${bookmark.id}">
2        <g:renderErrors as="list" bean="bookmark" />
3        <g:formRemote name="editorForm"
4                      url="[action:'update',id:bookmark.id]"
5                      update="bookmark${bookmark.id}">
6            <g:render template="editor"
7                      model="[bookmark:bookmark,
8                                suggestions:suggestions]" />
9            <div id="editButtons">
10                   <g:submit name="save" value="Save" />
11                 <g:submitToRemote
12                       url="[action:'show',id:bookmark.id]"
13                       update="bookmark${bookmark.id}"
14                      name="cancel" value="Cancel" />
15           </div>
16 </g:formRemote>
17 </div>
```

The result of the changes made in Listing 9-15 is that when you click the Edit link you're presented with the editor template displayed inline within the bookmark list as shown in Figure 9-6.

In addition to this already slick usability enhancement, it would be handy if the inline editing feature used tags in the same way as the create view. To achieve this, you just need to place some suggestions in the model; you can reuse the `getSuggestions(bookmark)` method from Listing 9-6 once again (for the third time!) by overriding the scaffolded edit action, as shown in the example in Listing 9-16.

Listing 9-16. *The Overridden edit Action*

```
def edit = {
    def b = Bookmark.get(params.id)
    if(b) {
        return [bookmark:b, suggestions: getSuggestions(b) ]
    }
    else {
        render "bookmark not found "
    }
}
```

Bookmark List

Grails - edit | delete
Agile web framework

Title: Groovy

URL: http://groovy.codehaus.or

Notes:

Dynamic JVM language

Tags:

(Save) (Cancel)

Figure 9-6. *Inline editing of the bookmark list*

In a fairly familiar flow control scenario, you retrieve the Bookmark by ID and then create the model, adding the additional suggestions. Also, if a Bookmark instance is not found (maybe the user deleted it in one browser window and then switched to another one with an out-of-date state) you render a useful message to be displayed to the user.

The introduction of this feature has highlighted an interesting usability problem with updating content asynchronously. Having the edit dialog appear immediately has the side effect of creating a jerky UI. In this sense, it would be nice to be able to use some form of a transition such as a fade-in or a blind effect to introduce the editor gradually. In the next section I explore how this can be done.

Applying Effects

Another part of the Ajax revolution is the increased usage of animation or effects controlled via JavaScript. To this end, many of the Ajax libraries such as Dojo, Prototype, and Yahoo UI package a library of effects for making animations easier.

As of this writing, Grails does not integrate with any one effects library. However, this does not prevent you from using them, and some, such as Scriptaculous (http://script.aculo.us/), make it remarkably easy and syntactically concise.

To include Scriptaculous into the page you can add the following line to the head tag of the main layout located in grails-app/views/layouts/main.gsp:

```
<g:javascript library="scriptaculous" />
```

This will ensure that the Scriptaculous library and all its dependencies (including Prototype) are included in the page. For example, say you want the bookmark inline editor to expand from top to bottom like a roller blind. To do so, you first need to make the bookmark editor in the grails-app/views/edit.gsp start off invisible by setting the display:none CSS style, as in the following example:

```
<div id="bookmark${bookmark.id}" style="display:none;">
```

Once this is done you can use the `<g:remoteLink>` tag's `onComplete` event to apply the effect. Listing 9-17 demonstrates how this might be done.

Listing 9-17. *Effects with Scriptaculous*

```
<g:remoteLink onComplete="Effect.BlindDown('bookmark${bookmark.id}');"
                        action="edit"
                        id="${bookmark.id}"
                        update="bookmark${bookmark.id}">edit</g:remoteLink>
```

The result is a pleasant-looking little animation as the bookmark inline editor appears, which is a little bit more graceful than the jerkiness you get without the effect when the content changes to make room for the editor.

The `<g:remoteLink>` tag used here uses the `onclick` event handler of the HTML anchor tag. This is a common approach; but often it is much cleaner to use JavaScript itself to attach events to the markup. In the next section I explore how Grails can create JavaScript functions to assign to other events either inline or in JavaScript.

Working with JavaScript Events

Using HTML anchor tags is one way to create links to Ajax calls, but frequently you just want to attach functions to events that perform these calls. This is where the `<g:remoteFunction>` tag comes in, and it is with this tag that you are going to develop your bookmarks example application even further.

The `<g:remoteFunction>` tag creates a JavaScript function that can be used within any JavaScript event handler such as `onclick`. You're going to be using this tag to provide a preview feature. Essentially, you're going to provide a preview link that has an `onmouseover` event, which will load the bookmark into an embedded `iframe`. It will look something like the screenshot in Figure 9-7.

You'll then use the `onmouseout` event to hide the preview when the user is finished with it. First, however, you're going to implement a `preview` action that retrieves a bookmark and renders a snippet of markup that contains an `iframe` with the URL to preview. Why an `iframe` you say?

Well, one of the limitations of `XMLHttpRequest` is that it *cannot* access content that is loaded from another domain. This makes it useless for what you are trying to achieve, as pretty much every link is going to be outside the bookmarks application's domain. Luckily, `iframes` have no such limitation and hence can be utilized as shown in Listing 9-18.

Listing 9-18. *The Preview Action*

```
def preview = {
    def b = Bookmark.get(params.id)
    render {
        iframe(src:b.url,width:640,height:480,border:0, 'iframes not supported')
    }
}
```

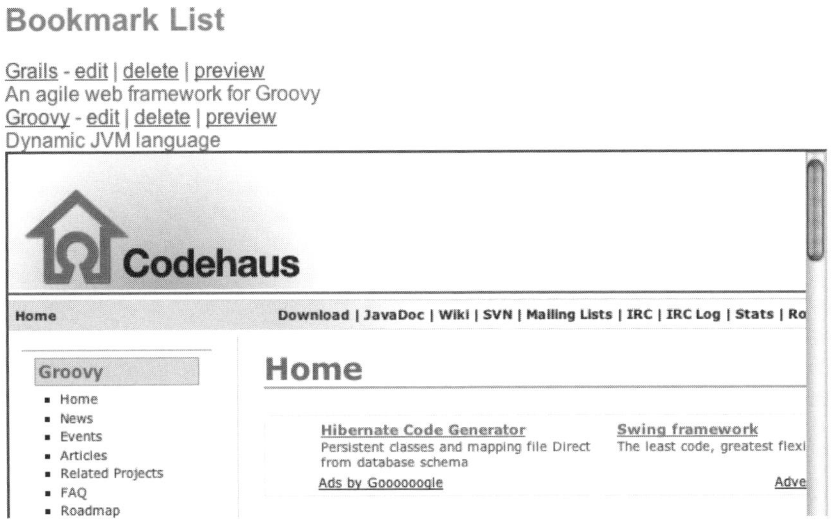

Bookmark List

Grails - edit | delete | preview
An agile web framework for Groovy
Groovy - edit | delete | preview
Dynamic JVM language

Figure 9-7. *The preview feature in action*

As it is such a small bit of markup there is little point in creating a template when you can use the convenience of the render method's markup building support. An example result for the code in Listing 9-18 would be something like the following (pretty-printed for easy reading):

```
<iframe src="http://grails.org" width="640" height="480" border="0">
    iframes not supported
</iframe>
```

The next step is to add the preview link to the template grails-app/views/bookmark/
_bookmark.gsp and attach the mouse events (and potentially onfocus and onblur too) to the necessary remote call. Listing 9-19 provides an example of the necessary code to implement the preview button.

Listing 9-19. *The Preview Button Code*

```
| <a href="#"
    onmouseover="${remoteFunction(
                    action:'preview',
                    id:bookmark.id,
                    update:'preview' + bookmark.id,
                     onComplete:'Effect.Appear(preview'+bookmark.id+')')}';"
    onmouseout="Effect.Fade('preview${bookmark.id}');">preview</a>
```

The code in Listing 9-19 appears directly after the Delete link and uses an Ajax call to load the preview and update a div that has an id attribute with a value of preview followed by the Bookmark instance's id property. It uses the <g:remoteFunction> tag's onComplete event to blend in the preview, and the onmouseout event on the anchor to fade out the preview when the user moves his or her mouse off the Preview link.

The last thing you need to do is provide the preview `div` that will be updated by the Ajax response to the same `Bookmark` template. Listing 9-20 demonstrates how this is done.

Listing 9-20. *The Preview div*

```
<div id="bookmark${bookmark.id}">

    ...
    <div id="preview${bookmark.id}">
    </div>
</div>
```

That's it! Now when you move your mouse over the Preview link, a preview of the site will blend in and then fade away when you move your mouse away. Note that for the sake of brevity, the solution presented is likely not to be the most performant. In a real-world situation you could perform caching of the `iframe` elements inside a lookup table or hash with the URL being the key. This would avoid having to return to the server for every preview mouse event.

In the next section I explore another Ajax tag that solves the common use case of being able to submit a form asynchronously while including all of the form's elements in the submission.

Remote Form Submission

For the observant reader this may not be news to you but there are some other notable additions to the `edit` view in Listing 9-15. First is the usage of another Ajax tag called `<g:formRemote>` on lines 3 to 5, a reminder of which can be seen in Listing 9-21.

Listing 9-21. *The <g:formRemote> Tag*

```
3       <g:formRemote name="editorForm"
4                              url="[action:'update',id:bookmark.id]"
5                              update="bookmark${bookmark.id}">
```

The `<g:formRemote>` tag in Listing 9-21 creates a regular HTML form that submits the fields nested within it using an asynchronous Ajax call to an action called `update`. In the next step you are going to call the `update` action on the `BookmarkController`, and all of the form data will be passed exactly like a regular form submission.

In addition, the `<g:formRemote>` tag has an `update` attribute exactly the same as the other Ajax tags, which is used to update the surrounding `bookmark div` with the contents of the response. The only thing you have to do is override the scaffolded `update` action to make it render a bookmark snippet as the response, instead of redirecting to the `show` action as it does now. The example in Listing 9-22 demonstrates how to do this.

Listing 9-22. *Overriden update Action*

```
def update = {
    def b = Bookmark.get(params.id)
    if(b) {
        b.properties = params
        if(b.save()) {
            render(template:'bookmark', model:[bookmark:b])
        }
        else {
            render(view:'edit', model:[bookmark:b])
        }
    }
}
```

Notice that the only real difference between the default scaffolded update action in Listing 9-22 is that you have replaced the redirect with a call to the render method that uses the pre-existing bookmark template (located at grails-app/views/bookmark/_bookmark.gsp).

Now you can edit and update bookmarks directly within your bookmark list.

■**Tip** The <g:formRemote> and <g:remoteLink> tags will link and submit forms without Ajax. If used carefully, you could develop applications that work when Ajax is not available, such as in older browsers or those with JavaScript disabled.

The buttons that manage this remarkable feat can be found toward the bottom of the updated edit view in Listing 9-15. The first form element is a regular HTML Submit button that will submit the form when clicked. The second form element, however, is another Ajax tag that goes by the name of <g:submitToRemote>, which creates a Submit button that can submit the form to another action entirely using Ajax.

In this case we've implemented a Cancel button by reusing the previously redundant show action and view. The show view, found at grails-app/views/bookmark/show.gsp, is modified to simply render another template:

```
<g:render template="bookmark" model="[bookmark:bookmark]" />
```

You now have a functional Cancel button that will revert the bookmark back to its original state prior to clicking the Edit link using Ajax. It is interesting to note at this point how you have gradually migrated the code generated by scaffolding, described in Chapter 5, to suit your needs. This clearly demonstrates just how powerful the concept of scaffolding can be to help you on your way to being productive and to give you a starting point to build from.

A Note on Ajax and Performance

It is important to note the impact that the use of Ajax has on the performance of an application. Given the number of small snippets of code that get rendered, it will come as little surprise that Ajax applications have to deal with a significantly larger number of requests.

What you have seen so far in this chapter could almost be seen as the naïve approach to Ajax development. You have waved the Ajax magic wand over your application with little consideration to some of the performance implications.

Nevertheless, it is not too late to take some of these things into account. There are a number of techniques that you can use to reduce the number of requests an Ajax application performs before you start throwing more hardware at the problem.

The first thing to remember is that an Ajax call is a remote network call and therefore expensive. Those who have developed with EJB will begin to recall some of the patterns used to optimize EJB remote method calls. Things such as the Data Transfer Object (DTO) are equally applicable in the Ajax world.

Fundamentally, the DTO pattern serves as a mechanism of batching operations into a single call and passing enough state to the server for several operations to be executed at once. This pattern can be equally effective in Ajax, given that it is better to do one call that transmits more information than a dozen small ones.

In addition, another popular technique is to move more complexity onto the client. Given that Ajax clients, in general, occupy a single physical page, a fair amount of state can be kept on the client. What I'm talking about here is *caching*. Caching is probably the most important technique in Ajax development and, where possible, should be utilized fully to cache results from the server.

A good candidate for caching in our example application is the preview feature that uses an onmouseover event. Clearly the dangers of mouse events are that they can be executed several times in succession. Here you could have done the initial query and cached the response, and then subsequent calls would retrieve the cached version.

Note, however, there is a downside to this approach, as the result is a fat client that is very much dependant on an environment—the browser—that is beyond your control. Hence, you will face the usual cross-browser challenges, as well as other issues such as unexpected behavior of the Back and Forward buttons in browsers, difficulty in creating automated unit tests, and potential for some hard to find bugs.

Needless to say, whichever technique you use, it will pay dividends in the long run, and the server infrastructure guys will love you for it. The users of your application will also appreciate the faster response times and interactivity of the site.

Summary

In this chapter you learned about the extensive range of adaptive Ajax tags that Grails offers and how to apply them to your bookmarks application to create a more useable interactive interface. On this particular journey, you also explored advanced Grails development, learning a lot more about how controllers, templates, and the render method function in combination.

You also saw how to gradually refactor a scaffolded application by taking the original bookmarks application and building on it from its humble scaffolded beginnings. In the last few chapters you've very much been involved with the web layer of Grails with controllers, GSP, tag libraries, and Ajax. Now, however, it is time to take a diversion as we start to explore what more Grails has to offer with services and jobs.

CHAPTER 10

■■■

Services and Jobs

A common pattern in the development of enterprise software is the so-called service layer that encapsulates a set of business operations. With Java web development, it is generally considered good practice to provide layers of abstraction and reduce coupling between the layers within an MVC application.

The service layer provides a way to centralize application behavior into an API that can be utilized by controllers or other services. Many good reasons exist for encapsulating logic into a service layer, but the following points are the main drivers:

- There is a need to centralize business logic into a service API.

- The use cases within your application operate on multiple domain objects and model complex business operations that are best not mixed in with controller logic.

- Certain use cases and business processes are best encapsulated outside of a domain object and within an API.

If your requirements fall into one of the preceding categories, creating a service is probably what you're after. Services themselves often have multiple dependencies; for example, a common activity for a service is to interact with the persistence layer whether that is straight JDBC or an ORM system like Hibernate.

Clearly, whichever system you use you are potentially dependent on a data source or a session factory or maybe just another service. Configuring these dependencies in a loosely coupled way has been one of the main challenges facing early adopters of J2EE technology.

Like most software development challenges the problem space here is solved by a software design pattern called Inversion of Control (IoC), or dependency injection, and projects such as Spring aim to ease this burden by providing an IoC container.

Grails itself uses Spring to configure itself internally, and it is this foundation that Grails builds on to provide *services by convention*. Nevertheless, let's jump straight into looking at what Grails services are and how to create a basic service.

Service Basics

Services, like other Grails artifacts, follow a convention and don't extend any base class. For example, say we decide to move much of the bookmarks application's business logic into a service; we would need to create a class called BookmarkService located in the grails-app/services directory.

Unsurprisingly, there is a Grails target that allows convenient creation of services. Building on what was just mentioned, to create the BookmarkService, we can execute the create-service target, which will prompt us to enter the name of the service as demonstrated in Listing 10-1.

Listing 10-1. *Running the create-service Target*

```
$ grails create-service
Buildfile: /Developer/grails/src/grails/build.xml

init-props:

create-service:
    [input] Enter service name:
bookmark
    [copy] Copying 1 file to /Developer/grails-apps/bookmarks/grails-app/services
    [echo] Created service: grails-app/services/BookmarkService.groovy

internal-create-test-suite:
    [echo] Created test suite: grails-tests/BookmarkTests.groovy
```

Here we enter the text "bookmark" as the name of the service, and the target will create the class automatically and put it in the right place. The result will resemble something like the following:

```
class BookmarkService {
    def transactional = true
    def serviceMethod() {

    }
}
```

Our service contains one method, which is just a placeholder for a real method. The more interesting aspect is the transactional property.

Transactions

As mentioned previously, services often encapsulate business operations that deal with several domain objects. If an exception occurs while executing changes, you don't want any prior changes committed to the database.

Essentially, you want an all-or-nothing approach, also known as a *transaction*. Transactions are essential for maintaining database integrity via their *ACID properties*, which have probably been covered in every book that has used a relational database. Nevertheless, we'll take a quick look at them here. ACID stands for *atomicity, consistency, isolation,* and *durability*.

Atomicity: This refers to how operations on data within a transaction must be *atomic*. In other words, all tasks within a transaction will be completed or none at all, thus allowing *rollback* of changes.

Consistency: This requires that the database be in a consistent state *before* and *after* any operations occur. There is no point attempting to complete a transaction if the database is not in a legal state to begin with, and it would be rather silly if an operation left the database's integrity compromised.

Isolation: This refers to how transactions are isolated from all other operations. Essentially, this means other queries or operations should never be exposed to data that is in an intermediate state.

Durability: Once a transaction is completed, durability guarantees that the transaction cannot possibly be undone. This is true even if system failure occurs, thus ensuring the committed transaction cannot at this point be aborted.

So how does all this relate to the `transactional` property? Well, when set to `true`, the methods of the service are configured for transaction demarcation by Spring. What this does is create a Spring proxy that wraps each method call and provides transaction management.

Grails handles the entire automatic runtime configuration for you, leaving you to concentrate on simply writing the logic within your methods. If the service does not require any transaction management, setting the `transactional` property to `false` can disable transactions.

Controllers and other Grails artifacts will, of course, need to get hold of a reference to the singleton `BookmarkService`. In the next section, we explore how Grails' underlying Spring container handles this through *dependency injection*.

Services and Dependency Injection

It is important to note that services are *singletons*, which means there is only ever one instance of a service. So how do we go about getting a reference to a service within a controller, for example? Well, as part of Spring's dependency injection support, Spring has a concept called *autowiring* that allows dependencies to automatically be injected by name or type.

Grails services can be injected by name into a controller. For example, simply by creating a property with the name `bookmarkService` and a type of `BookmarkService` within the bookmark controller, the `BookmarkService` instance will automatically be available to the controller. Listing 10-2 demonstrates how this is done.

Listing 10-2. *Injecting a Service Instance into a Controller*

```
class BookmarkController {
    BookmarkService bookmarkService
    ...
}
```

The convention used for the name of the property is basically the property name representation of the class name. In other words, it is the class name with the first letter in lowercase following the JavaBean convention for property names. You can then invoke methods on the singleton `BookmarkService` instance, even though we have done nothing to explicitly look it up or initialize it. The underlying Spring IoC container handles all of this automatically.

Note Given we're dealing with web applications, which are by nature multithreaded, access to local fields needs to be synchronized due to services being singleton. This is important; as with any multithreaded environment, if you don't synchronize access, fields could be modified concurrently, causing inconsistencies within your application or exceptions to be thrown. Alternatively, you could avoid local fields altogether and save yourself the hassle of remembering to synchronize access.

The same convention can be used to inject services into other services, hence allowing your services to interact within one another. Now that you understand the basics of services, we're going to move on to looking at an example of implementing a service.

Services in Action

One common use of services is to provide an API that reads data from and writes data to an external API. As mentioned previously, this could be straight JDBC or an ORM system. However, it could also be an external web service, and that is what we are going to look at in the following example.

Social bookmarking is a competitive market, and since the launch of our bookmarks application, the powers that be have decided that it would be a good thing to integrate with another popular service called del.icio.us (http://del.icio.us). Luckily, del.icio.us provides a nice web API that uses a secure HTTPS protocol and XML to provide access to bookmarks.

The idea here is to provide a way for users to access their bookmarks on del.icio.us as well as our new bookmarks application. To facilitate this, if a user registers with the same user details on the bookmarks application, we want to be able to display the most recent bookmarks that user has registered on del.icio.us and also integrate del.icio.us bookmarks in our search feature.

Clearly, intermingling all of this logic into a controller would be foolish, as we may wish to reuse the API in other applications (something that we will be looking at in the next chapter). So what we're going to do is implement a service that handles the communication with the del.icio.us API by running the grails create-service target. Listing 10-3 demonstrates this in action.

Listing 10-3. *Running the create-service Target*

```
$ grails create-service
Buildfile: /Developer/grails/src/grails/build.xml

init-props:

create-service:
    [input] Enter service name:
delicious
    [copy] Copying 1 file to /Developer/grails-apps/bookmarks/grails-app/services
    [echo] Created service: grails-app/services/DeliciousService.groovy
```

```
internal-create-test-suite:
    [echo] Created test suite: grails-tests/DeliciousTests.groovy
```

Here we enter the text "delicious" in the same way as the previous bookmark example, and the result is a service called `grails-app/services/DeliciousService.groovy`:

```
class DeliciousService {
    boolean transactional = true
    def serviceMethod() {

    }
}
```

The `DeliciousService` is going to be using an external web service that will have its own transaction management policies, so having `transactional` set to `true` is not necessary. Listing 10-4 shows how to disable transactions by setting the `transactional` property to `false`.

Listing 10-4. *Disabling Transaction Demarcation*

```
class DeliciousService {
    boolean transactional = false
    ...
}
```

The current del.icio.us API, located at the address `https://api.del.icio.us/v1`, provides a number of web service methods for retrieving all bookmarks (or *posts* in del.icio.us lingo) or the most recent posts, to name just a couple of examples.

Crucially, however, it uses HTTPS for communication in combination with basic authentication to log in and retrieve user posts. The regular `java.net.URL` package does not provide any built-in support for HTTPS, and although support can be added via the Java Secure Sockets Extension (JSSE), possibly the easiest way to implement HTTPS communication is via the Jakarta Commons HttpClient library available from `http://jakarta.apache.org/commons/httpclient/`.

Follow the links on this site to download the latest HttpClient release (I used release 3.0 in the examples to follow) and place the enclosed JAR file within the `lib` directory of the bookmarks application as shown in Figure 10-1.

As Figure 10-1 demonstrates, a second JAR file from the Jakarta Commons project, called Commons Codec, is also needed. This file, which can be downloaded from `http://jakarta.apache.org/commons/codec/`, provides support for the Commons HttpClient's Base64 encoding functionality. For our purposes, all we need to know is that it is an additional dependency that we need within the `lib` directory.

Dependencies in place, let's move directly on to the example, starting with a new addition to the search feature.

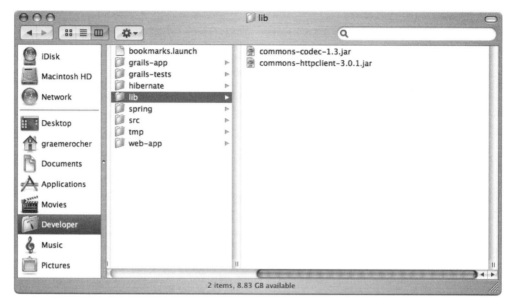

Figure 10-1. *Jakarta Commons HttpClient and Codec JAR files*

Example A: Extended Search Capability

The first bit of functionality we want to add is to augment the existing search feature to allow the bookmarks application to search del.icio.us posts as well as regular bookmarks. Figure 10-2 provides an example of the effect we want to achieve.

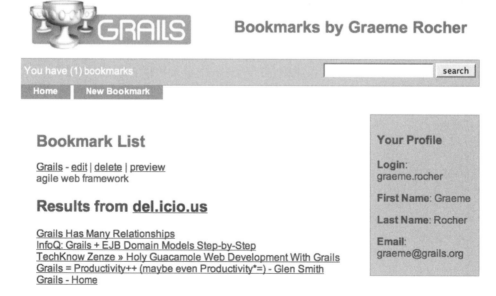

Figure 10-2. *Example of extended del.icio.us search*

To get these results, I entered "grails" in the search box. Since I am already a del.icio.us user (see `http://del.icio.us/graeme.rocher`) and have registered with the same details for the bookmarks application, I received additional results from del.icio.us as well as those I'd already created.

So how do we make this magic happen? Well, the del.icio.us API provides a mechanism for searching posts by tag using the `https://api.del.icio.us/v1/posts/all` web service method (henceforth simply referred to as `posts/all`). It supports an optional tag parameter, thus allowing us to search bookmarks on del.icio.us by tag. Perfect for what we need.

The `posts/all` call produces an XML response that resembles something like the following:

```
<posts tag="" user="graeme.rocher">
  <post href="http://grails.org/" description="Grails - Home"
  hash="6cfedbe75f413c56b6ce79e6fa102aba" tag="groovy grails"
  time="2005-11-29T20:30:47Z" />
  <post href="http://groovy.codehaus.org"
  description="Groovy - Home"
  hash="ca1e6357399774951eed4628d69eb84b"
  tag="groovy grails java" time="2005-11-29T20:30:05Z" />
</posts>
```

Essentially, what we have is one or many `post` elements that have an `href` attribute containing the link and a `description` attribute describing the link. What we need to do is translate this XML format into something our application will understand.

If you think about it, calling del.icio.us is going to involve some pretty repetitive things. We're going to need to do the following:

1. Create a URL to the API potentially containing parameters.

2. Execute a secure HTTPS call to the URL.

3. Parse the XML response.

Clearly, this sounds like a case for creating some sort of reusable code and in fact is a perfect job for closures. We're going to implement a private method within the `DeliciousService` that provides a reusable way to call the del.icio.us API. The method in question is called `withDelicious`, presented in Listing 10-5, and is an example of an advanced use of closures.

Listing 10-5. *Implementing del.icio.us Integration*

```
1 import org.apache.commons.httpclient.*
2 import org.apache.commons.httpclient.auth.AuthScope
3 import org.apache.commons.httpclient.methods.GetMethod
4
5 class DeliciousService {
6     boolean transactional = false
7
```

```
8     // a constant for the API location
9     static final API = "https://api.del.icio.us/v1"
10
11    private withDelicious(Map args,Closure callable) {
12        if(!args.user)
13            throw new IllegalArgumentException("Arg [user] is required")
14
15        // build the URL
16        def url = "${API}/${args.name}?"
17        args.params?.each { key,val ->
18            url+="&$key=$val"
19        }
20
21        // create Http client
22        def client = new HttpClient()
23        client
24          .state
25          .setCredentials( AuthScope.ANY,
26             new UsernamePasswordCredentials( args.user.login,
27                                              args.user.password))
28
29        def get = new GetMethod(url)
30        get.doAuthentication = true
31
32        // execute HTTP GET call
33        client.executeMethod(get)
34
35        // invoke callable closure
36        callable( new XmlSlurper().parse(get.responseBodyAsStream) )
37    }
38 }
```

That's probably a lot to swallow, so let's step through the code so you understand what's going on. First off, thanks to Groovy's seamless Java integration, we are able to import and use the Jakarta Commons HttpClient library with ease on lines 1 to 3. We then define a static constant to the del.icio.us API:

```
9     static final API = "https://api.del.icio.us/v1"
```

Notice in Groovy how simple it is to define constants, as there is no need to define the type and the default modifier is public, unlike in Java. Stepping through the withDelicious implementation, we define the method as taking two arguments:

```
11    private withDelicious(Map args,Closure callable) {
```

The first argument is a map that allows us to supply pseudo-named arguments to the method, while the second argument is a callable closure. We'll get to how we use this in a minute, but first let's continue to step through the code with lines 12 and 13 providing some validation and lines 15 through 19 building up the URL to the del.icio.us API call:

```
15        // build the URL
16        def url = "${API}/${args.name}?"
17        args.params?.each { key,val ->
18            url+="&$key=$val"
19        }
```

Here we use the API constant and a name argument within the args map to define the base URL. If there is a params argument within the args map, we then anticipate that it too is a map and iterate over each key and value appending the parameters to the API URL.

Once we have a URL, we can now send the HTTP request using Commons HttpClient:

```
21        // create Http client
22        def client = new HttpClient()
23        client
24          .state
25          .setCredentials( AuthScope.ANY,
26            new UsernamePasswordCredentials( args.user.login,
27                                             args.user.password))
```

First, we create the HttpClient instance and set some credentials on it using the login and password supplied by the user argument of the args map. The user argument is an instance of the User class from the bookmarks domain model. Next up, we execute an HTTP request using a GET method (as opposed to POST):

```
29        def get = new GetMethod(url)
30        get.doAuthentication = true
31
32        // execute HTTP GET call
33        client.executeMethod(get)
```

In this example, we create an org.apache.commons.httpclient.methods.GetMethod instance from the URL and set it to perform authentication. We then execute the method using the HttpClient class on line 33. Finally, we get to use the callable closure and invoke it:

```
36        callable( new XmlSlurper().parse(get.responseBodyAsStream) )
```

Interestingly, we use a Groovy class called groovy.util.XmlSlurper to parse the response XML into an object model representation. The XmlSlurper class is one of the amazing classes providing by the Groovy GDK for working with XML. Among other things, it allows you to use GPath to navigate an XML document.

■**Note** Recall that GPath is Groovy's equivalent to the XML technology XPath, and it provides a subtle expression language for navigating object graphs like an XML document.

The method uses a lot of advanced Groovy concepts that may be a little challenging to digest without a little more context, but in a moment we will look at how we use the withDelicious method to process the XML parsed by XmlSlurper into an object model we can work with.

Thanks to closures, we have provided an amazingly simple way to invoke the del.icio.us web service API. Listing 10-6 shows the `withDelicious` method in action.

Listing 10-6. *Finding All Bookmarks for a Tag*

```
1 class DeliciousService {
2    ...
3    def findAllForTag(String tag, User user) {
4        return withDelicious(name:"posts/all", user:user, params:[tag:tag]) { xml ->
5            def bookmarks = []
6            xml.post.each { p ->
7              bookmarks << new Bookmark(title:"${p.@description}",
8                                              url:new URL("${p.@href}"))
9            }
10            return bookmarks
11        }
12    }
13    ...
14 }
```

In Listing 10-6, we implement our first public method, called `findAllForTag`, that returns all the bookmarks from del.icio.us for the specified tag name and `User`. The method uses the `withDelicious` method, passing the name of the web service method to call as "post/all", the `User` instance, and a tag parameter.

Notice how Groovy allows us to provide a clean syntax to specify the named arguments that automatically get translated into a map and passed as the first argument to the method. In addition, the last argument to the method is the callable closure!

This is the closure that is invoked by the `withDelicious` method with the resulting XML from the del.icio.us response supplied as an argument to the closure. We then see the magic of the `XmlSlurper` in action within the body of the closure:

```
5        def bookmarks = []
6        xml.post.each { p ->
7            bookmarks << new Bookmark(title:"${p.@description}",
8                                            url:new URL("${p.@href}"))
9        }
10        return bookmarks
```

Here we create an empty list on line 5, and then simply refer to the `post` element inside the XML on line 6, and it returns a list of all `post` elements, thus allowing us to iterate over them. On line 7 we append each `Bookmark` instance to the list for each post returned by the del.icio.us XML using the left shift operator (`<<`) to perform the append operation.

In addition, when creating the `Bookmark` instances, we are able to refer to the attributes of each `post` element in the XML using Groovy's special @ field reference syntax. How does this compare to your experiences parsing XML in Java? Thanks to the dynamic nature of Groovy XML, parsing finally feels natural!

Now that we have converted the del.icio.us XML into our native domain model, we are ready to display the bookmarks in the view. First, however, we need to update the `BookmarkController` to invoke the `DeliciousService`. Listing 10-7 provides an example of how to add the `DeliciousService` as a property on the `BookmarkController` and then call it within the `search` action.

Listing 10-7. *Calling the DeliciousService from a Controller*

```
class BookmarkController {
    DeliciousService deliciousService
    ...
    def search = {
        ...
        def fromDelicious = null
        try {
            fromDelicious = deliciousService.findAllForTag(params.q, session.user)
        }
        catch(Exception e) {
            log.error('Failed to invoke del.icio.us: ' + e.message, e)
        }

        render(view:'list',model:[ bookmarkList:bookmarks.unique(),
                                    deliciousResults:fromDelicious ] )
    }
}
```

Remember that the `DeliciousService` instance is automatically injected into the `BookmarkController` by Spring, so all we have to do is invoke it, passing the search query as the tag name and the user located in the session. We then add the resulting bookmarks to the returned model.

■**Note** The code in Listing 10-7 uses a try/catch block under the assumption that occasionally something may go wrong when communicating with the del.icio.us API. Under this circumstance, we don't want the entire application to fail, hence the code simply logs the error when it occurs.

To finish up, we need to update the list view located in the grails-app/views/bookmark directory. All we need to do is check whether there are any deliciousResults in the model and render them as the results using the regular bookmark template. Listing 10-8 shows how this is done.

Listing 10-8. *Updated list View*

```
...
<g:render template="bookmark" var="bookmark" collection="${bookmarkList}" />

<g:if test="${deliciousResults}">
    <h2>Results from
        <a href="http://del.icio.us/${session.user.login}" target="_blank">
            del.icio.us
        </a>
    </h2>
    <g:render template="bookmark" var="bookmark" collection="${deliciousResults}" />
</g:if>
```

That's it! All and all you have learned a lot about services and what their place in the world is. Groovy's amazingly concise syntax and powerful XML processing features make it a extremely elegant language for communicating with web services such as that offered by del.icio.us.

■**Tip** The del.icio.us API uses a REST-like approach to web services. *REST* defines an architecture for creating web services using simple XML, a convention-based URL system, and HTTP. However, it is not the only standard; there are others such as SOAP and XML-RPC. Luckily, Groovy provides support for both through Groovy SOAP (http://groovy.codehaus.org/Groovy+SOAP) and the XML-RPC module (http://groovy.codehaus.org/XMLRPC).

The journey through our wave of feature enhancements doesn't end here, however. In the next section, you'll learn how to truly leverage the power of closures by extending the bookmarks application to display recent del.icio.us posts.

Example B: Latest del.icio.us Posts

We could have stopped this demonstration of services before this section, but since you've had a little exposure to closures, it is worth exploring their usefulness further and at the same time adding a new feature to the bookmarks application.

The feature in question is the ability to display the five most recent posts from the registered users del.icio.us account on the main bookmark screen as shown in Figure 10-3.

 **Bookmarks by Graeme Rocher**

You have (2) bookmarks   [   ] [search]

Home   **New Bookmark**

Bookmark List

Grails - Home - edit | delete | preview
Agile web framework
Groovy - edit | delete | preview
Dynamic language for the JVM

Latest from del.icio.us

Groovy - memorizable.org - The Flash Card Wiki - Groovy Flash Cards
jQuery: New Wave Javascript
Grails Has Many Relationships
InfoQ: Grails + EJB Domain Models Step-by-Step
TechKnow Zenze » Holy Guacamole Web Development With Grails

Your Profile

Login:
graeme.rocher

First Name: Graeme

Last Name: Rocher

Email:
graeme@grails.org

Figure 10-3. *Displaying the latest del.icio.us posts*

Once again, the del.icio.us API provides a web service method to facilitate this new addition called `https://api.del.icio.us/v1/posts/recent` (from now on referred to as `posts/recent`). The `posts/recent` web service method also accepts a `count` parameter to specify how many posts we need.

Since we've already implemented the `withDelicious` method, calling `posts/recent` to retrieve the top five most recent posts becomes trivial, as Listing 10-9 demonstrates.

Listing 10-9. *Retrieving the Latest del.icio.us Posts*

```
class DeliciousService {
    ...
    def findRecent(User user) {
        return withDelicious(name:"posts/recent",
                             user:user,
                             params:[count:5]) { xml ->
            def bookmarks = []
            xml.post.each {
                bookmarks << new Bookmark(title:"${it.@description}",
                                          url:new URL("${it.@href}"))
            }
            return bookmarks
        }
    }
    ...
}
```

In Listing 10-9, we create a findRecent method on the service that accepts a User domain object. We then call the withDelicious in the exact same manner as the findAllByTag method, except we change the name of the call to posts/recent and send the count parameter with a value of 5 to return only the top five most recent posts.

Next we need to update the BookmarkController's list action to return any del.icio.us results in the model as well as the normal bookmarks. Listing 10-10 provides an example of how this is done.

Listing 10-10. *Adding del.icio.us Posts to the list Action*

```
class BookmarkController {
    ...
    def list = {
        ...
        def fromDelicious = null
        try {
            fromDelicious = deliciousService.findRecent(session.user)
        }
        catch(Exception e) {
            log.error('Failed to invoke del.icio.us: ' + e.message, e)
        }

        [bookmarkList: Bookmark.findAllByUser(session.user, params ),
         deliciousList: fromDelicious ]
    }
}
```

Here we call the DeliciousService instance, passing the User in the session, and then add the results to the model. Finally, the grails-app/views/bookmarks/list.gsp view needs updating to display the latest del.icio.us posts if there are any as shown in Listing 10-11.

Listing 10-11. *Add del.icio.us Posts to list View*

```
<g:if test="${deliciousList}">
    <h2>Latest from
        <a href="http://del.icio.us/${session.user.login}"
            target="_blank">del.icio.us</a>
    </h2>
    <g:render template="bookmark" var="bookmark" collection="${deliciousList}" />
</g:if>
```

Although we have successfully implemented the feature, this is where it starts to get interesting. The observant reader may have noted that the closure passed to the withDelicious method, which extracts the bookmarks from the del.icio.us XML response, is identical for both calls in Listings 10-6 and 10-9.

It seems like a waste to have to repeat ourselves like this, especially if you recall closures can be assigned to variables. The reason this is significant is that it is also possible to define a closure that is a constant, hence avoiding unnecessary object creation. In Listing 10-12, we do just this by creating an EXTRACT_BOOKMARKS constant.

Listing 10-12. *Closures As Constants*

```
class DeliciousService {
    ...
    static final EXTRACT_BOOKMARKS = { xml ->
        def bookmarks = []
        xml.post.each {
            bookmarks << new Bookmark(title:"${it.@description}",
                                      url:new URL("${it.@href}"))
        }
        return bookmarks
    }

    def findRecent(User user) {
        return withDelicious( name:"posts/recent",
                                user:user,
                                params:[count:5],
                                EXTRACT_BOOKMARKS)
    }
    def findAllForTag(String tag, User user) {
        return withDelicious( name:"posts/all",
                                user:user,
                                params:[tag:tag],
                                EXTRACT_BOOKMARKS)
    }
    ...
}
```

This example clearly demonstrates the power of closures when used as *reusable code blocks*. We're able to reuse a snippet of logic as a constant called EXTRACT_BOOKMARKS (highlighted in bold) instead of unnecessarily repeating ourselves.

Closures provide much more than just the ability to perform iterations and looping (a common usage pattern admittedly), and although at first the potential usages don't always immediately become clear, once you understand their power, you'll be using them at every opportunity.

As with any code, it is important to consider how to automate testing, and hence it would be useful to write some unit tests to assert the behavior of the bookmarks application's del.icio.us integration. In the next section, we explore how to go about doing this.

Testing the Service

As with controllers, when you create a service, a blank unit test case is created for you. In the case of the DeliciousService, this is called grails-test/DeliciousTests.groovy. Since Grails unit tests are also configured via Spring, we can inject the DeliciousService instance into its test case in the same way as we would with a controller, thus allowing us to test the logic as in Listing 10-13.

Listing 10-13. *Unit Testing the DeliciousService*

```
class DeliciousTests extends GroovyTestCase {

    DeliciousService deliciousService

    void testFindAllForTag() {
        assert deliciousService != null
        def user = new User(login:'graeme.rocher',password:'...')
        def bookmarks = deliciousService.findAllForTag('grails',user)
        assert bookmarks.size() > 0
        def b = bookmarks.find { it.url == new URL("http://grails.org/") }
        assert b != null
    }
}
```

The test in Listing 10-13 is rather specific to my del.icio.us account; nevertheless, it serves to illustrate how to go about testing a service.

This marks the end of our coverage on services (although we'll be revisiting them in Chapter 11). In the next section, we look at another common activity in enterprise application development: scheduling repetitive tasks or *jobs.*

Scheduling Jobs with Quartz

A job is a task that needs to be performed at a set time or interval. Jobs are scheduled and managed by a job scheduler. As with other features in Grails, job support is provided by leveraging a robust existing library in the Quartz project (http://www.opensymphony.com/quartz/). Quartz is an enterprise job scheduler that can be integrated into any Java application to provide scheduling support.

Grails takes advantage of this power by providing *jobs by convention*. In other words, Grails provides a way to create jobs as classes that follow a set convention, and then configuration is handled for you automatically by the Grails runtime configuration engine and Quartz.

Let's start off by looking at the basics: how to create and schedule a simple job.

Simple Jobs

To start off, we're going to look at how to create a simple job that is executed in a timed interval. This could be every few seconds, hours, or days. First, however, we need to create the job, which we can again do via a Grails target.

The target in question is called grails create-job, and to demonstrate it in action, we create a job called "simple," as Listing 10-14 illustrates.

Listing 10-14. *Creating the simple Job*

```
$ grails create-job
Buildfile: /Developer/grails/src/grails/build.xml

init-props:

create-job:
    [input] Enter job class name:
simple
     [copy] Copying 1 file to /Developer/grails-apps/bookmarks/grails-app/jobs
     [echo] Schedules job created: grails-app/jobs/SimpleJob.groovy
```

Grails will create a new directory (if it doesn't already exist) called `grails-app/jobs` and place the newly created job within it. The resulting job will look something like the following code:

```
class SimpleJob {
    def timeout = 1000

    def execute() {
       // execute task
    }
}
```

By default the job is configured to start immediately upon loading and execute every second. The `timeout` property is specified in milliseconds, so in the preceding example this equates to a 1-second interval between executions.

Essentially, every second the `execute` method of the job will be called by the job scheduler. What you do within the `execute` method is entirely up to you. It could be some system maintenance task or maybe the execution of scheduled reports.

Occasionally, it's useful for a job to only start after a set period of time; this is where the `startInterval` property comes in. Like the `timeout` property, `startInterval` accepts a timing in milliseconds:

```
def startInterval = 10000
```

Here the job will only execute 10 seconds after the scheduler first loads. The scheduler is, of course, started when a Grails application first loads. Jobs can also optionally be placed in groups and given a name using the name and group properties. Listing 10-15 shows how this is done.

Listing 10-15. *Job Naming and Grouping*

```
class SimpleJob {
    def name = "MyJob"
    def group = "MyGroup"
    ...
}
```

This will become more relevant when in the section "Interacting with the Scheduler" later in this chapter. For the moment, however, it is time to look at an alternative way to schedule jobs that users of Unix's `crontab` command will be familiar with.

Cron Jobs

If you recall earlier, one potential usage of jobs is to schedule reports to be executed. The nature of reports, however, is that they tend to be executed at a set time rather than an interval. The time they are scheduled to be executed may represent the most inactive period for the web application.

Clearly, this type of use case warrants a different mechanism than the interval-based one we have seen with the simple job in the previous section. Luckily, the creators of the Unix cron utility have already thought about this and created a concept called a *cron expression*.

A cron expression represents a firing schedule, for example, "at 10:30 p.m. every last Sunday of the month," and is represented by six or seven fields representing seconds, minutes, hours, day of the month, month, day of the week, and year (optional), respectively. For example, the cron expression from the aforementioned English language version would be

```
0 30 22 ? * 1L
```

This may seem a little baffling at first, but there is method to the madness. Table 10-1 should make things a little clearer.

Table 10-1. *Cron Expression Fields*

Field Name	Allowed Values	Allowed Special Characters
Seconds	0–59	, - * /
Minutes	0–59	, - * /
Hours	0–23	, - * /
Day of month	1–31	, - * ? / L W C
Month	1–12 or JAN–DEC	, - * /
Day of week	1–7 or SUN–SAT	, - * ? / L #
Year (optional)	Empty or 1970–2099	, - * /

Essentially, each field in the cron expression relates to one of the rows in the left column in the order in which it is defined. The second column of allowed values is simple enough, but it is the special characters (some of which are used in the example expression) that might not be so clear:

- The asterisk (*) character is like a wildcard and means any value is allowed. It appears in the example expression to specify every month.

- The question mark (?) character is only applicable to the day-of-week and day-of-month fields and cannot be specified by both at the same time. It is used to allow no specific value in either field. The example expression indicates there is no specific value for the day-of-month field.

- You can use a comma (,) character to specify a group of values. For example, the value SUN,THU,FRI in the day-of-week field translates to "on the days Sunday, Thursday, and Friday."

- A range of values can be specified using the hyphen (-) character in the middle of two values. For example, if you only want the job to execute on working days, you could do MON-FRI in the day-of-week field.

- The forward slash (/) character allows increments to be specified in any of the fields. For example, if you have a frequently executed job, you may want to have a value of */15 in the seconds field, which means to execute the job on the seconds 0, 15, 30, and 45.

- The L character is an interesting one as it generally is shorthand for "last," and if placed in either the day-of-week or day-of-month fields on its own, it means the last day of the week or month, respectively. However, this behavior changes if it is included *after* another character. The example specifies 1L in the day-of-week field, which means "the last Sunday of the month."

- Next, we have the W character that, when appended to the end of another character, means "the nearest weekday to the given day." For example, using 3W will result in the nearest weekday to the third of the month. If the third is a Sunday, this will be Monday; otherwise, if it's a Saturday, the job will execute on a Friday. In addition, W can be used in combination with L in the form LW to indicate the last weekday of the month.

- Finally, the # character is used in the middle of two numbers such as 5#2, which translates to "the second Thursday of the month." With this character, it is important to remember that if the second number is out of range, the job will never be executed.

So now that you have garnered some knowledge about cron expressions, let's have a look how you go about specifying them in a Grails job, as shown in Listing 10-16.

Listing 10-16. *The simple Job Is No Longer So Simple*

```
class SimpleJob {
    def cronExpression = "0 0 6 * * ?"
    ...
}
```

Here we have removed the timeout property and provided a cronExpression property that tells the job to execute at 6 a.m. every day. Again, the remaining configuration is handled for you at runtime.

There is plenty more information on Quartz and cron expressions on the Quartz web site, which is worth familiarizing yourself with. However, Table 10-2 presents some examples taken from the Quartz Javadoc of various possible cron expressions and their meaning.

Table 10-2. *Example Cron Expressions*

Expression	Meaning
0 0 12 * * ?	Fire at 12 p.m. (noon) every day.
0 15 10 ? * *	Fire at 10:15 a.m. every day.
0 15 10 * * ?	Fire at 10:15 a.m. every day.
0 15 10 * * ? *	Fire at 10:15 a.m. every day.
0 15 10 * * ? 2005	Fire at 10:15 a.m. every day during the year 2005.
0 * 14 * * ?	Fire every minute starting at 2 p.m. and ending at 2:59 p.m. every day.
0 0/5 14 * * ?	Fire every 5 minutes starting at 2 p.m. and ending at 2:55 p.m. every day.
0 0/5 14,18 * * ?	Fire every 5 minutes starting at 2 p.m. and ending at 2:55 p.m., AND fire every 5 minutes starting at 6 p.m. and ending at 6:55 p.m. every day.
0 0-5 14 * * ?	Fire every minute starting at 2 p.m. and ending at 2:05 p.m. every day.
0 10,44 14 ? 3 WED	Fire at 2:10 p.m. and at 2:44 p.m. every Wednesday in the month of March.
0 15 10 ? * MON-FRI	Fire at 10:15 a.m. every Monday, Tuesday, Wednesday, Thursday, and Friday.
0 15 10 15 * ?	Fire at 10:15 a.m. on the fifteenth day of every month.
0 15 10 L * ?	Fire at 10:15 a.m. on the last day of every month.
0 15 10 ? * 6L	Fire at 10:15 a.m. on the last Friday of every month.
0 15 10 ? * 6L 2002-2005	Fire at 10:15 a.m. on every last Friday of every month during the years 2002, 2003, 2004, and 2005.
0 15 10 ? * 6#3	Fire at 10:15 a.m. on the third Friday of every month.

Clearly, cron jobs provide a lot of power at your fingertips, and it would be silly not to take advantage of at least some of it for the bookmarks application. In the next section, we'll be taking a look at how we can apply what we know so far about jobs to allow users of the bookmarks application to schedule e-mail notifications.

Jobs in Action

To demonstrate how jobs can be used, we're going to add a new feature to the bookmarks applications that allows user to *subscribe* to certain tag names. Then when other users create bookmarks that use the tags a user has subscribed to, he or she will receive a weekly e-mail with a list of bookmarks that other users have created for the tags they are interested in.

In essence, this is similar to what a weekly reporting system might do and thus serves as a good example use case. To enable this feature, we'll be adding a Subscriptions menu item to the Bookmark List page (see Figure 10-4).

Figure 10-4. *The new Subscriptions menu item*

The new Subscriptions link will take you to a page that allows users to manage the tags that they are subscribed to. The page in question will display a simple HTML list of tag names, but we'll be using some Ajax techniques you learned in the previous chapter to spice things up. Figure 10-5 shows what the subscription management feature will look like in practice.

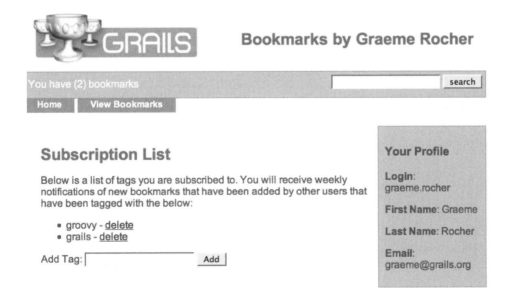

Figure 10-5. *The Subscription management page*

Before we can get going with the UI side of things, we need to make some alterations to the bookmarks application's domain model, which the next section covers in detail.

Updating the Domain Model

First up, we need to extend our domain model to add the concept of subscriptions. To do so, we'll create a Subscription class that relates a User to the Tag he or she is subscribed to. The UML diagram in Figure 10-6 illustrates the relationships between Subscriptions, Tags, and Users.

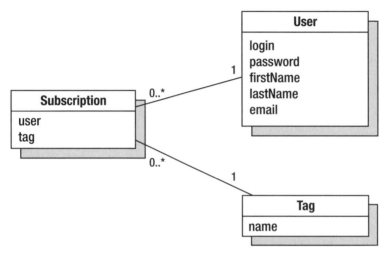

Figure 10-6. *Subscription class diagram*

A User can have zero to many Subscription instances, while a Subscription relates to exactly one User and one Tag. Once again, we can call on grails create-domain-class to help us out, but once created, the final Subscription class will look something like the following:

```
class Subscription {
    def belongsTo = [User,Tag]

    User user
    Tag tag

    String toString() { "$tag" }
}
```

Here we add a toString implementation that uses the Tag to represent the Subscription. Among other things, this allows us to easily represent a subscription in the view.

Implementing a Controller

Now that the domain model has been amended, we should create a new SubscriptionController that allows us to manage user subscriptions. To do so, we can use the grails generate-controller target to create a basis from which we can work.

Given how simple the Subscription domain model is, most of the actions generated prove unnecessary, so we can remove all except the list, delete, and save actions.

Still, it's important to note that even though we are throwing away most of what the generated controller does, it provided us with a starting point that represents a time savings, however small.

Moving on, we need to make significant modifications to the SubscriptionController. For one, we don't want to list all Subscription instances, but only those relating to the user in the session. Hence we modify the list action appropriately as in Listing 10-17.

Listing 10-17. *Modified SubscriptionController list Action*

```
def list = {
    [ subscriptionList: Subscription.findAllByUser( session.user,params ) ]
}
```

Quite simply, we change the call to Subscription.list() to use a dynamic finder that searches for all subscriptions by user. This is then returned as the resulting model, which the view can display.

Of course, we haven't created the view yet. This is something we will get to in a moment. For now, we need to continue adapting SubscriptionController to our needs with the next target being the delete action, as shown in Listing 10-18.

Listing 10-18. *Modified SubscriptionController delete Action*

```
def delete = {
        def subscription = Subscription.get( params.id )
        subscription?.delete()
        render(template:"subscription",
                   var:"subscription",
                   collection:Subscription.findAllByUser( session.user ))
}
```

Since we are going to use Ajax to manage the addition and deletion of subscriptions, the existing flow control is unnecessary, so we adapt the delete action to simply attempt a delete if the object is not null. This is done through clever use of the safe dereference operator in the code highlighted in bold.

Here the safe-deference operator will gracefully not call the delete() method on the Subscription object if it is null instead of the usual ugly NullPointerException. Finally, we use the render method to render a snippet of markup using a subscription template. We'll have a look at the details of this template later in the section, but fundamentally it will be used to update a list of subscriptions using Ajax.

Finally, the save action needs to be amended to use the User in the session and locate a Tag for a specified tagName parameter. Also, a user shouldn't be able to create the same subscription twice, so we can add a little logic to handle that. Listing 10-19 brings all of these concepts together as an example.

Listing 10-19. *Modified SubscriptionController save Action*

```
def save = {
    def t = Tag.findByName(params.tagName)
    if(!t)t= new Tag(name:params.tagName).save()

    if(!Subscription.findByUserAndTag(session.user,t))
        new Subscription(user:session.user, tag:t).save()
```

```
        render(template:"subscription",
                    var:"subscription",
                    collection:Subscription.findAllByUser( session.user ))
    }
```

Highlighted in bold is the check to see whether the Subscription already exists. Remember that null evaluates to false in Groovy, so we can use a finder this way inside an if block. Like the delete action, the save action will render the user's subscriptions at the end using the subscription template.

Those three concise actions make up the functionality of the controller, but remember, to get it to participate in our login mechanism, it has to extend SecureController. All in all, the results of our efforts can be seen here:

```
class SubscriptionController extends SecureController {
    def list = {
        [ subscriptionList: Subscription.findAllByUser( session.user,params ) ]
    }
    def delete = {
        def subscription = Subscription.get( params.id )
        subscription?.delete()

        render(template:"subscription",
                    var:"subscription",
                    collection:Subscription.findAllByUser( session.user ))
    }
    def save = {
        def t = Tag.findByName(params.tagName)
        if(!t)t= new Tag(name:params.tagName).save()

        if(!Subscription.findByUserAndTag(session.user,t))
            new Subscription(user:session.user, tag:t).save()

        render(template:"subscription",
                    var:"subscription",
                    collection:Subscription.findAllByUser( session.user ))
    }
}
```

With the controller done, we have successfully implemented the necessary server-side logic. Now let's move on to the view side of things in the next section.

Creating the View and Template

Right, now it is time to create the Ajax-inspired view. The first thing to do is create the link from the Bookmark List page to the Subscriptions page. This requires the addition of a new menu item:

```
<span class="menuButton">
    <g:link controller="subscription" action="list">Subscriptions</g:link>
</span>
```

The thing that is important to note here is the `controller` attribute. Remember, the `BookmarkController` creates the Bookmark List page, so if we were to omit this attribute, it would be assumed that we were linking to the `list` action within the `BookmarkController`.

To create a link to the `SubscriptionController` as desired, we need to explicitly define the controller name as this example demonstrates. Once we have a link in place, we need to create the view for the `list` action. This needs to be created in the `grails-app/views/subscription` directory and called `list.gsp` per the convention.

The easiest thing to do is to simply copy the `grails-app/views/bookmark/list.gsp` view and then modify it to our needs as shown in Listing 10-20.

Listing 10-20. *The Subscription list View*

```
1  <html>
2    <head>
3        <meta http-equiv="Content-Type" content="text/html; charset=UTF-8"/>
4        <meta name="layout" content="main" />
5        <title>Subscription List</title>
6    </head>
7    <body>
8      <div class="nav">
9          <span class="menuButton">
10             <a href="${createLinkTo(dir:'')}">Home</a>
11           </span>
12         <span class="menuButton">
13           <g:link controller="bookmark" action="list">View Bookmarks</g:link>
14         </span>
15     </div>
16     <div class="body">
17       <h1 id="title">Subscription List</h1>
18       <g:if test="${flash.message}">
19           <div class="message">
20                 ${flash.message}
21           </div>
22       </g:if>
23       <p>Below is a list of tags you are subscribed to. You will receive
24            weekly notifications of new bookmarks that have been added by
25            other users that have been tagged with the following:
26       </p>
27       <ul id="subscriptions">
28         <g:render template="subscription" var="subscription"
29                     collection="${subscriptionList}" />
30       </ul>
31       <p>
```

```
32          <g:formRemote name="addTag" url="[action:'save']"
33                                                     update="subscriptions">
34              Add Tag: <g:textField name="tagName" />
35                              <g:submitButton value="Add" />
36          </g:formRemote>
37              </p>
38          </div>
39      </body>
40  </html>
```

The main areas of interest are highlighted in bold. First, on line 27, we create a new HTML list element with an ID of subscriptions. This is the element that will be updated by our Ajax requests when adding and removing subscriptions.

Next, on lines 28 and 29, we have a call to the <g:render> tag that uses the same subscriptions template as the one referenced in the previous section when creating the save and delete actions of the SubscriptionController:

```
<g:render template="subscription" var="subscription"
                        collection="${subscriptionList}" />
```

This does the job of rendering the initial list of subscriptions for the user to view when the page first loads. It takes the subscriptionList model object, which is a java.util.List returned by the list action, and applies the subscription template to each subscription in the list.

Finally, on lines 32 to 36, we have a form that uses Ajax to asynchronously add new subscriptions to the list using the save action developed in the previous section:

```
<g:formRemote name="addTag" url="[action:'save']"
                                    update="subscriptions">
    Add Tag: <g:textField name="tagName" />
                <g:submitButton value="Add" />
</g:formRemote>
```

The <g:formRemote> tag is set to update the subscriptions HTML list element with the contents of the response. What we haven't yet looked at is the subscriptions template that is used to render the list of subscriptions by the save and delete actions.

The template in Listing 10-21, which is saved to grails-app/views/subscription/ _subscription.gsp, is remarkably simple; it creates an HTML list element for each subscription.

Listing 10-21. *The Subscription Template*

```
<li>${subscription} -
    <g:remoteLink action="delete"
                        id="${subscription.id}"
                        update="subscriptions">delete</g:remoteLink>
</li>
```

The interesting part is the <g:remoteLink> tag, which again uses Ajax to delete a subscription and then update the subscriptions HTML list. So far we have achieved much in the way of adding the ability to manage user subscriptions, but I have yet to cover how to go about scheduling a job to send subscription notifications.

In the next sections, we will look at doing just this and at the same time get to work with some pretty advanced Groovy subjects like more on closures, builders, and Groovy Mocks.

Scheduling the Job

Before we start, here's a recap on the goal of our task: what we want to achieve is the ability to e-mail users bookmark links that are related to the tags they have subscribed to. In other words, if they're interested primarily in topics related to Groovy, they could subscribe to the tag groovy, after which any new Groovy bookmarks will be sent to them in a weekly e-mail.

So the job itself needs the capability to send e-mail. There are a number of ways to do this in Groovy, but since we've already embraced the Jakarta Commons libraries in this example, we'll be using Commons E-mail.

The Commons E-mail library is available via the Apache Jakarta web site at the address `http://jakarta.apache.org/commons/email/`. Once downloaded, place the enclosed JAR file inside the `lib` directory of the bookmarks application. In addition, Commons E-mail is dependent on two libraries available from Sun:

- *The JavaBeans Activation Framework* (`http://java.sun.com/products/javabeans/jaf`): JAF is a standard extension to the Java platform that lets you take advantage of standard services to determine the type of an arbitrary piece of data, encapsulate access to it, discover the operations available on it, and instantiate the appropriate bean to perform the operation(s).

- *JavaMail API* (`http://java.sun.com/products/javamail/`): The JavaMail API provides a platform-independent and protocol-independent framework to build mail and messaging applications.

As part of the downloaded archives for each of these frameworks, you will find two JAR files called `activation.jar` and `mail.jar`, which again need to be placed within the `lib` directory of the bookmarks application. The `lib` directory should now resemble something like the one in Figure 10-7.

Once this has been set up, go ahead and create a new job for monitoring subscriptions using the `grails create-job` target you learned about earlier. Listing 10-22 shows how this is done.

Listing 10-22. *Creating the Subscriptions Job*

```
$ grails create-job
Buildfile: /Developer/grails/src/grails/build.xml

init-props:

create-job:
    [input] Enter job class name:
subscription
    [copy] Copying 1 file to /Developer/grails-apps/bookmarks/grails-app/jobs
    [echo] Schedules job created: grails-app/jobs/SubscriptionJob.groovy
```

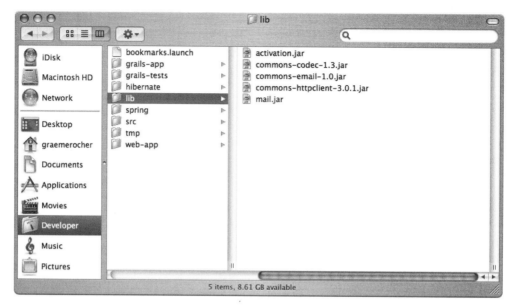

Figure 10-7. *The bookmarks lib directory*

When prompted, enter "subscription" and press the Return key. The target will create a new job called grails-app/jobs/SubscriptionJob.groovy. What we want the job to do is send a weekly e-mail to all subscribed users. For the sake of this example, we'll be sending the e-mails on Friday, as the powers that be feel people are more likely to do a little more browsing on the last day of the working week!

To summarize the use case, the job needs to do the following:

1. Find all the users with subscriptions.

2. For each user, get all the tags he or she is subscribed to.

3. Find any bookmarks that have been created in the last week and have been tagged with any of the subscribed to tags.

4. Send an e-mail to each user containing the bookmark links.

First, however, let's configure the job correctly so that it uses a cron expression to execute at 6 a.m. on each Friday of the month. Listing 10-23 provides an example that fulfills this use case.

Listing 10-23. *SubscriptionJob with Cron Expression*

```
class SubscriptionJob {
    def cronExpression = "0 0 6 ? * FRI"
    def execute() {
        // execute job
    }
}
```

This cron expression says, "Execute at 6 a.m. on Friday of each week of the month." Now that we have this in place, let's start the implementation of the execute method. The first job was to locate all users who have subscriptions. To do this, we're going to use a criteria query, as this allows us to use projections on the Subscription class to obtain a distinct list of user properties within it:

```
def criteria = Subscription.createCriteria()
def subscribedUsers = criteria.list {
        projections {
                distinct("user")
        }
}
```

Here we use the distinct projection that behaves in the same way as the SQL distinct keyword by selecting all distinct user properties from the Subscription class. Once we have this list of subscribed users, we can iterate over them using Groovy's each method:

```
subscribedUsers.each { user ->
```

For each User, we need to obtain a list of tags he or she is subscribed to. This can be achieved with a combination of a dynamic finder and GPath:

```
def subscribedTags = Subscription.findAllByUser(user).tag
```

Here we retrieve all subscriptions for the User, and the appended reference to the tag property automatically creates a list of tag instances thanks to GPath. The next requirement is to find all bookmarks that have been created in the last week and have been tagged with one of the tags in the subscribedTags variable we created in the last step. This is a perfect job for criteria:

```
def criteria = Bookmark.createCriteria()
def now = new Date()
def bookmarks = criteria.list {
        notEqual("user", user)
        between("dateCreated",now-7,now)
        tags {
                inList("tag", subscribedTags)
        }
}
```

Here we create a criteria instance that has three elements:

```
notEqual("user", user)
```

First, we execute a call to notEqual that ensures bookmarks that are created by the user aren't sent to him or her, as there is no need for a user to see his or her own bookmarks again!

```
between("dateCreated",now-7,now)
```

Next we use the Date instance created earlier to add a clause that will only include bookmarks for the last seven days. Groovy has an overloaded subtraction operator that allows you to subtract a number that represents days from an existing date. By subtracting 7 from the current time, we get a date that represents a week ago.

```
tags {
     inList("tag", subscribedTags)
}
```

Here we create a `criteria` element that relates to the `tags` property of the `Bookmark` class. Remember, `Bookmark` instances can have many `TagReference` instances via the `tags` property. Given that each `TagReference` has a `tag` property, the preceding clause essentially says that the `tag` property of each `TagReference` must be in the list of subscribed tags we retrieved earlier.

What this does is allow us to query the `tags` *association* to ensure we only get `Bookmark` instances that are tagged appropriately.

Right, now that we have a list of bookmarks that need to be delivered to a user being iterated over, we need to consider how we're going to send the e-mail. To have a bit of fun and explore the possibilities that Groovy builders offer, we're going to use one to build the e-mail.

What we're going to do is implement a `sendMail` method that takes the `User` to which the mail is being sent, the subject of the e-mail, and crucially a *closure* that represents the body of the e-mail. If you recall in Chapter 2 I introduced builders, and more specifically the Groovy `MarkupBuilder` that allows the construction of markup such as HTML programmatically. We're going to use this capability as a way of generating an HTML e-mail to send to each user.

We're then going to use the HTML e-mail features of the Commons E-mail library to deliver said e-mail. Let's have a look at the definition of the `sendMail` method in full and then we'll step through the code so you can see exactly what's going on. Listing 10-24 provides the full example.

Listing 10-24. *The sendMail Method*

```
 1 def sendMail(User to, String subject, Closure bodyContent) {
 2      def sw = new StringWriter()
 3      def mkp = new groovy.xml.MarkupBuilder(new PrintWriter(sw))
 4      mkp.html {
 5          body(bodyContent)
 6      }
 7
 8      def email = new org.apache.commons.mail.HtmlEmail(
 9                                  hostName: EMAIL_SERVER,
10                                  subject : subject,
11                                  htmlMsg    : sw.toString()
12      )
13
14      email.setFrom("noreply@bookmarks.grail.org" , "Grails Bookmarks")
15      email.addTo(to.email, "$to")
16      email.send()
17 }
```

As mentioned previously, the `sendMail` method accepts three arguments: the `User` to send the e-mail to, the subject of the e-mail as a `String`, and the body of the e-mail as a closure. The first thing that it does is use Groovy's `MarkupBuilder` to output the e-mail to a `StringWriter` instance on lines 2 to 6. The crucial bit happens on the following lines:

```
4        mkp.html {
5             body(bodyContent)
6        }
```

Here we use the MarkupBuilder to construct the HTML e-mail and pass the bodyContent closure into the call to the body tag. The resulting output will look something like this:

```
<html>
   <body>
        <!-- output from the bodyContent closure here -->
   </body>
</html>
```

Next we construct the e-mail to send using the Commons E-mail API's org.apache.commons.mail.HtmlEmail class on lines 8 to 12. We use Groovy's additional default constructor to initialize the HtmlEmail instance with the following property values:

- The hostName property is set to an EMAIL_SERVER constant, the value for which points at the e-mail server. In our application, this is set to localhost for a locally configured SMTP server.

- The subject of the e-mail is set to the subject argument that was passed in via the sendMail method's argument list.

- The htmlMsg property is set to the output from the StringWriter that was written to by the MarkupBuilder.

Finally, on lines 14 to 16 we set a default "from" address to some made-up address and add the User instance's e-mail address as the address to send to. We then simply execute the send() method on the email instance to send our e-mail.

Now let's see the usage of the sendMail method and the power of Groovy builders in action. Remember that builders use Groovy's closure support plus method calls to create a tree-like structure. Since closures can also be references like a regular variable, we can use this to implement methods that use builders under the hood.

Using this feature, we can dynamically create an HTML e-mail using the builder syntax and the sendMail method. Listing 10-25 shows how this is done.

Listing 10-25. *Calling the sendMail Method*

```
if(bookmarks) {
    sendMail(user,"Latest Bookmarks") {
        p("Hi ${user.firstName}!")
        p("""Below are some recent bookmarks
            for the tags you're interested in!""")
        for(b in bookmarks) {
            p {
                a(href:b.url, b.title)
            }
        }
```

```
            p("Enjoy the bookmarks!")
            p("The Bookmarks Team")
        }
    }
}
```

Here if there are any bookmarks to send to the subscribed user, we invoke the sendMail method, passing the user to send the bookmarks to, a subject of "Latest Bookmarks," and a closure that uses the MarkupBuilder syntax to construct an HTML e-mail.

The resulting e-mail will look something like the following:

```
<html>
    <body
    <p>Hi Graeme!</p>
    <p>Below are the most recent bookmarks for the tags you're interested in!</p>
    <p><a href="http://grails.org">Grails - Home</a></p>
    <p><a href="http://groovy.codehaus.org">Groovy - Home</a></p>
    <p>Enjoy the bookmarks!</p>
    <p>The Bookmarks Team</p>
    </body>
</html>
```

The HtmlEmail class also allows you to specify an alternative text e-mail if the user's e-mail client does not support HTML mail. For the sake of brevity, however, I have left this out. We've got to use quite a few advanced Groovy features in this example, including builders, for not only the HTML e-mail, but also construction of a complex criteria query. The full listing of what we have achieved can be seen here:

```
class SubscriptionJob {
    static final EMAIL_SERVER = "localhost"

    def cronExpression = "0 0 6 ? * FRI"
    def name = "subscriptionJob"
    def group = "bookmarks"

  def execute() {
     def criteria = Subscription.createCriteria()
     def subscribedUsers = criteria.list {
         projections {
             distinct("user")
         }
      }
      subscribedUsers.each { User user ->
          def subscribedTags = Subscription.findAllByUser(user).tag

          criteria = Bookmark.createCriteria()
          def now = new Date()
          def bookmarks = criteria.list {
```

```
                    notEqual("user", user)
                    between("dateCreated",now-7,now)
                    tags {
                         inList("tag", subscribedTags)
                    }
              }
           if(bookmarks) {
                sendMail(user,"Latest Bookmarks") {
                    p("Hi $user!")
                    p("""Below are some recent bookmarks
                             for the tags you're interested in! """)
                      for(b in bookmarks) {
                           p {
                                a(href:b.url, b.title)
                            }
                        }
                    p("Enjoy the bookmarks!")
                    p("The Bookmarks Team")
                }
            }
        }
    }

    def sendMail(User to,String subject,Closure bodyContent) {
        def sw = new StringWriter()
        def mkp = new groovy.xml.MarkupBuilder(new PrintWriter(sw))
        mkp.html {
             body(bodyContent)
        }
        def email = new org.apache.commons.mail.HtmlEmail(
                                      hostName: EMAIL_SERVER,
                                      subject : subject,
                                      htmlMsg    : sw.toString()
                          )
        email.setFrom("noreply@bookmarks.grail.org" ,
                          "Grails Bookmarks Application")
        email.addTo(to.email, "$to")
        email.send()
    }
}
```

Given that we're doing some relatively complex queries and object graph navigation, the preceding code is amazingly concise, thanks to all the syntax advancements in Groovy. Like any piece of complex code, it is important to think about ways to unit test.

Yes, even jobs need to be unit tested, but because of the way a job has a single point of entry (the execute method) and no returned result, it would be rather pointless just executing the job and hoping that it works. To thoroughly test that the preceding code is doing what it should, we need to use mocks, and more specifically dynamic Groovy Mocks!

Testing the Job

As with services and controllers, when we create a job, a test case is automatically created for us. In this case, the test case in question is called grails-test/SubscriptionTests.groovy. What we want to test is that when user A has a subscription and user B adds a new bookmark, user A will receive an e-mail when the job is executed.

Of course, the test should not assume there is a working SMTP server configured, as this will be left to the *integration* tests.

■**Note** Integration tests differ from unit tests in that they are exclusively run on the production environment to check that dependent services such as the database, SMTP servers, remote connections, and so on are operating correctly. Unit tests, on the other hand, are important to test the flow of logic within an application.

To get around this little problem and to make sure we're properly testing the *logic* of the code, we're going to use a Groovy Mock to *mock* the behavior of the HtmlMail class from Commons E-mail. You've already been exposed to mocks in Chapter 6, but you'll see more of them in action here.

Needless to say, the first thing to do, as in Listing 10-26, is define a test case for the execute method of the job.

Listing 10-26. *The Job Test Case*

```
class SubscriptionTests extends GroovyTestCase {
    void testExecute() {
        // test stuff here
    }
}
```

Now we need some test data. We're going to create two dummy users, one of which is subscribed to a tag called grails. Listing 10-27 provides an example of how easy it is to create test data with Grails.

Listing 10-27. *Creating the Dummy Users and Subscription*

```
1 def userA = new User(login:"graeme",
2                                         password:"graeme",
3                                         firstName:"Graeme",
4                                         lastName:"Rocher",
5                                         email:"graeme@grails.org").save()
6        // create a tag
7        def t = new Tag(name:"grails").save()
8        // create the subscription for the user to the tag
9        def s = new Subscription(user:userA,tag:t).save()
10
```

```
11      // create another user that is going to create a bookmark that
12      // the other user should receive notification of
13      def userB = new User(login:"other",
14                              password:"other",
15                              firstName:"other",
16                              lastName:"user",
17                              email:"other@grails.org").save()
```

What we have achieved here is to create two User instances, the first of which is subscribed to a tag called grails on line 9. The use of Groovy's default constructor for defining the property values plus the inline calls to the save method make it remarkably easy to create test data.

However, our job, excuse the pun, is not yet complete. What we want to do is test that when user B creates a new bookmark, user A will receive an e-mail notification when the job is executed. To do this, we need to simulate user B creating a new bookmark as in Listing 10-28.

Listing 10-28. *Creating a New Bookmark for User B*

```
// create a new bookmark tagged with Grails.
def b = new Bookmark(title:"Grails Download Page",
                        url:new URL("http://grails.org/Download"),
                        notes:"",
                        user:userB)

// here we tag the bookmark with the subscribed-to tag
b.addTagReference(new TagReference(user:userB,tag:t))
b.save()
```

OK, that's the test data done. So now let's start with some testing. First we want to test that the job actually sends mail. To do this, we're going to use the groovy.mock.interceptor. MockFor class. As discussed in Chapter 6, what this does is create a dynamic Groovy Mock that will intercept calls to the target class:

```
def emailMock =
        new groovy.mock.interceptor.MockFor(org.apache.commons.mail.HtmlEmail)
```

In the preceding example, I have used fully qualified class names, but please feel free to include imports if you so choose. Nevertheless, what this will do is create a stub for the HtmlEmail class, which we can then *use*. First, however, as the example in Listing 10-29 demonstrates, we need to *mock* the method calls to this class and test the incoming data.

Listing 10-29. *Testing Method Calls Using the HtmlEmail Mock*

```
emailMock.demand.setFrom { String addr, String name ->
        assert addr == "noreply@bookmarks.grail.org"
        assert name == "Grails Bookmarks Application"
}
emalMock.demand.addTo {  String addr, String name ->
        assert addr == userA.email
        assert name == userA.toString()
}
```

```
emailMock.demand.send {
        return true
}
```

Here we make sure that the "from" address is the made-up address defined earlier (this could be a constant by the way), and then we check that the "to" address set is user A's e-mail address. Remember that the Groovy Mock uses the demand property on mocks followed by the method name and a closure to replace a call to the real HtmlEmail method. Also, if the method *is not* executed at all, the test will fail.

The last "demand" of the test is that the send method is called. Since we know that the test will fail if it is not called, we can just use an empty closure, although in this case we have returned true just to increase clarity. So that's that; now all we need to do is execute the job and check that it works as expected with the test data in Listing 10-30.

Listing 10-30. *Testing the Job*

```
def job = new SubscriptionJob()
emailStub.use {
    job.execute()
}
```

Finally, in Listing 10-30, to test the job, we simply create a new instance and then *use* the emailMock to execute it. Within the scope of the closure passed to the use method, Groovy will mock the calls to the HtmlMail class dynamically. Our testing endeavors have not finished here, however; after all, you can never have too many tests. What the tests so far haven't achieved is to test the contents of the e-mail that is being sent out to make sure that it contains the relevant link.

To do this, we're going to mock the job class itself, specifically the sendMail method. In Listing 10-31, we create a new mock called sendMailMock that handles the intricacies of this task.

Listing 10-31. *Mocking the sendMail Method*

```
def sendMailMock = new MockFor(SubscriptionJob)
sendMailMock.demand.sendMail { User user, String subject, Closure bodyContent ->
        println("Checking generated email")

    def sw = new StringWriter()
    def mkp = new groovy.xml.MarkupBuilder(new PrintWriter(sw))
    mkp.html {
        body(bodyContent)
    }
    assert sw.toString()
        .indexOf('<a href="http://grails.org/Download">Grails Download Page</a>')
}
```

In this example, we create another MockFor instance for the SubscriptionJob class and then demand the sendMail method be called. We can then validate the closure that is passed to the method by outputting to a string and then checking the contents. Clearly, you could go a lot further in testing the structure of the e-mail and what not, possibly even involving XML parsers. For the purposes of this example, however, this is enough to get the general picture.

Executing the mock is then done in the same way as in the previous example:

```
sendMailStub.use {
    job.execute()
}
```

Once again, here is the complete code listing for the unit tests that we've developed through the course of this section:

```
import groovy.mock.interceptor.StubFor

class SubscriptionTests extends GroovyTestCase {

void testExecute() {
    def userA = new User(login:"graeme",
                             password:"graeme",
                             firstName:"Graeme",
                             lastName:"Rocher",
                             email:"graeme@grails.org").save()
    // create a tag
    def t = new Tag(name:"grails").save()
    // create the subscription for the user to the tag
    def s = new Subscription(user:userA,tag:t).save()

    // create another user that is going to create a bookmark that the
    // other user should receive notification of
    def userB = new User(login:"other",
                             password:"other",
                             firstName:"other",
                             lastName:"user",
                             email:"other@grails.org").save()

    // create a new bookmark tagged with Grails.
    def b = new Bookmark(title:"Grails Download Page",
                             url:new URL("http://grails.org/Download"),
                             notes:"",
                             user:userB)

    // here we tag the bookmark with the subscribed-to tag
    b.addTagReference(new TagReference(user:userB,tag:t))
    b.save()
    def emailStub = new StubFor(org.apache.commons.mail.HtmlEmail)
    emailStub.demand.setFrom { String addr, String name ->
        println("Checking from address")
        assert addr == "noreply@bookmarks.grail.org"
        assert name == "Grails Bookmarks Application"
    }
```

```
        emailStub.demand.addTo {  String addr, String name ->
            println("Checking to address")
            assert addr == userA.email
            assert name == userA.toString()
        }
        emailStub.demand.send {
            return true
        }
      def job = new SubscriptionJob()
      emailStub.use {
            job.execute()
      }
    def sendMailStub = new StubFor(SubscriptionJob)
    sendMailStub.demand.sendMail { User user,
                                        String subject,
                                        Closure bodyContent ->

        println("Checking generated email")

        def sw = new StringWriter()
        def mkp = new groovy.xml.MarkupBuilder(new PrintWriter(sw))
        mkp.html {
            body(bodyContent)
        }
        assert sw.toString()
                    .indexOf('<a href="http://grails.org/Download"> ')
    }
    sendMailStub.use {
            job.execute()
    }
    }
  }
}
```

And that concludes this example of jobs in action. Everything you have seen so far has assumed that jobs are configured at development time, but occasionally it is useful to create jobs at *runtime*. In the next section, we'll be looking into how to go about interacting with the Quartz scheduler to achieve exactly this.

Interacting with the Scheduler

Quartz and its scheduler control all jobs in Grails. The scheduler itself is an instance of org.quartz.Scheduler, a rich interface for managing jobs that are currently executing and adding new jobs at runtime. The interface is a little too rich to list here, but feel free to browse through the methods via the Quartz web site: http://www.opensymphony.com/quartz/api/org/quartz/Scheduler.html.

If you recall, I mentioned that you could give a job a name or place it in a group. This comes in handy when interacting with the scheduler. More specifically, the scheduler has methods to retrieve existing jobs by name and group.

First and foremost, though, you need to understand how to obtain a reference to the scheduler. The Spring container once again manages this for us, so obtaining a reference is a simple matter of defining the appropriate property in a controller-of-service class:

```
org.quartz.Scheduler quartzScheduler
```

The property will then automatically be set for you, and once obtained you can start interacting with the scheduler. To start off with, let's take a look at how to obtain *existing* jobs from the scheduler. The scheduler provides a number of useful methods to achieve this including those in Listing 10-32.

Listing 10-32. *Methods for Getting Jobs from the Scheduler*

```
class Scheduler {
    ...
    String[] getJobNames();
    String[] getJobGroupNames();
    JobDetail getJobDetail(String jobName, String jobGroupName);
    ...
}
```

The getJobDetail(jobName,jobGroupName) method will retrieve the org.quartz.JobDetail instance for a specified name and group. The JobDetail describes the job to be executed including information about the class that executes the job. Remember the name and group relate to the name and group properties defined when we create a job. For example, retrieving the SubscriptionJob could be done with the following:

```
def jobDetail = quartzScheduler.getJobDetail("subscriptionJob","bookmarks")
```

Every JobDetail in Quartz when registered with the scheduler is associated with a *trigger*. A trigger is an instance of the org.quartz.Trigger interface and is responsible for activating the job.

For example, once we obtain a reference to a JobDetail, we can then register new triggers that fire at certain times as in Listing 10-33.

Listing 10-33. *Registering New Triggers*

```
def trigger = TriggerUtils.makeDailyTrigger(11, 45)
  trigger.startTime = new Date()
  trigger.name = "myTrigger"

quartzScheduler.scheduleJob(jobDetail, trigger)
```

The example in Listing 10-33 introduces another useful class, org.quartz.TriggerUtils, that contains various methods for constructing Trigger instances, one of which is shown in the example. Here we make a new Trigger that will execute the job daily at 11:45 a.m. The Trigger is then registered with the scheduler using the JobDetail instance.

■**Note** As of this writing, Grails does not provide support for persistent jobs (although this support is planned), hence if you require jobs registered at runtime to survive between server restarts, you will need to manage their state explicitly.

Of course, registering a new job is not all that is possible, and in the next few sections you'll see what else can be accomplished with the scheduler.

Pausing and Resuming Jobs

As well as allowing new jobs to be registered, the scheduler also allows control over existing jobs including pausing jobs that are currently scheduled. To pause all jobs currently scheduled, the pauseAll method could be used:

```
quartzScheduler.pauseAll()
```

Unsurprisingly, there is also a corresponding resumeAll method that will resume all scheduled jobs:

```
quartzScheduler.resumeAll()
```

Sometimes, however, it is useful to pause only a single job or *group* of jobs. This can be achieved with the pauseJob and pauseJobGroup methods:

```
quartzScheduler.pauseJob("subscriptionJob","bookmarks")
quartzScheduler.pauseJobGroup("bookmarks)
```

The first statement will pause the subscriptionJob within the bookmarks group, while the second will pause all jobs within the bookmarks group. Note that pausing a job or group of jobs will not stop *currently executing* jobs from running.

Triggering a Job

If for some reason you need to execute a job immediately and hence cannot wait for any predefined trigger, the scheduler provides methods to do just this. The aptly named triggerJob method should do the trick nicely:

```
quartzScheduler.triggerJob("subscriptionJob","bookmarks")
```

Adding and Removing Jobs

You've already seen one way of scheduling jobs with the scheduleJob method; however, the addJob method provides a way to add new jobs or replace existing ones. Essentially, the addJob method takes two arguments: a JobDetail instance and a Boolean value that dictates whether it should replace an existing job of the same name and group.

To understand it, you need to explore how to create a JobDetail instance in the first place. At its simplest, the JobDetail class accepts three arguments: the name of the job, the group of the job, and a class that implements the org.quartz.Job interface, the definition of which is shown in Listing 10-34.

Listing 10-34. *The org.quartz.Job Interface*

```
interface Job {
    void execute(JobExecutionContext context);
}
```

Therefore, to add a job, you have to first define a class that implements this interface and then register it with the scheduler using a JobDetail bean.

■**Note** A typical way to create objects at runtime that implement a single method interface in Java would be to use an anonymous inner class, but unfortunately, as of this writing, Groovy doesn't support anonymous inner classes. As an alternative, you can have multiple class definitions in a single .groovy file, and in addition there may be support in the future for Groovy to be able to convert a closure into a single method interface.

Looking back at the bookmarks application, a possible use case here may be to allow users to manage the day that they receive e-mail notifications. Maybe the default Friday is inconvenient, and they would prefer to receive the e-mail on a Tuesday.

You could alter the SubscriptionJob to implement the org.quartz.Job interface as in Listing 10-35.

Listing 10-35. *Making SubscriptionJob Implement org.quartz.Job*

```
class SubscriptionJob implements org.quartz.Job {
    ...
    void execute(JobExecutionContext context) {
      ...
    }
}
```

The changes can be seen in bold with the addition of the implements keyword and the JobExecutionContext parameter to the execute method. Now we can add the job at runtime to the scheduler potentially based on user input preferences. Listing 10-36 looks at a potential action that could be added to the SubscriptionController to allow users to schedule their subscriptions.

Listing 10-36. *Scheduling Jobs at Runtime*

```
class SubscriptionController {
    org.quartz.Scheduler quartzScheduler
    ...
    def scheduleAlerts = {
        def jobDetail = new JobDetail("${user.login} Job",
                                      "bookmarks",
                                      SubscriptionJob)
        quartzScheduler.addJob(jobDetail, true)
```

```
        def dayOfWeek = params.dayOfWeek ? params.dayOfWeek.toInteger() : 1
        def trigger = TriggerUtils.makeWeeklyTrigger(dayOfWeek,6, 0)

        trigger.startTime = new Date()
        trigger.name = "${user.login} Trigger"
        quartzScheduler.scheduleJob(jobDetail, trigger)
    }
}
```

Here we implement a scheduleAlerts action in the SubscriptionController that creates a JobDetail bean using the user's login name and then uses a dayOfWeek parameter that represents the numbers 1 through 7 to create a Trigger for the job.

Once created, it duly schedules the job, which will be executed per the user's preferences. To later remove this job, we could use the deleteJob method:

```
quartzScheduler.deleteJob("${user.login} Job", "bookmarks")
```

Alternatively, if you only want to remove the trigger so that the job is no longer scheduled for execution, you could use unscheduleJob:

```
quartzScheduler.unscheduleJob("${user.login} Trigger", "bookmarks")
```

Well, that is it for jobs for now. Another thing to remember is that Grails provides the convenience of being able to define jobs by convention; however, the full power of Quartz and all its enterprise features are still fully available for you to manipulate and use. All and all, this makes for a pretty powerful and easy-to-use combination!

Summary

In this chapter, we tackled some more advanced concepts in services and jobs. In addition, to make it even more interesting, we mixed in some Groovy closures, builders, and mocks. The important thing to remember is where services and jobs are applicable, and the examples in this chapter served well in pointing out some common use cases.

We used services to integrate nicely with an external web service API and jobs to implement e-mail notifications that could easily be seen as reports. Of course, these are not the only areas where they will serve you well.

As far as services go, they serve as a great way of abstracting code to encapsulate any kind of business logic that you don't want intermingled with controller logic. Jobs, on the other hand, are great for code that needs to be executed in scheduled intervals like maintenance tasks and reports. Needless to say, services and jobs are yet another tool in the toolbox for developing the components that make up web applications today.

This has amounted to the most advanced chapter in this book so far. Nevertheless, it leads nicely into the next chapter, where we start to look at how to integrate Grails with Java.

■ ■ ■

## CHAPTER 11

Java Integration

One of the current never-ending battles being fought within the development community is the age-old debate of dynamically typed languages vs. statically typed languages. On one side of the battlefield you have those who believe dynamic typing is the only way to be productive. On the other hand, many argue that static typing is the only sane way to maintain control of a project's source code.

Unfortunately, both parties may well have missed the boat, because, really, to get the most benefit as a programmer from both types of languages you have to choose the *right tool for the job*. That tool may well be a dynamically typed language for one use case, and it may require stricter groundings in static typing for another. There is no hard and fast rule; it is more about learning and understanding the use cases and how to apply language choices.

Nevertheless, increasingly as a developer you will find yourself using both static and dynamic typing, and it is this *blended* approach to development that will help you get the most benefit from both paradigms. Of course, if you are using Java, you want to reduce the burden of switching from one language to another; and it is here where Groovy stands head and shoulders above other expressive languages on the JVM.

Server-Side Java Integration

Java integration is the key driver behind both Groovy and Grails, and its importance cannot be underestimated. Groovy already provides Grails with an advanced level of Java integration by seamlessly interoperating with the Java object model. A Groovy object is a Java object, and vice versa.

With Groovy you can do the following:

- Implement a Java interface with Groovy and call it from Java without the Java code knowing any better

- Extend abstract Java classes in Groovy and interoperate with the Java superclass transparently

- Import any Java class into Groovy without requiring any *special* directive found in other scripting languages on the JVM

These points are just a few of the possibilities and are the main drivers behind the Groovy language. Dierk Koenig, author of *Groovy in Action* (Manning Publications), described Groovy's goals in the form of a very revealing graph shown in Figure 11-1.

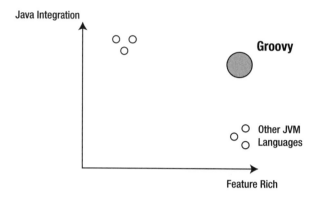

Figure 11-1. *Java dynamic language landscape from* Groovy in Action *by Dierk Koenig*

This diagram is a representation of the landscape of dynamic languages on the JVM. Essentially, many languages, represented by the small dots, are *either* feature rich *or* have tight Java integration. Groovy on the other hand has both feature richness *and* Java integration.

So what defines feature richness for a dynamic language? To be compared with languages such as Smalltalk, Ruby, and Python, a language needs to support concepts such as closures, metaprogramming, and advanced language constructs for common types such as maps, lists, ranges, and regular expressions.

What about Java integration? A dynamic language with tight Java integration should have a similar syntax, use the same APIs, and compile down to byte code for object model compatibility.

Groovy tries to solve all of these scenarios by providing powerful, dynamic concepts with a Java-like syntax that extends to the existing Java APIs while maintaining byte code compatibility.

Object model and API integration come into play again when you move to server-side Java programming. Sure frameworks such as Rails, Django, and TurboGears could be ported to the Java language, but it would require re-creating and crucially relearning much of what is already very mature in the Java platform.

Java, and more specifically Java Enterprise Edition, has APIs for database connectivity for working with HTTP requests, and for pretty much everything else you can think of. Instead of reinventing these APIs and forcing companies to reinvest in training around a new technology set, Grails *reuses* the JDBC API, the Servlet API, and others.

In fact you've already seen loads of Java integration throughout this book. The frameworks that Grails is built on top of, such as Spring, Hibernate, Quartz, and SiteMesh, are all written in Java, and yet they're completely unaware that they are configuring objects written in Groovy.

Why should they care? After all a Groovy object *is* a Java object. Grails takes Java integration even further by embracing the dominant Java web technology stack in Spring and Hibernate for dependency injection and ORM support, respectively. In the next few sections you'll see examples of how Grails allows the seamless interchange between Groovy and Java components.

The advantage of this approach is that if you have a particularly complex piece of functionality that would benefit from the advanced code navigation and refactoring capabilities that modern Java IDEs possess, you can use Java code. On the other hand, for a more simplistic approach, which covers the majority of cases, you have the power of a dynamic language such as Groovy at your fingertips.

ORM Integration with Hibernate

So far in Chapter 4 you saw how Grails integrates with Hibernate by providing an alternative mapping mechanism that uses convention instead of configuration. What's not tackled in that chapter is that this integration doesn't preclude you from using one of Hibernate's other mapping strategies.

Essentially, Hibernate defines two built-in mapping strategies. The first and most common is to use XML mapping files that define how an object is mapped to its related database table. In the next section you will see how this can be achieved with Grails to gain greater flexibility and control over the mapping options available to you.

Mapping with Hibernate XML

Although Hibernate XML is not nearly as concise and simple to work with as GORM, what it does provide is *flexibility*. Flexibility allows fine-grained control over how a class is mapped onto the underlying database. For example, having this control over the mapping allows you to map Grails onto legacy database systems.

To explore this capability in detail you're going to map a couple of your current bookmark application's domain classes with XML instead of GORM. The important point in the previous section is that you don't have to map *all* classes with Hibernate; you can mix and match where you feel it's appropriate. This allows GORM to handle the typical case, and Hibernate to do the heavy lifting.

To get going, the first thing you need to do is create the `hibernate.cfg.xml` file within the hibernate directory of the bookmarks application. Figure 11-2 shows an example of how do to this.

Figure 11-2. *The hibernate.cfg.xml file*

The `hibernate.cfg.xml` file serves to configure the Hibernate `SessionFactory`, which is the class used by Hibernate to interact with the database via sessions. Grails, of course, manages all this for you via the dynamic persistent methods discussed in Chapter 4.

All we're concerned with at this point is mapping classes from the domain model onto tables in a database. As it stands, the content of the `hibernate.cfg.xml` file looks something like Listing 11-1.

Listing 11-1. *The hibernate.cfg.xml File*

```
<?xml version="1.0" encoding="UTF-8"?>
<!DOCTYPE hibernate-configuration PUBLIC
        "-//Hibernate/Hibernate Configuration DTD 3.0//EN"
        http://hibernate.sourceforge.net/hibernate-configuration-3.0.dtd">
<hibernate-configuration>
    <session-factory>
            <!-- Mapping goes here -->
    </session-factory>
</hibernate-configuration>
```

At the moment there is merely an empty configuration file. To map individual classes it is good practice to create individual mapping files for each class and then *refer to* them in the main `hibernate.cfg.xml` file.

To do this, amend the `hibernate.cfg.xml` file according to Listing 11-2.

Listing 11-2. *Adding Mapping Resources to hibernate.cfg.xml*

```
<?xml version="1.0" encoding="UTF-8"?>
<!DOCTYPE hibernate-configuration PUBLIC
        "-//Hibernate/Hibernate Configuration DTD 3.0//EN"
        "http://hibernate.sourceforge.net/hibernate-configuration-3.0.dtd">
<hibernate-configuration>
    <session-factory>
        <mapping resource="User.hbm.xml"/>
    </session-factory>
</hibernate-configuration>
```

An additional mapping is defined in bold with a new mapping resource reference for the `User` class. Of course, the `User.hbm.xml` file does not yet exist at this point, so you need to create it. Figure 11-3 demonstrates what the state of the directory structure should look like after you've created the mapping file.

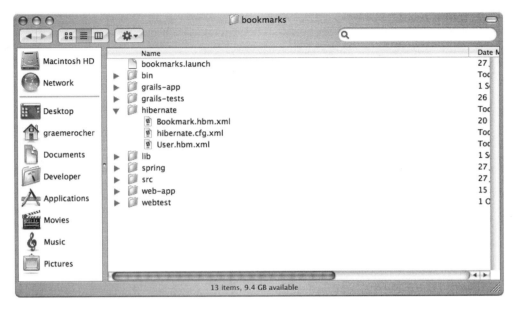

Figure 11-3. *Hibernate config with mapping files*

Mapping files contain the actual mappings between object model and relational table. They're normally located in the same package as the mapped class and follow the naming convention of the class. For example, the mapping file that handles the User mapping is User.hbm.xml, the contents for which can be seen in Listing 11-3.

Listing 11-3. *The User.hbm.xml Mapping File*

```
1 <?xml version="1.0"?>
2 <!DOCTYPE hibernate-mapping PUBLIC
3         "-//Hibernate/Hibernate Mapping DTD 3.0//EN"
4         "http://hibernate.sourceforge.net/hibernate-mapping-3.0.dtd">
5 <hibernate-mapping>
6     <class name="User" table="user_table" lazy="true">
7         <comment>The User domain object</comment>
8
9         <id name="id" column="user_id">
10            <generator class="native"/>
11        </id>
12        <natural-id mutable="true">
13            <property name="login"
14                             length="10"/>
15        </natural-id>
16        <property name="password"
17                        not-null="true"
18                        length="15"
19                        column="u_pwd"/>
```

```
20          <property name="email"/>
21          <property name="firstName" column="u_first_name"/>
22          <property name="lastName" column="u_last_name"/>
23      </class>
24 </hibernate-mapping>
```

The previous code maps the User class onto a table called user_table that has a natively generated identifier, on line 9, and a *natural identifier*. A natural identifier, shown on line 12, is a property or a combination of properties that is unique to an instance of the User class. In this case, the login property is unique for each User instance and hence has been identified as the natural identifier. Figure 11-4 shows what the mapped-to table will look like.

Table - user_table

user_id	login	u_pwd	email	u_first	u_last

Figure 11-4. *The User mapping table*

As with many databases there has been little care toward consistency of column naming in the User table; hence, using Hibernate as a mapping strategy grants you the flexibility to still use Grails on tables such as these.

Hibernate will create unique and not-null constraints when creating the database schema for the natural identifier. To get the User domain class to work with this mapping requires two minor amends. First, since you're mapping explicitly, GORM won't automatically inject the identifier property, so you have to add that manually.

Secondly, Hibernate recommends implementing equals and hashCode based on the natural identifier where possible. In fact, this is recommended even without Hibernate in place. Listing 11-4 shows the amends made to the User domain class to complete this example.

Listing 11-4. *User Domain Class Modifications*

```
class User {
    Long id
    ...
    boolean equals(obj) {
        if(this==obj) return true
        if(!obj || obj.class != this.class) return false
        return login?.equals(obj.login) ? true : false
    }
    int hashCode() {
        return login ? login.hashCode() : super.hashCode()
    }
}
```

Although not strictly necessary, or even enforced by Hibernate, implementing `equals` and `hashCode` will help Hibernate behave correctly when dealing with collections of objects and querying.

So that's that. Now all you have to do is start up the bookmarks application again using the `grails run-app` target and everything will work in exactly the same way. The only difference of course is that the `User` class is now using a different mapping strategy.

With that strategy covered, let's move onto another alternative mapping strategy that uses annotations in the next section.

EJB3-Compliant Mapping

EJB 3.0 has taken much inspiration from Hibernate in its latest incarnation. In many senses EJB 3.0 is a response to Hibernate's market dominance by attempting to make an API that has the same feel of Hibernate but is vendor-neutral.

One part of the specification is the Java Persistence API, or JPA, that defines a set of annotations for persisting POJO objects using object-relational mapping. Although Grails doesn't support JPA directly (this support is on the roadmap), what you can do is write EJB 3.0–*compliant* entity beans using JPA annotations. As well as annotations, JPA uses Java's generics feature to establish the type of objects contained within collections and other generic interfaces. Generics were added to Java to increase type safety and avoid unnecessary casting when working with generic objects such as the collections API.

■**Note** Annotations and some of the other features in this section, such as generics, were introduced in Java 5.0, hence the examples in this section require a Java 5.0 virtual machine. A full discussion on annotations and generics is beyond the scope of this book, but some good documentation on the subject is available at Sun's Java site at `http://java.sun.com`.

In the next example, you're going to use JPA annotations to migrate the bookmarks application's existing GORM domain classes into a Java-based domain model with EJB3 annotations.

To get started, make sure you have the bookmarks application imported into Eclipse as described in Chapter 3.

Next, create new Java classes within a package called `org.grails.bookmarks` for each of the equivalent GORM domain objects in `grails-app/domain`. Save them under the `src/java` tree using the New Java Class dialog shown in Figure 11-5.

The previous screenshot shows how to create the `Bookmark` class within the aforementioned package. Repeat the process of creating classes for each of the GORM domain objects until Eclipse's Package Explorer shows a source structure something like Figure 11-6.

New Java Class

Java Class
Create a new Java class.

Source folder:	test/src/java	Browse...
Package:	org.grails.bookmarks	Browse...
☐ Enclosing type:		Browse...

Name: Bookmark

Modifiers: ● public   ○ default   ○ private   ○ protected
             ☐ abstract ☐ final   ☐ static

Superclass: java.lang.Object   Browse...

Interfaces: Add...

                                                        Remove

Which method stubs would you like to create?
             ☐ public static void main(String[] args)
             ☐ Constructors from superclass
             ☑ Inherited abstract methods
Do you want to add comments as configured in the properties of the current project?
             ☐ Generate comments

                                              Cancel   Finish

Figure 11-5. *The Eclipse New Java Class dialog*

Figure 11-6. *The Bookmark and User classes*

Now it's time to write some Java code. First open up the User class and add the @Entity annotation to the class name. To get the class to compile correctly you will need to import the javax.persistence.Entity annotation as per Listing 11-5.

Listing 11-5. *The Class User.java*

```
package org.grails.bookmarks;

import javax.persistence.Entity;
import javax.persistence.Table;

@Entity
@Table(name="user_table")
public class User {
  // class body
}
```

As the previous code example shows, you will also need to use the @Table annotation to specify the table name previously used in the section "Mapping with Hibernate XML."

■**Note** The downside of the annotation approach is that your domain model is no longer free of persistence logic. In other words, by adding annotations specific to persistence you are polluting your domain model with information about the technical environment. This reason alone has seen many stick with Hibernate XML mapping even though annotation mapping is arguably simpler.

Now create private fields that match the names of the previous User GORM domain class as per Listing 11-6.

Listing 11-6. *The User Entities Fields*

```
package org.grails.bookmarks;
...
public class User {
      private Long id;
      private String login;
      private String password;
      private String firstName;
      private String lastName;
      private String email;
}
```

Once this has been done you need to create public getters and setters for each field so that the User class becomes a fully fledged JavaBean. Eclipse can help you out here by accessing the Source / Generate Getters and Setters menu option. This will make each field into what is known as a *property*.

Once the properties have been generated you need to annotate certain properties with additional information defining their purpose, starting with the id property in Listing 11-7.

Listing 11-7. *The id Property*

```
@Id
@Column(name="user_id")
@GeneratedValue
public Long getId() {
    return id;
}
```

In Listing 11-7 the id property is the primary key; it maps to a column called user_id; and its value is generated natively by the database. Next, the User class's login property needs to be unique for each User instance. Listing 11-8 shows how to make sure the login property doesn't exceed a specified length and is unique.

Listing 11-8. *The login Property*

```
@Column(nullable=false,unique=true,length=10)
public String getLogin() {
    return login;
}
```

The password, firstName, and lastName properties require different column names. Again, you can adjust this by using the @Column annotation as shown in Listing 11-9.

Listing 11-9. *Mapping Individual Columns*

```
@Column(name="u_first_name")
public String getFirstName() {
    return firstName;
}
@Column(name="u_last_name")
public String getLastName() {
    return lastName;
}
@Column(name="u_pwd")
public String getPassword() {
    return password;
}
```

You will, of course, have to add the imports for the @Column, @GeneratedValue, and @Id annotations used so far, but Eclipse or any good IDE will likely do this for you. Once complete, the new EJB3-compliant User class will look like the following:

```
package org.grails.bookmarks;
import javax.persistence.Column;
import javax.persistence.Entity;
import javax.persistence.Table;
import javax.persistence.GeneratedValue;
import javax.persistence.Id;
```

```java
@Entity
@Table(name="user_table")
public class User {
    private Long id;
    private String login;
    private String password;
    private String firstName;
    private String lastName;
    private String email;

    @Id
    @Column(name="user_id")
    @GeneratedValue
     public Long getId() {
        return id;
     }
     public void setId(Long id) {
        this.id = id;
     }
     @Column(nullable=false,unique=true,length=10)
     public String getLogin() {
        return login;
     }
     public void setLogin(String login) {
       this.login = login;
     }
     public String getEmail() {
        return email;
     }
    public void setEmail(String email) {
       this.email = email;
     }
     @Column(name="u_first_name")
     public String getFirstName() {
        return firstName;
     }
     public void setFirstName(String firstName) {
         this.firstName = firstName;
     }
     @Column(name="u_last_name")
      public String getLastName() {
          return lastName;
      }
      public void setLastName(String lastName) {
         this.lastName = lastName;
      }
      @Column(name="u_pwd")
```

```
    public String getPassword() {
        return password;
    }
    public void setPassword(String password) {
        this.password = password;
    }
}
```

Moving on to the Bookmark class again, much of the mapping is similar in terms of the need to define the @Entity annotation above the class name, having an @Id with a @GeneratedValue, and, of course, needing to import the annotation classes.

The main difference between the Bookmark EJB3 mapping and the GORM is how relationships are defined. Listing 11-10 presents the key areas of the Bookmark mapping with a @OneToMany annotation to define the one-to-many relationship to the TagReference type and a @ManyToOne annotation for the many-to-one User association.

Listing 11-10. *Example Associations in the Bookmark.Java Class*

```
...
@Entity
public class Bookmark {
    private Long id;
    private URI url;
    private String title;
    private String notes;
    private String type = "general";
    private Date dateCreated = new Date();
    private User user;
    private Set<TagReference> tags;

    @OneToMany(cascade=CascadeType.ALL)
     public Set<TagReference> getTags() {
         return tags;
    }
    @ManyToOne
     public User getUser() {
         return user;
    }
    ...
}
```

Notice how *generics* are used in Listing 11-10 to associate the java.util.Set to the TagReference type. Generics are a way in Java 5 to ensure type safety when working with "generic" APIs such as the collections API, which java.util.Set is a part of. They also reduce the need for unnecessary casting to different types.

The remaining mappings are much the same and are simply variations of the previous. In this sense you can see why; although not nearly as verbose as Hibernate XML, EJB3 mapping still violates the Don't Repeat Yourself (DRY) principal by requiring the developers to repeat themselves for each annotation definition.

Nevertheless, EJB3 entities do play well with existing IDE tools and refactoring technologies and in this sense it may be worth sacrificing the convenience of GORM for the easy code navigation and refactoring capability of Java entities.

The complete listing of the remaining entities for the bookmarks application, excluding the User class that you saw in Listing 11-6, can be seen here:

```java
package org.grails.bookmarks;

import java.net.URI;
import java.util.Date;
import java.util.Set;

import javax.persistence.CascadeType;
import javax.persistence.Column;
import javax.persistence.Entity;
import javax.persistence.GeneratedValue;
import javax.persistence.Id;
import javax.persistence.ManyToOne;
import javax.persistence.OneToMany;

@Entity
public class Bookmark {

    private Long id;
    private URI url;
    private String title;
    private String notes;
    private String type = "general";
    private Date dateCreated = new Date();
    private User user;
    private Set<TagReference> tags;

    @OneToMany(cascade=CascadeType.ALL)
    public Set<TagReference> getTags() {
        return tags;
    }
    public void setTags(Set<TagReference> tags) {
        this.tags = tags;
    }
    @Id
    @GeneratedValue
    public Long getId() {
        return id;
    }
}
```

```java
        public void setId(Long id) {
            this.id = id;
        }
        public Date getDateCreated() {
            return dateCreated;
        }
        public void setDateCreated(Date dateCreated) {
            this.dateCreated = dateCreated;
        }
        @Column(nullable=true)
        public String getNotes() {
            return notes;
        }
        public void setNotes(String notes) {
            this.notes = notes;
        }
        public String getTitle() {
            return title;
        }
        public void setTitle(String title) {
            this.title = title;
        }
        public URI getUrl() {
            return url;
        }
        public void setUrl(URL url) {
            this.url = url;
        }
        @ManyToOne
        public User getUser() {
            return user;
        }
        public void setUser(User user) {
            this.user = user;
        }
    public String getType() {
        return type;
    }
    public void setType(String type) {
        this.type = type;
    }
}
// TagReference.java
package org.grails.bookmarks;

import javax.persistence.Entity;
import javax.persistence.GeneratedValue;
```

```java
import javax.persistence.Id;
import javax.persistence.ManyToOne;

@Entity
public class TagReference {
    private Long id;
    private Bookmark bookmark;
    private Tag tag;
    private User user;

    @ManyToOne
    public Bookmark getBookmark() {
        return bookmark;
    }
    public void setBookmark(Bookmark bookmark) {
        this.bookmark = bookmark;
    }
    @Id
    @GeneratedValue
    public Long getId() {
        return id;
    }
    public void setId(Long id) {
        this.id = id;
    }
    @ManyToOne
    public Tag getTag() {
        return tag;
    }
    public void setTag(Tag tag) {
        this.tag = tag;
    }
    @ManyToOne
    public User getUser() {
        return user;
    }
    public void setUser(User user) {
        this.user = user;
    }
    @Override
    public String toString() {
        return this.tag.getName();
    }
}

// Tag.java
package org.grails.bookmarks;
```

```java
import javax.persistence.Entity;
import javax.persistence.GeneratedValue;
import javax.persistence.Id;

@Entity
public class Tag {
    private Long id;
    private String name;
    @Id
    @GeneratedValue
    public Long getId() {
        return id;
    }
    public void setId(Long id) {
        this.id = id;
    }
    public String getName() {
        return name;
    }
    public void setName(String name) {
        this.name = name;
    }
    @Override
    public String toString() {
        return name;
    }
}
// Subscription.java
package org.grails.bookmarks;

import javax.persistence.Entity;
import javax.persistence.GeneratedValue;
import javax.persistence.Id;
import javax.persistence.ManyToOne;

@Entity
public class Subscription {

    private Long id;
    private User user;
    private Tag tag;
    @Id
    @GeneratedValue
    public Long getId() {
        return id;
    }
```

```
    public void setId(Long id) {
        this.id = id;
    }
    @ManyToOne
    public Tag getTag() {
        return tag;
    }
    public void setTag(Tag tag) {
        this.tag = tag;
    }
    @ManyToOne
    public User getUser() {
        return user;
    }
    public void setUser(User user) {
        this.user = user;
    }
}
```

With that rather long listing out of the way, there are a few things left to do to complete the migration to EJB3 entities. First, you need to update each DataSource in the grails-app/conf directory to tell Grails that you want to use an annotation configuration strategy. Listing 11-11 shows the necessary changes to the development DataSource.

Listing 11-11. *Specifying the Annotation Configuration Strategy*

```
import org.codehaus.groovy.grails.orm.hibernate.cfg.*
class DevelopmentDataSource { // Groovy
    def configClass = GrailsAnnotationConfiguration
    ...
}
```

With that done, the hibernate.cfg.xml located in the hibernate directory needs updating to reflect the fact that you are no longer using Hibernate XML mapping. Listing 11-12 shows the update Hibernate configuration file with each class referenced using the class attribute of the mapping tag.

Listing 11-12. *Updated hibernate.cfg.xml File*

```
<?xml version="1.0" encoding="UTF-8"?>
<!DOCTYPE hibernate-configuration PUBLIC
                "-//Hibernate/Hibernate Configuration DTD 3.0//EN"
                "http://hibernate.sourceforge.net/hibernate-configuration-3.0.dtd">
<hibernate-configuration>
    <session-factory>
        <mapping package="org.grails.bookmarks"/>
        <mapping class="org.grails.bookmarks.Bookmark" />
        <mapping class="org.grails.bookmarks.User" />
```

```
            <mapping class="org.grails.bookmarks.Tag" />
            <mapping class="org.grails.bookmarks.TagReference" />
            <mapping class="org.grails.bookmarks.Subscription" />
    </session-factory>
</hibernate-configuration>
```

The previous mapping simply tells Hibernate which classes are persistent, and the configuration of the mapping is then delegated to the annotations contained within the classes themselves.

You now need to delete the GORM domain classes in grails/domain, since their Java brethren have superseded them. Once done, the last thing to do is to update the controllers, tag libraries, services, and unit tests to include imports to the new package, simply by adding the following line to the top of each file:

```
import org.grails.bookmarks.*
```

You can now start Grails using grails run-app, and the bookmarks application will operate as if nothing has changed. The remarkable thing here is that the domain classes are written in Java and yet all of the dynamic finder and persistence methods work as if by magic.

Grails is an *unobtrusive* framework, and by that I mean that it doesn't require your domain objects to have any knowledge of the framework itself. Grails will magically inject the necessary behavior to support dynamic persistence and query methods into each Java EJB3 entity using Groovy's Meta Object Protocol.

Grails' unobtrusive nature makes it an appealing proposition, as you can essentially reuse an existing Hibernate domain model and get all the benefit of the dynamic nature of Grails when you need to. On the other hand, if you want to switch over to use Struts or Spring MVC, you can use the *same* domain model, as there are no framework specifics tying domain objects to Grails.

This is an incredibly powerful concept and one of the defining aspects of Grails that sets it apart from other frameworks and allows you to operate using a blended approach. By *blended* I mean having the *choice* to use static typing when you want to or, if you so choose, harnessing the power of dynamic typing when it suits your needs.

Before I continue, there is one thing that you should do just to be sure that your application is working exactly as it was before you migrated the domain model: execute the tests. In fact, if you execute grails test-app at this point, you will get a number of failures. Why? During the migration you lose the power that GORM's constraints mechanism offers.

So how do you create constraints for EJB3 entities? In the next section I tackle this very issue.

Using Constraints with POJO Entities

Clearly, one of the powerful features of Grails is its constraints mechanism (discussed in Chapter 4). It allows a flexible way to specify meta-information about a class that can then be used in features such as validation and scaffolding. The reason there are failing test cases, as mentioned at the end of the previous section, is that your validation logic for the Bookmark class is no longer working due to missing constraints.

Why is it not working? Quite simply because it is not there! Java doesn't support closures or builders so you can't just include the necessary code inside a Java class. Luckily, however, Grails has an elegant solution to this problem, again based on the convention approach.

What you need to do is create a new Groovy *script* in the same package and directory (yes, a Groovy file is now placed under src/java/...) as the class for which the constraints are being applied. The scripts name needs to start with the name of the class and end with `Constraints`. Figure 11-7 shows a new Groovy script called `BookmarkConstraints.groovy`.

Figure 11-7. *Creating the BookmarkConstraints.groovy script*

The reason the previous file is a script is that it doesn't really make sense to define an entirely new class just to define constraints on an existing class. All you are really interested in is applying a set of constraints in the same form as seen inside GORM classes. Listing 11-13 shows how to apply constraints within the `BookmarkConstraints.groovy` script.

Listing 11-13. *Applying Constraints to the Bookmark Class*

```
package org.grails.bookmarks
constraints = {
    url(nullable:false)
    title(blank:false)
    rating(range:1..10)
    type(inList:['blog','article','general','news'])
    notes(maxLength:1000)
}
```

The previous constraints definition is all that the file contains: no class definition, no configuration, quite simply the constraints that apply to the `Bookmark` class. At run time, Grails will load and execute this script to retrieve the constraints that apply to the `Bookmark` class, hence allowing Java domain classes to have constraints in the same format as GORM classes.

Now if you execute `grails test-app`, all tests will pass with flying "green" colors. That's not the end of your Hibernate exploration, however; in the next section, you'll see how to interact with the `SessionFactory` directly with Spring and Hibernate.

Retrieving the SessionFactory

The Hibernate `SessionFactory` is the class used to create Hibernate `org.hibernate.Session` instances. A Hibernate `Session` can in turn be used to read and write objects to the database. For the most part, Grails provides enough dynamic methods for you to not have to deal with the relatively more complex API that the `Session` object offers.

Nevertheless, if you *really* need to access the `SessionFactory` from a Grails controller or service, all you need to do is create a property called `sessionFactory` as per the following example:

```
SessionFactory sessionFactory
```

The underlying Spring container will then inject the `SessionFactory` instance into your class, making it available at run time. One possible usage is to have finer-grained control over transaction management if service classes don't totally fulfill your needs.

■**Note** To participate in session-per-request processing, which ensures a shared session across the entire length of a request, it is recommended that you use Spring's `HibernateTemplate` class when working directly with the `SessionFactory`.

A full discussion on the Hibernate API is really beyond the scope of this book, however, given the popularity of Hibernate, you won't find yourself searching for documentation for too long.

Obtaining the `SessionFactory` in the aforementioned way works thanks to Spring and its transparent dependency injection capability. In the next section, you'll see what else you can achieve with Spring to further integrate Grails with existing Java technologies.

Dependency Injection with Spring

The Spring Framework really embraced the move in the Java industry to POJO-based, lightweight programming. Although, as developers have discovered, as a Spring application grows in complexity, the XML configuration required to develop Spring applications can start to feel anything but lightweight.

For the most part, with Grails you don't have to expose yourself to Spring XML if you so choose. However, if you are willing to delve into the underlying Spring runtime configuration, there are some powerful possibilities at your disposal.

In the next section, you'll see how to register a bean with Grails' underlying Spring container and also explore some useful beans that you may want to obtain from the Grails application context.

Getting Hold of Useful Beans

Grails uses the Spring Framework in a number of ways. Many of the core Spring APIs are used internally to help with resource management, data binding, and so on. Grails also uses Spring's Inversion of Control (IoC) container to automatically configure itself at run time.

During this automatic run-time configuration, a number of useful beans are created that you may want to get a reference to. The following list of bean names, which is by no means comprehensive, will give you an idea of what's available:

sessionFactory: The org.hibernate.SessionFactory instance used by Grails for Hibernate integration. You may want to obtain a reference to this bean for a number of reasons, including the ability to work directly with the Hibernate API, obtain metadata about persistent classes, and so on.

dataSource: An instance of javax.sql.DataSource. This bean is useful when you want to directly perform SQL queries, maybe to optimize queries that produce a large number of results such as reports. You can call the getConnection method on the dataSource to obtain a JDBC Connection object and go from there.

messageSource: An instance of org.springframework.context.MessageSource used to resolve i18n messages from Grails message bundles (see Chapter 8 for information on i18n).

transactionManager: Spring's org.springframework.transaction.Platform➡ TransactionManager that is used to manage transactions in things such as services. You can use this bean in combination with Spring's org.springframework.transaction. support.TransactionTemplate to have finer-grained control over transactions.

classLoader: The central groovy.lang.GroovyClassLoader instance used across Grails to manage class loading. This class loader is responsible for loading all Grails artifacts at startup time and hence contains references to all Grails classes.

exceptionMappings: An instance of org.springframework.web.servlet.handler. SimpleMappingExceptionResolver used to map exceptions onto appropriate views. By default it contains only a single mapping, "java.lang.Exception=/error", that resolves all exceptions to the Grails default error view. You can customize this behavior if you want specific exceptions mapped to specific views. For example, you could define something like "org.grails.bookmarks.iSecurityException=/login" to handle logins.

quartzScheduler: The Quartz org.quartz.Scheduler bean that manages scheduled jobs. Using the scheduler is covered in Chapter 10 on services and jobs.

grailsApplication: An instance of org.codehaus.groovy.grails.commons. GrailsApplication that provides a central interface for obtaining information about Grails artifacts such as domain classes, controllers, and so on.

That's a pretty long list of useful beans. Nevertheless, to provide a little clarity, the Java class in Listing 11-14 shows how you would obtain a reference to the `javax.sql.DataSource` instance. If you need to know how to obtain the same reference within a Groovy class, take a look at Chapter 10 on services and jobs.

Listing 11-14. *Using Spring Dependency Injection*

```
package org.grails.bookmarks.dao;

import javax.sql.DataSource;
import java.sql.Connection;
import org.grails.bookmarks.Simple;

public class SimpleDAO implements Simple {
        private DataSource dataSource;
        public setDataSource(DataSource ds) {
                this.dataSource = ds;
        }
        public void executeReport() {
                Connection c = this.dataSource.getConnection();
                // do something with connection
                ...
        }
}
```

■**Tip** If you're looking for an easier way to deal with JDBC from Java, take a look at Spring's `org.springframework.jdbc.core.JdbcTemplate` class. Alternatively, if you're writing a DAO like in Listing 11-14 with Groovy, Groovy has excellent support for SQL with the `groovy.sql` package. There is excellent information on Groovy SQL in *Groovy in Action* by Dierk Koenig, and in the IBM developerWorks article "Practically Groovy: JDBC Programming with Groovy" by Andrew Glover (`http://www-128.ibm.com/developerworks/java/library/j-pg01115.html`).

The example in Listing 11-14 shows a hypothetical DAO class that implements a pretend interface called `Simple`. The technique in Listing 11-14 is called *dependency injection* because the class instance has no awareness of Spring or the dependencies that are injected into it. All dependencies are resolved at run time. Dependency injection is the mostly commonly used technique when working with Spring and allows your application to be abstracted away from the underlying configuration strategy.

Now, to configure the `SimpleDAO` classes dependency on the `javax.sql.DataSource`, open up the `spring/resources.xml` file shown in Figure 11-8.

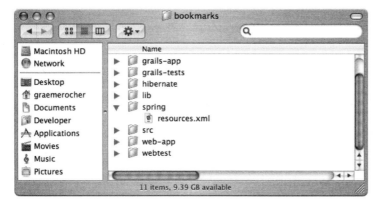

Figure 11-8. *The Spring resources.xml File*

The bean definition for the SimpleDAO class needs to look something like Listing 11-15.

Listing 11-15. *The SimpleDAO Bean Definition*

```
<bean id="simple" class="org.grails.bookmarks.dao.SimpleDAO">
      <property ref="dataSource" />
</bean>
```

Once configured in resources.xml you can then obtain a reference to the simple bean in any Grails artifact by defining a property that is of the type and name of the simple bean. In the following example I use the bean's Simple interface, thus the code that uses the interface is completely unaware of the underlying implementation:

```
org.grails.bookmarks.Simple simple
```

An alternative approach to using dependency injection as detailed in Listing 11-16 is to use Spring's factory support via the org.springframework.context.ApplicationContextAware interface. Listing 11-16 shows the modifications to SimpleDAO to support this approach.

Listing 11-16. *Using ApplicationContextAware*

```
...
import org.springframework.context.*;

public class SimpleDAO implements Simple, ApplicationContextAware {
      private ApplicationContext applicationContext;
      public setApplicationContext(ApplicationContext ctx) {
            this. applicationContext = ctx;
      }
      public void executeReport() {
            DataSource ds = (DataSource)this.applicationContext
                                             .getBean("dataSource");
```

```
                Connection c = ds.getConnection();
                // do something with connection
                ...
        }
}
```

The differences in the way the `DataSource` is resolved in Listing 11-14 are highlighted in bold. This technique follows the Service Locator pattern (defined in *Design Patterns* by the Gang of Four) and is another type of IoC that differs from dependency injection, in that you have to interact directly with a factory-like API to obtain your objects. The downside of this approach is that you need to work directly with Spring APIs and therefore are bound to Spring unless you refactor later on.

Overriding Bean Definitions

Obtaining beans is clearly useful for customizing existing ones, however, sometimes customization of the Grails runtime configuration is not enough. This is where overriding comes in handy.

Essentially if you create a bean definition in `spring/resources.xml` that matches the name of one of the beans Grails configures at run time, the bean definition will be overridden. One such scenario where this may be useful is if you are in an environment where the network administrators in your business control the data sources you are able to access.

All you are given is a Java Naming and Directory Interface (JNDI) resource name of the data source to look up. In this scenario you can use Spring's `org.springframework.jndi.JndiObjectFactoryBean` factory bean to look up the data source as demonstrated in Listing 11-17.

Listing 11-17. *Looking up a JNDI Object*

```
<bean id="dataSource" class="org.springframework.jndi.JndiObjectFactoryBean">
  <property name="jndiName" value="jdbc/myDataSource"/>
</bean>
```

Notice how the name of the bean is the same as the bean configured by Grails at run time. This will cause the runtime bean definition to be overridden by the definition in Listing 11-17 and therefore the data source used by Grails to be the one supplied via JNDI.

Again, this is another useful feature, but what if you just want to obtain a reference to a Grails service inside a Java class? In the next section I explore this option.

Using Spring Controllers with Grails

Say one day you decide that you want to invoke the `DeliciousService` that you developed in Chapter 10 from a Java class. Since Groovy compiles directly to byte code, the integration overhead to do this is minimal.

First, let's define a more generic interface in Java that encapsulates the basics of the `DeliciousService`. The methods on the `DeliciousService` are fairly generic and there may well be a circumstance where you could provide an alternative implementation. The new interface is called `org.grails.bookmarks.IBookmarkService`, the details of which are shown in Listing 11-18.

Listing 11-18. *The org.grails.bookmarks.BookmarkService Interface in Java*

```java
package org.grails.bookmarks;

import java.util.List;
/**
 * A generic interface for different types of Bookmark services
 *
 * @author graemerocher
 */
public interface IBookmarkService {

    /**
     * Finds a list of the most recent Bookmark instances for the specified
     * User
     * @return A List of Bookmark instances
     */
    List<Bookmark> findRecent( User user);

    /**
     * Finds a list of all the Bookmark instance for the specified Tag and User
     * @return A List of Bookmark instances
     */
    List<Bookmark> findAllForTag( String tag, User user);
}
```

Next, you need to implement this interface in the DeliciousService Groovy class. One inconsistency between the interface and the current implementation of the DeliciousService is that the Groovy version doesn't declare any types. Fortunately, since Groovy supports static typing, this can be corrected by merely changing the method signatures as per Listing 11-19.

Listing 11-19. *Updated DeliciousService Groovy Class*

```groovy
...
class DeliciousService implements IBookmarkService {
    List findAllForTag(String tag,User user) {
        ...
    }
    List findRecent(User user) {
        ...
    }
}
```

The changes in the previous listing show the updates made to the DeliciousService class in bold, in order to align it with the interface defined in Listing 11-18. Note that Groovy doesn't yet have the concept of generic types (and may never have), so you can merely omit these and still implement the interface.

The service itself can then be retrieved in one of two ways that you've already seen in the previous section. Listing 11-20 shows the two techniques available, assuming you have configured your bean in `spring/resource.xml`.

Listing 11-20. *Retrieving the DeliciousService Bean in Java Code*

```
...
// Using Dependency Injection
private IBookmarkService deliciousService
public void setDeliciousService(IBookmarkService bs) {
        this.deliciousService = bs;
}
...
// Using Inversion of Control
this.deliciousService = (IBookmarkService)applicationContext
                                                .getBean("deliciousService")
```

The previous Java code shows how to retrieve the `DeliciousService` instance. Since it now implements the `org.grails.bookmarks.IBookmarkService` Java interface it can merely be cast to the interface in Java and called without Java having any awareness that it is actually invoking a Groovy class.

To understand how to inject Grails services into Java objects a little better, say one day it is decided that it will be useful to provide a unified POX (Plain Old XML) API onto the bookmarks application that allows a user to read his or her del.icio.us bookmarks as well as those registered on the bookmarks application. What you could do is create *another* Grails service that implements the `IBookmarkService` interface.

To do this, execute the `grails create-service` target and type in the name **bookmark**. The result will be a file called `grails-apps/services/BookmarkService.groovy` that defines a `BookmarkService` class. Since you want to implement the same interface defined in Listing 11-18, you can simply provide an implementation that queries the existing domain model. Listing 11-21 shows the implementation of the `IBookmarkService` interface.

Listing 11-21. *The BookmarkService Implementation*

```
import org.grails.bookmarks.Bookmark
import org.grails.bookmarks.User
import org.grails.bookmarks.Tag

class BookmarkService implements org.grails.bookmarks.IBookmarkService {

    boolean transactional = false
```

```
    List findAllForTag(String name ,User user) {
        def tag = name? Tag.findByName(name) : null
        if (user) user = User.findByLogin(user.login)
        List bookmarks  = Collections.EMPTY_LIST
        if(tag && user) {
            def criteria = Bookmark.createCriteria()
            bookmarks = criteria.list {
                eq('user',user)
                tags {
                    eq('tag', tag)
                }
            }
        }
        return bookmarks
    }

    List findRecent(User user) {
        def now = new Date()
        if (user) user = User.findByLogin(user.login)
        if (user) {
            return Bookmark
                    .findAllByUserAndDateCreatedBetween(user, now-7, now)
        }
    }
}
}
```

The previous example shows how simple Grails makes implementing a typical service that, when written in Java, would likely require a lot of ORM-specific code. The findAllForTag implementation uses a criteria instance to search for all the Bookmark instances for a specified User instance and tag name.

The findRecent method, on the other hand, just uses a dynamic finder to find all Bookmark instances created within the last week. With that out of the way, you're going to implement the bookmark application's API with a Spring controller.

The Spring controller is going to use the two Grails services to produce an XML stream written to the response. To facilitate this you're going to use the XStream library that allows Java (and Groovy) objects to be easily converted to and from XML.

Download the XStream JAR from http://xstream.codehaus.org and place it within the lib directory of your Grails application. I use version 1.2 in these examples. Now create a new Java class within the src/java directory of your Grails application called org.grails.bookmarks. api.BookmarkXmlController. The screenshot in Figure 11-9 shows what your Eclipse Package Explorer should look like.

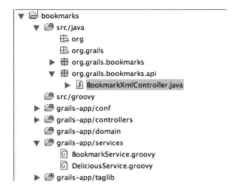

Figure 11-9. *The BookmarkXmlController in Package Explorer*

Now the first thing you need to do is implement the interface `org.springframework.web.`
`servlet.mvc.Controller` as required by all Spring controllers. Listing 11-22 shows how to
provide a basic implementation that does nothing.

Listing 11-22. *Implementing the Spring Controller Interface in Java*

```
package org.grails.bookmarks.api;
import org.springframework.web.servlet.ModelAndView;
import org.springframework.web.servlet.mvc.Controller;
import javax.servlet.http.HttpServletRequest;
import javax.servlet.http.HttpServletResponse;
public class BookmarkXmlController implements Controller {
     public ModelAndView
                   handleRequest(HttpServletRequest request,
                                         HttpServletResponse response)
                                                throws Exception {
          return null;
     }
}
```

Since the previous basic implementation is not going to do exactly what you want, let's
begin adding the necessary functionality, starting with defining a couple of constants for the
API calls to handle:

```
private static final String BOOKMARK_API_ALL = "/api/all";
private static final String BOOKMARK_API_RECENT = "/api/recent";
```

Next you need to specify the controller's dependencies on the two Grails services as JavaBean
properties so that they can be injected by Spring as per Listing 11-23.

Listing 11-23. *The Grails Service Dependencies*

```
private IBookmarkService deliciousService;
private IBookmarkService bookmarkService;

public void setBookmarkService(IBookmarkService bookmarkService) {
    this.bookmarkService = bookmarkService;
}
public void setDeliciousService(IBookmarkService deliciousService) {
    this.deliciousService = deliciousService;
}
```

Remember Grails uses injection by name so the names of the JavaBean properties have to match the convention in the class names of the Grails services. Alternatively, you could implement the `ApplicationContextAware` interface and look the service beans up explicitly in the Service Locator style described in Listing 11-16.

Now let's start implementing the `handleRequest` method of the `Controller` interface from Listing 11-22. Given that it is rather pointless to process the request without it having been authenticated first, you need to assert that there is a `User` in the session and if not, return an error. Listing 11-24 shows the code to do this and also the generic `writeError` method introduced to provide error handling.

Listing 11-24. *Ensuring There Is a Logged-in User Using the API*

```
User user = (User)request
                          .getSession()
                          .getAttribute("user");
if(user == null) {
    writeError("No user in session. Please authenticate first.", response);
}
else {
  ...
}
...
private void writeError(String message, HttpServletResponse response) {
    response.setContentType("text/xml");
    PrintWriter w;
    try {
        w = response.getWriter();
        w.write("<error message=\"");
        w.write(message);
        w.write("\" />");
    } catch (IOException e) {
        throw new RuntimeException(
            "Problem sending <error> tag to response: " +e.getMessage(),
            e);
    }
}
```

The writeError method in the previous listing will write some XML to the response in the following form:

```
<error message="Something went horribly wrong" />
```

It is then the responsibility of the client to handle the resulting error gracefully when communicating with the API. Moving on to the remainder of the handleRequest method, since you're going to be providing functions to retrieve the most recent bookmarks and all the bookmarks for a specific tag, you need some way of evaluating the request path.

You could evaluate the request path by hand, but Spring provides a fantastic class called org.springframework.web.util.UrlPathHelper that has been designed for exactly this purpose. Listing 11-25 uses its getLookupPathForRequest method, which will return the path relative to *the controller* of the request.

Listing 11-25. *Looking Up the Request Path*

```
UrlPathHelper helper = new UrlPathHelper();
String path = helper.getLookupPathForRequest(request);
```

Once a path has been established for the request, you can now evaluate it and act on the path's value appropriately. In a more complex situation, you may simply have a different controller implementation for each individual API call, but since you only have two API functions to provide, you can encapsulate both in a single controller. Listing 11-26 shows how the path is evaluated using the constants you defined previously.

Listing 11-26. *Handling API Calls*

```
List<Bookmark> bookmarks = new ArrayList<Bookmark>();
boolean success = false;

If(path.equals(BOOKMARK_API_RECENT)) {
    success = handleFindRecent(user, bookmarks);
}
else if(path.equals(BOOKMARK_API_ALL)) {
    String tag = request.getParameter("tag");
    success = handleFindAll(tag, user, response, bookmarks);
}
else {
    writeError("API call ["+path+"] not supported.", response);
}
```

This listing shows how the controller delegates control to two private methods called handleFindRecent and handleFindAll when the request matches a relevant API call. Otherwise, it simply reuses the writeError method defined earlier in Listing 11-24 to return a response.

The handleFindRecent method is the simplest one and just adds the results of calls to both the deliciousService and the BookmarkService to the bookmarks list defined on the first line of Listing 11-26. If successful, the method will return true and assign the local variable success to true. You will see the significance of this in Listing 11-29; in the meantime, Listing 11-27 shows the handleFindRecent method's definition.

Listing 11-27. *The handleFindRecent Method*

```
private boolean handleFindRecent(User user, List<Bookmark> bookmarks) {
        bookmarks.addAll( deliciousService.findRecent(user) );
        bookmarks.addAll( bookmarkService.findRecent(user) );
        return true;
}
```

The handleFindAll method is a little more complicated, as it provides error handling for the case where no tag parameter is specified. Listing 11-28 shows it in action.

Listing 11-28. *The handleFindAll Method*

```
private boolean handleFindAll(String tag,
                                              User user,
                                              HttpServletResponse response,
                                              List<Bookmark> bookmarks) {
     if(StringUtils.isBlank(tag)) {
            writeError("Tag parameter not specified", response);
            return false;
     }
     else {
            bookmarks.addAll( deliciousService.findAllForTag(tag,user) );
            bookmarks.addAll( bookmarkService.findAllForTag(tag,user) );
            return true;
     }
}
```

With the results of the calls to the BookmarkService and DeliciousService in hand and the success variable set to true, it is time for XStream to come into play. As already mentioned, XStream provides a way to convert Java objects to XML. The code in Listing 11-29 shows how easy it makes creating the XML response.

Listing 11-29. *Using XStream to Write a Response*

```
if(success) {
        response.setContentType("text/xml");
        XStream xs = createSerializer();
        xs.toXML(bookmarks, response.getWriter());
}
...
```

```
private XStream createSerializer() {
      XStream xs = new XStream();
      xs.alias("bookmark", Bookmark.class);
      xs.alias("bookmarks", List.class);
      xs.omitField(Bookmark.class, "user");
      xs.omitField(Bookmark.class, "tags");
      return xs;
}
```

The XStream object's toXML method does all the magic for you; all you have to do is initialize it appropriately. You've done that in a method called createSerializer that provides appropriate names for the List and Bookmark classes and omits the user and tags properties from the Bookmark class, as there is no need to expose User details via this API, and the individual tags are not needed either.

The full listing of what you have achieved with the Spring BookmarkXmlController class is shown in the following code, with a little bit of exception handling thrown in for good measure:

```java
package org.grails.bookmarks.api;
import java.io.*;
import java.util.*;
import javax.servlet.http.*;
import org.apache.commons.logging.*;
import org.grails.bookmarks.*;

import org.apache.commons.lang.StringUtils;
import org.springframework.web.servlet.ModelAndView;
import org.springframework.web.servlet.mvc.Controller;
import org.springframework.web.util.UrlPathHelper;
import com.thoughtworks.xstream.XStream;

public class BookmarkXmlController implements Controller {

      private static final Log LOG = LogFactory.getLog(BookmarkXmlController.class);
      private static final String BOOKMARK_API_ALL = "/api/all";
      private static final String BOOKMARK_API_RECENT = "/api/recent";

      private IBookmarkService deliciousService;
      private IBookmarkService bookmarkService;

      public void setBookmarkService(IBookmarkService bookmarkService) {
          this.bookmarkService = bookmarkService;
      }
      public void setDeliciousService(IBookmarkService deliciousService) {
          this.deliciousService = deliciousService;
      }
```

```java
    public ModelAndView handleRequest(
                             HttpServletRequest request,
                             HttpServletResponse response) throws Exception {
        User user = (User)request
                                  .getSession()
                                  .getAttribute("user");
        if(user == null) {
            writeError("No user in session. Please authenticate first.",
                          response);
        }
        else {
            UrlPathHelper helper = new UrlPathHelper();
            String path = helper.getLookupPathForRequest(request);
            List<Bookmark> bookmarks = new ArrayList<Bookmark>();

            try {
                boolean success = false;
                if(path.equals(BOOKMARK_API_RECENT)) {
                    success = handleFindRecent(user, bookmarks);
                }
                else if(path.equals(BOOKMARK_API_ALL)) {
                    String tag = request.getParameter("tag");
                    success = handleFindAll(tag, user, response, bookmarks);
                }
                else {
                    writeError("API call ["+path+"] not supported.", response);
                }
                if(success) {
                    response.setContentType("text/xml");
                    XStream xs = createSerializer();
                    xs.toXML(bookmarks, response.getWriter());
                }
             }
            catch(Exception e) {
                LOG.error("Error invoking bookmark services: " +
                              e.getMessage() , e);
                writeError("Bookmark service is currently unavailable."+
                              " Please try again later",response );
            }
        }
        return null;
    }

    private boolean handleFindRecent(User user,
                                        List<Bookmark> bookmarks) {
        bookmarks.addAll( deliciousService.findRecent(user) );
        bookmarks.addAll( bookmarkService.findRecent(user) );
```

```java
            return true;
    }

    private boolean handleFindAll(String tag,
                                             User user,
                                             HttpServletResponse response,
                                             List<Bookmark> bookmarks) {
        if(StringUtils.isBlank(tag)) {
            writeError("Tag parameter not specified", response);
            return false;
        }
        else {
            bookmarks.addAll( deliciousService.findAllForTag(tag,user) );
            bookmarks.addAll( bookmarkService.findAllForTag(tag,user) );
            return true;
        }
    }
    /**
     * Creates a XStream serializer
     */
    private XStream createSerializer() {
        XStream xs = new XStream();
        xs.alias("bookmark", Bookmark.class);
        xs.alias("bookmarks", List.class);
        xs.omitField(Bookmark.class, "user");
        xs.omitField(Bookmark.class, "tags");
        return xs;
    }
    /**
     * Writes the error response
     */
    private void writeError( String message,
                                    HttpServletResponse response) {
        response.setContentType("text/xml");
        PrintWriter w;
        try {
            w = response.getWriter();
            w.write("<error message=\"");
            w.write(message);
            w.write("\" />");
        } catch (IOException e) {
            throw new RuntimeException(e.getMessage(),e);
        }
    }
}
```

So how do you get this Java controller to interact with the Grails services that it depends on? This is where Spring comes in. The Grails directory structure comes with a spring directory that contains a file called resources.xml. Open up this file and register the bean definitions provided in Listing 11-30.

Listing 11-30. *Registering the Controller*

```
<!-- Bookmark API controller -->
<bean id="bookmarkAPI"
          class="org.grails.bookmarks.api.BookmarkXmlController">
      <property name="deliciousService" ref="deliciousService" />
      <property name="bookmarkService" ref="bookmarkService" />
</bean>
<bean id="urlMappings"
          class="org.springframework.beans.factory.config.PropertiesFactoryBean">
      <property name="properties">
          <value>
              /bookmark/api/**=bookmarkAPI
          </value>
      </property>
</bean>
```

There are a few key points about this listing. First off, you're *referencing* the deliciousService and bookmarkService beans without them actually being defined within resources.xml. Don't worry about this though, as Grails will create these bean definitions at run time; you just have to reference them.

Second, the urlMappings bean is a bit special, as it provides any additional URL handlers that Grails should use when configuring itself internally. In the definition, you've told Grails and its underlying Spring MVC framework to map all requests below the path /bookmark/api to the bookmarkAPI controller.

What you have in the end is a Spring controller written in Java being provided dependencies that are written in Groovy and configured at run time by Grails. If you log in and create a few bookmarks, then subsequently access the http://localhost:8080/bookmarks/bookmark/api/recent URL, you'll get a result such as the following:

```
<bookmarks>
    <bookmark>
        <id>1</id>
        <url>http://grails.org</url>
        <title>Grails</title>
        <notes></notes>
        <type>general</type>
        <rating>1</rating>
        <dateCreated class="sql-timestamp">2006-10-09 21:37:35.254</dateCreated>
    </bookmark>
    ...
</bookmarks>
```

So how would you go about calling this API? Open up a new command window in the root of the bookmarks application and type **grails console** to load the Grails interactive console window. In the console that opens, execute the script in Listing 11-31, assuming you have the bookmarks application running and have registered with the appropriate details.

Listing 11-31. *A Simple API Script*

```
import org.apache.commons.httpclient.*
import org.apache.commons.httpclient.methods.GetMethod

server = "http://localhost:8080/bookmarks"
login = "graeme.rocher"
password = "test"
// login, not very securely!
client = new HttpClient()
get = new GetMethod("$server/user/login?"+
                                "login=${login}&"+
                                "password=${password}")
client.executeMethod(get)
get = new GetMethod( "$server/bookmark/api/recent" )
client.executeMethod(get)
xml = new XmlSlurper().parseText(get.responseBodyAsString)
xml.bookmark.each {
    println it.title
    println it.url
}
```

The previous example script uses the Apache HttpClient API that ships with Grails to initiate a stateful communication. It first performs a login by requesting the login page and passing relevant credentials. Once the login is complete, it then requests the API and parses the XML response.

Clearly, the example in Listing 11-31 is simply for illustrative purposes, and in the real system you would likely use a more secure authentication scheme. Nevertheless, it serves to illustrate the API you've created, which others can now consume.

While we're on the topic of secure authentication schemes, in the next section you'll see a more advanced usage of Spring that configures the Acegi Security system to support declarative security in the bookmarks application.

Using Acegi Security with Grails

Acegi is a declarative POJO-based security framework for Spring. It allows login and security to be configured in the Spring application context at a number of levels, including web security and even instance-based security.

It is actually a little bit of a pain to configure, since it is incredibly flexible. In this sense, it is almost the complete opposite of the DRY and "convention over configuration" approaches and violates these paradigms at multiple levels. Nevertheless, it is incredibly powerful, and Grails is all about being simple on the surface, while flexible and powerful underneath.

Grails gives you the *choice* as to whether you want to implement a simpler solution to security, such as the security interceptor implemented in Chapter 7, or to configure flexible declarative security if you so choose.

The example in this section demonstrates how you can use Spring to customize and inject behavior into a Grails application.

The first point to note is that Acegi requires an instance of the org.springframework.web. context.ContextLoaderListener configured in web-app/WEB-INF/web.template.xml. This is done for you when you create the bookmarks application using grails create-app. However, if you create a Grails application with a servlet version lower than 2.4, like in the following command, the ContextLoadListener will not be used, since listeners do not work consistently across all Servlet 2.3 containers:

```
grails -Dservlet.version=2.3 create-app
```

In other words, creating a Grails application with this target will *not* work with Acegi and Servlet versions 2.3 and below. With that inconvenience out of the way, let's look at how to set up Acegi to work with the current bookmarks application.

The first thing to do is to add the concept of a Role to the org.grails.bookmarks.User entity. A Role allows you to group users according to categories that may have a defined set of privileges or access rights. Listing 11-32 shows the modifications made to the User class.

Listing 11-32. *Roles in the User Class*

```
...
public class User {
    public enum Role { ROLE_ANONYMOUS,
                                ROLE_GENERAL_USER,
                                ROLE_ADMIN,
                                ROLE_SUBSCRIBER,
                                ROLE_THIRD_PARTY_INTEGRATION };
    ...
    private String role = Role.ROLE_GENERAL_USER.toString();
    public String getRole() {
        return role;
    }
    public void setRole(String role) {
        this.role = Role.valueOf(role).toString();
    }
}
```

The previous listing shows how you use a Java 5 enum to add support for the different role names. The role property itself is a string that must be one of the enum's values. You could, of course, have an entirely separate enum class that persists to its own table, but for now this is the simplest possible solution. You can always refactor later.

> **■Note** If you were implementing these Role features in Groovy, you could use strings in combination with the inList constraint described in Chapter 5 on scaffolding as an alternative to enums, which aren't supported by Groovy at the moment.

The next step is to set up the Acegi servlet filter to intercept all calls to the bookmarks application. Opening the web-app/WEB-INF/web.template.xml file and adding the filter definition in Listing 11-33 can do this.

Listing 11-33. *The Acegi Filter Definition*

```
<filter>
    <filter-name>Acegi Filter Chain Proxy</filter-name>
    <filter-class>
       org.acegisecurity.util.FilterToBeanProxy
    </filter-class>
    <init-param>
        <param-name>targetClass</param-name>
        <param-value>
             org.acegisecurity.util.FilterChainProxy
        </param-value>
    </init-param>
</filter>

<filter-mapping>
       <filter-name>Acegi Filter Chain Proxy</filter-name>
       <url-pattern>/*</url-pattern>
</filter-mapping>
```

What the previous listing does is ensure that the Acegi filter is executed for each request. The filter mapping's url-pattern element, highlighted in bold, uses the /* wild card to ensure this happens.

Now open up the spring/resources.xml file and add the bean definitions in Listing 11-34 to the Spring context.

Listing 11-34. *The userDetailsService and AuthenticationProvider Beans*

```
<bean
     id="daoAuthenticationProvider"
     class="org.acegisecurity.providers.dao.DaoAuthenticationProvider">
     <property name="userDetailsService">
         <ref bean="userDetailsService"/>
     </property>
</bean>
```

```
<bean id="userDetailsService"
    class="org.acegisecurity.userdetails.jdbc.JdbcDaoImpl">
    <property name="dataSource" ref="dataSource" />
    <property name="usersByUsernameQuery">
      <value>SELECT login,u_pwd,1 FROM user_table WHERE login = ?</value>
    </property>
    <property name="authoritiesByUsernameQuery">
      <value>SELECT login, role FROM user_table WHERE login = ?</value>
    </property>
</bean>
```

The daoAuthenticationProvider bean in the previous listing references a bean called
userDetailsService that is an instance of org.acegisecurity.userdetails.jdbc.JdbcDaoImpl.
This implementation references the Grails dataSource bean and uses a simple SQL query to
look up a user's login details and obtain their role.

The userDetailsService abstraction allows you to configure *how* users are looked up. In
the previous example, JDBC is being used to query the database, but this could easily be
swapped out to another authentication mechanism. In fact, Acegi provides different *providers*,
the details of which can be found within the org.acegisecurity.providers package, to authentic
against commonly used authentication and authorization technologies such as LDAP (Lightweight
Directory Access Protocol) and JAAS (Java Authentication and Authorization Service).

Next, you need to register an Acegi ProviderManager, defined in Listing 11-35, that manages
the different authentication providers, such as the daoProvider, also in Listing 11-35. The bean
definition shows how this can be accomplished.

Listing 11-35. *The Acegi ProviderManager*

```
<bean id="authenticationManager"
        class="org.acegisecurity.providers.ProviderManager">
    <property name="providers">
      <list>
        <ref bean="daoAuthenticationProvider"/>
        <bean
            class="org.acegisecurity.providers.anonymous.Anonymous ➡
AuthenticationProvider">
            <property name="key"><value>anonymous</value></property>
        </bean>
      </list>
    </property>
  </bean>
```

Notice how in Listing 11-35 the authenticationManager bean references the
daoAuthenticationProvider bean you defined earlier, *as well as* another inline bean called
AnonymousAuthenticationProvider. This provider is responsible for allowing access to certain
resources that don't require a login.

Acegi has a concept of *voters* where you register various voters that have the option to
veto a request to access resources. Listing 11-36 shows how to create a bean called
accessDecisionManager that decides about access based on a user's role and authentication status.

Listing 11-36. *The accessDecisionManager Bean*

```
<bean id="accessDecisionManager" class="org.acegisecurity.vote.UnanimousBased">
    <property name="allowIfAllAbstainDecisions">
       <value>false</value>
    </property>
    <property name="decisionVoters">
       <list>
         <bean class="org.acegisecurity.vote.RoleVoter" />
         <bean class="org.acegisecurity.vote.AuthenticatedVoter" />
       </list>
    </property>
  </bean>
```

The RoleVoter, defined in the previous code, is responsible for ensuring that only users within a correct role are allowed access to *allowed resources*. So how do you define the allowed resources? This is where the FilterSecurityInterceptor class comes in handy, as shown in Listing 11-37.

Listing 11-37. *The filterInvocationInterceptor Bean*

```
1  <bean
2     id="filterInvocationInterceptor"
3     class="org.acegisecurity.intercept.web.FilterSecurityInterceptor">
4        <property name="authenticationManager">
5           <ref bean="authenticationManager"/>
6        </property>
7        <property name="accessDecisionManager">
8            <ref bean="accessDecisionManager"/>
9        </property>
10        <property name="objectDefinitionSource">
12           <value>
13              CONVERT_URL_TO_LOWERCASE_BEFORE_COMPARISON
14              PATTERN_TYPE_APACHE_ANT
15
16              /bookmark/**=ROLE_GENERAL_USER
17              /tag/**=ROLE_GENERAL_USER
18              /subscription/**=ROLE_GENERAL_USER
19              /admin/**=ROLE_ADMIN
20              /premium/**=ROLE_SUBSCRIBER
21              /api/**=ROLE_THIRD_PART_INTEGRATION
22              /user/**=IS_AUTHENTICATED_ANONYMOUSLY
23           </value>
24        </property>
25    </bean>
```

The filterInvocationInterceptor defined in Listing 11-37 uses Ant-like path matches to define which resources are accessible by which roles. For example the bookmark application's current controller URIs such as /bookmark, /tag, and /subscription are all accessible via the ROLE_GENERAL_USER role on lines 16 through 19.

To provide examples of other possible use cases there is a path for /admin/* assigned to the ROLE_ADMIN role for administrators, potentially a ROLE_SUBSCRIBER role for premium paid customers on line 20, and a special role for users of the bookmark application's web service API on line 21.

In addition, the UserController's actions, found under the /user URI, are allowed to authenticate anonymously on line 22. Note that because in your domain model you defined a one-to-one relationship between User and Role (i.e., a single User has a single Role), by having just a single role property, it would be impossible to have a User having multiple roles. Yes, another reason to refactor in the future!

Moving on, the next thing you need to do is define the necessary filter bean definitions to tie all this together. The key ones here are anonymousProcessingFilter, authenticationProcessingFilter, and exceptionTranslationFilter in Listing 11-38.

Listing 11-38. *Key Acegi Filters*

```
1 <bean
2    id="anonymousProcessingFilter"
3    class="org.acegisecurity.providers.anonymous.AnonymousProcessingFilter">
4    <property name="key" value="anonymous" />
5    <property name="userAttribute"
6      value="anonymousUser,ROLE_ANONYMOUS" />
7 </bean>
8
9 <bean
10   id="authenticationProcessingFilter"
11 class="org.acegisecurity.ui.webapp.AuthenticationProcessingFilter">
12    <property name="authenticationManager"
13                    ref="authenticationManager" />
14    <property name="authenticationFailureUrl"
15                    value="/user/login?login_error=1" />
16    <property name="defaultTargetUrl" value="/bookmark/list" />
17    <property name="filterProcessesUrl"
18                    value="/j_acegi_security_check" />
19 </bean>
20
21  <bean
22        id="exceptionTranslationFilter"
23    class="org.acegisecurity.ui.ExceptionTranslationFilter">
24    <property name="authenticationEntryPoint">
25      <bean
26        class="org.acegisecurity.ui.webapp.AuthenticationProcessing ➥
FilterEntryPoint">
27        <property name="loginFormUrl" value="/user/login" />
28        <property name="forceHttps" value="false" />
29      </bean>
```

```
30    </property>
31    <property name="accessDeniedHandler">
32      <bean
33        class="org.acegisecurity.ui.AccessDeniedHandlerImpl">
34        <property name="errorPage" value="/user/accessDenied" />
35      </bean>
36    </property>
37  </bean>
```

Some crucial stuff is happening in the previous listing. First, the anonymousProcessingFilter is responsible for assigning anonymous credentials to a user who has not yet logged in. The authenticationProcessingFilter contains some important properties such as the following:

authenticationFailureUrl: This is the URL to which the request is redirected to if login fails. Typically it is just the login page itself. You've set it to the existing bookmark application's /user/login page.

defaultTargetUrl: The default target URL property on line 16 defines where to redirect the request following a successful login. You've set it to the bookmark application's list page at /bookmark/list.

filterProcessesUrl: The filter process URL is where the login form has to submit to in order to process a login. In this case you've left it as the recommended default of /j_acegi_security_check.

Next, in Listing 11-38 is the exceptionTranslationFilter that defines what should happen when certain exceptions are thrown. In this case you've defined the authentication entry point as the existing login page on line 27, and on line 34 you provide a URL to handle *access denied exceptions.* Access denied exceptions occur when a user is logged in but attempts to visit a URI that he or she doesn't have permission to view.

There are a few remaining filters that need to be defined, the details are shown in Listing 11-39.

Listing 11-39. *Remaining Acegi Filters*

```
<bean id="securityContextHolderAwareRequestFilter"
    class="org.acegisecurity.wrapper.SecurityContextHolderAwareRequestFilter" />

  <bean id="httpSessionIntegrationFilter"
        class="org.acegisecurity.context.HttpSessionContextIntegrationFilter">
        <property name="context">
            <value>org.acegisecurity.context.SecurityContextImpl</value>
        </property>
  </bean>

  <bean id="logoutFilter"
    class="org.acegisecurity.ui.logout.LogoutFilter">
    <constructor-arg value="/user/logout" />
    <constructor-arg>
```

```
    <list>
      <bean
        class="org.acegisecurity.ui.logout.SecurityContextLogoutHandler" />
    </list>
  </constructor-arg>
</bean>
```

Listing 11-39 shows the securityContextHolderAwareRequestFilter bean that decorates the request to allow you to retrieve information about the logged-in user using regular Servlet API methods such as getRemoteUser and isUserInRole(String role).

There is also an httpSessionIntegrationFilter bean that provides integration with the standard HttpSession instance by retrieving and storing the user's SecurityContext within the session. Finally, the logoutFilter bean allows the definition or a URI to handle a logout request.

The final thing left to do to the Spring configuration is to put all of these Acegi filters together into a filter chain. Listing 11-40 shows how to use Acegi's FilterChainProxy class to achieve this.

Listing 11-40. *Configuring the Acegi filterChainProxy*

```
<bean
    id="filterChainProxy"
    class="org.acegisecurity.util.FilterChainProxy">
    <property name="filterInvocationDefinitionSource">
        <value>
         CONVERT_URL_TO_LOWERCASE_BEFORE_COMPARISON
         PATTERN_TYPE_APACHE_ANT
        /**=httpSessionIntegrationFilter,
            logoutFilter,
            authenticationProcessingFilter,
            securityContextHolderAwareRequestFilter,
            anonymousProcessingFilter,
            exceptionTranslationFilter,
            filterInvocationInterceptor
        </value>
    </property>
</bean>
```

So that is the Spring configuration. As with many things with Spring, much of Acegi's configuration is merely boilerplate and the initial configuration time far outweighs the long-term maintenance effort. As you can imagine, adding new roles and configuring them would simply be a matter of updating the filterInvocationInterceptor bean in Listing 11-40; the rest of the code would remain largely unchanged.

Nevertheless, the whole job is not yet complete. You now need to update the SecureController class you developed in Chapter 7, as it is no longer responsible for authentication. All it needs to do is look up the already authenticated User as per Listing 11-41.

Listing 11-41. *Updated SecureController*

```
import org.grails.bookmarks.*
abstract class SecureController {
    def beforeInterceptor = {
        if(!session.user) {
            session.user = User.findByLogin(request.remoteUser)
        }
    }
}
```

Here, all it does is look up the User object from the request's remoteUser property. Acegi's request decorator will ensure that the remoteUser property returns the username of the authenticated User. Next, the UserController needs updating, as you can now remove the handleLogin action from it, and you need to provide an accessDenied action to handle the case where someone is attempting to access an unauthorized area of the site.

Listing 11-42 shows the accessDenied action that will simply redirect the request to the BookmarkController, since you know that the BookmarkController is viewable by all users in the ROLE_GENERAL_USER role.

Last but not least, the login view located at grails-apps/views/user/login.gsp needs to now submit to the Acegi authentication URL in order for users to be able to log in successfully. Listing 11-42 shows the updates to the form within the login view to support this.

Listing 11-42. *Acegi Authenticating login View*

```
<form action="${request.contextPath}/j_acegi_security_check">
    <p>
        <label for="login">Login:</label>
        <input type="text" name="j_username" />
    </p>
    <p>
        <label for="password">Password:</label>
        <input type="password" name="j_password" />
    </p>
    <input class="button" type="submit" value="Login" />
</form>
```

And that's it. You now have fine-grained declarative control of authentication and roles within the bookmarks application. Not only that, authentication could be delegated to any LDAP-compliant software (see http://en.wikipedia.org/wiki/Ldap for a list of supporting vendors) or an application server using JAAS, to name just a couple of possibilities.

Although the configuration is rather heavy, the important fact to gather from this example is how Grails offers you the *flexibility* to harness the underlying configuration APIs, while still shielding you away from this complexity for the common case.

The stark reality is that sometimes to create flexible systems, you have to do a certain amount of configuration. Since Grails leverages Spring to achieve this flexibility, it opens up a whole world of possibilities in terms of Enterprise Application Integration (EAI).

In the next section you'll take a look at SOAP, one of the enablers of EAI, with a technology that provides the ability for disparate languages to communicate with one another. More specifically you'll see how to expose a Grails service as a SOAP service.

Exposing a SOAP Service with XFire

The XFire project is an effort to create a lightweight SOAP framework that is both easy to use and highly efficient. In addition, it features strong Spring integration that you can take advantage of to expose the `BookmarkService` implemented in Listing 11-21.

Before getting started, however, you need to download XFire from `http://xfire.codehaus.org` (I use version 1.2.2 in these examples). Once you download it, you will need to place XFire and its related dependencies within the `lib` directory of the bookmarks application. The dependencies required are the following:

- `jaxen-1-1-beta-9.jar`: A general-purpose XPath engine for Java

- `jdom-1.0.jar`: The JDOM parser for XML

- `stax-api-1.0.1.jar`: The Streaming API for XML (StAX) is an API for the pull-parsing of XML

- `wsdl4j-1.5.2.jar`: An API for working with Web Services Description Language (WSDL)

- `wss4j-1.5.0.jar`: An implementation of the WS-Security API

- `wstx-asl-3.0.1.jar`: The open source Woodstox implementation of the StAX API

Once you've copied all the previous dependencies into your `lib` directory it should look like the screenshot in Figure 11-10.

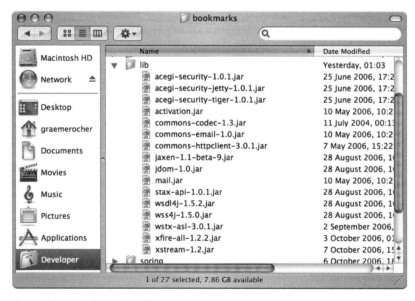

Figure 11-10. *XFire dependencies placed in the lib directory*

Now you need to make some modifications to the `web-app/WEB-INF/web.template.xml` file that is used to produce the `web.xml` file required by the Servlet specification.

Open it up and make the following change to the `contextConfigLocation` context parameters as shown in Listing 11-43.

Listing 11-43. *Updated contextConfigLocation*

```
<context-param>
  <param-name>contextConfigLocation</param-name>
  <param-value>/WEB-INF/applicationContext.xml
    classpath:org/codehaus/xfire/spring/xfire.xml</param-value>
</context-param>
```

The changes are highlighted in bold in the previous listing and merely serve to load the XFire Spring integration bean definitions. Now add an additional servlet mapping that you will use as part of the URL location for the SOAP service directly below the other servlet mappings as per Listing 11-44.

Listing 11-44. *Additional Servlet Mapping*

```
<servlet-mapping>
    <servlet-name>grails</servlet-name>
    <url-pattern>/services/*</url-pattern>
</servlet-mapping>
```

The next part of the configuration involves the `spring/resource.xml` file. Firstly, to allow the SOAP service to be available without the need to authenticate, you need to tell Acegi to authenticate anonymously for the service's URL. To do so, add the following line to the `objectDefinitionSource` property in Acegi:

```
/services/**=IS_AUTHENTICATED_ANONYMOUSLY
```

Now add the following bean definition that uses the Spring `XFireExporter` class to automatically configure a SOAP service for the Grails `BookmarkService`. Listing 11-45 shows the bean definition.

Listing 11-45. *The SOAP Service Bean*

```
<bean id="bookmarkSoapService"
        class="org.codehaus.xfire.spring.remoting.XFireExporter">
  <property name="serviceFactory">
     <ref bean="xfire.serviceFactory"/>
  </property>
  <property name="xfire">
     <ref bean="xfire"/>
  </property>
  <property name="serviceBean">
     <ref bean="bookmarkService"/>
  </property>
```

```
    <property name="serviceClass">
        <value>org.grails.bookmarks.IBookmarkService</value>
    </property>
</bean>
<bean
    id="urlMappings"
    class="org.springframework.beans.factory.config.PropertiesFactoryBean">
    <property name="properties">
        <value>
            /bookmark/api/**=bookmarkAPI
            /services/BookmarkService=bookmarkSoapService
        </value>
    </property>
</bean>
```

The previous listing shows how to configure a bookmarkSoapService bean, which is then added to the urlMappings bean definition you created earlier. Now this is probably enough to get started straight away, however, you're really only interested in a subset of the properties on the Bookmark class. So to avoid passing unnecessary information, you're going to implement an XFire Aegis mapping file for the Bookmark class.

Aegis is XFire's technology for defining the XML to object marshaling rules. In other words, it helps XFire understand how to convert an object into a suitable XML format.

To do so, create a new file in the same package as the Bookmark class called Bookmark.aegis.xml. Populate the contents of the file as per Listing 11-46.

Listing 11-46. *The Bookmark Aegis Mapping File*

```
<mappings
    xmlns:xsi="http://www.w3.org/2001/XMLSchema-instance"
    xsi:schemaLocation="http://xfire.codehaus.org/schemas/1.0/mapping.xsd">
    <mapping>
        <property name="id" ignore="true" />
        <property name="title" />
        <property name="url"  />
        <property name="rating" ignore="true"  />
        <property name="dateCreated" nillable="true" ignore="true" />
        <property name="notes" ignore="true" nillable="true" />
        <property name="user" ignore="true" nillable="true"/>
        <property name="tags" ignore="true"
         componentType="org.grails.bookmarks.TagReference"/>
    </mapping>
</mappings>
```

The mapping file in the previous listing provides information about which properties may be null and which ones should be ignored when sending and receiving the response. With that out of the way, start the Grails server and navigate to the URL http://localhost:8080/bookmarks/services/BookmarkService?wsdl. The resulting XML is the web service definition that provides information about the web service for clients to be able to invoke it. It is rather verbose to list here and includes everything from the methods and their signatures to the types of the objects returned.

The WSDL is meant to be language-neutral and hence is too detailed to list here, but what you will do is create a SOAP client that takes advantage of this information. To get started, make a copy of the bookmarks application directory and call the directory `bookmark-client`. Now remove all the bean definitions in the `spring/resources.xml` file in the bookmark-client project and replace them with a single bean definition as per Listing 11-47.

Listing 11-47. *The Bookmarks Client Application's resources.xml*

```
<import resource="classpath:org/codehaus/xfire/spring/xfire.xml"/>
<bean
    id="bookmarkClient"
    class="org.codehaus.xfire.spring.remoting.XFireClientFactoryBean"
    singleton="true"
    lazy-init="true">
        <property name="serviceClass">
                <value>org.grails.bookmarks.IBookmarkService</value>
        </property>
        <property name="wsdlDocumentUrl">
            <value>
             http://localhost:8080/bookmarks/services/BookmarkService?wsdl
            </value>
        </property>
    </property>
</bean>
```

The `resources.xml` file now contains a single bean definition for the bookmark client. This uses a Spring factory bean called `XFireClientFactoryBean` that constructs a client from the WSDL definition supplied by the `wsdlDocumentUrl` property. In this case, for testing purposes, you've simply supplied the URL of the locally running Grails server.

Now start up a console instance using the `grails console` target. Once loaded, type the short script in Listing 11-48 into the console and run it.

Listing 11-48. *The Bookmark SOAP Client*

```
client = ctx.getBean("bookmarkClient")
bookmarks = client.findRecent(user)
bookmarks.each {
    println(it.title)
    println(it.url)
}
```

The Grails console has an implicit Spring application context instance called `ctx` that you are able to retrieve the bean instance from and then simply invoke methods on, as if it were a regular object. The SOAP service then returns `Bookmark` instances to the client, and all the conversion to and from XML is handled transparently.

Summary

In this chapter, you learned the fundamental message behind Grails, even if you didn't realize it until now. Essentially, Grails strives to make the common, repetitive tasks that Java developers face every day ridiculously simple.

On the other hand, Grails provides all the underlying power and flexibility that you get in traditional Java web frameworks. Need to integrate with an LDAP directory? No problem. Want to expose a SOAP API onto a Grails service? That's possible too. In fact, whatever you can configure with Spring can be integrated with Grails.

In addition, you found out that you can write your domain model in Java and *still* take advantage of all the advanced Grails features such as dynamic finders, criteria, and scaffolding. Grails takes integration with Java extremely seriously, with the whole goal being to provide an environment for blended development. This also makes committing to Grails a safe choice, since you can always revert back to Java partially or totally without excessive costs.

The reality is that there are many cases where static typing is the better choice, and conversely, there are many where dynamic typing is favorable. Groovy and Grails provide a platform to use a mix of approaches that allows you to switch between environments without requiring a large mental shift or making you deal with incompatibilities between programming platforms and paradigms.

Index

You Need the Companion eBook

Your purchase of this book entitles you to buy the companion PDF-version eBook for only $10. Take the weightless companion with you anywhere.

We believe this Apress title will prove so indispensable that you'll want to carry it with you everywhere, which is why we are offering the companion eBook (in PDF format) for $10 to customers who purchase this book now. Convenient and fully searchable, the PDF version of any content-rich, page-heavy Apress book makes a valuable addition to your programming library. You can easily find and copy code—or perform examples by quickly toggling between instructions and the application. Even simultaneously tackling a donut, diet soda, and complex code becomes simplified with hands-free eBooks!

Once you purchase your book, getting the $10 companion eBook is simple:

❶ Visit **www.apress.com/promo/tendollars/**.

❷ Complete a basic registration form to receive a randomly generated question about this title.

❸ Answer the question correctly in 60 seconds, and you will receive a promotional code to redeem for the $10.00 eBook.

2560 Ninth Street • Suite 219 • Berkeley, CA 94710

eBookshop

THE EXPERT'S VOICE™

Offer valid through 6/07.